TOURISM, TECHNOLOGY AND COMPETITIVE STRATEGIES

Auliana Poon

BA, MSc (Economics), PhD (Tourism)

Managing Director
Caribbean Futures Ltd
(Trinidad and Germany)

j

15

CIU

CAB INTERNATIONAL

CABI is a trading name of CAB International

CABI Head Office
Nosworthy Way
Wallingford
Oxfordshire OX10 8DE
UK

CABI North American Office
875 Massachusetts Avenue
7th Floor
Cambridge, MA 02139
USA

Tel: +44 (0)1491 832111
Fax: +44 (0)1491 833508
Email: cabi@cabi.org
Web site: www.cabi.org

Tel: +1 617 395 4056
Fax: +1 617 354 6875
Email: cabi-nao@cabi.org

ISBN-13: 978-0-085198-950-1
ISBN-10: 0-085198-950-0

First published 1993
Reprinted 1994, 1996, 1998, 2002
Transferred to print on demand 2006

Printed and bound in the UK by Antony Rowe Limited, Eastbourne.

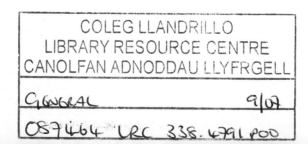

CONTENTS

Acknowledgements   vii

PART I: INTRODUCTION

1. TOURISM IN CRISIS   3
   1.1   Introduction   3
   1.2   Mass Tourism   4
   1.3   Limits to Growth   5
   1.4   Future Growth Prospects   7
   1.5   Seeds of Change   9
   1.6   New Consumers   9
   1.7   New Technologies   11
   1.8   A New Global 'Best Practice'   13
   1.9   Tourism will Lead the New 'Best Practice'   15
   1.10   Tourism in Transition   16
   1.11   New Tourism   17
   1.12   The Implications of New Tourism   18
   1.13   The End of Mass Tourism?   21
   1.14   Competitive Strategies – Key to Success   24
   1.15   What is to Come?   25

PART II: OLD AND NEW TOURISM

2. MASS TOURISM   29
   2.1   Introduction   29
   2.2   The Historical Setting   30
   2.3   Mass Tourism Defined   32
   2.4   The Evolution of Mass Tourism   33
   2.5   Frame Conditions   35
   2.6   Consumers   38

2.7   Technology   41
2.8   Mass Tourism Forces in Europe and the USA   48
2.9   Mass Tourism Forces in the USA   51
2.10 Mass Tourism Forces in Europe   56
2.11 Summary   59

3. GLOBAL IMPERATIVES   62
3.1   Introduction   62
3.2   Environmental Limits to Growth   63
3.3   The Microelectronics Revolution   70
3.4   Birth of a New Paradigm   73
3.5   Lessons from the Manufacturing Sector   79
3.6   Summary   83

4. GLOBAL TRANSFORMATION   84
4.1   Introduction   84
4.2   New Tourism Defined   85
4.3   Emergence of a New Tourism   86
4.4   New Consumers   90
4.5   New Technologies   92
4.6   New Production Practices   94
4.7   New Management Techniques   96
4.8   New Frame Conditions   98
4.9   Summary   108

PART III: DRIVING FORCES

5. NEW CONSUMERS   113
5.1   Introduction   113
5.2   The New Tourists   114
5.3   More Experienced Travellers   116
5.4   Changed Values   122
5.5   Changed Lifestyles   128
5.6   Changing Demographics   134
5.7   More Flexible Consumers   139
5.8   More Independent Consumers   140
5.9   Old and New Tourism at Work   141
5.10 Old and New Tourists Compared   144
5.11 New Tourists in the Family Islands   146
5.12 Old and New Tourism in the Bahamas   151
5.13 Summary   151

6. TECHNOLOGY CHANGES TOURISM   153
6.1   Introduction   153

6.2	An Information-intensive Industry	153
6.3	A System of Information Technology	156
6.4	Adoption is System-wide	158
6.5	Rapid Diffusion of Technology	158
6.6	Technology Impacts in Tourism	161
6.7	Increased Efficiency	163
6.8	Improved Quality	164
6.9	New Services	164
6.10	Flexible Holidays	167
6.11	A New Industry Best Practice	169
6.12	Conclusions	171
7.	**TECHNOLOGY IN ACTION**	172
7.1	Introduction	172
7.2	The Tourism Production System (TPS)	172
7.3	Technology in Production	173
7.4	Airline CRSs	178
7.5	Technology in Travel Agencies	190
7.6	Technology in Tour Operations	193
7.7	Technology in Hotels	194
7.8	Conclusions	201
PART IV:	**COMPETITIVE STRATEGIES**	
8.	**COMPETITIVE SCENARIO**	205
8.1	Introduction	205
8.2	The Tourism System	206
8.3	The Industry Value Chain	208
8.4	New Tourism Changes the Value Chain	214
8.5	Diagonal Integration	215
8.6	Strategic Responses for Industry Players	228
8.7	Summary	234
9.	**COMPETITIVE STRATEGIES FOR INDUSTRY PLAYERS**	236
9.1	Introduction	236
9.2	Competitive Strategies	236
9.3	Put Consumers First	240
9.4	Be a Leader in Quality	254
9.5	Develop Radical Innovations	266
9.6	Strengthen Your Strategic Position	275
9.7	Summary	282

PART V: THE FUTURE

10.   STRATEGIES FOR TOURISM DESTINATIONS   287
     10.1   Introduction   287
     10.2   Tourism – Blessing or Blight?   288
     10.3   Competitive Strategies are Necessary   291
     10.4   Put the Environment First   294
     10.5   Make Tourism a Lead Sector   306
     10.6   Strengthen Marketing and Distribution Channels   323
     10.7   Build a Dynamic Private Sector   329
     10.8   Summary   336

References and Further Reading   337

Index   360

ACKNOWLEDGEMENTS

I cannot take credit for all of the ideas contained in this book: I have merely brought together the concepts, philosophies and tools that others have developed. If I have contributed anything, it is applying them to the tourism industry and organising them under readily understandable concepts of 'old tourism' and 'new tourism'.

It was nearly 10 years ago when I embarked on a journey of no return — a journey through the highways and byways of the travel and tourism industry. During this short journey, I have met hundreds of people and exchanged thousands of ideas. This book is a culmination, rather, a celebration of, those many business people, experts, employees, politicians, academics and ordinary people whom I have had the pleasure of meeting, exchanging ideas and even disagreeing with from time to time.

It is virtually impossible to acknowledge the countless individuals from whose knowledge and experience this book has benefited. However, I would like to make a small start, in the hope that I will be forgiven by those whose names have inadvertently slipped my pen.

I would like to begin by thanking Trevor Farrell who encouraged me to pursue a doctorate after completing with distinction the MSc (Economics) degree at the University of the West Indies, Trinidad. My doctoral work at Sussex University, England, was made possible by the Government of Trinidad and Tobago, through funds provided by the European Economic Community under the LOME II programme.

At the Science Policy Research Unit, Sussex University, I became fascinated by Schumpeterian notions of innovation, long waves, paradigm shifts and more specifically, the microelectronics revolution. The idea of making tourism the focus of my doctoral work came later only when the implications of the microelectronics revolution for small Caribbean-type economies became apparent. At first, the idea of linking tourism and technology seemd rather absurd — but time has proven to be the real judge of that! Sincere thanks are due to Carlotta Perez and Chris Freeman who gave their unending support and encouragement to follow tourism and technology's unbeaten path.

I would like to thank the many willing organizations and their respective fellows and librarians who kindly provided information for this book, namely:

American Express, USA and UK
American Hotel and Motel Association, USA
Brighton Polytechnic, UK
Caribbean Development Bank, Barbados
Caribbean Hotel Association, Puerto Rico
Caribbean Tourism Organization, Barbados and USA
CARICOM Secretariat, Guyana
General Agreement on Trade and Tariffs, Geneva
European Economic Community, Belgium
Institute of Development Studies, Sussex University, UK
International Labour Organization, Barbados, Trinidad and
    Switzerland
Organization of American States, USA
PROGRES Research Program on the Service Economy, Switzerland
Reed Travel Group, USA
Science Policy Research Unit, Sussex University, UK
Studienkries für Tourismus (StfT), Germany
Tour and Travel News, USA
Tourism Canada, Canada
Tourism Society, UK
Travel and Tourism Research Association, USA
Travel Trade Gazette, UK
Travel Weekly, USA
United Nations Conference on Trade and Development, Switzerland
United Nations Economic Commission for Latin America and the
    Caribbean, Trinidad
University of Berne, Switzerland
University of Surrey, UK
University of the West Indies, Trinidad and Barbados Campuses,
    West Indies
US Department of Transportation, USA
US Travel Data Center, USA
World Tourism Organization, Spain
World Travel and Tourism Council, UK

Portions of this book originally appeared in the following publications:

Annals of Tourism Research

Belize Tourism Link
Business Barometer
Caribbean Affairs
Caribbean Contact
CARICOM Perspectives
Progress in Tourism, Recreation and Hospitality Management
Tourism Management
Trinidad Express
World Development

Grateful acknowledgement is made to these publishers for permission to reprint previously published materials.

Special thanks are due to the Caribbean Tourism Organization, the United Nations Development Programme and the World Tourism Organization for permission to use the results of work carried out by the author between 1988 and 1990 in the Caribbean region.

The *West Indian Commission* has graciously consented to allow the publication of results of a commissioned study on *Tourism as an Axial Product — Potential for Linkages and Development of Services*, which was prepared by me in September 1991.

I would also like to acknowledge the following publishers and organizations whose information has been reproduced in the book:

Motivation and satisfaction of visitors to the Bahamas, Stopover Exit Survey 1991, Bahamas Ministry of Tourism, the Bahamas.

Information on Belize national parks, Belize Audubon Society, Belize City, Belize.

Chart on 'Tourism-Who Benefits?', *Christian Conference of Asia*, Report of a Workshop on Tourism, 1980, Manila.

Classification of Services, *General Agreement on Trade and Tarfifs*, Geneva, 1991.

Information on Japanese travel patterns, Japanese Overseas Travel, Japan Travel Bureau Inc., 1990, Japan.

Table on the stages of technology usage in hotels, by Paul Gamble in 'Innovation in Innkeeping', *International Journal of Hospitality Management*, Inaugural issue, 1991.

Table on Information Technology and the Third Wave, from Freeman and Perez 1988, in *Structural Crises of Adjustment: Business Cycles and Investment Behaviour*, Francis Pinter, UK.

Information on German travel patterns, Reisanalyse 1990 and 1991, *Studienkreis für Tourismus*, Germany.

Excerpt from an article by Jost Krippendorf, entitled Ecological approach to tourism marketing, *Tourism Management* 8(2), 1987.

Information on multinational corporations in international tourism,

United Nations Center on Transportational Corporations, 1982, USA

Information on demographic patterns in the USA *Discover America 2000*, United States Travel Data Center, 1989.

In addition, my sincere gratitude is due to the following industry experts and academics who made time to read and comment on draft chapters of the book:

Chris Freeman and Carlotta Perez, Science Policy Research Unit, UK

Rolf Freitag, European Travel Data Centre, Germany

David Gilbert and Chris Cooper, Surrey University, UK

Jean Holder, Victor Curtin and Arley Sobers, Caribbean Tourism Organization, Barbados

Jafar Jafari, Annals of Tourism Research, USA

Jost Krippendorf, formerly University of Berne, Switzerland

Luiz Moutinho, Cardiff Business School, Wales

Bill Niles, Reed Travel Croup, USA

Armin Vielhaber, Director of StfT and Heinz Hahn, former Director, StfT, Germany

Stephen Wheatcroft, Aviation and Tourism International, UK

Others from whom I have benefited through discussions and personal communication are:

Andrew Barnett, Martin Bell, Giovani Dosi, Kurt Hoffman, Robin Mansell, Jeff Oldham, Keith Pavitt, Roy Rothwell and Luc Soete from SPRU, UK

Geoffrey Barrett and Gabriel Lee, EEC, Belgium

John Bell, CHA, Puerto Rico

John Bessant, Howie Rush and Marian Whitaker of Brighton Polytechnic, UK

Ian Betrand, Francis Lewis, Bentley Roach and Ted Webb, BWIA International, Trinidad and Tobago and UK

Byron Blake and Roderick Sanatan, Caricom Secretariat, Guyana

Compton Bourne, Winston Dookeran, Norman Girvan, Ralph Henry, Ainsley O'Riley, Dennis Pantin, Brinsley Samaroo, Eric St Cyr and Roy Thomas, University of the West Indies, Trinidad and the Bahamas

Maura Brassil, Family Islands Promotion Board, Miami

Don Brice, William Demas, Marshall Hall, Alister McIntyre and Philip Nassief, West Indian Commision, Barbados

Paul Chen Young, Executive Director, Eagle Merchant Bank, Jamaica

Susan Cook, US Travel Data Center, USA

Emmanuel De Kadt, Raphie Kaplinsky and Robin Murray, IDS, Sussex

Edwin Carrington, former Secretary General, African, Caribbean and Pacific States Secretariat (ACP), Belgium

Martin Elder, *Travel Agent* magazine, USA

Terrance Farrell, Central Bank of Trinidad and Tobago

Douglas Frechtling, former Director, US Travel Data Center, USA

Alan Fredericks, *Travel Weekly*, USA

Chuck Gee, University of Hawaii, Hawaii

Jose-Ignacio Estevez and Mathias Meyer, Inter-American Development Bank, USA

Hugo Souza and other staff at the Inter-American Bank

Cord Hansen-Sturm and Richard Selton, New School for Social Research, USA

Anthony Hill, former permanent representative to Jamaica at the United Nations, Switzerland

Bernard Hoeckman and Raymond Krommenacker, GATT, Switzerland

Kirk Iffil, International Financial Corporation, USA

Jerry Landress, *Tour and Travel News*, USA

Bruno Lanvin and Murray Gibbs, United Nations conference on Trade and Development, UNCTAD, Switzerland

Gotz Link, Deutsche Stiftung für internationale Entiwicklung, Berlin, Germany

Marcella Martinez, Marcella Martinez Associates Inc., USA

Victor Middleton, World Travel and Tourism Environment Research Centre (WTTERC), UK

Juan Rada, International Management Institute, Switzerland

Brian Samuel, Business Advisory Services, Barbados

Rohinton Sethna and Dennis Benn, UNDP, Barbados and USA

Naresh Singh, Caribbean Environmental Health Institute, St Lucia

Staff and directors of the Bahamas Ministry of Tourism, the Bahamas

Wong Seng Hong, Hooi Ling Foo Lim, other staff and directors of the National Computer Board, Singapore

Singapore Tourism Promotion Board, Singapore

Martin Stabler and Ludmilla Teuting, *Tourism With Insight*, Germany

Garnet Woodham, IADB representative, the Bahamas

Eugenio Yunis, former Chief of the Americas, WTO.

I would also like to thank the many hotels throughout the Caribbean and elsewhere as well as travel agencies, tour operators, airlines, cruise operators and others within the industry from whom I have gained invaluable insights into the workings of the industry. This fraternity is far too large to list individually.

Sincere thanks are also due to the board of directors and the staff of the Caribbean Tourism Organization (CTO) with whom I have had the pleasure of working from 1988 to 1990. The CTO experience opened the Caribbean tourism industry in all of its splendour, with all of its problems and opportunities. I would like to specially thank Jean Holder, Secretary General of the CTO, who allowed me the flexibility to carry out pioneering work in many aspects of the Caribbean tourism industry.

I am also grateful to the Belize Tourism Industry Association (BTIA) and USAID with whom I worked as tourism advisor. The Belize experience made clear to me the potential for ecotourism as well as the real constraints and opportunities associated with building a 'new tourism', particularly in a newly-emerging tourism destination.

On the other hand, my experience with working with the National Computer Board and the Tourism Promotion Board in Singapore, helping in a small way to prepare Singapore for 'the next lap', has been invaluable in revealing how a tiny island state can use information technology for competitive success.

I have also benefited tremendously from various assignments undertaken for the Inter-American Development Bank, Washington, the Bahamas and Trinidad and Tobago and Barbados. Working with Ivan Laughlin and Roger Turton, my *Caribbean Futures* partners in Trinidad, has also been a source of tremendous inspiration.

I would like to gratefully acknowledge Nadine Godwin, Managing Editor of *Travel Weekly* who kindly agreed to read most of the draft chapters and made valuable comments. I would also like to thank the *Caribbean Futures* team who worked on the book: Ian David provided research assistance; Akusomcpeith (Felix) O Tau assisted in editing the book and improving its style; Roseline Poon assisted in the final edits and preparation for publication. Ursula Potthoff-Sewing assisted in proofreading some of the text.

I am also thankful to those who influenced my early development — Sr Regina, the principal and the staff of Providence, also Clifford Dalip and Jack Warner of St James Polytechnic Institute.

Sincere appreciation to my parents who made it all possible in the first place: my mother, Veronica, who is virtually always there, even when we are miles apart; and my father, Achan, whose unending love and admiration for his five daughters has always taught us that each one of us is special.

Four of my very dear friends, Eric Adams, Christian Lassalle, Elizabeth Parsan and Ana Romero have been a constant source of support and encouragement.

I would like to thank my publisher Tim Hardwick of CAB International. One could not have wished for a more efficient or understanding publisher.

Finally, I would like to sincerely thank my husband and former colleague at Sussex University, Christian Potthoff-Sewing. Christian has developed a profound appreciation for my work. He has read many chapters of this book and provided valuable insights. Above all he is patient and understanding. I thank him especially for letting me be.

A. Poon

I
INTRODUCTION

1

TOURISM IN CRISIS

1.1. INTRODUCTION

The tourism industry is in crisis – a crisis of change and uncertainty; a crisis brought on by the rapidly changing nature of the tourism industry itself. In the year 2000, tourism will look nothing like it used to be. The industry is in metamorphosis – it is undergoing rapid and radical change. New technology, more experienced consumers, global economic restructuring and environmental limits to growth are only some of the challenges facing the industry. Creative gales of destruction and more stormy weather lie ahead. The era of sunny weather management is over.

The transformation today is rather different from the hiccups of 1973–1974 (oil crisis), 1980–1981 (mild recession) and 1991 (the Gulf War). In those periods, everyone suffered – and they suffered equally. In addition, it was only a matter of time before players recovered from these bouts of indigestion. Today, however, recovery will neither be easy nor certain. Today, the industry is being transformed – the rules of the game are changing, and they are changing for everyone. Some players are winning; others are dying.

Today, winning does not just mean surviving: it means *leading* – it means becoming a leader in a new and profoundly changed tourism industry. Competitive strategies are more important than ever to ensure that industry players and tourism destinations stay ahead of the game: for to lead is to win.

The crisis of the tourism industry is a crisis of *mass tourism*; for it is mass tourism that has brought social, cultural, economic and environmental havoc in its wake, and it is mass tourism practices that must be radically changed to bring in the new. Perhaps it is best to begin with an examination of the culprit – mass tourism.

3

1.2. MASS TOURISM

Mass tourism was the logical outcome of key social, economic, political and technological influences after the Second World War (see Fig. 1.1). Mass tourism took off with the jet aircraft in 1958. Post-war peace and prosperity, paid holidays, charter flights and cheap oil lubricated the wheels of tourism change. Sun-lust and inexperienced tourists, together with the availability of cheap package tours to sun destinations and the diffusion of 'plastic' cards ensured the demand for mass tourism. Technology also facilitated the development of mass tourism for it made possible the standardization, management and distribution of mass tourism services on a global scale.

By the mid-1970s, mass tourism was the order of the day. Mimicking mass production in the manufacturing sector, tourism was developed along assembly-line principles: holidays were standardized and inflexible; identical holidays were mass produced; and economy of scale was the driving force of production. Likewise, holidays were consumed *en masse* in a similar, robot-like and routine manner, with a lack of consideration for the norms, culture and environment of host countries visited.

Within two short decades, the tourism industry became mass, standardized and rigidly packaged. The industry offered a limited range of inflexible travel and holiday options to a seemingly identical group of mass travellers. By the 1970s and early 1980s, mass tourism was 'best practice'. In other words, mass tourism became the organizational and managerial common sense for best productivity and most profits in the industry.

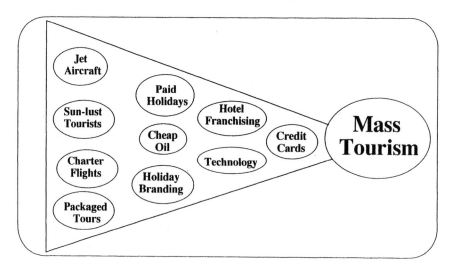

Fig. 1.1. Mass tourism forces.

So pervasive was the tendency toward mass production, standardization and rigid packaging that not even *sex tourism* could escape its overwhelming impact. Of the Japanese all-male tour party in the Philippines, for example, it is documented that:

> ... there are a number of private houses which cater to Japanese tourists. In this case the tourist bus travels around the sites of the city and at some stage calls in at the private house through a back door. The group troops into the building and are told that they have an hour. Behind closed doors and windows they choose a girl. An hour later the bell rings, they march out to the bus and continue their tour of the city.
>
> (O'Grady, 1981)

Several key forces were responsible for the spread of mass, standardized and rigidly packaged tourism.

1. *Consumers*: sun-lust, sex-starved and inexperienced mass consumers.
2. *Technology*: jet aircraft, automobile, computer reservations and accounting systems, credit cards.
3. *Production*: cheap oil, charter flights, packaged tours, hotel over-building, mass production.
4. *Management*: economies of scale, hotel and holiday branding; promotional air fares, mass marketing.
5. *Frame conditions*: post-war peace and prosperity, paid holidays, regulation of air transportation, incentives to attract hotel chains to establish operations in many 'sun' destinations and the world over.

In North America and Europe, different agents facilitated the development and spread of mass tourism. In the USA, multinational hotel chains, airlines and automobiles, were the main vehicles driving the tourism industry. In Europe, by comparison, tour operators, charter flights and package tours to Mediterranean 'sun' destinations, were the key agents in the rapid growth of mass tourism. With growth came much destruction: destruction to the ecology, the environment, the compromising of indigenous cultures, the 'flesh trade', crime, deviance, new diseases and a whole lot more (see Chapter 10).

One of the key questions today is: 'Will mass tourism continue its socially, culturally and environmentally destructive patterns of growth or are the days of mass tourism numbered?'

1.3. LIMITS TO GROWTH

Tourism is a doubled-edged sword – it can be a potential blessing and it can be a blight. Many tourism destinations benefit from the flows of tourists and the hard currencies they bring. However, they have not completely avoided some of tourism's negative consequences – prostitution, crime, deviance, environmental degradation, commercialization of culture and changing societal norms and values (see Chapters 3 and 10). These factors, if left unchecked, will continue to limit the growth of the tourism industry.

The energy-and-environment-intensive production patterns of mass tourism place enormous stress on the natural assets of the industry. Mass tourism destroys exactly what it seeks – such things as quiet, solace, pristine cultures and landscapes, unpolluted waters, intact reefs, fishes, turtles, mountains, ski slopes, wildlife and virgin forests.

The impacts of three decades of mass tourism have been far-reaching – particularly for tourism-dependent economies with fragile environments, cultures and infrastructures. The negative impacts of tourism – from pollution to prostitution – are significant. Mass tourism has already begun to rear its ugly head on the ski slopes of Switzerland, in the Caribbean sea, along the Adriatic coast, in the Himalayas, on the sleazy streets of Bangkok and elsewhere. One observer sees host countries 'training for revolt' if mass tourism continues its mass destruction (Krippendorf, 1987a).

Concern for the environment is at an all-time high and growing. The fact is that fires in the Amazon, the destruction of the ozone layer, acid rain, 'macro pollution', and skyrocketing world population threaten not only the tourism industry but the existence of man and woman on Planet Earth (see, for example, the King and Schneider report to the Club of Rome, 1991). Growing concerns about environmental destruction will limit the further growth of the tourism industry. New and more sustainable patterns of development are critically important if the industry is to survive over the long term.

Environmental limits to growth hold several important lessons for the tourism industry:

1. Tourism cannot afford to continue its environmental-intensive pattern of growth.
2. Limits to growth increasingly question mass-tourism methods of production and consumption.
3. Call it by any name – soft tourism, ecotourism, sustainable tourism, new tourism, responsible tourism – environmentally sound tourism is not just a fad. It has to become a way of life if the industry and indeed this planet is to be sustained. There is no other choice.
4. Positive actions taken by host countries such as Belize, Bermuda and Trinidad and Tobago (see Chapter 10), together with actions by funding agencies and the 'greening' of the private sector (such as the Canadian Pacific Hotels and Resorts), provide the first set of signals ushering in a new approach to tourism development. These actions are by no means

enough to save the tourism industry – far less the world. More initiatives by public- and private-sector bodies are necessary.

5. New tourism can play a leading role in providing and promoting more sustainable patterns of development and in saving Planet Earth. Tourism must be allowed to play this role.

1.4. FUTURE GROWTH PROSPECTS

In 1950, a mere 25 million persons crossed international borders; by 1990, 425 million persons travelled abroad and in the year 2000, this figure is expected to reach 637 million (World Tourism Organization, 1990). When it is considered that international arrivals account for a mere 10% of all tourism flows, the tourism industry (domestic and international) is enormous. Employing some 130 million people world-wide and generating over US$3 trillion in gross sales for 1992, the travel and tourism industry is already the largest in the world. In Britain, Germany, Japan and the USA, more adults have travelled during 1988 than visited a library, attended a sporting event or have gone to see a play or concert (American Express Global Travel Survey, 1990).

That the industry will continue to grow is not in question (Fig. 1.2). However, it is increasingly evident that:

- the *rate* of growth will slow down;
- the *distribution* of growth will shift; and
- the *direction* of growth will change.

The golden age of tourism is over: the age of unlimited growth and the exploitation of the environment as though it were nobody's business, is rapidly drawing to a close. The world economy is in 'structural recession'. This has become a 'necessary evil' the world economy continues to battle with geo-political restructuring (the new Germany, break-up of the Soviet Union and the emergence of new countries in Europe); as producers in many parts of the world continue to battle with new competition from Japan and elsewhere; as they adapt to new technologies and more demanding consumers; and as they continue to shift their production structures to reflect the new realities of flexible production (see Chapter 3). This adjustment process is bound to take a temporary toll on the tourism industry: a short- to medium-term slowdown in the industry's growth is therefore expected. Closer to home, increasing tourism fatigue, environmental degradation, noise, congestion at airports and the negative socioeconomic consequences of tourism in host countries continue to put a damper on mass tourism's further growth.

International Tourism Arrivals
1950-2000

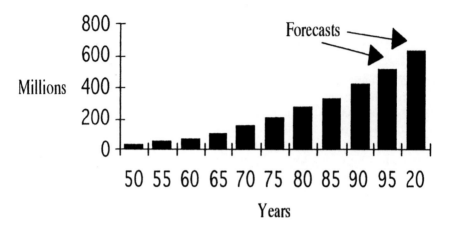

Fig. 1.2. Predicted growth in tourism.
- Leisure time is still increasing internationally.
- Despite temporary slowdown, incomes will grow.
- Changes in the value structure: from having to being.
- There is no substitute for the travel experience.
- As the markets in developed countries near maturity, new wealthy regions
  with strongly growing demand for travel are emerging.

While growth is expected to slow, this will not be the case for all
participants. Indeed some industry players (cruise ships and all-inclusive
resorts) and tourism regions (Asia) will experience greater than average
growth and others will grow far slower than they would like. In the
Caribbean, for example, cruise ships and all-inclusive hotels are proving to
be real competitors to conventional hotels. In so far as the World Tourism
Organization predicts that the most successful tourism-receiving region will
be Asia/Oceana: its share of international tourist arrivals is expected to
rise from 14.7% in 1989 to 21.9% in the year 2000. Asia/Oceana's share
of world tourism receipts is expected to be even more marked: increasing
from 19.5% in 1989 to 30.5% in 2000. Other regions recording higher-
than-average growth in terms of arrivals are likely to be the Americas
(including the Caribbean) and Africa.

More important than slow growth and shifting distribution of growth is
the fact that the direction of tourism growth will change. This is funda-

mentally important because the change in direction will be such that industry players will not be able to capture market share by continuing to dish out the mass tourism products and services they have grown accustomed to doing. Players will need to change their production and management practices in order to become leaders in a radically changing tourism industry.

1.5. SEEDS OF CHANGE

Just as post-war peace, the jet engine and cheap oil fuelled tourism's growth, today, equally compelling forces are shaping the industry. Pressures for change come both from within and from outside the industry (Table 1.1). The most important *internal* forces of change are new consumers and new technologies. From the *outside*, environmental limits to growth and the emergence of a new global 'best practice' of flexible production will profoundly change the tourism industry. A new tourism is already emerging – a tourism that is flexible, sustainable and individual-oriented. In addition, new industry practices for best productivity and most profitability will consist of customization, market segmentation, total quality management (TQM), employee empowerment, zero defection, yield management, *diagonal integration*, strategic alliances and information partnerships (see Chapter 9). Diagonal integration is a process by which firms use information technologies (for example CRSs) to logically combine the provision of services (for example travel + insurance + credit cards + travel agencies) for best productivity and most profits.

Table 1.1 Key forces shaping tourism

Internal	External
New consumers	Limits to growth
New technologies	Emergence of a new global best practice

1.6. NEW CONSUMERS

Changes in consumer behaviour and values provide a critical driving force for the new tourism. New tourists are fundamentally different from the old (Table 1.2). They are more experienced, more 'green', more flexible, more

Table 1.2 Old and new tourists compared

Old tourists	New tourists
Search for the sun	Experience something different
Follow the masses	Want to be in charge
Here today, gone tomorrow	See and enjoy but do not destroy
Just to show that you had been	Just for the fun of it
Having	Being
Superiority	Understanding
Like attractions	Like sports
Precautious	Adventurous
Eat in hotel dining room	Try out local fare
Homogeneous	Hybrid

independent, more quality conscious and 'harder to please' than ever before.

The motivations of the old tourists are different from those of the new. For the old tourists, travel was a novelty; it mattered not where they went, once they got to a warm destination and could show others that they had been there. Quality of services was relatively unimportant. Vacation was an escape from work and from home. By contrast, vacation is an extension of life for the new tourists. New tourists go on vacation to experience something different. For the new tourists, quality and value for money are a premium.

Old tourists tended to be homogeneous and predictable. If they went first class, they went first class all the way. They felt secure by travelling in numbers. They took vacations where everything was pre-paid and pre-arranged. New tourists, on the other hand, are not like their predecessors; rather, they are spontaneous and unpredictable. They are hybrid in nature and do not consume along linear predictable lines. The hybrid consumer may want to purchase different tourism services in different price categories for the same trip (e.g. travel tourist class and stay in a five-star hotel). These new consumers want to be different from the crowd. They want to affirm their individuality and they want to be in control.

Demographic changes are also reflected in the new consumers – the population is ageing, household size is decreasing and more income is available per household. Changing lifestyle and changing demographics of the new tourists are creating demand for more targeted and customized holidays. Families, single-parent households, people whose children have left home, 'gourmet' babies, couples with double income and no kids

(DINKS), young urban upwardly mobile professionals (YUPPIES) and modern introverted luxury keepers (MILKIES) are examples of lifestyle segments. Suppliers will have to pay far more attention to consumer psychographics (the way consumers think, feel and behave) than they have hitherto done.

1.7. NEW TECHNOLOGIES

Information technology and tourism seem to be unlikely, if not unthinkable, bedfellows. The partnership of technology and tourism conjures images of computer-aided hospitality, robot-guided tours and humanless hotels. The apparent mismatch between tourism and technology can be reconciled when it is considered that:

1. Tourism is an extremely information-intensive industry.
2. The rapid development of information technologies facilitates the speed and efficiency with which the industry's information is processed, stored, retrieved, distributed and otherwise manipulated.

The partership of information technology and tourism has grown even stronger since the deregulation of the US airline industry in 1978 (see Chapter 4). Deregulation has made information technologies even more indispensable to the tourism industry. It has further complicated the playing field with a large volume and wide array of rapidly changing information; such include new airlines, new fares, new routes, forever-changing prices, more alternatives, more confusion and a whole new vocabulary (yield management, no frills, frequent-flyer awards, display bias, halo effect). It is not surprising that technology has had to come to the rescue. Consider that:

1. It is not a computer or telephone or video brochure or teleconferencing that is being used by the industry, but a *whole system* of computer and communication technologies. These include: computerized reservation systems; electronic funds transfer; digital telephone networks; smart cards; satellite printers; mobile communications, and more more (see Chapter 6).
2. It is not airlines or hotels or travel agencies or cruise ships that are using the technology, but *all* of them. All players will have to become users of information technology in order to ensure their own survival and competitiveness. Information technology will leave no player in the travel and tourism industry untouched. No player will escape its impacts.

Many industry players are already users of information technologies:

1. *Travel agents*: use computerized reservation systems to obtain information, make bookings and sell travel;

2. *Hotels*: use the technologies to carry out their front office, back office and food and beverage operations; to entertain their guests and to distribute their bed nights in the marketplace;

3. *Airlines*: use information technologies for almost every aspect of their operations – from schedule generation to flight planning, reservations, sales and analysis.

Already, almost all travel agencies in the US are linked to computerized reservations systems (CRSs). At the same time, airlines are technology leaders in the industry and CRSs have emerged as the dominant technology (see Chapter 7). Technology has advanced so rapidly that it is not only possible for visitors to find out the price, availability and location of their future vacation spot but the technology is already available on systems such as SabreVision to allow clients to take a visual tour of the hotels they will stay at, to pre-view the beds they will sleep in and to visit the rain forest they will walk in, before departure!

There are ten key characteristics of information-technology applications to the tourism industry.

1. The technology is well-developed.

2. A system of information technology is diffusing.

3. All players are users of technology.

4. Diffusion is rapid.

5. Computerized reservations systems have emerged as the dominant technology.

6. CRSs have become profit centres in their own right.

7. Technology creates a new basis for competition.

8. Technology will not alter the human content of tourism – rather, it will infect its core information-intensive functions (management, marketing, distribution, sales).

9. The greatest impact of technology will be in the area of distribution and sales.

10. Technology makes it possible to:

    (a) Increase efficiency of production;

    (b) Provide better quality services;

    (c) More effectively market and distribute services in the marketplace;

    (d) Release human hours for 'high touch' services; and

    (e) Generate completely new and flexible services (e.g. 'mix and match' holidays, teleconferencing, mobile communications (sky and boat telephones).

Information technology (IT) is having three profound implications for the travel and tourism industry:

1. IT changes the rules of the game.

2. IT is substantially altering the role of each player in the value-creation process of the industry (see Chapter 8).

3. IT facilities the production of new, flexible and high-quality travel and tourism services that are *cost-competitive* with mass, standardized and rigidly packaged options. CRSs, for example, reduce the cost to owning airlines of making a booking from US$7.50 to US$0.50c and they increase travel agency productivity by 42% (see Chapters 6 and 7).

4. IT helps to engineer the transformation of travel and tourism from its mass, standardized and rigidly packaged nature into a more flexible, individual-oriented, sustainable and diagonally integrated industry (see Chapters 4, 6 and 8).

1.8. A NEW GLOBAL 'BEST PRACTICE'

The power of information technology goes beyond the hardware and the software that the tourism industry has begun to use. At the heart of all information technology developments – from flexible manufacturing systems (FMS), robots and personal computers to computerized reservations systems (CRS) – is microelectronics.

Microelectronics is as significant today as cotton and pig iron, coal, railways, steel and oil that fuelled the industrial revolution between the 1770s and 1830s, Victorian prosperity between the 1830s and the 1880s and the golden age of full employment between the 1940s and the 1980s. The microelectronics revolution is therefore significant, not only for the technological possibilities that it brings but, more profoundly, because of its role in ushering in the whole new age of development – the information age. The information age brings a whole new paradigm of development.

A paradigm can be described as an 'ideal' pattern or style of productive organization or best technological 'common sense' that prevails at the time (Perez, 1983). A paradigm therefore refers to the prevailing 'best practice' that is applicable in almost any industry and everywhere. During the post-war period, for example, mass production was best practice: it was the prevailing common sense for best productivity and most profitable practice for automobile producers, for clothing manufacturers, for chemical companies, for producers of fast-moving consumer goods (e.g. washing powder and toothpaste) and for many others. From the 1930s to the 1980s, mass production represented the ideal organizational and managerial 'common sense' for best productivity and most profit.

Today, mass production is no longer the prevailing common sense. It is rapidly giving way to flexible production. The paradigm of flexible production is radically transforming the prevailing engineering and managerial common sense in almost every industry (Freeman and Perez, 1988). With mass production, profits were made from the replication of massive

Table 1.3 Old and new best practice compared

Old best practice	New best practice
Mass production	Flexibility, specialization
Mass markets	Niche markets, customization
Labour is a variable cost	Labour is human capital
There is one best way	A better way can always be found
Stocks held 'just in case'	Stocks delivered 'just in time'
People fixed to positions	Variable posts, adaptable people
Tolerance for rejects	Strive for 'zero defects', 'zero rejects'
Stockpiling and markdowns	Innovation
Materials and energy-intensive	Materials and energy-saving; information-intensive

quantities of identical units, realizing tremendous scale economies and low unit cost of production. It was very much a numbers game – companies battled for market share and competed on price, mark-downs and stock-piling. With flexible production, companies compete on quality; they listen to consumers; and attempt to satisfy their needs as closely as possible – customization, market segmentation and diagonal integration are the order of the day. Production is very much consumer-driven. Some of the salient features of the new paradigm of flexible production are:

- Product variety and specialization;
- Flexible systems and adaptable procedures;
- Niche markets, customization;
- Widespread delegation of decision-making;
- Much in-house training and re-training of people;
- Variable posts and adaptable people;
- Innovation; and
- Market segmentation.

Table 1.3 compares some of the principles of the old mass-production paradigm with that of flexible production. It can be observed that, with the old best practice of mass production, stocks were held 'just in case'; while with the new practice of flexible production, stocks are delivered 'just in time'. Also, in the old practice of mass production, labour is treated as a variable cost, a 'disposable' item. Flexible producers, by contrast treat labour as human capital and the key to quality.

Flexible production is already a way of life for Japanese automobile manufacturers. Perhaps the most striking difference between mass production and flexible (lean) production lies in their ultimate objectives.

> Mass-producers set a limited goal for themselves – 'good enough', which translates into an acceptable number of defects, a maximum acceptable level of inventories, a narrow range of standardized products .... Lean producers, on the other hand, set their sights explicitly on perfection: continually declining costs, zero defects, zero inventories, and endless product variety.
>
> (Womack *et al.*, 1990)

In fact, it is the Japanese that perfected the concept of 'lean production' (Womack, *et al.*, 1990). The Japanese adopted Kaizen (continuous improvement) as their guiding philosophy (Imai, 1986) and have succeeded in producing smaller, more fuel-efficient and quality competitive cars. It is not surprising, therefore, that 'in 1973, 12% of US consumers felt that Japanese cars were of better quality than US ones, but by 1983 that figure had risen to 40%.' (Bessant, 1991). The Japanese success in the automobile industry is partially due to their quick adoption and perfection of the principles of flexible production (see Chapter 3 and Chapter 9). It is not surprising that old-style, mass-production manufacturers such as General Motors (GM) in the USA are having a hard time recovering from Japanese competition. The Japanese success with flexible production in the automobile industry has some important lessons for the tourism industry.

The Japanese equivalents in the travel and tourism industry are holiday-makers – players whose business it is to make, market, distribute and deliver holiday experiences. Holiday-makers, include cruise ships, Disney-land and other similar-themed entertainment complexes, and all-inclusive establishments such as *Club Med* (France), *SuperClub* (Jamaica) and *Sandals* (Jamaica). The drive toward continuous quality improvement and flexible production is being adopted by holiday makers and is largely responsible for their tremendous success compared with other industry players. Like the Japanese, holiday-makers increasingly fill the quality gap in the travel and tourism industry (see Chapter 9). Holiday-makers produce quality holiday experiences at prices which are cost-competitive with mass, standardized and rigidly-packaged options. The innovative and fast-moving cruise lines are already taking away business from unimaginative and backward land-based hotels on many Caribbean islands and indeed elsewhere.

1.9. TOURISM WILL LEAD THE NEW 'BEST PRACTICE'

The tourism industry was following the manufacturing sector when it adopted the principles of mass production – a principle to which it was ill-suited. For travellers are not mass, standardized and rigidly packaged by nature. They never were. They were simply forced by the economics of mass production to consume standardized packaged travel and leisure services because they were darn cheap! Today, the inherent information-intensity and human-intensity of tourism, as well as the natural indivi-duality of its consumers, make the industry an ideal candidate for flexible organization, management and production. Tourism is therefore expected to be a lead sector in mastering the principles of flexible production. While tourism followed manufacturing during the last couple of decades, in the decades to come, tourism could well lead the manufacturing sector along the path of flexible production.

Cruise lines are the leaders in flexible production in the tourism industry. Not only do cruise ships offer the flexibility of varied ports of call, but they offer the flexibility of varied activities and attractions at each port of call (including cruises to nowhere). Cruise ships also have the flexibility to source materials and labour on a global scale (much like multinational corporations operating in the manufacturing sector); to dispose of their garbage flexibly (at sea when no one is looking); as well as to the flexibility to avoid taxation (through registration of ships in tax-free locations). In addition, cruise ships have begun to segment the market in a major way: Club Med, Star Quest and Windstar offer romance under sail; Renais-sance, Crystal and Seabourne offer sophistication; Lindbar and Frontier offer adventure; Windjammer Barefoot offers active holidays; Carnival offers fun and entertainment; Radisson Diamond offers business and incentive travel; and Ocean Quest specializes in diving. Cruise ships are *mass customizing* the market as they are able to use the enormous scale economies from their large size to produce flexible holidays at relatively low prices to a large number of clients.

1.10. TOURISM IN TRANSITION

The travel and tourism industry has not escaped the impacts of the Gulf War, the two oil crises, the jet aircraft or the build-up of algae in the Adriatic sea. Nor will it escape the overwhelming impacts of information technology, the 'greening' of consumers and the overpowering imperative toward the new global 'best practice' of flexible production.

The tourism industry has begun to change its course radically. In fact, the five key forces that created mass tourism in the first place, are them-selves changing (Fig. 1.3). From Figure 1.3, it can be seen that new frame conditions such as airline deregulation, economic restructuring, environ-mental awareness, consumer protection and the increased spread and flexibility of vacation days, are giving rise to a new tourism. On the

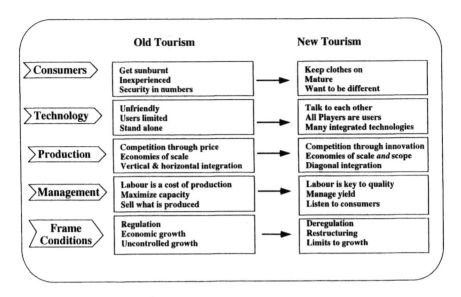

	Old Tourism	New Tourism
Consumers	Get sunburnt Inexperienced Security in numbers	Keep clothes on Mature Want to be different
Technology	Unfriendly Users limited Stand alone	Talk to each other All Players are users Many integrated technologies
Production	Competition through price Economies of scale Vertical & horizontal integration	Competition through innovation Economies of scale *and* scope Diagonal integration
Management	Labour is a cost of production Maximize capacity Sell what is produced	Labour is key to quality Manage yield Listen to consumers
Frame Conditions	Regulation Economic growth Uncontrolled growth	Deregulation Restructuring Limits to growth

Fig. 1.3. Old and new tourism compared.

management and production sides, price competition is giving way to quality competition, and producers are moving away from just selling what they produce as they begin to *listen* to consumers (see Chapter 4). Together, these developments are beginning to signal the end of mass tourism.

1.11. NEW TOURISM

The widespread adoption of a new industry 'best practice' constitutes a 'new tourism'. Many signs of the new tourism are already apparent:

- the demand for independent holidays is growing;
- the demand for choice and flexibility is greater than it has ever been;
- information technologies are rapidly diffusing (96% of all US travel agencies are linked to CRSs);
- CRSs are becoming the flexible alternative to package holidays;
- the rate of growth of the traditional sun package tour business is declining;
- there is increasing environmental planning and control of tourism in host countries (Belize, Bermuda);
- there is increasing segmentation of vacation markets which cater to lifestyle characteristics (DINKS, YUPPIES, MILKIES); and

- the travel behaviour and motivation of tourists are changing (shorter breaks, activity-oriented).

Some signals are very weak and only just beginning to take hold (the decline of the package tour), others are more apparent (technology adoption) and yet others are not immediately visible (the power of the new green consumers).

New tourism exists if and where the following six conditions hold:

1. The holiday is flexible and can be purchased at prices that are competitive with mass-produced holidays (cruises *v.* land-based holidays).
2. Production of travel and tourism-related services are not dominated by scale economies alone. Tailor-made services will be produced while still taking advantages of scale economies where they apply (yield management).
3. Production is increasingly driven by the requirements of consumers.
4. The holiday is marketed to *individuals* with different needs, incomes, time constraints and travel interests. Mass marketing is no longer the dominant paradigm.
5. The holiday is consumed on a large scale by tourists who are more experienced travellers, more educated, more destination oriented, more independent, more flexible and more green.
6. Consumers look at the environment and culture of the destinations they visit as a key part of the holiday experience.

Old industry practices of mass marketing, standardization, limited choice and inflexible holidays are no longer 'common sense'. Tourism is taking on a greener, more individual, flexible and, segmented character. Industry players are also diagonally integrating to control the value creation process of the industry (see Chapter 8). The winners will be the leaders of these new tourism practices.

1.12. THE IMPLICATIONS OF NEW TOURISM

New tourism will change the boundaries of the tourism industry and radically alter the position of industry players. Players closest to consumers (e.g. travel agents, hotels, cruise ships) and those in control of the industry's information (e.g. those that own CRSs) are expected to gain. CRSs will increasingly become the flexible alternative to pre-packaged holidays offered by tour operators. *The role of tour operators is expected to decline in importance.* It is no longer relevant whether a company is an airline, a travel agent, hotel or tour operator. What becomes more relevant are the *activities* along the value chain that they control.

These changes imply a radical transformation of the opportunities available to the various players in the tourism industry. New functions and demands will emerge (e.g. quality control, flexible holidays), while at the same time other key activities will become less important (e.g. pre-packaged tours). Thus, the position of each player within the value chain will have to be re-thought. In addition, as the rules of the game continue to change, the pressures of cooperation and/or concentration are likely to be more intense.

Diagonal integration – a process whereby firms use information technologies to logically combine services for best productivity and most profitability – will be one of the most significant developments in the international travel and leisure industry. Diagonal integration will become a key tool for controlling the process of value creation in the tourism industry. It will continue to blur the boundaries among industry players and make the travel and tourism industry a system of wealth-creation. Already, the boundaries within the tourism industry, and between this industry and others, are becoming increasingly blurred. Players are crossing each others' borders more than ever before: banks move into travel agencies; insurance companies acquire hotel interests; airlines provide credit cards; department stores operate travel agencies; and pleasure-boat companies move into hotels.

The industry, as a result of this trend, will become more *'systems'-like* in nature. One of the key implications of the trend towards diagonal integration is that competitors will increasingly come from outside the industry. Equally, diagonal integration will offer opportunities for travel and tourism players to move into other industries, particularly services.

New tourism holds a number of key implications for industry players. In what follows, we will briefly examine some of the implications for tour operators, travel agents, and hotels.

1.12.1. Tour Operators

Several of the value-creating activities of tour operators will decline in importance – particularly those of packaging, risk brokerage and distribution. These functions are being increasingly superseded by computerized reservation systems. In response to the declining importance of key activities, tour operators will have to take action on several fronts. They will have to:

- create more flexibly packaged holidays;
- expand their information functions (e.g. provide computerized reservation niches for specific products or destinations);
- develop creative relationships with travel agencies (selected agents could have the option of flexibly packaging holidays on-line from the tour operator's portfolio); and

- control the quality of the product at all levels.

Quality control at all crucial phases in the delivery of the holiday will become a key source of competitive advantage for tour operators. Tour operators will have to take a far broader view of the holiday that they deliver. They will have to find ways of better controlling and influencing the product delivered to consumers.

1.12.2. Travel Agencies

The importance of travel agency reservations, ticketing the client advice functions are all expected to grow in importance. Already travel agencies handle a large and growing proportion of airline bookings. In creating more value from these activities, travel agencies will have to use their CRSs creatively and provide the information that consumers want.

It is to ensuring the satisfaction of the travel consumers that agencies must give priority in order to ensure their own long-term survival and competitiveness. *The ability of travel agents to acquire, provide and transmit unbiased information in a courteous, efficient and timely manner will be key to their competitive success.* Indeed, a competitor agency will be able to copy a convenient 'high-street' location, subscribe to the same airline reservation system and place satellite printers in their corporate clients' offices. However, a competitor will have tremendous difficulty in copying travel agency personnel who place the interest of the consumers first, causing them to be loyal.

New opportunities for travel agencies to create value will emerge in the areas of packaging and in the representation of services other than those of tour operators. Travel agencies will have the information at their finger-tips to provide flexible itineraries. Strategically, through cooperation with other agencies, agents can increase buying power with airlines and other suppliers in order to obtain competitive prices for package components. This will allow travel agencies the avenue to provide competitively priced, flexible holiday packages. Travel agencies will also find it profitable to represent other services such as cruise ships, pleasure boats, car-rental companies, hotels, spas and other segments that will grow in importance in the travel and leisure industry.

1.12.3. Hotels

Hotels will no longer be able to leave their marketing to tour operators or their reservation systems. They will have to get closer to their consumers and to travel agents in the market place. This is the only way that hotels will be able to adjust effectively their products to suit their changing clients.

Being close to consumers and supplying the experiences they want have become so important that hotels can no longer simply sit back and expect their rooms to be sold.

One of the key ingredients in the success of Sandals and SuperClub all-inclusive hotels in the Caribbean, for example, is the strong links they have established with travel agents in the marketplace. Nothing is left to chance. Sandals and SuperClub employ sales agents in the marketplace whose business it is to travel the length and breath of the USA (and increasingly European) markets to educate travel agents about their product, new services, new properties and new experiences being offered.

Hotels will have to work more closely with their guests, *listen* to them and modify the services they offer to meet the new demands. Hotels will also have to identify market niches, segment the market and provide the experiences that consumers want and for which they are willing to pay.

1.12.4. The Winners and the Losers

Although travel agents, hotels and cruise ships are closest to the consumer and are thus expected to increase their influence on the industry's value-creation, this will not happen automatically. The current dominance of airlines over the industry's CRSs is no accident. CRSs are the results of strategic decisions and continuous investments initiated by US airlines beginning more than a decade ago. Similarly, cruise ships, hotels, resorts, theme parks, travel agencies and suppliers on site will all have to make strategic moves and undertake strategic investments and build strategic alliances in order to ensure their own competitive success.

The very same logic holds for tour operators. Although the role of the tour operator is expected to decline, this will not be the case for all operators. While the role of the tour operators in their conventional roles of 'middle men', capacity buying and holiday packaging are likely to decline, their role could increase as they seek to control other wealth-creating activities within the industry (e.g. CRSs, flexible holidays, on-line holiday packaging, hotels and travel agency operations). Competitive strategies are key determinants of competitive success – for industry players and for tourism destinations.

1.13. THE END OF MASS TOURISM?

Mass tourism will not disappear altogether or be completely replaced by the new tourism. However, the *rate of growth* of new tourism will rapidly outpace that of the old (Fig. 1.4). The future growth prospects of old and new tourism can be compared with *typewriters* and *computers*. While there

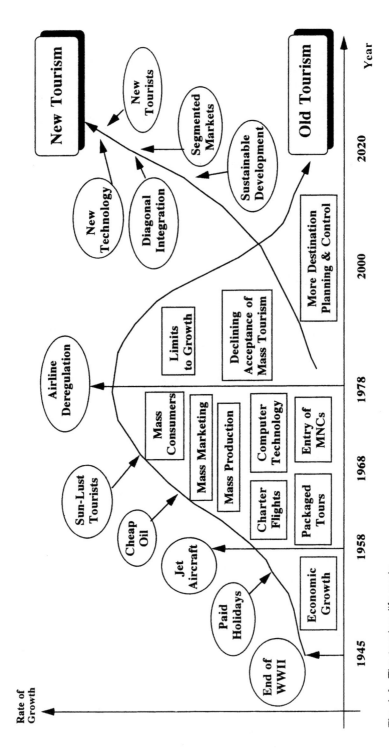

Fig. 1.4. The tourism life cycle.

will continue to be a market for typewriters (mass tourism), the growth of new computers (new tourism) will be far greater. Having used typewriters and then been exposed to the power of computers, users will be unwilling to go back to the old way. This exact logic holds for old and new tourism.

Also as new demand is fuelled by population growth and the opening up of new markets in Eastern Europe, Asia, the Pacific and Africa, the demand for rigidly packaged holidays to sun destinations could surge. In time, these consumers will become more experienced, more mature, more green, more flexible and more discerning. They will advance to higher levels of consumption, as signified by flexible, independent and more environmentally sound vacations. And, of course, once bitten, there will be no turning back.

Moreover, there is growing evidence that new consumers are quick to learn and they will not necessarily have to pass through the era of rigidity and mass environmental destruction before they are 'born again' (see Chapter 5). The sheer fragility of the environment will not tolerate it. New markets, for example, the Eastern European countries and Japan, will not first have to re-invent the wheel – in other words to make their experiences with mass tourism before they move on to the new. In fact, first-timers provide some of the best markets for the new tourism. As we will see in Chapter 5, the mass search for the sun is neither a driving factor in the vacation pursuit of the Japanese nor the former East Germans. Rather, sightseeing, relaxation and sport, on the part of the Japanese, and the need to visit friends and relatives and to experience nature, on the part of the former East Germans, are the prime motives of travel by these new groups of travellers.

Computers, like the new tourism, signal the beginning of a new paradigm – a new best practice and new opportunities for consumption. Computers allow for flexibility and make it possible for flexibility to be obtained at prices that are cost-competitive with mass, standardized and rigidly packaged options. Growth in the new flexible options will be tremendous.

Companies and countries dependent on tourism will have to take strategic decisions as to which route they pursue or what combinations of the old and new tourism they choose to develop. Taking a conscious strategic decision to develop a new tourism is critically important for industry players and for destinations. As a tourism destination, the Commonwealth of the Bahamas provides an excellent example of the importance and benefits of new tourism (the Family islands), when compared with old tourism (Nassau). The Bahamas offers important lessons both for old tourism destinations as well as would-be or soon-to-be new tourism destinations (see Chapter 5).

Corporate entities and countries cannot afford to let the new tourism happen to them. They must make it happen. They must be leaders in the new tourism. Otherwise, they will be left behind.

1.14. COMPETITIVE STRATEGIES – KEY TO SUCCESS

To stay ahead of the game, industry players must develop and implement new strategies. Competitive strategies are conscious policies and proce-dures developed by companies in order to 'strategically align themselves with the turbulent environment and select appropriate strategies to create defensible competitive positions' (Tse and Olsen, 1991). The more rapid the changes in the firm's environment, the more important the conscious strategy formulation and implementation becomes. The travel and tourism industry is undergoing rapid and radical transformation. Therefore, competitive strategies are more important than ever for the survival and competitiveness of industry players.

Generic competitive strategies of cost-leadership, differentiation and focus (Porter, 1987) have been developed for the manufacturing sector. These have limited applicability to the tourism industry, however. Even with cost-leadership, a unique product, or superior focus, the producers of *typewriters* (old tourism), for example, would have limited success in the face of the rapid diffusion and declining cost of *computers* (new tourism). In this case, radical innovation – the introduction of new and unprece-dented products to the market – is of critical importance.

Industry players as well as tourist destinations will have to follow a number of principles in order to compete successfully in today's tourism market place. For competitive success, industry players will have to:

- put consumers first;
- be leaders in quality;
- develop radical innovations;
- strengthen the firm's strategic position within the industry's value chain.

Those companies that develop the capability to implement these strategies most efficiently will be successful.

For tourist destinations to be competitive, they will also have to follow a number of key principles. They will have to:

- put the environment first;
- make tourism a lead sector;
- strengthen the distribution channels in the marketplace; and
- build a dynamic private sector.

Successfully implementing these strategies will place tourist destinations firmly in the camp of new tourism – a tourism that is sensitive to the environment and the people of the country; a tourism that is sustainable; a tourism that is able to transform tourism-dependent and vulnerable island economies into viable entities.

1.15. WHAT IS TO COME?

This book provides important insights and analysis of key issues facing the tourism industry:

- why did the American Express Optima Card fail?
- why are cruise ships the Japanese equivalents in the tourism industry?
- why do all-inclusive hotels out-perform conventional hotels?
- why is information technology taking the tourism industry by storm?
- why do some airlines make more money from their CRSs than from their principal activity of transporting passengers?
- why are buildings getting smarter?
- why are resort offices developing in Japan?
- why is Club Med shifting from the sexy formula which made it famous and now wants to attract the 'fat rich guy who wants to eat all day'?
- why the power of the new, green consumer should not go unnoticed?
- why are some companies empowering their employees to do anything to satisfy their customers – which includes picking up the bill, if necessary
- why are some airlines dying and fewer will be flying?

This book will guide readers through the evolution of mass tourism (Chapter 2) and the transformation toward a new tourism (Chapter 4). The book carries out a detailed analysis of the key imperatives for change – limits to growth and the emergence of a new global 'best practice' (Chapter 3), new consumers (Chapter 5) and new technologies (Chapters 6 and 7). Chapter 8 identifies the important trend towards 'diagonalization' in the tourism industry and explores the implications of new tourism for tour operators, travel agents and hotels. Finally, competitive strategies for industry players and tourism destinations are explored in Chapters 9 and 10.

II
OLD AND NEW TOURISM

2

MASS TOURISM

2.1. INTRODUCTION

Tourism was brought sharply into international focus at the end of the Second World War. Within a mere 20 years of the industry's take-off, international tourism displayed nearly all the characteristics of its manufacturing counterpart – it was *mass, standardized* and *rigidly packaged.* By the mid-1970s, tourism was being produced along assembly-line principles, similar to the automobile industry, with tourists consuming travel and leisure services in a similar robot-like and routine manner.

Today mass tourism is no longer common sense. The factors that caused mass tourism (e.g. frame conditions such as cheap oil and paid holidays, mass consumers, computer technology and standardized production and management practices) are themselves changing. Understanding the evolution of mass tourism, and the factors that created it, are key to understanding the industry's transformation. Building a capacity to respond to the changes taking place in the international tourism industry and to play a lead role in the creation of a new best practice, will be key determinants of competitive success in tourism – for regions, for countries, and for industry players.

This chapter will demonstrate that mass tourism was the logical outcome of key social and economic influences at the time. It will show how and why post-war prosperity, together with paid holidays, the jet aircraft, packaged tours, sun-lust tourists and other developments, gave birth to mass tourism. It will also be shown how the forces of mass tourism took on different roles and significance in the USA and Europe.

2.2. THE HISTORICAL SETTING

Tourism harks back to the conquests of Alexander the Great (356–323 BC) and the subsequent development of the Hellenistic urban system (Turner and Ash, 1975, p.20). It is argued that tourism requires both large claustrophobic cities and the means to escape from them, both of which were present in Greece during this period.

Within modern times, the notion of tourism is closely linked to the idea of the 'Grand Tour', which spanned the 16th to 19th Centuries. The Grand Tour is 'a tour of certain cities in Western Europe undertaken primarily, but not exclusively, for education and pleasure' (Towner, 1985, p.301). This later era of grand tourism was typified by long, expensive, 'classical' and 'romantic' visits, mainly by the British aristocracy, to France, Italy, Germany, Switzerland and the Low Countries. Over time, and with the rise of the middle professional class, the Grand Tour was patronized by a wider segment of the population. Nonetheless, only 3–4% of the population represented the nucleus from which Grand Tourists might have been drawn (Towner, 1985, p.306). The golden age of the Grand Tour was the 18th Century, particularly the 30 years before the outbreak of the French Revolution in 1789. By the 1830s, the length of the Grand Tour fell from an average of 40 months in the mid-16th Century to an average of only 4 months (Towner, 1985, p.316).

The growth of tourism to 'mass' proportions as it is known today, has its foundation in several timely innovations: technologically in the field of transportation; and in the existence of a critical facilitating force, entrepreneurship – in the person of Thomas Cook.

In 1815, 1 year after the Battle of Waterloo ended the Napoleonic wars, the first channel crossing by steamer was made (the site of the battle itself becoming a major tourist attraction). By 1821, a regular service was operated between the ports of Dover and Calais. In 1828 the first railways were laid in France and Austria, and in 1844 the railway reached Switzerland. 'This revolution in Transport technology and the low cost, speed and efficiency that it provided, led to an immediate expansion of European tourism' (Turner and Ash, 1975, p.52).

Complementing transportation technology was the existence of entrepreneurial talent, 'initiative' and 'organizing genius' in the person of Thomas Cook. 'His originality lay in his methods, his almost infinite capacity for taking trouble, his acute sense of the needs of his clients, his power of invention and his bold imagination' (Young, 1973, p.21). It has been written that 'the father of modern tourism was unquestionably Thomas Cook' (English, 1986, p.3). 'Cook was the perfect entrepreneur, a brilliant opportunist, quick to sense the need of his clientele ...' (Turner and Ash, 1975, p.52). He was a true Schumpeterian entrepreneur – a leader, a 'disturber of the peace', who had the initiative, authority, foresight, intuition and psyche to carry out innovations.

Thomas Cook organized travel on a scale that had never been seen before. He heralded an era of organized, large-scale, relatively cheap tourism, spread across national, regional and international destinations. If Europe had the 'hot spots' for the Grand Tourists, the opening of the Far East, India and America, were the hallmarks of the Cook era. Until the early 1860s, Britain remained the main field of Cook's activities; in 1862 he moved into Europe; he moved into America in 1866; took his first round-the-world trip in 1872; reached India and the Far East by the 1880s; and the first Cook hotel was established at Luxor (Egypt) in 1887.

In 1862, the first true package tours were provided by Cook – all the details of transport and accommodation were pre-arranged for tourists who were, generally, of modest means. Spurred on by his example and the profits made by this entrepreneur, many imitators entered the fray. Turner and Ash write, for example, that 'it was not long before his example was imitated; in 1863, the Stangen Travel Agency was established in Breslau. Stangen soon moved his centre of operation to Berlin and became a successful rival to Cook' (Turner and Ash, 1975, p.54). By taking advantage of 19th-Century advances in transport technology, Thomas Cook and Son had effected a revolution in tourism by the end of the century. No longer the preserve of the wealthy and the leisured, tourism was now an industry. While an average of 257 people per annum took part in Grand tourism during the 1547–1840 period (Towner, 1985), Cook had taken 20000 people to the *Paris Exhibition* of 1897 – such was the magnitude of his entrepreneurial prowess.

Despite the leaps and bounds that the industry experienced, tourism, until the 1930s, was still a matter of trains, boats and coaches. Travel by water transportation was a very important form of tourism during the 1920s and 1930s. The ships themselves were a form of floating hotel, where the act of travel was equated with tourism. Travel was seen as an end in itself. As if the industry has gone full circle, today, cruise tourism is one of the fastest growing segments of the international tourism industry.

It was in 1950 that the first package holiday built around air transport was organized. This was undertaken by Vladimir Raitz, a Russian émigré educated at the London School of Economics. His successful company, Horizon Holidays (now merged with Thomson, the largest UK operator) was one of the top three tour operators in Britain. By the 1960s, the package holiday business began to use air transport in a major way as Raitz's competitors, spurred on by his success, also began using the aircraft.

Still, foreign travel in the 1930s remained a luxury commodity within the reach of only a privileged few having both plenty of free time and considerable purchasing power. This picture was to change when, coupled with post-war peace and prosperity, came innovations in aircraft technology and changes in labour legislation, which provided paid holidays, and the development of the package tour. Aided by these innovations, mass tourism had arrived.

2.3. MASS TOURISM DEFINED

Mass tourism is a phenomenon of large-scale packaging of standardized leisure services at fixed prices for sale to a mass clientele. Mass tourism refers to key characteristics that the international tourism industry displayed during the 1960s, 1970s and 1980s. Mass tourism exists if the following conditions hold.

1. The holiday is standardized, rigidly packaged and inflexible. No part of the holiday could be altered except by paying higher prices.
2. The holiday is produced through the mass replication of identical units, with scale economies as the driving force.
3. The holiday is mass marketed to an undifferentiated clientele.
4. The holiday is consumed *en masse*, with a lack of consideration by tourists for local norms, culture, people or the environments of tourist-receiving destinations.

Standardization and rigidity are very clear characteristics of package tours offered on a large scale. An inclusive charter tour provides the same level of transportation, accommodation, meal and transfer services to all clients who pay the same price, visit the same sun destination, sunbathe on the same beaches, sleep in the same high-rise hotels and in the same type of beds, read the same tourist brochures, visit the same sites, stay the same length of time, take the same kinds of photographs and even buy the same souvenirs.

Within the confines of mass, standardized and rigidly packaged tourism, choice, individuality, personalized services and flexibility are just not possible (or where possible, it is at horrendous prices compared with the package price). There is little place within mass tourism for the individual who wishes to be different from the crowd, who wishes to use different accommodation or participate in different holiday activities. It is true that many tourists have avoided the 'mass' tourist holidays and many have used the relatively cheap services of mass tourism as launching pads for their own vacations. However, in the 1960s and the 1970s, these were the exceptions rather than the common trend.

Commenting on the trend toward mass tourism, Turner and Ash wrote:

> The people-processors hate individual tourists, especially those with quirks and idiosyncrasies (though the computer is helping the

industry handle such non-conformists). The individual needs as much attention as a flock of mass tourists, so he offers disappointing returns.

(Turner and Ash; 1975, p. 108)

Mass tourism certainly had its time and place. Today the tourism industry is in crisis. Mass tourism is no longer best practice. Conditions that gave birth to it – the frame conditions, consumers, technology, production and management practices – are themselves changing. Understanding how mass tourism came about and why it was best practice at the time are key to understanding why the international tourism industry is being transformed and the shape that the new best practice is taking.

2.4. THE EVOLUTION OF MASS TOURISM

Mass tourism is a product of the late 1960s and early 1970s. Several factors came together to create mass tourism. These factors are summarized in Figure 2.1.

From Figure 2.1, it can be seen that several interrelated developments in the world economy produced mass tourism. Important circumstances (e.g. post-war peace and prosperity, paid holidays, governments' promotion of tourism and generous incentives offered by developing countries to attract international hotel chains) provided the necessary conditions within which mass tourism flourished. Sun-lust and inexperienced mass consumers also aided the creation of mass tourism. While on the technology front, the jet aircraft, computers and reservations systems facilitated its development. In the area of production, cheap oil, charter flights, package tours, standardization, economies of scale and mass production helped in its maturation. Management practices of franchising mass marketing and vertical and horizontal integration also played their role in the creation and spread of mass tourism.

None of these conditions on its own could have produced mass, standardized and rigidly packaged (MSRP) tourism. However, the combination of these factors, together with the timing of their respective developments, provided both necessary and sufficient conditions for MSRP tourism to take off.

Different factors played relatively different roles in producing mass tourism. In the USA, for example, international hotel chains, airline oligopolies, business travel, the car, domestic tourism, short breaks and travel and entertainment cards were important forces for mass tourism. In Europe, tour operators, charter flights, holiday travel (as opposed to business), intra-European travel to Mediterranean sun destinations and long-stay holidays were the driving forces.

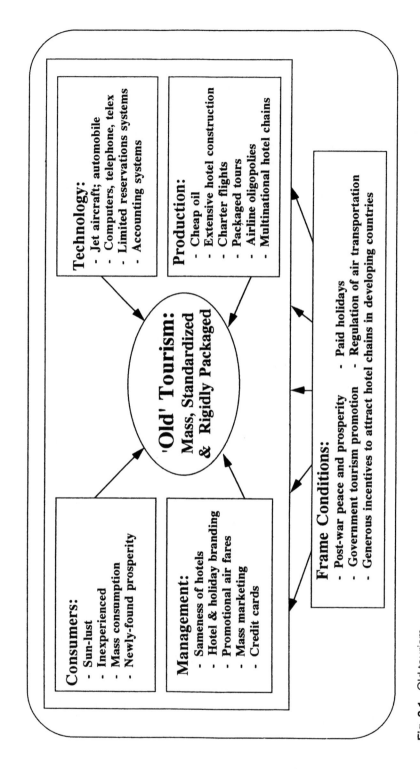

Fig. 2.1. Old tourism.

2.5. FRAME CONDITIONS

'Frame conditions' refer to factors within the social, economic and institutional framework of the world environment that are conducive to the development of tourism. Frame conditions normally lie outside the control of the tourism industry but have tremendous impacts on the industry's growth and development. Frame conditions that facilitated the growth of tourism include post-war peace and prosperity, paid holidays, increased leisure time, and a governmental framework of incentive legislation, tourism promotion boards and ministries of tourism.

2.5.1. Post-war Peace and Prosperity

A major impetus to tourism's growth was provided by a very congenial sociopolitical framework that delivered peace and prosperity to the world economy. The world economy recovered from the major depression of the 1930s, and sustained peace finally returned at the end of the Second World War in 1945. The stability and growth of the world economy were additionally promoted by the Marshall Plan, Keynesian-inspired economic policies and the strength of the American economy. At this time, oil, the main source of industrial energy, was cheap and plentiful. Energy at the right price was abundantly available to meet all the transportation requirements of a growing industry. As a result, industries flourished, economies grew and affluence increased. This opened up new travel possibilities for many citizens of the world.

2.5.2. Labour Legislation/Paid Holidays

In the field of labour legislation, two important advances were made: paid annual holidays and the 40-hour working week. In 1936, at the instigation of its trade union representative, the International Labour Organization (ILO) adopted the first convention that was to promote paid holidays and later on, paid annual vacations. The French government in 1936–1937 instituted annual paid holidays. After the First World War, starting in the 1930s and gathering force in the 1940s, 2–3 weeks annual paid holidays became the norm. It was the coming of paid annual holidays that has had the real impact on the development of long-haul vacation trips such as exist between Europe and the Caribbean and Pacific islands. The introduction of paid holidays and paid annual vacations were important innovations in Labour Law, since by the 1940s only 14 countries had enacted general legislation on paid holidays (World Tourism Organization, 1978, p. 31). Then in 1938, the Fair Labour Standards Act in the USA mandated the working week to be 40 hours. These two significant social innovations provided more time for non-work leisure activities as well as the necessary incomes with which to spend in the pursuit of them.

2.5.3. Government Promotion of Tourism

In the inter-war years, governments of developed countries began to recognize the importance of tourism to the economy – particularly as an item in the balance of payments. This recognition of the importance of tourism was stimulated in the period of post-war reconstruction in the 1950s. Promotional activities of European national tourist offices were at the time directed mainly towards the North American market.

By the 1960s, many developing countries had come to the realization that tourism could help them to generate much-needed income, employment and foreign exchange. For example, in Indonesia's first 5-year development plan (1968–1973) tourism was adopted as a strategy for economic development (Noronha, 1979, p. 180). Tourism was considered a welcome saviour in these economies at a time when:

- primary commodity exports were declining;
- many governments were eager to diversify their skewed baskets of primary exports (e.g. sugar, cocoa, coffee, citrus, bananas); and
- disillusionment with attempts at import substitution and industrialization in Latin America and the Caribbean was beginning to set in.

This conviction was not at all surprising at a time when tourism was, as it still is, considered 'a promising new resource for economic development' (Organization for Economic Corporation and Development, 1966, p. 7).

Based on this view, the 1960s became a time when many developing countries rushed to establish boards and ministries of tourism. Young (1973, p. 1) observes that 'the importance of tourism is gradually being recognized and, in many countries, particularly in developing ones, it now warrants a ministry all to itself'. Development corporations for the promotion of hotel and other infrastructure investments and generous tax incentives to foster and induce foreign capital to develop tourism, were the order of the day. These policies very naturally complemented the globalization drives of multinational corporations in the hotel sector.

The very nature and emphasis on tourism development in developing countries' reinforced the trend toward mass, standardized and rigidly packaged tourism. It should be considered that, at the time, governments and private sectors, were often firmly wedded to the equation: *volume = benefits.* The more flights, the more hotels, the more tourists, the more advertising, the more promotions and the more public relations there were, the more profits, incomes, employment and foreign exchanges would accrue to the country.

The institutional framework within which governments and companies operated in the development of their tourism sectors was also conducive to the development of an industry oriented along mass-production lines. For example, a hotel of 'international standard' by definition cannot be less than 100 rooms, it must have air conditioning, a lift and a swimming pool. Many governments and companies contemplating entry into the tourist business, hardly considered anything less than the international standard. It should also be considered that large projects (be they iron and steel mills, airports or large tourist resorts) were always safe investments for governments in political terms. It is within this context of 'the more the merrier', 'more is better', and the idea of attracting 'plenty plenty' tourists, that mass tourism, with its standardized and inflexible consequences, was allowed to flourish.

2.5.4. Generous Incentives for Hotel Chains

Another important frame condition in the making of mass tourism was the existence in developing countries of several generous incentives that encouraged multinational hotel chains to invest in the replication of their standardized facilities throughout the developing world. This included repatriation of profits, cash grants, assistance with project financing, equity participation, loan guarantees, tax-free bonds, underwriting share issues, tax holidays, investment and other tax credits, accelerated depreciation, double taxation relief, special currency exchange rates, infrastructure construction, leasing of properties, marketing support, development of amenities, training and the development of special institutions. By 1978, multinational corporations accounted for 43.9% of total hotel rooms in the Philippines; 61.0% in the Seychelles; 49.7% in the Senegal; 33.4% in Venezuela; 31.0% in Jamaica; and 42.6% in Trinidad and Tobago (United Nations Center on Transnational Corporations, 1982).

Table 2.1 shows the importance of multinational hotels in different parts of the world. It can be seen that multinational corporations played a major role in the hotel industry of developing regions. MNCs accounted for 16% of the hotel stock in the Middle East, and 16.6% and 17.7% of total hotel rooms in Asia and Africa respectively. Particularly because of its proximity to the USA (the franchising and MNCs capital of the world) the Caribbean region had the highest penetration (35.6%) of multinational hotel rooms. When it is considered that hotel chains (e.g. Club Mediterranée, Hilton Hotel, Holiday Inn and others) built identical hotels worldwide, developing 'sun' countries were initiated into mass tourism with large, standardized, hotels. Mass, standardized and rigidly packaged tour operators and tourists were soon to follow.

Table 2.1 Dominance of multinational hotels in 1978

Regions	Multinational-associated hotel rooms (as a percentage of all rooms)
Developed economies	2.1
Middle East	16.0
Asia	16.6
Africa	17.7
Latin America	4.6
Caribbean	35.6

Source: United Nations Center on Transnational Corporations, 1982.

2.6. CONSUMERS

In any industry, consumers are supposed to be the most important con-sideration – virtually the *raison d'être* for the industry's existence. In the period after the war, however, it was not the consumers, but rather, mass production, scale economies, product standardization and cheap prices that dictated the pace and direction of the growth of tourism, and indeed of all other industries. In other words, *mass tourism was producer- rather than consumer-driven.*

At the time, however, key characteristics of tourism's consumers allowed mass tourism to flourish on a global scale. Tourist's common search for the sun and their consumption of travel *en masse* played an important role in the development of mass, standardized and rigidly packaged tourism the world over. It is not that consumers were naturally undifferentiated and identical human beings. However, whatever individu-ality they possessed was simply subordinated to the greater logic of mass production and the new travel possibilities that cheap packaged holidays made possible.

2.6.1. Sun-lust Tourists

The fashion for the suntan was one of the profound changes in the attitude of tourism's pioneering elite – an attitude that was a complete reversal of the old (Turner and Ash, 1975, p.78). By the 1920s, the leisured class deliberately began to cultivate a darkened skin tone. Commenting on this radical transformation of ideals, Turner and Ash wrote:

In Roman times ladies of refinement had swathed themselves in the fine silks of the Kos to filter the coarsening rays; gardens and parks were provided with elaborately shaded walks, pergolas and colonnades.... Any deliberate cultivation of a tan would have savoured too much of identification with lower (largely rural) classes and coloured subject people. Thus the ladies of the British Empire in India did not relax the cumbersome properties of Victorian dress to suit the climate. Similarly, for the females of the landed aristocracy in Europe, a pale complexion was the symbol of their superior delicacy.

(Turner and Ash, 1975, p.79)

By the 1920s, the sun was not only an element of high fashion, but it was now sought after for precisely the reason it had been avoided – its simple virtues and its closeness-to-the-soil.

Today, industry observers agree that 'the most significant impulse in the development of tourism since the Second World War has been the search for the sun' (OECD, 1966, p.12; Peters, 1969). This can be readily seen when one considers that the movement of leisure travel has mainly been from the cold northern countries to the warm southern countries. It is also not surprising that Spain and Hawaii have become mass tourism destinations, rather than Norway and Alaska.

2.6.2. Mass Consumption

While the industry was not directly consumer-driven, a critical ingredient in the making of mass, standardized and rigidly packaged tourism, had to be the tourists – the ultimate consumer. This was because, ultimately, hotels, travel agencies, tour operators, airlines and governments were satisfying what became *effective demand* for this type of tourism – effective demand being the demand or desire for something, a demand backed by money and followed through with purchase.

The sociopsychological make-up of the consumer a generation ago was largely receptive to mass, standardized and inflexible tourism. This is largely due to the fact that workplaces and everything consumed by mass consumers – from automobiles, dishwashers and television sets to food and clothes – were already 'infected' by decades of mass production, mass marketing and mass consumption. Tourists logically followed in the foot-steps of mass production in the manufacturing sector. As a result, 25 years ago or thereabouts, many tourists did not mind being like everyone else: having the same washing machines or cars as others; eating cornflakes and drinking coca cola like everyone else; being on vacation in the same places as other tourists; or being part of the crowded tourism landscape – on the motorways, on the ski slopes or the beaches. After all, at the time, 'living up to the Jones's' was the consumers' best practice at the time. Copying other vacationers was natural.

If, 25 years ago, one went to a beach, a party or a social gathering, and it was not well patronized, 'crowded' or 'swinging', then one would immediately think that this was not the place to be; or the 'in place' to be; or the place where it was 'happening'. This was precisely the sociopsychological atmosphere of the time that allowed mass, inflexible and standardized tourism to flourish the world over.

This is not to say that international tourism before the 1980s was completely inflexible. Naturally, the more independent, educated and well-to-do citizens of the world took exceptions to this trend. However, what little flexibility did exist, was submitted to the greater logic of the mass production paradigm. The economics of large-scale mass production produced cheaper and more affordable holiday prices – and this made good economic sense. Thus cheap, standardized, affordable holidays were as much a part of the logic of the time as were the forces (e.g. economies of scale and profit) that drove producers to produce fixed, low-priced, affordable, holiday packages. It should also be remembered that after the Second World War holiday-making was just getting within reach of wider segments of the population.

2.6.3. Inexperienced Travellers

The existence of an inexperienced clientele also allowed mass tourism to flourish. Consumers often were more taken up with the novelty and excitement of travel to foreign destinations rather than which destinations they visited, the type of plane seats they had, the hotels they stayed at or the quality of services they received. Since there was no previous experience, consumers had nothing to go by – no real yardstick with which to measure quality. The inexperience of consumers thus provided fertile ground for the replication of standardized hotels across the globe. These hotels provided familiarity, safety and reassurance to consumers who were often visiting a foreign land for the first time. Identical hotels replicated across the globe virtually allowed mass tourists to feel 'at home'.

Inexperienced travellers, fearful of adventure, also encouraged the emergence of tour operators who mass-produced, standardized and rigidly packaged tours, removing any element of consumer risk. The tour operator would pre-test and pre-visit the destination and would normally have a hired representative in the destination – someone with a familiar face who spoke the same language and who could relate to the fears and anxiety of the inexperienced – providing an additional sense of security and an added incentive for mass tourism.

Inexperience, and the sense of insecurity bred by it, also complemented the phenomenon of group affinity, where one feels safer in an unfamiliar environment as a member of a group rather than as an individual traveller. In this respect it might be said that the mass tourists certainly tested the validity of the old saying that: 'there is safety in numbers'. It is therefore not surprising to find that the Japanese – the major new leisure class of the 1980s – began their penetration of new destinations in groups. Groups of camera-toting Japanese tourists may seem odd today to many Westerners who, as Western tourists, passed that stage 1–2 decades before. If the camera-toting Japanese tourists seem strange in the 1980s and 1990s, one can only wonder what perceptions the population of many developing sun-destinations had of masses of Western tourists in the 1960s and 1970s.

2.7. TECHNOLOGY

What the consumers perceived they wanted or needed at the time, on the demand side, were richly facilitated by technological possibilities on the supply side.

Important technological advances have had a very profound impact on the development of mass tourism. The development of the jet aircraft, plastic cards, and the applications of new computer technology facilitated the growth of mass tourism in no small measure. However, the technology did not create mass tourism; rather, technologies – the jet aircraft and computers – were the main instruments for the provision of mass tourism services. Computers were not developed because of the travel and tourism industry; rather, this industry became an essential user of technologies that were designed and developed for other sectors of the economy.

The application of computer technologies to the international tourism industry in the 1960s and 1970s had mainly the impact of improving the *efficiency* of production of mass tourism services. To some extent, technology applications also had the effect of improving the *quality* of tourism services provided. The impact of information technology in generating completely new services (e.g. airline computerized reservation systems and frequent flyer programmes) and in transforming the entire best practice of the tourism industry was to come in 1978 when the US government made considerable strides in deregulating the airline industry.

The role of technology in mass tourism was considerably different from its role today. In the 1960s and 1970s, tourism technologies were stand-alone items, incapable of interacting with human beings or with one another. Today, computers and communications technologies created by airlines are systems of wealth creation in themselves. They have now become indispensable to the industry (see Chapters 6 and 7).

2.7.1. Jet Aircraft

A very important impetus for the creation of modern-day mass tourism phenomenon was the advancement in air transportation technologies. Rapid advances were being made in the technologies of land and sea transport as well. However, in air-transport technology, 1958 was the turning point. 'The year 1958 ushered in a new era – the jet age – which revolutionized transportation the world over and changed long-held perceptions of time and space' (Robinson, 1983, p. 17).

Until 1958, the fastest commercial aeroplane in the US scheduled service was the Douglas DC-7, which averaged a 350 m.p.h. cruising speed. At that rate, it took the whole day to fly across the Atlantic. The intro-duction of jet aircraft – the Boeing 707 and the Douglas DC-8 – the following year changed all that. Cruise speed went up to 590 m.p.h. and travel time over long distances fell by 40%. The jet aircraft was not only almost twice as fast, it also offered *double the capacity* of the earlier piston-engine aircraft.

In 1958, both BOAC (now British Airways) and Pan Am began transatlantic jet services between New York and London and National Airlines launched the first domestic jet service between New York and Miami. By 1964, 72% of all air services were operated with jet aircraft (World Tourism Organization, 1966–1986, p. 29).

The efficiency of jets produced lower fares. The idea of the 'economy fare' was introduced in 1958 and this made travel available to more people. In addition, a wider range of routes was made possible. Accordingly, 'the jet was the catalyst for a prolonged travel boom' (Feldman, 1983, p. 124).

The average annual rate of growth of air transportation was 11.9% between 1958 and 1961 and 13.6% over the 1961–1964 period (figures for 1966 in World Tourism Organization, 1966–1986, p. 29). By 1966, it had been observed that international air traffic was growing faster than the rate of tourism movements itself. World tourist arrivals increased by 259% from 1950–1963 while the number of passengers carried on air services increased by 330% in the same period (World Tourism Organization, 1966–1986, p. 29).

The 1970s was the decade of the wide-bodied jets. Pan Am (no longer in operation) put the first B-747 in scheduled air service in 1970. The aircraft was certified to carry 490 passengers, weighed 710000 pounds (322340 kg), had a wing span of 195 feet (59.44 m), a length of 231 feet (70.41 m) and a height of 63 feet (19.20 m). It was the largest commercial transport in the world at the time of its introduction and carried a crew of 20.

In 1975, British Airways and Air France acquired their first faster-than-sound Concordes and sought to introduce them into the transatlantic market. In 1972, the US certificate carriers boarded more than 195 million passengers, and all the major carriers in the country were flying jets. There were 2239 jets in the airlines' fleets in 1968. By 1983, there were 10 472 jets in service. Commenting on 25 years of the jet age, *Travel Weekly* concluded that: 'for better or worse, air travel now catered to the mass market' (*Travel Weekly* 25th Anniversary Issue, 1983). And so it did.

Air travel played a critically important role in opening up tourism to developing countries. Indeed, it played a more vital role in the creation of international tourism in developing countries than in developed countries mainly because of the great distances of most developing countries from their developed-country tourists. The share of air travel in international tourist arrivals was 65.2% for the Bahamas; 83.1% for Barbados; 89.3% for Kenya; 97.9% for the Philippines; but as little as 10.9% for Italy and 25.8% for Spain (World Tourism Organization figures for 1977; see World Tourism Organization, 1966–1986).

While the jet aircraft changed long-held perceptions of time and place and was the catalyst for a prolonged travel boom, advances in micro-electronics and computers and communications technologies provided the wherewithal to manage this travel boom. Computers and communications technologies facilitated the globalization of the international tourism industry and greatly facilitated the distribution, control, management and coordination of tourism services across the globe. Plastic cards and other forms of electronic payment also facilitated the rapid growth and development of travel and related services.

2.7.2. Plastic Money

The year 1958 was significant for the travel and tourism industry not only because it was the year of the jet. It was the year that American Express launched its credit card. Diners Club was founded in 1950 and Carte Blanche (which with Diners Club is now owned by Citicorp) was created in 1959 by the Hilton Hotel Corporation. Around 1969 the bank cards entered the travel and entertainment arena. Bank America card (now Visa) and Master Charge (now Master Card) had been in existence for nearly a decade but had served almost exclusively as cards for small retail purchases.

Americans who travelled had to carry 'huge rolls of money', which was felt to be risky (Brower, 1983, p.284). It was found that credit cards provided a safe, easy, convenient and reliable method of facilitating travel and related payments before, during and after the journey. Credit cards have since grown in importance over time and are now a permanent fixture in the tourism landscape as travellers are increasingly urged not to leave home without them. The plastic card has created 'a revolution in payments for those on the move' (Cullen, 1988, p.65).

Credit cards got off to a slow start in the travel and tourism industry as major airlines were not convinced that the cards would generate more business. It was a major breakthrough in 1964 when American Express won acceptance by American Airlines. By February 1965, it was reported that air travel was the fastest growing segment of the credit-card business. Today, credit-card payment is one of the fastest if not the fastest growing sector of the payment business, especially among the higher spending business travellers who use plastic to pay for about two-thirds of business expenditure at hotels and restaurants.

The use of plastic cards in travel payments differs across regions and within individual countries. Europe lags behind the USA in credit card ownership. Within Europe, the UK has the highest concentration of credit cards per head of population (a total of about 25 million cards), while in West Germany, Eurocheque is the most popular form of payment (Cockrell, 1987, p. 33) – Germans use credit cards to pay for only 5% of costs when on holiday (de Coster, 1990, p. 56).

Information technology lies at the basis of other payment systems such as electronic funds transfer, the validation and authorization of credit-card transactions, cash-dispensing machines, travellers cheques and the myriad of consumer services related to lost or stolen cards and cheques. All of these services and the technology on which they are based facilitate payment transactions in the travel and tourism industry. They play an important role in the rapid growth and development of the industry.

2.7.3. Computer Technology

There are fundamental differences in the role that technologies play in the old tourism and in the new (Fig. 2.2). A full exposition of the transformation from the old to new tourism is contained in Chapter 4.

In the 'old' mass standardized and rigidly packaged (MSRP) tourism, technologies are used to facilitate the mass production of tourism services and to control the production process. Computers also assist with internal management functions of accounting, financial control and payroll. In the 'new' flexible, segmented and diagonally integrated (FSDI) tourism, technology takes on an entirely different role. Technologies in the new tourism are used to manage capacity, optimize yield and get closer to clients. The focus of technology applications in the new tourism is on global networks, communications and value creation.

From the 1960s to the early 1980s, technology usage by the tourist industry was principally aimed at *facilitation* – facilitating the rapid growth of mass tourism on a global scale. The use of technology by the tourism industry before 1978 was therefore limited. The technology users in the old

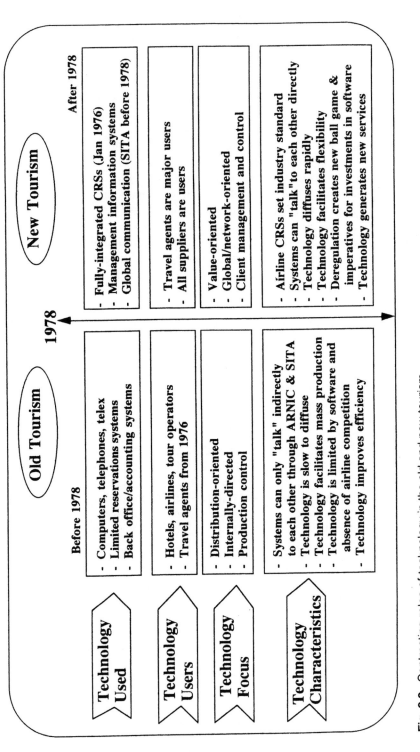

Fig. 2.2. Contrasting roles of technology in the old and new tourism.

tourism were limited to airlines, hotel chains, car-rental companies and tour operators (mainly, European).

By comparison, in the new tourism, travel agents are major users of technology (e.g. for computerized reservations terminals) and play an even more important role in the value chain of the travel industry. In addition, other service providers such as cruise ships, car-rental companies and pleasure boats are users of the industry's computerized reservations technologies. Even champagne and flower services, tourist boards, independent resorts, theme parks and other suppliers are represented on CRSs.

Technologies used in the old tourism were embodied in stand-alone delinked equipment such as telephones, computers, telex, back office accounting and management systems. The reservation systems used by the industry at the time were also limited in their ability to communicate with each other as well as their inability to operate in real time. It meant that if a booking for 20 rooms was made with Hotel X this information was not automatically reflected in Hotel X's room inventory; that information was relayed from the agency's CRS to the hotel at some later point.

Typically, airlines, hotels and tour operators developed their own dedicated systems. One airline system, for example, could not 'talk' to another airline system, far less to hotels and tour operators' systems. The carriers communicated with each other through Arnic and Sita, but this was not on a real-time basis. From one airline or hotel reservation system, one had only limited capability of checking availability on other airlines or hotel properties. This could make the job of the travel agent unnecessarily cumbersome because several telephone calls might have to be made for a single enquiry, booking or sale, if the CRS showed that products were sold out when in fact they were still available directly from the supplier.

In the 1960s and 1970s, information technologies mainly played a facilitating role in the international tourism industry. It allowed the tourism industry to reap tremendous productivity increases within the confines of the mass, standardized production practices – a production practice that was the industry's best practice at the time. The technology itself did not create mass, standardized and rigidly packed tourism, it merely facilitated its development.

Technology applications in the old tourism (1960s and 1970s) had the effect mainly of improving the efficiency of tourism services and facilitating mass production, scale economies and low costs of production. Computer technologies facilitated the mass production of tourism services. Technology allowed tourism producers to plan better, manage and control their activities at a global level. Technology facilitated the standardization and replication of facilities and services on a global scale. Technology facilitated the distribution of product in international markets and was used to improve the efficiency of services provided to consumers.

Technology made it relatively easy, for example, for major international hotel chains to manage information to disaggregate in detail all aspects of the operation of a hotel, franchise the concept, mass produce identical hotel rooms across the globe and yet succeed in achieving identical services, standards, facilities, fixtures, fittings and amenities and all affiliated properties. At the same time, functions such as buying, reservations, training, accounting, planning and marketing were centralized, allowing hotel chains to reap enormous economies of scale through their operations.

To some extent, the development of information technologies also increased the quality of services. One must remember that the rationale for mass production was not the improvement of quality, but lowering the costs of production, reaping economies of scale and offering low prices to an inexperienced clientele. It is only with the entry of competitors where low costs are no longer sufficient to generate a competitive edge, that attention to quality, product differentiation, innovation, the generation of new services and paying attention to the consumer become critical to the competitive process. This was not to happen until the early 1980s.

The year 1978 was a major turning point for the tourism industry. In a very real sense, airline deregulation created the imperative for the extensive development of CRSs by airlines. Before deregulation, airlines, fares, route structures were generally fixed, regulated, predetermined and largely predictable. Deregulation spawned increased competition that resulted in several new routes, new services, new schedules, new destinations, new fares and even new airlines. Moreover, the travel environment became more flexible and unpredictable with mergers, bankruptcies and take-overs, airlines adding and dropping routes, frequent price changes, frequent flyer programmes, last-minute discounted seats becoming quite prevalent.

After 1978, the international tourism industry needed something as powerful as computerized reservation systems simply to keep track of all the new information and to satisfy consumers. Since 1978, technology diffusion in tourism has been rapid. Nearly all of travel agencies in the USA are now linked to airlines' computerized reservations systems (CRSs). CRSs provided by the airline industry, especially since deregulation, have dramatically improved matters. Travel agents can now look, book and sell at the CRS terminal without making a telephone call. They can check inventories of more suppliers, they can book more hotels, car rental and other services required by the modern traveller as well as more 'tailor-made' holidays.

The impact of technology applications in the new tourism has also been tremendous. Improvements have been made on all fronts – improvements in the efficiency of production and the quality of services provided as well as the generation of completely new services. CRSs today allow airlines and other users more directly to monitor, manage and control their capacity (yield management) and their clients (frequent flyer programmes).

Tourism suppliers are now better able to match their output with the needs of their ever-changing clientele – a marriage that has increasingly become a critical success factor in tourism.

It is the diffusion of a system of information technologies throughout the international tourism system that, on the supply side, is driving the transformation of the international tourism industry (see Chapter 6). The mass globalization of the tourism industry would not have taken place at the speed and intensity that it did were it not for the technologies to facilitate and control it.

2.8. MASS TOURISM FORCES IN EUROPE AND THE USA

The USA and Europe accounted for a significant proportion (96%) of world tourism arrivals in 960 (World Tourism Organization, 1966–1986). There are fundamental differences in the way in which mass tourism was developed in the USA and Europe: hotels and tour operators, for example, played different roles and assumed varying levels of importance in the shaping of mass tourism. Figure 2.3 illustrates the main differences between the European and American tourism industries.

In the USA, the major players in the creation of mass tourism were hotel chains and airlines. US hotel chains, through branding and the replication of a standard product across the globe, provided consumers with the safety and confidence for them to travel *en masse*. The brand name provided the assurance and familiarity in a 'home away from home' atmosphere.

Tour operators played a similar role in the development of mass tourism in Europe to that played by hotel chains in the USA. In Europe, tour operators, by creating cheap package tours using charter air services, were the main instrument of mass tourism. They were able to offer similar levels of security and certainty that US hotel chains offered. This they achieved through the branding of holidays, selecting hotels and destinations, guaranteeing standards and taking the risks and responsibility for delivering the holiday promised.

The European packaged holidays invariably included charter flights. This was another major difference between the mass tourism forces in the USA and Europe. Travel in Europe was mainly intra-European in nature, often involving air transportation to the Mediterranean sun destinations. In the USA, by contrast, it was domestic holiday travel and business travel that were the industry's driving force. It was therefore the car, rather than charter flights, that provided the impetus to North America's tourism industry. The car still dominates travel in the USA today. Over three-quarters of all personal trips taken in 1987 were by car, truck or recrea-

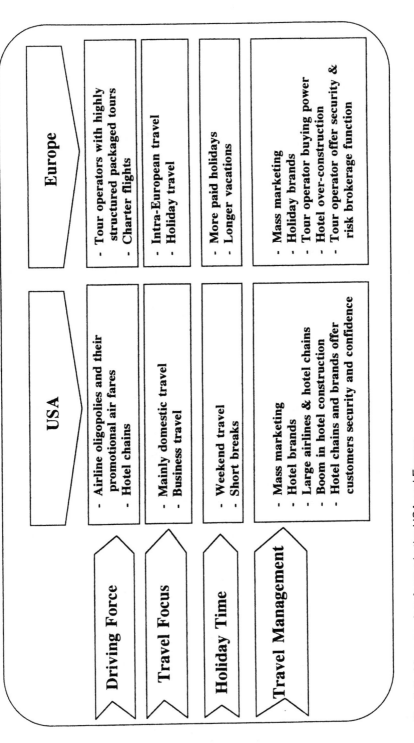

Fig. 2.3. Mass tourism forces in the USA and Europe.

	USA	Europe
Driving Force	- Airline oligopolies and their promotional air fares - Hotel chains	- Tour operators with highly structured packaged tours - Charter flights
Travel Focus	- Mainly domestic travel - Business travel	- Intra-European travel - Holiday travel
Holiday Time	- Weekend travel - Short breaks	- More paid holidays - Longer vacations
Travel Management	- Mass marketing - Hotel brands - Large airlines & hotel chains - Boom in hotel construction - Hotel chains and brands offer customers security and confidence	- Mass marketing - Holiday brands - Tour operator buying power - Hotel over-construction - Tour operator offer security & risk brokerage function

tional vehicle (US Travel Data Center, 1989). As such, hotels did not take on a tour packaging function as the tour operators did in Europe. Instead, they set up roadside motels and city hotels, many of which could be reached by car. As a result, the tour operator industry in North America has been nowhere near as active as its European counterparts.

Another difference in the way in which mass tourism developed between Europe and North America is in the area of paid holidays. American employers continued to offer fewer vacation days than was typical in Europe. While many Europeans enjoyed between 3–5 weeks holiday during the 1960s and the 1970s (and today many more enjoy 6–8 weeks paid holidays plus a 13th salary*) in the USA, 2 weeks of paid holiday is still the norm for many workers. As such, the travel focus of North Americans was mainly on weekend travel and the short breaks. By contrast, European travel was for much longer periods, although today short breaks are a growing feature of European travel.

However, while there were differences in the way mass tourism developed in North America and Europe, the management of mass tourism was similar on both continents. Both engaged in mass marketing. In their respective markets, they mass produced identical tourism services for an undifferentiated group of mass tourists.

Economies of scale and standardization were achieved through *hotel* branding in the USA and *holiday* branding in Europe. In the USA, hotel brands such as Holiday Inn and Hilton Hotel were developed, while in Europe holiday brands included, for example: Club Mediterranée and Nouvelle Frontiers in France; Holland International in Holland; Thomson Holidays, International Leisure Group and Horizon Holidays in the UK; and NUR, Dr Tigges, Trans Europa, Meyers Welt Reisen and Jahn Reisen in Germany.

Mass production was achieved through large, concentrated and integrated airline and hotel structures in North America and in Europe mainly by the tour operators' tremendous airline and hotel-buying power. International hotel franchising in North America was paralleled by the development of Mediterranean destinations for mass travellers in Europe. The tendency toward the over-building of hotels was prevalent both in North America and Europe.

It is very important to grasp the differences between the American and European travel market and the different forces that led to the old mass, standardized and rigidly packaged tourism. Fundamental differences also exist between both continents in the development of the new flexible, segmented, environmentally friendly and diagonally integrated tourism.

---

*13th salary refers to holiday pay in Germany.

2.9. MASS TOURISM FORCES IN THE USA

A number of production and management imperatives in the USA gave birth to mass tourism in America. These included the dominant position of airlines and multinational hotel chains, promotional air fares, mass marketing, hotel branding and hotel franchising. All of these factors played significant roles in determining the rate and direction of growth of the international tourism industry. In the case of franchises, for example, they facilitated the standardization and assembly line production of hotels, thereby allowing hotel chains to project a brand image, while obtaining tremendous economies of scale in advertising identical outlets around the world.

2.9.1. Airlines

In the airline industry, antitrust immunity preserved an oligopolistically structured industry from the Chicago Convention until deregulation in 1978. There has been a great deal of concentration of airline operations since the arrival of the jet aircraft in 1958. In 1961, the merger of United (with a 14000-mile route system) and Capital (with a route system of 7000 miles) made the surviving carrier, United, the largest air carrier in terms of route miles, aircraft, personnel and potential passenger traffic (*Travel Weekly*, 1983). Northeast merged into Delta in 1972, and the American/Trans-Caribbean merger took place in 1970 giving American Airlines its first access to the Caribbean, then controlled by Eastern. Delta also merged with Western and Northwestern with Republic and Pan American Airways with National. Several other mergers also took place. This produced a concentrated airline industry, with carriers exercising a great deal of control over the rate and direction of growth of the tourism industry. An analysis of the patterns of related activities of selected airlines concluded that 'airlines have become the driving force in tourist activities', with the majority of them exercising varying degrees of control over tour operators and hotels (Clairmonte and Cavannah, 1984, pp. 250–254).

It was found, moreover, that airlines have very diversified portfolios of activities. Of 22 major airlines analysed in 1984, 72.7% were involved in tour operations; 86.3% had hotel interests; 13.6% had interests in car rentals; 68.1% were associated with other airlines; and all of them (100%) had other related interests (Clairmonte and Cavannah, 1984). Such related interests included miscellaneous activities such as catering, international merchant banking, worldwide aviation insurance and re-insurance.

Airlines were instrumental in the vertical and horizontal integration of the travel and tourism industry (see Chapter 8). They provided the services for mass tourism and exercised a great deal of control over the rate and direction of growth of the industry. That airlines today dominate the CRSs of the travel industry is certainly no surprise – it is a reflection of the historical dominance of air transportation in the development of the tourism industry. The power of the airlines in the USA paralleled the power of tour operators in Europe.

2.9.2. Promotional Fares

Apart from the purely technological advances in aircraft design and operations, innovative pricing was an important ingredient in the creation of mass travel. The World Tourism Organization observed that 'the volume of air traffic passengers is closely related to the total cost of the holiday' (figures for 1972 in World Tourism Organization, 1966–1989, p. 46).

Tourism is a luxury item that responds very well to price. It is both price and income elastic. This means that a marginal change in consumers' incomes or the price of a holiday will result in a more than proportionate change in their effective desire to consume travel. In his econometric analysis of international travel, Artus (1972, pp. 579–614) estimated price elasticities for expenditures on foreign travel by Europeans at between −3.58 and −2.61; while income elasticities were estimated between 2.30 and 1.16. This means that a unit rise in the price of travel will bring about a decrease in the quantity of travel demanded by a factor of between 2.61 and 3.58. Similarly, a unit rise in income will bring forth between twice or three times as much travel. In other words, cheaper prices for travel bring forth proportionately greater travel demand by consumers.

The economy fare was introduced in 1958 and the fare structure has constantly been modified to attract a wider proportion of the population. A number of promotional fares were introduced to encourage tourist traffic. Besides the normal first-class and economy fares, there were excursion rates, such as the advance purchase excursion (APEX) fare, group fares and the inclusive tour excursion (ITX) fare. These promotional tariffs had a very important effect on the number of travellers and, consequently, the load factors that these airlines were able to obtain.

Inclusive tours have thus made international travel accessible to an increasing range of socioeconomic groups. 'The relatively low fares of inclusive tour charters have been a major factor influencing the growth of tourism' (World Tourism Organization, 1966–1986). This organizational innovation (inclusive tours), together with the emergence of charter-class fares (ITX), charter carriers and tour operators, ensured the services for mass tourism.

The objective of promotional fares was not to reduce the cost of travel to those who could already afford to buy travel (e.g. business travellers). Rather, they aimed at making travel available to more people. An APEX fare, for example, is a restrictive fare: tickets for travel have to be bought in advance, they are not subject to change, have limited availability, and can incur the penalty of no refund. By its very restrictive terms, the APEX fare ensures that the business clientele are largely unable to benefit from the low fare. This is due to the fact that business trips usually require more flexibility and are subject to short planning horizons. For vacation travel, the reverse may be true.

The ITX fare was also a very important innovation. The ITX fare is a charter-class rate offered to tour operators who organized inclusive tours and it was very important for the tourist industry at the time. These special tour-basing fares made it possible for tour operators to offer inclusive tours. Before 1962 the North Atlantic charter market was dominated by International Air Transportation Association (IATA) scheduled airlines. These scheduled airlines performed the dual role of providing scheduled and non-scheduled (charter) services. It was only during 1963–1968 that charter (non-schedule, non-IATA) carriers entered the air transportation market, opening up the new possibility of inclusive tours which tour operators quickly seized.

Technological changes in air transportation as well as marketing innovations in the promotion and pricing of air travel, laid the foundation for mass, large-scale transportation and tourism. Jet aircraft and jumbo jets made it physically possible to transport larger numbers of passengers. Innovative pricing policies made it possible for ordinary people to buy air transportation and to travel *en masse* to an increasing number of distant destinations. These air components of mass tourism were complemented by developments in the hotel industry – specifically the emergence of multinational chains.

2.9.3. Multinational Hotel Chains

Multinational hotel chains were important agents for the delivery of mass, standardized and rigidly packaged hotel bed-nights across the globe. They emerged primarily to satisfy the global demand that mass tourism fuelled. Hotel chains expanded rapidly and built thousands of properties all over the world. The case of the Holiday Inn hotel chain clearly demonstrates this.

In 1952 Holiday Inn built its first unit. In 1964 number 500 was completed, and in 1968 number 1000 appeared. In 1968, Holiday Inn opened its first European motel in Holland. The company invaded Japan in 1973, and the following year reached South America. By 1981, the chain had 212 motels overseas in 58 countries (Luxenberg, 1985, pp. 112 and 210). Holiday Inn is the largest corporate hotel chain in the world with 370081 rooms in 1900 hotels worldwide (*Travel Industry World Year-*

book, 1991). In 1988, Holiday Inn generated system wide sales of US$5.4 billion.

At the end of 1978, it is estimated that 81 multinational hotel chains from 22 countries were associated with 1025 hotels abroad and 270 646 rooms (Table 2.2). The USA was the clear leader in the development of international hotel brands. Europe lagged behind. Thus while the USA accounted for 56.2% of all rooms in multinational hotel companies outside the chains' home countries, Europe accounted for 32.6% of all rooms of leading hotel chains outside the chains' homeland.

Multinational hotel chains were a phenomenon not only of the developed countries. Many countries in the developing world had their own multinational hotel companies operating in other parts of the world. They included India, Colombia, Mexico and Guatemala. However, these accounted for a mere 4% of total hotel rooms in multinational corporations' affiliated hotels overseas (see Table 2.2).

Up to the early 1960s, the developed countries and the higher-income developing areas attracted most of the activities of multinational hotel chains, but in the following decade there was a remarkable growth of new associations in Africa, Asia and Oceana (UNCTC, 1982, p. 24). In developed countries, ownership or part ownership accounted for 47.8% of multinational hotel involvement; leasing 11.9%; management contracts, 23.5%; and franchising, 16.8%. After 1975, 65.4% of all multinational

Table 2.2 Market share of leading hotel chains by region, 1978

Countries	Number of multinational hotel corporations	Number of associated hotels abroad	Number of rooms represented	Percentage share of rooms (%)
USA	22	508	152 118	56.5
France	8	156	35 374	13.1
UK	13	147	31 765	11.7
Other Europe	14	87	21 190	7.8
Japan	7	23	9093	3.4
Other developed market economies	8	65	10 557	3.9
Developing countries	9	37	10 549	3.9
Total	**81**	**1025**	**270 646**	**100.0**

Source: United Nations Center on Transnational Corporations, 1982.

hotel involvement in the hotel sector in developed countries were through management contract (UNCTC, 1982, p. 24).

Through their operations on a global scale, multinational hotel chains were able to achieve considerable scale economies in three critical areas of operation:

- mass marketing;
- buying power; and
- distribution and reservations systems.

Emulating mass production in the manufacturing sector, multinational hotel chains standardized, mass-produced and mass-marketed tourism on a global scale. Franchises were the main instruments used by multinational hotels to mass-produce standardized (branded) hotel bed-nights across the globe.

2.9.4. Hotel Branding/Franchising

Franchises allowed hotel chains to produce and to standardize hotel products by replicating details of site, layout of buildings, furnishings, fixtures, price, the quality of service, management, food, and other areas. The details of the hotel and its service are disaggregated and very well defined so that each segment could be measured and regulated. This definition, measurement and regulation formed the basis of the franchise and the stardization procedures contained therein.

Since the franchise system is based upon the replication of near-identical hotels the world over, the franchiser obtained considerable benefits from marketing the same standard principle worldwide. In addition, the need for standardized facilities, equipment and materials meant that purchasing power was consolidated on a global level, with the benefit of lower average costs, lower prices to consumers and complete control.

In a detailed cost–benefit analysis of the Trinidad Hilton Hotel, it was observed that:

> The hotel is run on a standardized system that has been developed
> by the company; most of the furnishings, operating equipment,
> china, glass, etc., are purchased through the central purchasing office
> in New York; some food is obtained locally and some flown in from
> the USA.
>
> (Forbes, 1977, p. 17)

This franchising mechanism, together with the availability of electronically powered communications equipment to link the worldwide chain of franchises, provided the basis for standardization and mass production of tourist accommodation the world over. The rapid expansion of these chains and their franchising principle was a major force in the development of a mass-tourism industry. The impact of franchises on a global scale was overwhelming and, while they satisfied the needs of mass tourism, their impact upon the communal environment was far from satisfactory. As one observer puts it, the growth of these chains resulted in:

> ... stultifying homogenization of products and communities. They destroy a sense of community by mass-producing environments that minimize personal contact. Moreover, since employees and managers are forced to operate inside a straitjacket of corporate regulations, franchisees have little chance to tailor their units to their own taste or local preference.
>
> (Luxenberg, 1985)

2.9.5. Mass Marketing

Mass marketing involves the sale of identical goods and services to a seemingly identical group of consumers. Two key factors are usually present in mass marketing. These are:

- large numbers of identical consumers; and
- large-scale production of identical units.

Both of these factors were present in the development of the tourism industry in the post-war period leading up to the 1980s. Hotel and holiday branding by multinational hotel chains in the USA and tour operators in Europe, respectively, allowed for the replication of standardized holidays internationally. Mass, inexperienced sun-lust tourists, together with paid holidays and post-war prosperity, produced large numbers of apparently identical consumers ready and willing to buy standardized travel options. Tourism services were thus mass marketed both in Europe and the USA as a result of these two essential mass-marketing factors.

2.10. MASS TOURISM FORCES IN EUROPE

A number of production and management imperatives gave birth to mass tourism in Europe. These included the role and importance of tour operators, the development of charter flights, package tours, holiday branding, mass marketing, hotel *over-construction* and the development of Mediterranean sun destinations for mass consumption.

All of these factors played significant roles in determining the rate and direction of growth of the international tourism industry. Tour operators, for example, were very instrumental in the transmission of mass tourism. In the case of charter flights in Europe, there exists a direct correlation between the destination's popularity with the mass market and the percentage of charter flights to the total air traffic of that destination. On the other hand, promotional fares, mass production and packaged tours were important factors in democratising travel, bringing it within the reach of wider, mass segments of the population. The package tour itself removed the risks associated with travel to distant and foreign lands and encouraged the increased consumption of travel.

2.10.1. Tour Operators and Package Tours

Tour operators are essentially wholesalers who put together the separate elements that normally make up a tour or travel package. Inclusive tours are vacations arranged by a tour organizer where the cost includes air transportation, accommodation, board, and ground transfers, with sight-seeing tours and other destination services as optional extras. The tour operator 'packages' these services and sells them to the consumer for a single inclusive price. The tour organizer obtains considerable savings on each element of the package because these services must be procured and paid for in advance and they are usually bulk purchases (e.g. the special ITX fare from the airline). Some of these savings are passed on, in the form of lower prices, to the consumer. The price of a package tour is usually considerably less than buying and packaging the elements of a vacation for oneself. Tour operators were key agents in the transmission of mass, standardized and rigidly packaged tourism.

The idea of buying a package of transportation, accommodation, and perhaps some ancillary services such as ground tours, became established in Western Europe in the 1960s. Package holidays were extensively used by tourists from the Northern industrial countries of Scandinavia, West Germany and the UK. These packages concluded at resorts in the Mediterranean. By the late 1960s, the emergence of the inclusive tour as a principal medium in holiday travel in Europe had been established. Thus by 1965, just over 1 million holiday visits to Western Europe from the UK were inclusive tours by charter – already twice the number of independent air holidays. By 1970, while the number of independent holidays by air remained at just over half a million, inclusive tours by air had doubled to 2 million in number (Burkart and Medlik, 1974, p. 32).

Tour operators, spurred on by success over time, amassed considerable buying power over air seats and hotel capacity. Most European tour operators also had their own charter airlines and considerable interests in hotel properties in the Mediterranean. Their advanced purchases of tourism services have considerably improved cash flow and planning by many suppliers, particularly hotels. Many operators also had substantial financial assets in the tourism industry and were able to accumulate considerably more economic power through their idle cash balances accruing from pre-paid holidays.

There were several incentives for tourists to buy these package tours rather than incur the higher risks and costs of doing it for themselves. With the package tour, the risks associated with travel (i.e. uncertain accommodation on arrival in a tourist destination, unknown terrain and disaster) as well as the cost of travel were considerably less to the consumer. Tour operators were the true risk brokers and price setters of the travel industry.

The package tour has brought travel within the reach of many who could normally not afford to take vacations abroad. By organizing large groups of tourists and transporting them from the tourist-generating country to a single destination in a host country and back again, tour operators have had a great impact on the volume of tourist traffic:

> The tour operators in the late 1970s were able to charter planes and guarantee more than 90% of capacity – compared with the average passenger load factor of 55% of capacity on scheduled flights in the 1960s.
>
> (UNCTC, 1982, p. 31)

2.10.1. Charter Flights

With the arrival of the jet aircraft, promotional fares, charter flights and inclusive tours, the novelty of air travel and tourism had begun to wear off. According to Burkart and Medlik (1974, p. 187), 'within the last 10 years, a holiday abroad has become as much a feature of the good life as a refrigerator or washing machine'. If innovations in air transportation (i.e. jet aircraft), marketing (i.e. promotional fares) and organization (e.g. inclusive tours) came together to create the phenomenon of mass, standardized and rigidly packaged tourism. Charter flights sealed the fate of tourism in Europe.

The very nature of a charter flight is that it is non-scheduled and low-cost and it operates on a limited and inflexible route structure. Thus charter flights differ from ordinary air services with their schedule, route structure and price. The purpose of a charter is to provide low-cost transportation to and from a tourist destination for holiday-makers. The idea is to obtain as high a load factor as possible (i.e. get as many people on the aircraft as possible) to benefit from scale economies and therefore lower prices per passenger. It is the achievement of high load factors (e.g. a full plane load) that makes it possible to lower the average price paid per consumer for a return flight.

Charter flights are a logical development of the mass air-transportation market. With the advent of the jet aircraft and the development of strategies by tour operators, the expansion of the charter market in the 1960s was very rapid. By 1967, charter operators had the same amount of the charter market as the scheduled operators, with each group carrying about 200000 passengers (figures for 1974 in World Tourism Organization, 1966–1986, p.50). By 1969, for the first time, the share of charter traffic exceeded 25% of the air transportation market in the USA.

In Europe, revenue passenger kilometres from charter operations increased nearly six-fold between 1963 and 1969, at an average annual rate of 35% per year (figures for 1976 in World Tourism Organization, 1966–1986, p.45). In 1971, charter carriers accounted for 32.2% of total air traffic, with Europe taking 63.4% of the total and North America accounting for the remaining 36.6%. The tendency of Europe to dominate the charter market continues to persist to the present. The availability of charter flights played an important role in the development of mass tourism in Europe.

That the jet aircraft was a progenitor of the mass tourism era can readily be understood when one examines the critical role that air charter flights played in the development of mass tourism destinations such as Spain. The importance of charter flights to the emergence of mass tourist destinations can be readily seen in this example. Spain was the first Mediterranean country to exploit its tourism resources in a major way, taking advantage of an increasingly wealthy Northern European population who were beginning to travel southward in search of the sun. Over the period 1964–1974, the percentage of charter traffic in the total air traffic to Spain averaged 69.5%. This percentage was even higher for individual resorts: 92.6% for Tenerife; 90.2% for Majorca; and 92.2% for Alicante (World Tourism Organization, 1978, pp.88–90).

Post-war prosperity, the arrival of the jet age (with the development of the jumbo jets in particular) brought developing countries, particularly Africa, Asia, the Caribbean and Pacific islands sharply into the international tourism focus. Relatively cheap long-distance travel, together with the incomes and desire to penetrate and explore new regions brought places like Bermuda, Bali, Acapulco and Jamaica onto the tourism map. At the same time, there was an annual flood of North Americans across the Atlantic, traditional destinations such as France and Italy became more widely visited, and the Mediterranean coast of Spain soon became a mass tourist destination for Northern Europeans.

2.11. SUMMARY

Over the past three decades, international tourism has generally displayed all the features of mass production: (i) holidays were standardized, rigidly packaged and inflexible; (ii) identical holidays were mass produced with scale economies as the driving force; (iii) holidays were mass marketed to an undifferentiated clientele; and (iv) holidays were consumed *en masse* with a lack of consideration for the norms, culture and environment of the host countries. Mass, standardized and rigidly packaged tourism (MSRP) became a key feature of the international tourism industry during the 1960s, 1970s and early 1980s. MSRP tourism was 'best practice'. It was organizational and managerial common sense for best productivity and most profits.

Important frame conditions created MSRP tourism: post-war peace and prosperity together with the emergence of paid holidays provided the atmosphere, income, time and inclination to travel.

Consumers themselves helped to create mass tourism. Inexperienced post-war tourists attracted by the idea and novelty of air travel and a common search for the sun ensured the effective demand for mass-tourism services. Many tourists at the time were more taken up with the novelty and excitement of travel rather than with the quality of the destination or where they went, the hotels they slept in, or the quality of services they received.

Identical hotel chains' strategy of franchising and international branding replication of hotels across the globe, provided familiarity, safety and reassurance to mass tourists – virtually allowing them to feel 'at home.'

Technology also facilitated the creation of MSRP tourism:

1. The year 1958 ushered in the jet age. The jet aircraft changed long-held perceptions of time and place and was the catalyst for a prolonged travel boom.
2. The development of plastic cards and other electronic methods of payment facilitated rapid growth and development of travel and related services.
3. Computer technology allowed tourism suppliers to better plan, manage and control their activities at a global level and facilitated the standardization, replication and management of facilities and services on a global scale.
4. Technology enabled the distribution of services in international markets and improved the efficiency of services provided to consumers.
5. The role of information technologies in transforming the tourism industry and in generating completely new services was to become more important in 1978, when an important frame condition changed – i.e. when the US government formally deregulated its airline industry.

Different *management and production* imperatives drove mass tourism in Europe and North America:

1. In the USA, international hotel chains branded hotels and mass-produced standardized accommodation the world over, while airlines, exercising oligopolistic power, controlled the rate and direction of tourism growth.

2. In Europe, tour operators branded holidays, controlled charter flights and, beginning with Spain, succeeded in making the Mediterranean the first mass tourism region in the world.

Mass tourism certainly had its time and place. Mass tourism was 'common sense'. It was the industry's and indeed the world's 'best practice'. Today, the tourism industry is in crisis. Mass tourism is no longer 'best practice'. Conditions that gave birth to mass tourism – the frame conditions, consumers, technology, and production and management practices – are changing.

Today, one is already witnessing a transformation toward new organizational and managerial principles for the best productivity and most profitable practice in the travel and tourism industry. Such new principles include quality, flexibility, environmentally sound, customization, innovation and diagonal integration.

Forces directing the transformation of travel and tourism stem not only from the industry's internal frame conditions such as its consumers and the management and production imperatives of its suppliers. Fundamental imperatives at the global level are also engineering the transformation of the travel and tourism industry. As these global imperatives are examined in Chapter 3, it will be shown that the travel and tourism industry was not alone in the adoption of mass-production principles. Neither will the industry be alone in the adoption of the new 'best practice' of flexible production. Flexible production is rapidly becoming the global 'best practice'. Flexible production is already common practice in the same industry that perfected mass production – the car industry. It has been perfected by the Japanese and remains a key source of their competitiveness. The Japanese experience in the automobile industry holds some key lessons for travel and tourism suppliers.

3

GLOBAL IMPERATIVES

3.1. INTRODUCTION

Tomorrow's world has its origins in the past. Today, it is being shaped by fundamental imperatives: (i) environmental limits to growth; (ii) the microelectronics revolution; (iii) the breakdown of the old mass-production paradigm and the birth of flexible production; (iv) the emergence of a new superpower in the country of Japan; (v) the ascendancy of the service economy; (vi) the melting away of the iron curtain and the break-up of the Soviet Union; (vii) the emergence of a United States of Europe; (viii) the re-unification of Germany; and (ix) the increasing liberalization of global trade and services.

In the past, tourism has been shaped by several compelling forces – post-war peace and prosperity, paid holidays, the development of the jet engine and the supply of cheap oil. Today it is being shaped by equally compelling forces – the microelectronics revolution, ecological concerns and a growing need to express individuality on the part of tourists. Global developments, from the computer revolution to growing concerns for the environment, have profound implications for the current and future growth of the travel and tourism industry. Understanding these developments will provide key insights into why the travel and tourism industry is on the brink of a major transformation, why conventional mass tourism could be dead within a few years, why ecotourism is more than just a fad, why information technology is currently taking the travel and tourism industry by storm, and why the travel and tourism industry will be a lead sector in the fifth wave.

This chapter will consider three of the key global influences impacting on the tourist industry: (i) the environmental limits to growth; (ii) the microelectronic revolution; and (iii) the birth of a new paradigm. Environmental limits to growth will put a damper on tourism's growth prospects, technology will open new production possibilities and the emergence of a new paradigm of flexible production will make tourism a lead sector in this, the fifth and current information technology wave.

3.2. ENVIRONMENTAL LIMITS TO GROWTH

Tourism is an environment-intensive industry. The natural environment is its most valuable yet most fragile asset. The environment is exactly what is sold. From the safaris, reefs, forests, flora, fishes, lakes, ski slopes, mountains, archaeological sites, beaches and isolated cays, to the wind, water and the sun, the natural environment is the most important attraction to holidaying in all parts of the world. The environment is an item of immense consumption. It is the final product.

Too much pressure on the environment can destroy it – if too heavily consumed it will perish. Thus, in order to preserve the natural environment, its consumption must be regulated. Therefore, limits on its use must be set.

Environmental limits to growth have important consequences for the future rate and direction of development of the travel and tourism industry. The sheer magnitude and intractability of environmental problems, increased environmental awareness among consumers, the rapid spread of environmental pressure groups, actions taken by tourism destinations such as Belize and Bermuda, the work of international funding agencies and the 'greening' of the private sector, all pressure the tourism sector into taking an environmentally responsible approach to its development.

3.2.1. The Gravity of the Problem

The gravity of the environmental problem cannot be overstated. In 1970, Dubois lamented the disturbing fact that:

> ... physical and mental characteristics of mankind were now being shaped by dirty skies and cluttered streets, anonymous high rises and amorphous urban sprawl; by social attitudes that are more concerned with things than with men; and by environmental ugliness and the rape of nature ...

(Dubois, 1970)

These concerns have been voiced by Stuart L. Udall, US Secretary of the Interior, in his 1966 address before the Long Island Conference on Natural Beauty. He quipped, to great approval 'if we weren't careful, we'd be remembered as the generation that put man on the moon while standing knee deep in garbage' (Dubois, 1970, p. 192).

Today, the destruction of the ozone layer, global waming, fires in the

Amazon, acid rain, 'macro pollution', the greenhouse effect, destruction of the world's rain forests and wildlife species and skyrocketing world population threaten the existence of man and woman on planet earth. According to Gilbert M. Grosvenor, President and Chairman of the National Geographic Society:

> During one brief century, mankind has passed the point of global opportunism and entered an era of global protection. There is hardly a place in this land where the lesson is not written plain for all to see ...

Environmental problems are cause for tremendous concern by international bodies, environmental pressure groups, consumers, school children and the population at large. There is growing awareness both of the interdependence of man and his environment as well as the interdependence of the world's peoples. So great is the concern, so grave and intractable the environmental problems, that international banks, lending agencies and governments of the western world have initiated debt for nature swaps to help save Brazil's and other countries' endangered rain forests. The simple logic is this: fires in the Amazon have implications not only for the people in Brazil but for all peoples on planet earth. The protection of the environment is now everybody's business.

3.2.2. Tourism Can Hurt the Environment

Environmental problems as they relate to tourism affect every part of the industry – from the boating and yachting sectors of the Caribbean and Pacific islands to the ski slopes of Europe, the jungles of South America, the safari parks of Africa, the mountains of India, the Barrier Reef of Australia, the historical ruins of Mexico, Peru, Egypt, Greece and Turkey.

Among the environmental and ecological problems encountered in many tourist destinations and brought about as a result of the development of tourism are:

1. *Poor sewage* infrastructure, management and planning for hotels and resorts, leading to the disposal of raw sewage and other pollutants directly into the sea, causing the pollution of beaches and bathing water and the destruction of marine life – for example, the high growth of algae in the Adriatic sea, which was brought to the public's attention in August 1988, directly affecting resorts such as Rimini and Riccione on the Romagna Coast (Becheri, 1991).

2. *Degradation of beaches and soil erosion* from construction too close to the shore line – for example, some hotels and resorts in the Caribbean region are experiencing a loss of sand and bathing area as the sea begins to reclaim some of the area, exposing ugly building foundations.

3. *Indiscriminate dumping of garbage* overboard cruise ships and pleasure boats (especially man-made substances such as plastics which are known to stifle aquatic life, in particular, young turtles). The problem of garbage dumping is particularly severe in the Caribbean area, especially along the main cruise ship route where plastic cups and other items bearing the ship's logo can be found floating around the pristine Family Island of the Bahamas and elsewhere.

4. *Unlawful spear fishing* 'just for fun', destroying invaluable underwater life. In the Caribbean, the French are identified as being particularly guilty of this environmentally unfriendly behaviour (Caribbean Tourism Organization, 1991a).

5. *Destruction of reefs and underwater life* as a result of commercialization through the exploitation of shells, black coral and other items to satisfy the souvenir trade; as well as through over-fishing, partly to feed the tourist population, and by the use of anchors.

6. *Over-use of natural areas* such as caves, national parks, wildlife reserves, isolated cays, bays and anchorages, as tourist attractions – even ecotourism attractions – which leads to serious environmental pressures.

7. *Noise pollution, overcrowding and congestion* at trafficked areas such as beaches, airports, roadways and historic attractions.

8. *Corrosion of ancient monuments* by acid rain and the long steady trek of tourists – for example, in the highly polluted city of Athens. Here tourist coaches are no longer allowed on the Acropolis hill, and it is estimated that buildings have suffered from more acid rain in the last 25 years than the preceding 2400 years (Smith and Jenner, 1989).

9. *Destruction of forests and mountains* from heavy usage and trekking by 'nature tourists' – for example, in the Himalayan mountains the destruction of large tracts of mountain have occurred as a result of the nature tourist's search for firewood (Dixit and Tüting, 1986).

10. *Pressures on protected areas and national parks* brought on by over-demand, inadequate management and funding and the sheer physical limits of these reserves.

11. *Marred landscapes* caused by skiing and unsympathetic design leading to topsoil erosion, mud slides, snow avalanches, the displacement of countless species of birds, mammals and plants.

12. *Use of snow cannons to create artificial snow* for ski resorts which 'apart from the noise nuisance and obvious unattractiveness, utilize millions of gallons of water, making sudden changes in the water levels in feeder lakes, disturbing the biologically most interesting elements of these lakes' (Smith and Jenner, 1989).

13. *Insistence on the eating of certain types of gourmet foods irrespective of the time of year* – for example, lobster-eating during the closed season, thereby creating a demand for the illicit trade and placing enormous strain on the wildlife population (it takes two to tango).

The current problem of the tourism industry and the delicate balance of development and conservation was recently documented in a well-researched BBC programme entitled, '*Wish You Weren't Here*' (BBC England, Monday 25 November 1991). Environmental problems caused or reinforced by tourism have merely served to compound the environmental problems already existing on a global scale (e.g. global warming, destruction of the world's rainforests).

3.2.3. Environmental Pressure Groups

> People everywhere are offended by pollution. They sense intuitively
> that we have passed beyond limits we should not have exceeded.
> They want to clean up the world, make it a better place, be good
> trustees of the earth for future generations.
>
> (James Gustave Speth, President of
> the World Resources Institute, 1988)

Currently there are several organized environmentalists, writers, magazines, consumers and other pressure groups working towards the goal of saving Planet Earth. Their numbers are growing. 'Greenpeace,' for example, stands for a safe and nuclear-free world, fresh air, clean water, and the protection of wildlife and their habitats. Other organizations with a similar mission include: the Audubon Society; the Caribbean Conservation Association; the Alliance of Small Island States; the Caribbean Natural Resources Institute; Club of Rome; Friends of the Earth; the World Conservation Unit; the Smithsonian Institute; the National Geographic Society; the International Union for Conservation of Nature and Natural Resources; Tourism Concern; the World Council of Churches; the World Resources Institute and the World Wildlife Foundation.

In the tourism field, the Studienkreis fur Tourismus (StfT) has pioneered a Sympathie Magazine, aimed at tuning travellers into other countries and people in an informative, entertaining and sympathetic way. Sympathie Magazines have been produced for destinations such as the Caribbean, Jamaica, Thailand, Kenya, China, Peru, Nepal, Jugoslavia, Greece, Turkey, Indonesia, and other countries. The Ecumenical Coalition of Third World Tourism and The Tourism with Insight group (a coalition of many institutions both in the developed and developing countries) have also produced a code of behaviour for tourists, host countries and businesses alike. The Audubon society has also issued a 'Travel Ethic for Environmentally Sound Travel', which aims at encouraging sustainable travel, strengthening the conservation effort and enhancing the natural integrity of places visited (National Audubon Society, 1989).

Many host countries also publish 'do's and don'ts' for visitors. For example, in Barbados tourists are not allowed to enter shops and supermarkets in bathing suits; and in the majority of Caribbean islands, nude bathing is prohibited. In Tobago there are penalties imposed on tourists and the local population if caught taking anything away from the reefs. All visitors to Tobago are made aware of this law on arrival on all British West Indian Airways (BWIA) flights from all destinations into Tobago.

3.2.4. Growing Consumer Awareness

All of these initiatives result in growing awareness of environmental problems on a global scale. They serve to reinforce the practice of environmentally sound living.

Today there is considerable and growing awareness of the environment and its fragility. The environmental movement is gaining in momentum as has never been seen before. Consumers in European societies, particularly in Western Europe, now practice conscious recycling techniques and try to ensure that their consumption patterns are not harmful to the environment. There is already a Green Consumer Guide that is a bestseller and the Green Consumer Supermarket Shopping Guide, which provides 'shelf by shelf recommendations for products which don't cost the earth' (Elkington and Hailes, 1989).

Indeed, consumers are more aware than ever before. 'Gallup' surveys in the USA conclude that more than 75% of US consumers include environmental considerations in their shopping decisions (cited in Kleiner, 1991, p. 39). Research also shows that 'public attention to environmental issues has not peaked and will continue to gain momentum (Roper Organization, cited by the US Travel Data Center, 1989, p. 13). Environmental consciousness is certainly spilling over to the tourism industry as witnessed by the increased demand for ecotourism and other forms of nature travel (World Wildlife Foundation, 1990).

3.2.5. The Greening of the Private Sector

There is also a growing 'greening' of the private sector. Producers are responding to consumer demands by producing recycled paper, phosphate-free soap powders, non-aerosol sprays, and other items that minimize the negative impacts on the environment. No longer does being green mean being a bunch of non-conformist revolutionaries trying to keep back the course of production through:

- protest voyage to a nuclear test zone, disrupting the test (the site at Amchitka on the Aleutian Islands is now a bird sanctuary);
- sending tiny inflatable boats to protect the whales, taking up position between the harpoons and the fleeing whales (today commercial whaling is banned);

- voluntarily placing bodies between the grafts of sea hunters and the helpless sea pups, calling off the hunt; and
- endangered protests against radioactive waste to secure prevention of dumping at sea (actual activities undertaken by Greenpeace, cited in the Greenpeace publication, *Thank God Someone's Making Waves*, undated).

Green today means money. It has become compatible with corporate interests. In describing what it means to be green, one author suggests that it is 'moving not only beyond the law but ahead of its industry and many of its consumers' (Kleiner, 1991, p. 38).

In the travel and tourism industry, there are weak but growing signals of an increasingly conscious private sector. Opportunities are emerging for new relationships between conservationists trying to protect areas and tour operators trying to bring more people to these areas. One tour operator, Journeys International, was formed as a non-profit travel organization: it simultaneously formed the Earth Preservation Fund to utilize a portion of the trip proceeds to support the areas where clients are taken. Other tour operators support the effort with donations (World Wildlife Foundation, 1990).

The Conservation Foundation Holiday Club launched by David Belamy in London in February, 1991, guarantees that for every booking made, £10.00 will be donated to the Programme for Belize (see Chapter 9). The Caribbean region is encouraged to conserve its environment by American Express, which has launched an annual conservation award for the best conserved historical site in any of the Caribbean Tourism Organization's 31 member-states. And there are other green initiatives. Chapter 10 provides some case examples of destinations that have begun to link tourism with the environment in a serious way.

3.2.6. Funding Agencies Foster Conservation

In addition to the conservation effort of tourist destinations, a number of other important efforts are in train by international funding agencies. These efforts are clearly evident in the Caribbean. Among the agencies making a positive contribution to the health of the tourism sector in the Caribbean are the Caribbean Development Bank (CDB), European Community (EC), Inter-American Development Bank (IDB), Organization of American States (OAS), United Nations Development Programme (UNDP) and the United States Agency for International Development (USAID).

The European Community, through the LOME Convention, has been in the forefront of providing funds to the Caribbean tourism sector. The role of tourism in the fourth and current LOME convention has changed considerably. From a situation where 'tourism was hardly mentioned at all', tourism now plays a significant role and special account is taken of its 'real importance' (Personal communication, Gabriel Lee, head, DG VIII, Division for Trade and Development with special responsibility for tourism, London, November 1991). The scope for tourism under LOME IV covers human resources and institutional support, product development, market development and research and information, paying particular attention to the need to fully integrate tourism into the social, cultural and economic life of the people. One of the most important aspects of the new tourism package is the emphasis on product development – the development of cultural heritage, ecological and environmental aspects of management, protection and conservation of flora and fauna, historical, social and other natural assets. A total of ECU 9 million is available for regional projects, while Caribbean islands (notably, Grenada and Trinidad and Tobago) have independently committed a large proportion of their national programmes to tourism.

A major EC initiative on the environment is being implemented in Grenada. In 1990, the Parliament of Grenada passed into law the National Parks and Protected Areas Act thereby setting the legal basis for the National Parks System – a system of national parks and protected areas, which, including 27 sites in Grenada and 16 in the sister island of Cariacou, amounts to 13% of the islands' land surface. One Park, the Levera National Park in Grenada, is being funded by the EC to the extent of 925 000 ECU (US$1.1 million) and is the first project by the EC of this nature in the context of development cooperation (Personal communication, J. Caloghirou, EC Delegation in Grenada, 1991).

The Inter-American Development Bank, Washington, has embarked on a lending programme to the tourism sector, based on requests by the respective governments. Environmental impact assessments are necessary conditions for loans to the sector. Preliminary work in Trinidad and Tobago has been completed and programmes for the Bahamas, Barbados, Jamaica and other islands are in progress.

The OAS has been instrumental on the environmental front and has been responsible for the development of proposals for national parks and protected areas in islands such as St Vincent and the Grenadines, St Lucia, Trinidad and Tobago and other islands. The OAS has also produced some seminal work on the cultural impacts of tourism in the Caribbean. A resident training expert at the CTO, with prime responsibility for training teachers to teach tourism and training the Caribbean tourism public sector, is also being funded by the OAS.

The CDB continues to support the Caribbean tourism industry through its support for the Caribbean Tourism Organization, where it funds tourism statistical programmes. It also provides soft loans and technical support to the hotel sector both directly and through its development bank members in many of the islands. The president of the Caribbean Development Bank,

Sir Neville Nicholls recognized in the 1980s that these loans and technical assistance have been of tremendous help to the region. When it is considered that 60% of the 120000 rooms in the Caribbean are located in establishments of less than 30 rooms and over 50% of the sector is locally owned, the importance of funding to the local sector is significant (Curtin and Poon, 1988). The International Financial Corporation (a World Bank affiliate), the European Investment Bank, the Commonwealth Development Corporation and the Caribbean Financial Services Corporation also provide support to the hotel and tourism sector in the Caribbean.

UNDP with the World Tourism Organization have been instrumental in initiating an ongoing programme at the CTO in Barbados that is aimed at the measurement of the economic impact of tourism and delivering technical assistance to its 29 member countries – now 31, including Cuba and Mexico.

USAID has also taken many initiatives in the Caribbean. It provided seed funding for the development of Tourism Action Plan Limited in Jamaica – a joint private/public sector body whose main responsibility is that of produce development (see Chapter 9 for more details); also funded, to the tune of US$250000, is a feasibility study of a regional Caribbean Tourism Promotion Campaign in 1988. At present, it has a very ambitious development programme in place in Belize, Central America and there are other USAID initiatives throughout the Caribbean.

3.3. THE MICROELECTRONICS REVOLUTION

While environmental constraints set limits to growth, the microelectronics revolution opens new opportunities, which, creatively utilized, can enhance the growth potential of the travel and tourism industry. Technological developments in the miniaturization of electronic components on a single chip has ushered in a revolution of tremendous magnitude. No one will escape its impact. Microelectronics has brought about a technological revolution that is influencing the behaviour of the entire economy.

Microelectronics has invaded almost every aspect of our daily lives – our homes, our places of work, our hotels, our travel agencies and our cars. It influences the way we spend money, how we cook and even the way we entertain ourselves. Microelectronic chips are in our cars, stereos, telephones, tools, toys, televisions, microwave ovens and computers. It is hard to think of anything that microelectronics has not as yet invaded. Microelectronics not only leads to the emergence of a new range of products, services, systems and industries in its own right, but it affects directly or indirectly almost every other branch of the economy (Freeman and Perez, 1988).

3.3.1. The Technology

Microelectronics has given birth to what is commonly referred to today as information technology (IT). IT is the collective term given to the most recent developments in the mode (electronic) and the mechanisms (computers and communications technologies) used for the acquisition, processing, analysis, storage, retrieval, dissemination and application of information. IT refers to the synthesis of electronics, computing and telecommunications technologies (Rada, 1984).

That information technology is heralded as *the* technology of this century, capable of having the most profound impacts upon manufacturing activities, service pursuits, employment and daily life as a whole, is due fundamentally to developments taking place in the related fields of computers and communications (Kobayashi, 1986). The principal technological foundation for computers and communications is microelectronic technology (Braun and Macdonald, 1982).

Electronics, computers and communication technologies are the key building blocks of information technology. These are briefly described below.

3.3.2. Electronics

Developments taking place in the design, production and use of electronic devices have progressed quantitatively and qualitatively at such a meteoric rate that it has created enormous potentials for their use, both in manufacturing and services (Bessant, 1991; Forrester, 1982).

The world has progressed from valve technology in the 1930s, transistors in the 1940s, integrated circuits in the 1950s, medium- and large-scale integration of electronic components on a single chip in the late 1960s, leading to the programmable microprocessor in 1971. Very-large-scale integration in the late 1970s and early 1980s, and ultimately, ultra-large-scale integration in the future, all open new production possibilities in all spheres of material life.

Developments in microelectronics have made possible small, reliable, high-powered and low-cost equipment, which can perform complex operations on digitally encoded data. Microelectronic chips lie at the heart of developments in information technologies such as computer-aided design and computer-aided manufacture (CAD/CAM), computer-aided quality control (CAQC), flexible manufactured systems (FMS), robots, personal computers, notebook computers, word processors, computerized reservations systems (CRSs), mobile communications, image communication, videotext and teleconferencing.

Our ability to generate, analyse, process, store and communicate information is greatly affected by developments taking place in computers and communications.

3.3.3. Computers

Developments from the tube and the transistor, to integrated circuits and very-large-scale integration of electronic components on silicon chips, have led us through four generations of computers with the fifth in the making. With each generation, the capacity of the computer to store, process, manipulate and display information has increased tremendously. As early as 1977, it was noted that:

> Today's microcomputer ... has more computing capacity than the first large electronic computer, ENIAC. It is 20 times faster, has a larger memory, is 1000 times more powerful, consumes the power of a lightbulb instead of a locomotive, occupies 1/30000 the volume and costs 1/10000 as much ...

(Noyce, 1977, p. 65)

Developments in computer technology remove the limitations in quantity, time and intelligence in the capacity to generate, process and store information (Kobayashi, 1986, p. 49). Computers are the key tools to quickly and efficiently · store, process, update and retrieve information contained in computer reservation systems (CRSs). With each generation of computers, computing power and performance have increased, while prices continue to fall. Computers are increasingly becoming a way of life – a tool for enhancing productivity in all sectors of the economy, a generator of new goods and services and a creator of new leisure pursuits.

3.3.4. Communications

Paralleling developments in electronics and advances in computers are developments in communications. In the communications field, the evolution of electronic technologies has given way to digital (as opposed to analogue) transmission systems. This has created the basis for many new information communication networks and their applications service systems. Representative examples of these developments are the integrated service digital networks, the value-added network, the direct broadcast satellite system, videotext (PRESTEL in the UK), teleconferencing, office automation, the corporate communication systems local area network and the wide area network. These systems have increased the speed and efficiency of information generation, transmission and storage at substantially reduced costs. These technological developments have made communications possible on a 'whenever, wherever and with whomever' basis.

3.4. BIRTH OF A NEW PARADIGM

As noted in Chapter 1 microelectronics today are as significant as the cotton and pig iron, coal, railways, steel and oil that fuelled the industrial revolution (1770s–1830s) Victorian prosperity (1830s–1880s) and the golden age of full employment (1940s–1980s). The microelectronics revolution is therefore significant not only from the technological possibilities that it brings but, more profoundly, because of its role in ushering in a new age of development – the information age. The information age brings a whole new paradigm of development – a paradigm with powers to transform production management and consumption 'best practices'; a paradigm with powers to determine the competitiveness of nations and dominance of the global marketplace, a paradigm that brings 'a unique new combination of decisive technical and economic advantages' (Freeman and Perez, 1988, p. 48).

A paradigm can be described as an 'ideal' pattern or style of productive organization or best technological 'common sense' that prevails at the time (Perez, 1983). A paradigm is really the prevailing common sense for the best productivity and most profitable practice. Mass production during the post-war period, for example, was best practice. From the 1930s to the 1980s, mass production – with its drive toward large-scale production, standardization and economies of scale – represented the ideal organizational and managerial 'common sense' for best productivity and most profit.

A paradigm change refers to 'a radical transformation of the prevailing engineering and managerial common sense for best productivity and most profitable practice, which is applicable in almost any industry' (Freeman and Perez, 1988, p. 48). In each new paradigm, a particular input or set of inputs – a 'key factor' of that paradigm satisfies the following conditions (Freeman and Perez, 1986):

1. Clearly perceived low and rapidly falling relative cost.
2. Apparently almost unlimited availability of supply over long periods.
3. Clear potential for the use or incorporation of the new key factor(s) in many products and processes throughout the economic system either directly or, more commonly, through a set of related innovations that both reduce the cost and change the quality of capital equipment, labour inputs and other inputs to the system.

Freeman and Perez contend that this combination of technoeconomic characteristics holds today for microelectronics (Freeman and Perez, 1986), and also held, until recently, for oil which underlay the post-war mass-production boom. Before that, and more tentatively, the 'key factor' was played by low-cost steel between the 1880s and 1940s, by low-cost

Table 3.1 Information technology leads the fifth wave

Character	Waves				
	First	Second	Third	Fourth	Fifth
Time frame	1770s and 1780s – 1830s and 1840s	1830s and 1840s – 1880s and 1890s	1880s and 1890s – 1930s and 1940s	1930s and 1940s – 1980s and 1990s	1980s and 1990s – 2040s and 2050s?
Description	Early mechanization	Steam power and railway	Electrical and heavy engineering	Fordist mass production	Information and communication technology
Main carrier branches	Textiles Textile machinery Iron-working Trunk canals Turnpike roads	Steam engines Steam ships Machine tools Railways World shipping	Electrical engineering Electrical machinery Cable & wire Heavy engineering Heavy armaments Steel ships Synthetic dye stuffs Electricity supply	Automobiles, trucks tractors, tanks aircrafts Motorized warfare Process plant Synthetic materials Petrochemicals Highways, airports Consumer durables	Computers, software Electronic capital goods Robotics Telecommunications equipment Optical fibres Digital communication networks Services, **tourism**
Key factors	Cotton	Coal	Steel	Oil	Microelectronics
Leading countries	Britain	Britain	Germany	USA	Japan

Source: Freeman and Perez, 1988; *Caribbean Futures*, 1991a.

coal and steam-powered transport in the 'Victorian boom' of the 19th Century; and by low-cost factory labour and cotton in the 'industrial revolution' at the end of the 18th Century (Freeman and Perez, 1986, p. 12). Table 3.1 provides a brief description of the phases (long waves) of development of the global economy, the role played by key factors and leading countries.

Microelectronics is as important today as coal, steam, steel and cotton of the past centuries. Microelectronics is the progenitor of the fifth and current wave – a wave that is also known as the 'information and communication wave', 'information technology paradigm' and 'flexible specialization'. Information technology lies at the heart of the fifth-wave paradigm. This information technology paradigm is marked by the rapid diffusion of information technologies throughout every aspect of production and material life in modern societies as a whole.

3.4.1. Mass Production

Before information technology, the technological regime that predominated in the post-war Fordist mass-production boom was one based on low-cost oil and energy-intensive materials (mainly petrochemicals and synthetics). It was led by giant oil, chemical, automobile and other mass durable goods producers. The 'ideal' type of productive organization at the plant level was the continuous-flow assembly-line turning out massive quantities of identical units. Mass-production corporations required a large number of consumers ready and willing to buy their output. The massive expansion of the market for consumer durables was facilitated by innovations in the financial system allowing for 'hire purchase' and other types of consumer credit. A ready market was also provided by the demand generated by incomes accruing to the large number of workers in middle-range skills in both blue- and white-collar employment who were required to churn out consumer durables at the factories. Mass production also required:

> ... a vast infrastructural network of motorways, service stations, airports, oil and petrol distribution systems, which was promoted by public investments on a large scale already in the 1930s, but particularly since the post-war period. At various times and in various countries, both civil and military expenditure of governments played a very important role in stimulating aggregate demand and a specific pattern of demand for automobiles, weapons, consumer durables, synthetic materials and petroleum products.
>
> (Freeman and Perez, 1986)

3.4.2. Limitations of Mass Production

Mass-production practices – continuous-flow process and assembly-line principles of full standardization of components and materials – were developed in order to overcome the limitations of scale of batch production.

Similarly, information-technology tools have evolved partially because of the limitations of the old mass-production paradigm. Dis-economies of scale and inflexibility of dedicated assembly lines and process plant could be partially overcome by flexible manufacturing systems, 'networking' and 'economies of scope'. The limitations on energy and materials intensity could not be conquered partially by electronic control systems and components. The limitations of hierarchical departmentalization could now be overwhelmed by 'systemation', 'networking' and integration of design, production and marketing.

3.4.3. The Information Technology Paradigm

Today, with cheap microelectronics widely available, with prices expected to fall even further and with related developments in computers and communications, it is no longer commonness to continue along the now expensive path of material-intensive inflexible mass production (Freeman and Perez, 1986). Moreover, with the increasing experience and sophistication of consumers, together with their changing values, lifestyles and demographic circumstances, there is an increased demand for more variety and better quality (see Chapter 5). Products and services that make intensive use of information and related technologies are expected to be the preferred choice for investment and will represent a growing proportion of a country's gross domestic product (GDP). The utilization of information technologies gives suppliers the flexibility and cost imperatives to supply the rapidly changing consumer demands.

Unlike the material-intensive inflexible mass-production regimes of the past, information-intensive organizations increasingly link design, management, production and marketing into one system – a process that may be described as systemation and goes far beyond the earlier concepts of mechanization and automation (Freeman and Perez, 1986).

Firms organized on this new basis, whether in the computer industry such as IBM, in the clothing industry such as Beneton, or in the aviation industry such as American Airlines, can produce a flexible and rapidly changing mix of products and services (Freeman and Perez, 1986). Growth tends to be increasingly led by the electronic and information sectors, taking advantage of the growing externalities of the telecommunications infrastructure, which, as the airline CRSs demonstrate, considerably reduces costs of access to the system for both producers and users of information (see Chapter 7).

The skill profile associated with the new information-technology paradigm changes from the concentration on middle-range craft and supervisory skills to increasingly medium-and-high-range qualifications. There is also a move from narrow specialization to broader, multi-purpose basic skills for information handling. Diversity and flexibility at all levels substitute for homogeneity and dedicated systems. The transformation of the profile of capital equipment is no less radical. Computers are increasingly associated with all types of productive equipment as in computer numerically controlled (CNC) machine tools, robotics and process control instruments, as well as with the design process through computer-aided design (CAD). According to some estimates, computer-based capital equipment accounted for nearly half of all new fixed investments in plant and equipment in the USA (Freeman and Perez, 1988).

The main carrier branches of the fifth wave are computers, electronic capital goods, software, telecommunications equipment, optical fibres, robotics, flexible manufacturing systems, ceramics, data banks, information services, digital communications network, satellites, travel, tourism and other services (see Table 3.1). Other sectors growing rapidly from a small base are third-generation biotechnology products and processes, space activities, fine chemicals and strategic defence initiatives. Some features of the tertiary or services sector in this wave are the rapid growth of new information services, data banks and software industries, integration of services and manufacturing in such industries as printing and publishing, rapid growth of professional consultancy, new forms of craft production linked to distribution. Travel and tourism services have a major role to play. Taking up the principles of mass production rather late, travel and tourism will be one of the leading sectors of the new wave.

3.4.4. Old and New Best Practice Compared

Flexible specialization is a production practice in which the focus is on variety, niche markets and customization. The style of operation in mass production is radically different from that in flexible production. In mass production, routines and procedures are standardized, there is one best way and a single top-down line of command. In flexible production, the procedures and systems used are adaptable and flexible, there is widespread delegation of decision-making and a philosophy that 'a better way can always be found' (Table 3.2). In mass production, stocks are held 'just in case' and corporations compete through full capacity utilization, cost cutting, over-production and mark-downs. In flexible production, firms compete through continuous innovation, improvements in quality, diversi-

Table 3.2 The old and new 'best practice' compared

Characteristics	Mass production	Flexible production
Production concept	Mass production	Flexibility, specialization
Products	Limited range of standardized products Mass markets	Product variety and specialization 'Niche' markets, customization
Style of operation	Standardized routines and procedures 'There is one best way' Single top-down line of command	Flexible systems/adaptable procedures 'A better way can always be found' Widespread delegation of decision-making
Manning and training	Labour as a variable cost Market provides most trained personnel People to fit fixed positions	Labour as human capital Much in-house training and re-training Variable posts, adaptable people
Equipment and investment	Dedicated equipment Each plant anticipates demand growth Strive for economies of scale	Adaptable/programmable flexible equipment Organic growth closely following demand Choice or combination of economies of scale and economies of scope
Production programming	Stocks held 'just in case' Tolerance on quality and rejects	Stocks delivered 'just in time' Strive for 'zero defects' and 'zero rejects'
Markets and customers	Manufacturers dominate retailers Producers dominate users Mass advertising	Retailers dominate Producers and users have two-way relations Firm rather than product advertising
Competitive strategy	Full capacity utilization Cost cutting and over-production Stockpiling and markdowns	Innovation Diversification Market segmentation

Source: Perez, 1986; UNDP/UNIDO, 1987; Poon, 1990.

fication and market segmentation. The manning and training methods, equipment and investment, production programming, customers and markets are also radically different in the old and new production best practices. These differences can be gleaned from Table 3.2, which compares the old 'best practice' of mass production with the new 'best practice' of flexible production.

3.5. LESSONS FROM THE MANUFACTURING SECTOR

The experience of the manufacturing sector, car manufacturing in particular, holds some very interesting lessons for tourism. Beginning with the development of the Ford T model in the 1920s, the manufacturing sector was undoubtedly the leader of mass production. Since the development of mass production, the manufacturing sector has not stood still. Technologies have continued to advance at an extraordinary rate and competition has intensified to satisfy more sophisticated consumers. It is therefore not surprising today that the automobile industry, particularly the Japanese industry, is in the forefront of new flexible production and management methods (Womack *et al.*, 1990). In this respect, there are a number of lessons that the travel and tourism industry can learn from its manufacturing counterpart.

It is useful at the outset to compare the manufacturing sector, with the travel and tourism industry. The automobile industry, as an example of a manufacturing enterprise, is an excellent reference point. A comparison can be made between automobiles and travel and tourism. This can be done by comparing the role of mass production and flexible specialization in both industries. The findings are very interesting as they point to the direction that the travel and tourism industry should take in the future.

Table 3.3 compares mass production practices of the travel and tourism industry and the automobile industry. It can be seen from this table that cars are produced in factories, while travel and tourism services are constructed in offices, hotels and resorts. Also, while dedicated machinery and assembly lines were the main instruments for the mass production of cars, packaged tours, charter flights, franchises, and holiday and hotel branding achieved a similar objective in the travel and tourism industry. The approach to the labour force is also very similar in the car industry and the travel and tourism industry. In the travel and tourism industry, labour is seasonal, turnover is high, flexibility is low and the industry has developed a reputation for the lowest-paying jobs. In the automobile industry mass production is facilitated by labour, which is conceived as little more than a cost of production. The consumers of cars are in many cases identical to those who purchased standardized

Table 3.3 Mass production: tourism and automobiles compared

Characteristics	Automobiles (1930s and 1940s–1980s and 1990s)	Travel and Tourism (1960s and 1970s–1980s and 1990s)
Production concept	Mass production	Mass tourism
Products	Limited range of standardized products Mass markets	Mass, standardized and rigidly packaged holidays, mass markets
Instruments of production	Dedicated machinery Assembly lines Factories	Packaged tours Charter flights Franchises Holiday branding Offices, hotels, resorts
Organization of production	Strive for economies of scale Anticipate demand growth Stocks held just in case	Scale economies are very important Anticipate demand, buy future capacity Hold holidays just in case
Manning and training	Labour as a variable cost People to fit fixed positions	Labour is seasonal High labour turnover Reputation for lowest-paying jobs Low labour flexibility
Marketing	Mass marketing Mass advertising	Mass marketing Mass advertising
Customers	Inexperienced, apparently homogeneous motivated by price	Inexperienced, apparently homogeneous sun-lust, predictable, motivated by price
Quality	Tolerance for some level of inferior quality and rejects	No difference

Source: Derived from Fig. 2.1 and Table 3.2.

Table 3.4 Flexible production: tourism and automobiles compared

Characteristics	Automobiles (1980s and 1990s–Future)	Travel and Tourism (1980s and 1990s–Future)
Production concept	Flexible production	Flexible travel and tourism options
Products	Product variety, specialization, 'niche' markets, customization	Flexible, segmented, customized, environmentally sound holidays
Instruments of production	Adaptable/programmable flexible equipment	Yield management Specialized operators Destination competence Independent holidays Greater role of suppliers and agents
Organization of production	Strive for economies of scale and scope Organic growth closely following demand	Scale and scope economies, flexibility Close to the market, diagonal integration
Manning and training	Labour as human capital Much in-house training and re-training Variable positions, adaptable people	Human resources strategies for the travel and tourism industry not yet clear
Marketing	Mass customization	Mass customization
Customers	Very experienced consumers	Experienced, independent, flexible, changed values, mature, responsible
Quality	Zero defects, zero rejects, continuous quality improvements	No comparable strategies for the travel and tourism industry are as yet apparent

Source: Derived from Fig. 2.1 and Table 3.2.

and rigidly packaged holidays. In fact, many tourists in the USA would have travelled to their rigidly packaged holiday with a mass-produced car. Other comparisons between travel and tourism and the car industry in the areas of production organization, customers, markets and quality can be gleaned from Table 3.3.

Table 3.4 compares flexible production in the travel and tourism industry and the car industry. The findings are very revealing. While flexible production in the car industry is facilitated by flexible and programmable equipment such as robotics, flexible manufacturing systems (FMS) and computer-aided design (CAD), in the travel and tourism industry, flexible production is facilitated through specialist operators, destination competence, independent holidays, yield management and a greater role of service suppliers (e.g. hotels) and travel agents. Information technology in the form of CRSs and various levels of computers and communication applications in hotels also plays an important role in increasing the flexibility of production and delivery of travel and tourism services.

The techniques adopted by the manufacturing sector in its approach to quality and human resources are very important and hold key lessons for travel and tourism suppliers. It is in these two areas perhaps more than any other that the travel and tourism industry has to learn from its manu-facturing counterparts. New 'best practices' approaches of automobile manufacturers to their work force include: (i) valuing labour as human capital; (ii) undertaking a great deal of in-house training and re-training to upgrade skills and quality; and (iii) creating variable positions and adaptable workers. As yet, there is no clear 'best-practice' strategy widely adopted by travel and tourism suppliers in the management of its human resources. Rather, old practices predominate.

In the pursuit of continuous improvement, the Japanese have devel-oped several systems and strategies specifically aimed at improving the quality of their goods. Such include zero defects, zero rejects as well as the whole concept of 'kaizen', which pervades their everyday life. Kaizen is the Japanese word for improvement – ongoing improvement involving both managers and workers. Kaizen reflects the typical Japanese way of running an enterprise, their approach as it were to the production process itself; this involves:

- customer orientation;
- total quality control (TQC);
- robotics;
- quality circles (QC);
- suggestion system;
- automation;
- total productive maintenance (TPM);

- just-in-time;
- zero defects;
- small-group activities;
- co-operative labour/management relations;
- productivity improvement; and
- new product development.

The travel and tourism industry as a whole has not developed a quality imperative comparable with car manufacturers where, in particular, the Japanese are the trendsetters. The possible exceptions are cruise ships, Disneyland and all-inclusive hotels (see Chapter 8). While package tours, charter flights, CRSs, 'mass tourism', deregulation, 'summer sun', sun lust and related concepts have entered the travel and tourism vocabulary, no equivalent for quality has as yet surfaced, except perhaps the concept of zero defection (see Chapter 9). Competitive strategies for travel and tourism will increasingly have to address the quality imperative.

3.6. SUMMARY

The international travel and tourism industry has been shaped in the past by several crucial factors – post-war peace and prosperity, the growth of paid holidays, the advent of the jet engine and production of cheap oil. Critical global forces – environmental limits to growth, the microelectronics revolution and the birth of a new 'technoeconomic paradigm' – will continue to shape its rate and direction of growth.

The travel and tourism industry was not alone when it adopted and modified principles of mass production. It was blazing the trail of a well tried and tested 'best practice' in the manufacturing sector. Nor will the industry be alone in its adoption of the principles of flexible production, which is rapidly becoming the new global best practice. Indeed, the travel and tourism industry will not escape the overpowering tendency toward flexible production; rather, the information-intensity and malleability of the industry makes it an ideal candidate for flexible organization, management and production practices.

The travel and tourism industry will be a lead sector in the current information technology wave.

4

GLOBAL TRANSFORMATION

4.1. INTRODUCTION

Old tourism was the logical outcome of key social and economic influences. Mimicking mass production in the manufacturing sector, mass tourism became *best practice*. Today, mass tourism is no longer common sense. The industry is in crisis as it searches for a new way.

International tourism is undergoing rapid transition to a new industry best practice. A new tourism is emerging – a tourism characterized by flexible, segmented and environmentally conscious holidays. Production and management practices of market segmentation, diagonal integration, customized services for large numbers of travellers, and innovation, are increasingly common sense for best productivity and increased profit.

This chapter will demonstrate how and why a new tourism is emerging. One of the best ways of describing the transformation from the old tourism to the new, is to compare the forces that gave rise to the old tourism with those giving rise to the new tourism. Five main impulses driving the new tourism are identified and examined. These are:

- new consumers;
- new technologies;
- new production practices;
- new management techniques; and
- changes in the industry's frame conditions.

This chapter will give particular emphasis to the industry's changed *frame conditions*. New consumers and new technologies are especially important forces driving the new tourism: new consumers are dictating the pace and direction of changes in the industry; while technology provides the flexibility to move with the market.

4.2. NEW TOURISM DEFINED

New tourism is a phenomenon of large-scale packaging of non-standardized leisure services at competitive prices to suit the demands of tourist as well as the economic and socioenvironmental needs of destinations. New tourism refers to key emerging characteristics of the tourism industry. As noted in Chapter 1 new tourism exists if the following conditions hold:

1. The holiday is flexible and can be purchased at prices that are competitive with mass-produced holidays.
2. Production of travel and tourism-related services are not dominated by scale economies alone. Tailor-made services will be produced while still taking advantages of scale economies where they apply.
3. Production is increasingly driven by the requirements of consumers.
4. The holiday is marketed to *individuals* with different needs, incomes, time constraints and travel interests. Mass marketing is no longer the dominant paradigm.
5. The holiday is consumed on a large scale by tourists who are more experienced travellers, more educated, more destination-oriented, more independent more flexible and more 'green'.
6. Consumers look at the environment and culture of the destinations they visit as a key part of the holiday experience.

One of the key characteristics of the new tourism is *flexibility* – flexible consumers, flexible services and the flexibility of producers to move with the market. The cornerstone of the industry's flexibility is information technology (IT). IT creates the flexibility to satisfy changing consumer needs at prices that are cost-competitive with mass-produced holidays. This practice is fundamentally different from the old paradigm where low-cost holidays were only possible within the confines of mass production, standardization and rigid packaging.

Information and communication technologies also allow producers to segment their markets and to match production more closely with the changing needs of their clients. Suppliers are now able to produce different travel, leisure and other related services (e.g. insurance and credit cards) along the same production line. Tourism now mimics flexible manufacturing and 'just-in-time' methods, which are now common practice in the automobile industry. What is unique about the growth of international tourism, however, is the speed at which it adopted the old mass-production manuacturing practices; the apparent short life cycle that mass production had in tourism; and the celerity with which the tourism industry is taking up the new production principle of flexibility.

As a new global best practice of flexible production takes hold, the travel and leisure sector will rapidly out-pace the manufacturing sector in adopting flexible production. Tourism will be a clear leader in the pack.

The marketing of the new tourism is also different from the old. In the old tourism, producers sold identical products to homogeneous groups of tourists. In the new tourism, there will be greater levels of market segmentation where travel and leisure services will increasingly cater to specific lifestyle characteristics of the new consumers. Marketing will be focused on the individual consumers, rather than on groups of undefined tourists.

Production will continue to be large-scale and global in nature and will take advantage of scale economies where they apply. It will, however, increasingly benefit from *scope economies* – economies associated with producing a *range* of items rather than producing a large quantity of identical units. While necessary, scale economies will no longer be sufficient to guarantee competitive success. Production will also be more flexible and closely geared to the changing needs of the consumers. *Mass customization* – the production and sale of large amounts of tailor-made services – will allow producers to supply flexible travel and tourism services to meet the demands of the new consumers. It will allow producers to supply travel and related services at prices that are competitive with mass-tourism services. Club Med is a good example for a supplier that has produced customized vacations for 'swinging singles' and marketed them to a large clientele. Cruise ships also provide an excellent example of mass customization. Armed with mega-ships and flexible itineraries, and a range of activities in which to participate at the various ports of call, cruise-holiday suppliers can offer a number of customized holidays to a large range of travellers.

4.3. EMERGENCE OF A NEW TOURISM

International tourism is undergoing rapid and radical transformation – a transformation into a new industry best practice or common sense.

As previously noted, five forces are driving the new tourism:

- consumers;
- technology;
- management techniques;
- production practices; and
- frame conditions.

These forces are summarized in Figure 4.1. It can be seen from the figure that new consumers and technologies are driving the new tourism, whilst new management techniques and production practices facilitate the development of the new services, and new frame conditions influence the speed and direction of the industry's change.

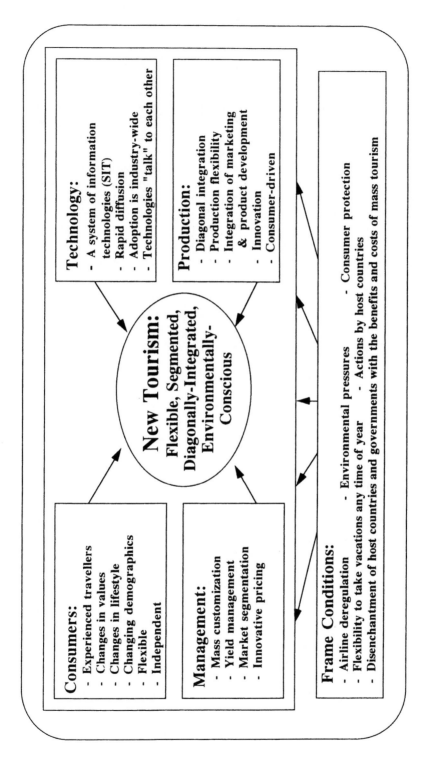

Fig. 4.1. Driving forces of the new tourism.

Changes in *consumer* behaviour and value provide the fundamental guiding force for the new tourism. New consumers are more informed and experienced travellers. They are products of universally accepted education. They have acquired changed values and lifestyles. They are products of changing population demographics. New tourists are flexible and more independent – they are hybrid consumers, spontaneous and unpredictable. They want to be active and in charge. They want to be different from the crowd. The increased travel experience, flexibility and independent nature of the new tourists are generating demand for more flexible holidays. Changing lifestyles and changing demographics of the new tourists are creating demand for more targeted holidays catering to their specific situations whether they be couples, families, single-parent house-holds, empty nesters, travellers and double income and no kids (DINKS), young upwardly mobile persons (YUPPIES) or modern introverted luxury keepers (MILKIES).

Changing values are also generating demand for a more environ-mentally conscious and nature-oriented holiday. That it is the consumers who are driving the new tourism is reflected in a statement by Sir Colin Marshall, Deputy Chairman and Chief Executive of British Airways, as he concluded the First Annual World Travel Market Lecture in London, 1990:

> ... aside from safety and security, the shape, scope and style of the airline industry in Europe and around the world should be regulated by one force only – the choice and the preference of the air travel consumer.

New technology provides yet another key impetus to the new tourism. It provides the wherewithal both to handle the high volumes of information that deregulation has produced (e.g. new fares, new airlines, new services) and the flexibility to cope with different and changing consumer require-ments. Technology diffusion in tourism is so rapid and so pervasive that no segment of the industry will remain untouched. It is not merely a telephone *or* computer *or* videotext *or* teleconferencing that is permeating the tourism industry, but a whole system of information technologies that can now 'talk' to each other. Technology creates a new basis for competition in the tourism industry and has become a key determinant of competitive success. It is now possible, given the state of technology, for industry players to itemize in minute detail the many travel and leisure opportunities open to the traveller, while at the same time list the tourist's every demand, note his every preference and expectation in the quest to satisfy.

New production practices are also characteristic of the new tourism. These include: diagonal integration, production flexibility and innovation. Production practices of mass customization increasingly allow producers to satisfy the 'quirks and idiosyncrasies' of the consumers at prices that are cost-competitive with mass-produced tourism and related services. Diagonal integration makes it increasingly common sense to link services such as financial services, insurance and travel, with tremendous synergies, systems gains and scope economies to be obtained from integrated production (see Chapter 8). In a constantly changing travel environment, innovation becomes an indispensable tool for survival.

Changed management techniques is another ingredient in the making of the new tourism. Management practices of mass customization, yield management, market segmentation and the integration of production and marketing are driving the new tourism. Producers increasingly allow consumers to dictate the character and pace of production. They make a greater effort to find out what the consumers want, to produce what consumers are demanding and to sell consumers what they want to buy. Mass customization and a proliferation and splintering of brands will be the order of the day in the new tourism. Products and services will be carefully dissected and finely tuned, to meet the needs of the new consumers.

Frame conditions are the fifth and final ingredient facilitating the new tourism. Deregulation of the airline industry, limits to growth, initiatives taken by host countries, consumer protection and the increasing spread and flexibility of vacation days, are creating the conditions within which the new tourism will flourish. Deregulation has equally opened a whole new ball-game in the industry and has ushered in new airlines, mega carriers, and increased price competition. A new and more vital role for computerized reservations systems has also been ushered in. All these developments are radically changing the face of tourism.

Limits to the growth of old tourism have begun to be felt; tourism fatigue has begun to set in, and a growing global environmental consciousness limits its growth still further. Increasing levels of consumer and environmental protection will lead to improved standards in the industry and ensure that production reflects consumer choices while remaining sensitized to the needs of the eco-system. The flexibility to take vacations at any time in the year, as is now the case in Britain, will lead to a more even flow of tourism, which will reduce the high levels of seasonality – a common characteristic of the tourism industry. This could lead to a more balanced flow visitors to resorts and attractions and lower the environmental effects of overcrowding, noise and other forms of pollution.

In what follows, the key changes in consumers, technology, management and production, and also the frame conditions that are changing tourism, shall be identified briefly.

4.4. NEW CONSUMERS

New consumers are fundamentally different from the old. Some of the main differences are summarized in Figure 4.2.

Old tourists were homogeneous and predictable. They felt secure when travelling in numbers and took vacations where everything was pre-paid and pre-arranged. New tourists are spontaneous and unpredictable. They are hybrid in nature and no longer consume along linear predictable lines. The hybrid consumer may want to purchase different tourism services in different price categories for the same trip. New consumers want to be different from the crowd. They want to assert their individuality and they want to be in control.

The motivation of the new tourists is different from those of the old. For the old tourists, travel was a novelty. Travel was almost an end in itself. It mattered not where the old tourists went, once they got to a warm destination and could show others that they had been there. Quality of service was relatively unimportant and vacation was an escape from the routinization of home and work. For the new tourists, however, vacation is an extension of life. It is a journey of discovery. Vacations are taken 'just for fun', rather than to show others that one has been there. New tourists go on vacation not to see and experience the things they are used to at home and to be surrounded by it in safety; rather, they go out to see something different, something that would expand their experience. For the new tourists, quality and value for money are a premium; and expressing their individuality at the destination, their ultimate pleasure.

The attitudes of the new tourists are also very different from that of the old. Old tourists had a healthy disregard for the environment and cultures of the host countries they visited. Today, with the new tourist, there is a growing 'see and enjoy, but do not destroy' attitude. And while old tourists imposed their values on the receiving destinations with a 'West is best' attitude, among the new tourists today, there is greater understanding and appreciation for the different. The new tourists are generally better educated and informed than were the old.

Old tourists were content to lie in the sun and get sunburnt. They were interested in visiting attractions, had little or no special interests and ate in the hotel dining room. For the new tourists, sun is still a necessary factor in the vacation pursuit; however, sun is not sufficient to satisfy their expectation. New tourists have special interests and are more adventurous (termed 'soft, medium and hard'). They like sport and want to be active. With respect to the sun, the new tourists are more concerned about the effects of overexposure to it and its link to health.

Six key attributes are characteristic of the new tourists:

- they are more experienced;

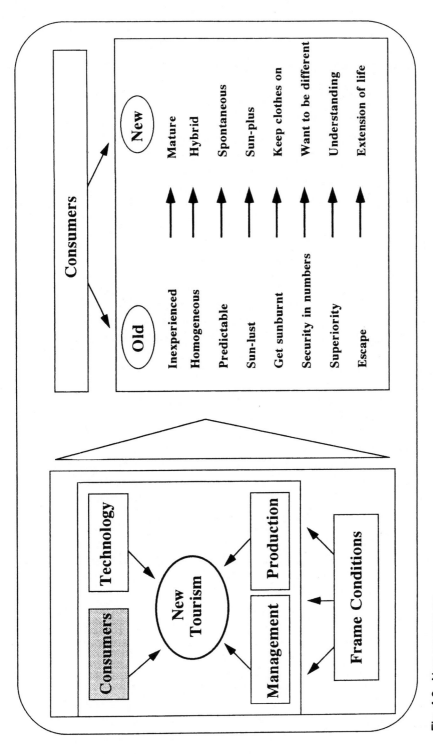

Fig. 4.2. New consumers.

Source: Krippendorf, 1987a; Poon, 1987a; *Economist*, 23 March 1991.

- they have changed values;
- they have changed lifestyles;
- they are products of changed demographics;
- they are flexible; and
- they are independent-minded.

These key characteristics of the new tourists are leading to the transformation of the old tourism best practice (see Chapter 5).

4.5. NEW TECHNOLOGIES

There are fundamental differences in the role that technologies play in the old tourism and in the new (Fig. 4.3).

In the old tourism, technologies were used to facilitate the mass production of tourism services. Computers assisted with internal management functions of accounting, financial control and payroll. In the new tourism, in addition to these standardized roles, technologies take on entirely new ones. Technologies in the new tourism are used to facilitate flexible production and to manage capacity, yield and clients. The focus of technological applications in the new tourism is on global networks, communications and value creation.

The technology users in the old tourism were limited to airlines, hotel chains and tour operators. In the new tourism, travel agents are major users of technology (e.g. computerized reservations terminals) and play an even more important role in the value chain of the travel industry (see Chapter 7). In addition, other service providers, such as cruise ships and pleasure boats are users of the industry's computerized reservations technologies. Even champagne and flower services, tourist boards, independent resorts, theme parks and other suppliers are represented on CRSs.

In the new tourism, technology is not used solely by travel agents *or* hotels *or* airlines *or* car rental *or* cruise ship companies *or* charter boat companies *or* tour operators, but by *all* of them. Moreover, each tourism segment's use of the new system of information technologies has implications for all other parts.

Technologies used in the old tourism were embodied in stand-alone, de-linked, equipment such as telephones, computers, telex, back-office accounting and management systems. The reservation systems used by the industry at the time were also limited in their ability to communicate with each other. Typically, airlines, hotels and tour operators developed their own dedicated systems. An airline system could check availability on other airlines or hotel properties but in relatively rudimentary ways. This made the job of the travel agent more cumbersome because of the frequency with which bookings were made by telephone even if there was a CRS on the premises.

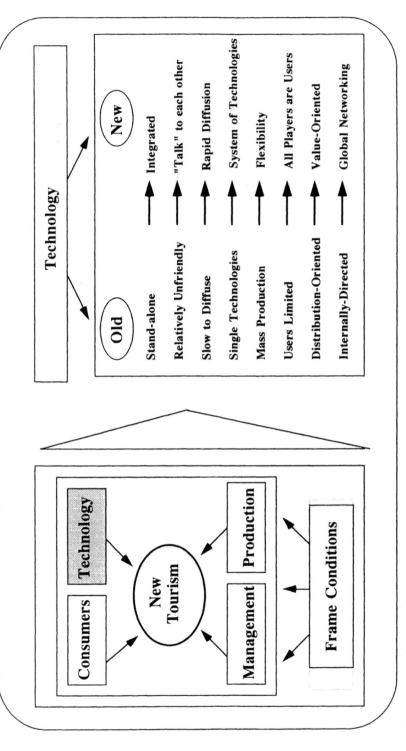

Fig. 4.3. New technologies.

In the new tourism, it is not a computer or telephone or video brochure that is being diffused, but a *whole system of evolving computer and communications technologies.* The components of the system of information technologies (SIT) being diffused in tourism include: (i) computerized reservation systems; (ii) teleconferencing; (iii) videotext; (iv) videos and video brochures; (v) computers; (vi) management information systems; (vii) airline electronic information systems; (viii) electronic funds transfer; (ix) digital telephone networks; (x) mobile communications (e.g. sky and boat phones); and (xi) interactive videotext. These technologies are diffusing very rapidly throughout the tourism industry. They promise to leave no player untouched.

4.6. NEW PRODUCTION PRACTICES

There are fundamental differences between the production 'best' practices between the old and new tourism (Fig. 4.4). Old tourism prospered in an environment where oil was cheap and plentiful and mass production was the order of the day. The environment was a promising new resource for exploitation – a factor of production. There were no special concerns for the environment. Producers and consumers had grown accustomed to life in a 'disposable society'. Today the tourism industry is faced with severe limits to growth and the environment is now a thing to be treasured.

In the 1960s, travel was still very much a novelty. Producers dictated the pace and pattern of production. The industry sold what it produced and consumers simply bought what was available. Production was dominated by large vertically integrated organizations – airlines, tour operators and hotel chains – and mass branding was best practice.

The new tourism will witness even more concentrated 'mega' forms – such as the recent merger of Thomas Cook (UK) and TUI (Germany) – and branding will take on even greater significance (see Chapters 8 and 9). The market, however, will not be dominated by a few large brands, but by a proliferation of different brands and subbrands, many of which could be owned by few entities. Holiday clubs, mega resorts, boutique hotels, cruise ships, pleasure boating and a number of other dedicated brands will experience tremendous growth.

Rigidly produced travel-and-tourism-related services will give way to more flexible products. Flexible production will be made possible through the rapid diffusion of information technologies throughout the tourism industry. Economies of scale, while necessary, will no longer be sufficient to guarantee success. Economies of scope – benefits from producing a range of items – will become increasingly important.

Horizontal and vertical integration – practices where firms come

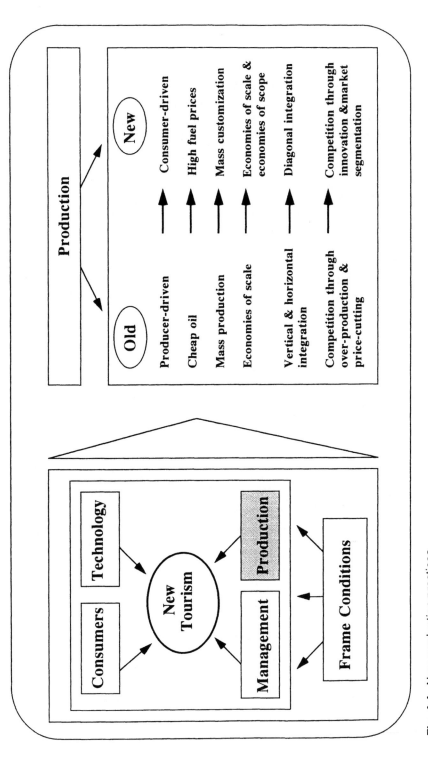

Fig. 4.4. New production practices.

together to control the market (concentration) and the stages of production respectively – will increasingly give way to diagonal integration. Diagonal integration, driven by information technologies, is a process by which service firms move into new and different activities, with tremendous systems gains, synergies and scope economies to be had from integration (see Chapter 7). For example, firms such as American Express can be integrated to produce a package of services including travel, insurance, real estate, financial services, investment services.

Credit cards and insurance services are not seen traditionally as a stage in the production of tour operator or airline services. However, information technologies make it increasingly possible to produce these marginally related services along the same production line with the same computer and communications infrastructure.

Competition in the new tourism will not be dominated by full capacity utilization, cost-cutting, over-production and price-cutting. Diversification, market segmentation, diagonal integration and total innovation will increasingly become best practice for competitiveness (see Chapter 8).

4.7. NEW MANAGEMENT TECHNIQUES

There are major differences in the management practices of the old tourism and the new tourism. In the old tourism, tourists were treated as a homogeneous mass of consumers (Fig. 4.5). In the new tourism, there is a greater emphasis on catering to the individual consumer. Producers increasingly allow consumers to dictate the character and pace of production.

There is much more research, analysis and monitoring of what consumers want. There is an attempt to produce what consumers want, rather than to sell them what is produced. New management styles focus on linking product development with marketing so as to allow the marketing function – the function closest to the consumer – to influence what is being produced. It is increasingly best practice to link product development with marketing, thereby allowing consumer signals to be brought directly to the arenas of production.

Mass customization and a proliferation and splintering of brands will be the order of the day in the new tourism. Products and services will be dissected carefully and finely tuned to meet the needs of the new consumers – needs that are increasingly determined with some degree of surgical precision. This practice is altogether different from the old tourism where a limited range of mass branded services were sold to assumedly identical travellers.

In the old tourism, management practices focused on maximizing

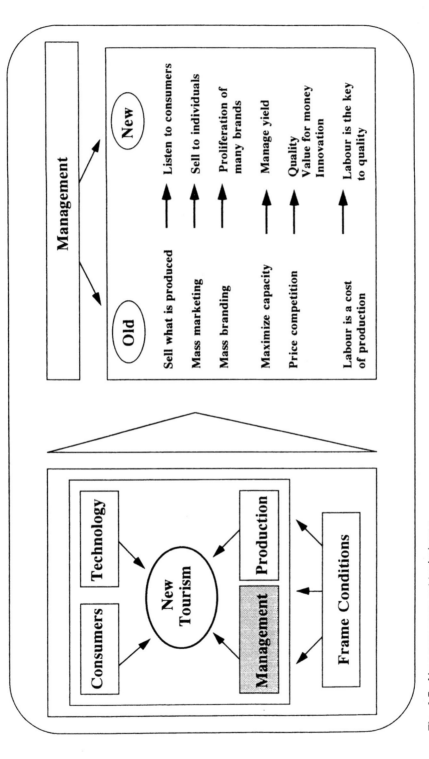

Fig. 4.5. New management techniques.

capacity – filling planes, coaches and hotels with any and every body. Today there is greater emphasis on maximizing yield, that is, maximizing the mix of customers who are serviced at any point in time.

Competitive strategies of the new tourism are no longer almost exclusively focused on cost and price-cutting strategies. Innovation, market segmentation, yield management, quality, value for money and technology play important roles in the competitive process of the new tourism.

4.8. NEW FRAME CONDITIONS

The final factor in the transformation of the tourism industry is the changing *frame conditions*, that is, the environment that supports change. The following account provides a detailed examination of the frame conditions that are facilitating the *new tourism*.

There are fundamental differences in the frame conditions that created the old tourism compared with those that are fostering the new. In most cases, the new frame conditions are a reversal of the old (Fig. 4.6).

Old tourism prospered in an environment of regulation, while deregulation of the airline industry and the financial-services sector are critical conditions facilitating the new tourism. Old tourism was facilitated by a political environment that extensively promoted tourism and an incentive structure that encouraged multinational corporations to replicate standardized hotels across the globe. Today, there is more planning and control. Disillusionment of host governments and populations with the limited economic benefits of tourism continues to put a damper on the further growth of mass tourism. Environmental limits to growth of the industry have also set in and there is increasing environmental awareness across the globe (see Chapter 3). Signs of the new environmental awareness are evident in the increasing trend toward:

- debt for nature swaps;
- the spread of environmental pressure groups;
- increased government regulation and planning of tourism; and
- consumer preference for environmentally friendly consumption.

Major initiatives and innovations in host countries (e.g. environmental audits, ecotourism, the creation and management of national parks and training, the development of the environment as a focus sector) are also driving the new tourism (see Chapter 9).

Socioeconomic conditions creating the new tourism are also different from what prevailed in the old tourism. Old tourism flourished in an environment of post-war peace, Keynesian-inspired economic growth, paid holidays and a global best practice of mass production. The new tourism

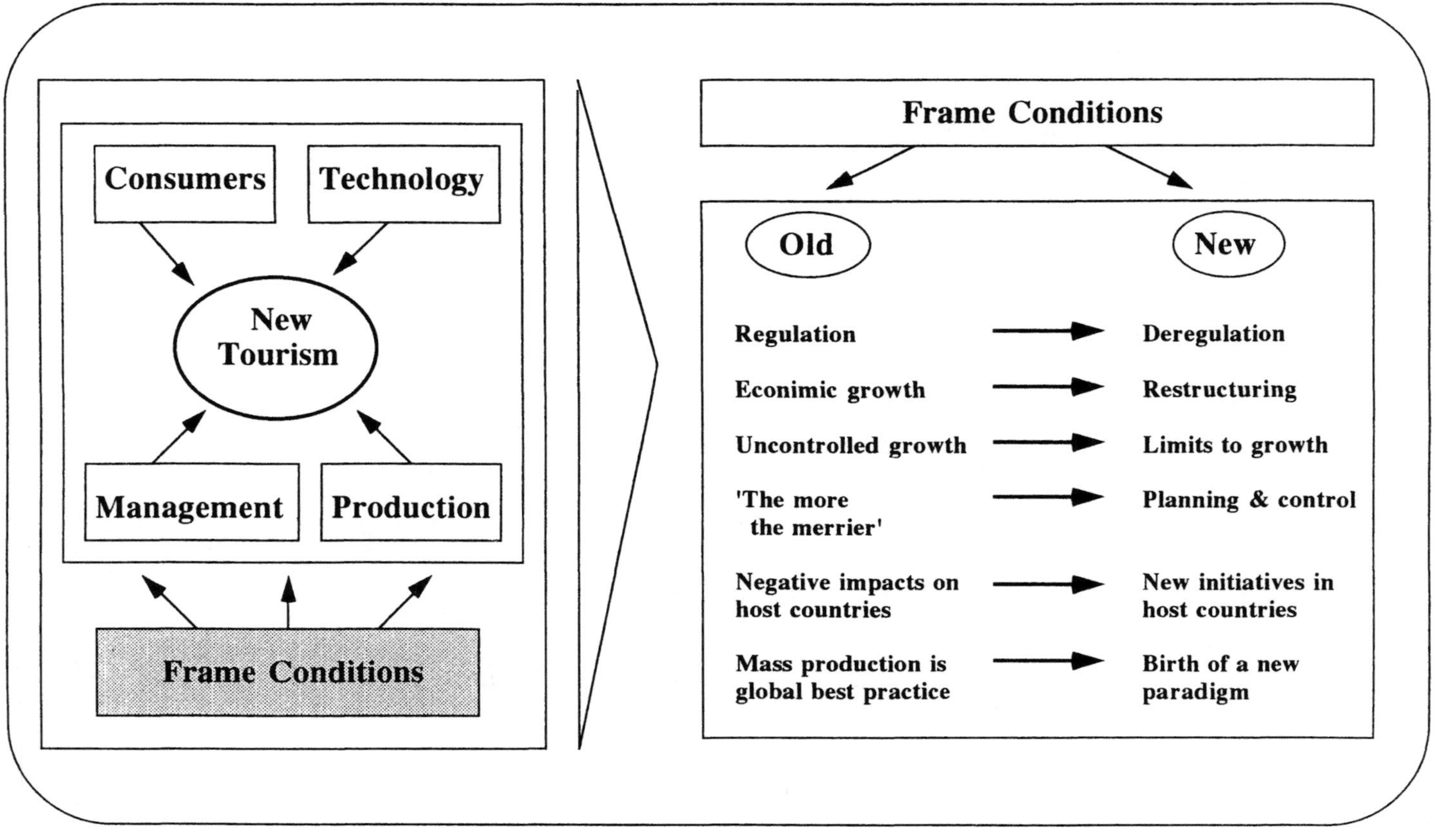
Consumers
Technology
New Tourism
Management
Production
Frame Conditions
Frame Conditions
Old
New
Regulation
Deregulation
Econimic growth
Restructuring
Uncontrolled growth
Limits to growth
'The more the merrier'
Planning & control
Negative impacts on host countries
New initiatives in host countries
Mass production is global best practice
Birth of a new paradigm

Fig. 4.6. New frame conditions.

emerges in a shrinking world, where the jet age and advances in information and communication technologies have produced a 'global village'.
New tourism is being weaned in a world where the Old Germany is now
replaced by a New Germany; where the enemy behind the curtain has
disappeared and a 'westernization rush' has taken over; where a new
economic superpower has emerged in the country of Japan, with roaring
Asian 'tigers' (e.g. Hong Kong, Singapore, Taiwan and South Korea)
following close behind. New tourism is being developed in a world where
growing debt in the developing world, environmental destruction, fires in
the Amazon, global warming, increased global competition and rapid
technological changes are challenging the global economy with economic,
political, personal and social restructuring. Finally, as we have seen in
Chapter 3, a new techno-economic paradigm is born, ushering in a new
best practice. The travel and tourism industry will be a lead sector in the
fifth and current information technology wave.

Key frame conditions – namely, airline deregulation, environmental
pressures and consumer protection – facilitating the emergence of a new
tourism. These are explained below.

4.8.1. Airline Deregulation

Airline deregulation in the USA has been heralded by some observers as
the greatest thing to happen the airline industry since the jet engine. The
year 1978 – the year the Airline Deregulation Act was passed – was indeed
a turning point. The subsequent years have been a period of 'unprecedented growth and radical change for all segments of the travel industry'
(Fleschner, 1988).

Prior to 1978, US airlines were rigidly regulated by the Civil Aeronautics Board (CAB). The CAB decided which airlines flew which routes,
and held veto power over all domestic fares. The CAB literally enforced a
differentiated oligopoly (Farris and Southern, 1981). Since airline fares had
to be approved by the CAB, each airline tried to compete on the basis of
cabin service, equipment, arrival/departure times, leg room, food, piano
bars, and so on. However, this competition was always of the 'non-price'
variety.

On 24 October 1978, President Carter signed into law the Airline
Deregulation Act, which would phase out the CAB and leave airlines free
to determine their own pricing and routes. The implementation of these
laws were to span over a period of 6 years ending 31 December 1984, with
the dismantling of the CAB and with the Department of Transportation
then carrying out the deregulation mandate.

The Airline Deregulation Act of 1978 had the avowed intention of:

encouragement, development and maintenance of an

air-transportation system relying on actual and potential competition
to provide efficiency, innovation, and low prices and to determine
the variety, quality and price of air transportation services.

(Khan, 1982)

According to Alfred Khan, the 'midwife of deregulation', airline deregulation had the following effects.

1. It permitted local service carriers to extend their operations into the
longer haul markets, taking business away from the trunk carriers to whom
they had, previously, dutifully delivered their traffic at the intermediate
points.
2. It permitted the mutual interpenetrating of markets by the trunk carriers
themselves, for example, the entry of Eastern, hitherto confined to north–
south operations, into the transcontinental routes.
3. It allowed the entry of new and very low-cost price-cutting competitors
like Air Florida, World and Capitol, on the long hauls, and Peoples
Express and New York Air, on the somewhat shorter routes [none of these
airlines are currently in business].
4. It removed from the goverment the responsibility of regulating prices or
routes, giving it to the airlines.

Deregulation had several profound implications for travel and tourism –
many of which are still being digested by the industry. Some of these
impacts are examined below.

4.8.1.1. A proliferation of information ensued

Tourism is already an information-intensive activity and one of the most
important effects of deregulation is that it produced more information than
ever before in the travel industry (see Chapter 6). According to J.W.
Marriot Jr:

> Today's travellers are not equal anymore. They are better educated,
> more well-trained about the mechanics of travelling, and less likely
> to accept standardization in the way they consume. They are not
> interested in having their needs and expectations met nearly; they
> expect that their needs and wants will be met exactly
>
> (Marriot, 1989, p. 291)

Deregulation had the further role of complicating the travel and tourism
industry, with the large volume and wide variety of rapidly changing information. Such new information included:

- new fares;
- new routes;
- new airlines;

- new prices;
- new arrival and departure times;
- new fare restrictions;
- new services;
- changes in fares, routes and airlines;
- more alternatives;
- more confusion;
- frequent-flyer programmes;
- new airlines no longer in operation; and
- a whole new vocabulary (SuperSavers, yield management, no frills, frequent-flier awards, virtual nesting, architectural bias, display bias, halo effect).

4.8.1.2. Technology lends a helping hand

Since deregulation, information technologies have become even more indispensable to the travel and tourism trade. This has led to the increased demand for IT tools with which to manipulate and distribute this increased volume and flow of information. Computerized reservation systems (CRSs) were one of the tools utilized by airlines to manage their post-deregulation affairs. The travel agency versions of these systems became a key marketing tool for airlines.

According to Nadine Godwin, managing editor of *Travel Weekly*, the proliferation of CRSs was stimulated to a large degree by the deregulation era (Personal communication, June 1991). Were it not for the existence of CRSs and other airline computer capabilities such as frequent-flyer programmes and yield management systems, Godwin argues that:

1. All changes (e.g. of prices, schedules and routes) would have moved more slowly.

2. Airlines would have been more cautious about starting or perpetuating fare wars.

3. Airline frequent-flyer programmes had they been created at all, would have been more rudimentary and probably less generous.

4. Code sharing – an arrangement between two airlines that allows one carrier to list its flights under the two-letter designation of another in order to benefit from on-line status for connections displayed in reservations systems – would be less important.

5. Without CRSs, new entrants would have had a harder time distributing through agents. CRSs provided them with virtual instant visibility.

6. Pasengers would have enjoyed fewer fare options over the past one-and-a-half decades.

7. CRSs profoundly influenced the complexity and shape of the airline industry.

4.8.1.3. Technology is not a panacea

While the importance of CRSs and the role of airline deregulation in speeding its adoption are undisputed, the relationship between CRS ownership and the success and failure of airlines is less clear. Airlines without CRSs will be at a clear disadvantage *vis-à-vis* their competitors. However, it does not necessarily follow that being an early or a major developer of a CRS guarantees success. One CRS founder, Eastern, is out of business and another TWA is in receivership. On the other hand, Delta had one of the weakest systems, DATAS II, and is still in business today (DATAS II has since merged with System One). CRSs, therefore, are not important for their own sake. They are important is shaping competitive advantages and affecting the structure of the industry (see Chapter 7).

It seems clear, therefore, that while technology is necessary for the success of carriers they are certainly not sufficient to guarantee success. Attention to the bottom line, marketing strategies, yield management, lean management, strategic alliances and acquisitions, information partnerships and diagonal integration are also key ingredients in the airlines' total game plan.

4.8.1.4. New forms of competition emerge

Airline deregulation has also altered the rules of the game within the industry. Airlines now no longer rely solely on advertising and quality of their service as their competitive weapons. Airlines can now alter their routes, services and price as they see fit. Deregulation has opened a new era of *price* competition in the airline industry. Completely new forms of competition, primarily *technology* competition, have also emerged within the deregulated travel environment.

4.8.1.5. Marketing takes on a new importance

Since prices were fixed by the CAB, there was little point in airlines spending considerable sums in aggressively marketing their products since prices could not be adjusted to recoup these costs. Deregulation changed all this. United Airlines, bouncing back from a mechanics strike in May 1989, in an attempt to regain market share, offered half-price coupons for the customers' next flight. Other airlines matched United's offer and a great coupon war ensued (*Travel Weekly*, 1988a).

In 1981, American launched a marketing blow that has since become a permanent and pervasive fixture of the travel industry. In May, American introduced AAdvantage, the first frequent-flyer programme that attempted to reward loyalty and to influence future travel choices of its customers with the promise of free travel. Since then, all major US airlines have developed frequent-flyer programmes. European airlines such as British Airways and Lufthansa are also experimenting with such programmes.

In the early 1980s, competition from lower-fare carriers such as Continental (bankrupt for the second time) and People's Express (now folded) led to a new fare-cutting spree in the industry. Trunk lines became more aggressive in pricing. In 1985, American introduced the Ultimate SuperSaver, a 25% non-refundable ticket with a 30-day advance purchase requirement. A completely non-refundable Maxsaver fare has also been introduced. In May 1992, American Airlines attempted to 'put value back into travel' by simplifying fares. This strategy did not work as other airlines did not follow suit, leading to summer sales throughout the USA market, mounting losses and a resumption of increased fare types by American Airlines to deal with the competition.

4.8.1.6. New airline affiliations formed

The onset of deregulation fostered new relationships and affiliations between and among airlines as well as with key industry players such as car rental companies, hotel chains, cruise lines, travel agencies and even banks (American Airlines and Citicorp).

Airlines saw marketing opportunities in offering frequent-flyers bonus miles to travellers who picked up rental cars at the airport. This led to affiliations between car rental companies and the major airlines. Airlines have also developed a number of code-sharing arrangements with other airlines in order to expand their own services, appearing to provide on-line connections.

Deregulation also affected the relationship between airlines and cruise lines. Cruise lines often included in their price an air ticket to the cruise departure point. When air fares became flexible, the cruise lines put pressure on carriers to lower their fares to high-volume cities such as Miami and San Juan.

Meanwhile, travel agencies became a critical link in the airlines' distribution system. The travel agency's share of airline ticket sales rose by 57% to 87% shortly after deregulation (Hitchins, 1991).

4.8.1.7. Mergers lead to mega carriers

One of the fundamental concerns that has emerged in the deregulated environment is *concentration*. According to one analyst, the great wave of deregulation in the late 1970s and early 1980s was predicated in the belief that 'replacement of the dead hand of regulation with the invisible hand of the free market would spur competition, enhance productivity and reduce prices' (*Business Week*, 1986, p. 48).

Speaking at a Conference on Trade in Services (Trade Policy Research

Center, 8 July, 1987), Daniel Kasper, Director of International Aviation for the US CAB from 1979–1983, put forward the view that:

> ... the spreading impact of deregulation is likely to transform the airline industry from its present, largely national, orientation to a truly global industry served by multinational airlines. Thus, by the year 2000 – and perhaps sooner – fewer than a score of large, multinational airlines are likely to provide most of the scheduled airline services between and within developed and major developing (non-communist) countries around the globe
>
> (Kasper, 1987)

Colin Marshall, executive vice-president of British Airways uttered not too dissimilar sentiments when he categorically stated:

> ... big airlines are getting bigger, the smaller are becoming far more alert and inventive in finding niches which they can occupy profitably, while the middle-sized airline increasingly finds with some desperation that it has nowhere to go ...
>
> (*Daily Telegraph* 24 April, 1987, p. 30)

By 1988, the airline industry had seen no less than 60 mergers of various types and sizes of carriers from different geographic regions in the USA. Among the major events were United's acquisition of Pan Am's Pacific Division in 1985, TWA's purchase of Ozark in 1986, Northwest's purchase of Republic, Texas Air's US$680 million acquisition of Eastern, and US Air's merger with Piedmont in 1987 (*Travel Weekly*, 1988a).

Instead of leading to a proliferation of carriers, deregulation boiled the industry down to a handful of mega carriers. Of 42 new entrants into the US airline industry after deregulation, only 12 were still flying by 1989 (*Travel Weekly*, 1988a). The six largest airlines in the USA carried 82.5% of the system's traffic in 1978; and in 1987, the six largest carried 77.3% of the traffic (Feldman, 1988).

4.8.1.8. The rise and fall of carriers

Business Week observed that there is mounting evidence that *a striking increase in concentration is starting to undermine deregulation's benefits* measured in terms of reduced prices and operating efficiencies, the latter having 'surpassed even the most optimistic projections' (*Business Week*, December 1986, p. 48). The oft-cited example of a failure brought about as a result of deregulation is People's Express, one of the most dynamic new airlines in decades. People's Express was brought over by Texas Air – itself no model of a financially successful airline, having placed Continental into bankruptcy twice and purchased the weak Eastern Airlines – and finally shut it down. It is lamented that 'not a single new player has challenged the leaders' and despite little evidence of monopoly profits, observers fear that top companies will soon use their power to arrest still-vigorous price competition (*Business Week*, December 1986, p.49).

4.8.1.9. Who benefits?

For the travelling public, the first few years of deregulation were like a dream come true. Lower air fares and increased flights were the order of the day.

One of the most difficult questions is determining whether consumers – supposedly the reason for deregulation – really end up benefiting from it. Some argue that deregulation has led to an explosion of travel. According to Michael Levine, one of the drafters of the Airline Deregulation Act, the benefits expected from deregulation had already been realized by 1985, with a higher level of air service overall, prices that benefit the consumers and a wide range of carrier choices (*Travel Weekly*, Deregulation Issue, 1985b). Other analysts demonstrate that there were similar rates of growth in revenue passenger miles before and after deregulation. For example, passenger miles grew 54% between 1979 and 1987 compared with the same 54% between 1969 and 1977 (*Travel Weekly*, 1988a).

With the considerable power that mega carriers have amassed, not only in the number of planes and route structures but control over computerized reservations systems, it remains to be seen what the future will hold for the new consumers.

4.8.1.10. Europe follows suit ... slowly

The winds of deregulation have blown slowly across the Atlantic. The question of concentration (and the consequent implications for monopoly profits and welfare) was one of the critical factors that Europe's airline policymakers took into consideration in their decisions to grant or veto mergers. With the British Airways (BA)/British Caledonia (BCAL) merger in the UK, considerations of concentration and monopoly power dominated the decision-making environment. This came in the wake of a government avowed policy (White Paper on Airline Competition, 1984) of promoting airline competition, where BCAL was identified as the major competitor to BA on scheduled routes. The decision by the Monopolies and Mergers Commission to allow the merger in 1987 – nearly 10 years after deregulation in the USA – was partially influenced by the need to strengthen the competitive position of BA in the face of increasing competition from US mega carriers. Interestingly, BA had a fleet size of 163 aircrafts while British Caledonia had one numbering 29, thus the merger in 1987 was chickenfeed by comparison to the fleet size of the US mega carriers.

Progress in liberalizing the European transportation market has otherwise been 'painfully slow' (Wheatcroft, 1990).

4.8.2. Coordination of Vacation Days

Another frame condition facilitating the emergence of a new tourism in keeping with the idea of a more sustainable tourism is the coordination of vacation holidays. The European Economic Community is currently attempting to coordinate the times when its populations take vacations in order to prevent the congestion of travel around the summer period. The French, for example, are in the habit of taking off for 4 weeks in August.

The flexibility to take vacations at any time in the year, as is now practised in Britain, will lead to a more even flow of tourism, which will reduce the high levels of seasonality – a common characteristic of the tourism industry. This could lead to a more balanced flow of visitors to resorts and attractions and lower the environmental effects of over-crowding, noise and other forms of pollution. For the new tourist, the coordination of vacation days, if successful, will lead to year-round, non-concentrated tourism compared to the seasonal, mass-consumption practice with its accompanying mentality.

4.8.3. Consumer Protection

There have been several attempts, particularly in Europe, to protect the interests of the travellers. The EC is in the vanguard of consumer protection in the travel and tourism industry. In 1987, starting in France, a blue flag scheme for beaches was developed for the dual purpose of rewarding environmentally sound resort areas while giving consumers an indication of the quality of the product they were consuming. More than 1000 flags were awarded in 1991 alone. There are controversies surrounding this scheme, with allegations that the scheme is 'not strict enough', 'misleading' and 'meaningless' (*Trade and Travel Gazette*, 1991a, p. 4). The main problems with the scheme arose in relation to the relative standards in North and South Europe; for while Mediterranean destinations were delighted with their awards, Germany's North Sea resorts, such as Schleswig Holstein, urged their members to scrap the flags because there was no common standard across Europe. Despite its difficulties, schemes such as these, and perhaps more stringent ones that will follow, are definitely in the consumers' interests.

The European Community package holiday directive is another attempt at consumer protection. The main tenet of the directive is that the tour operator should take more responsibility for how the holiday functions. European consumer ministers want there to be *unlimited liability* on a no-fault basis. To quote one analyst, 'The tour operator should be held legally responsible by their clients for anything that goes wrong on a holiday whether or not the negligence is that of one of their suppliers/ agents (i.e. the hotel, ground handler), if there is contributory negligence by the client or if there is no "fault" involved' (Peisley 1989a, p.61). The UK tour operators also produced a directive, already employed as a rule for business by many tour operators, the main points of which are:

1. If a client suffers from food poisoning or any accident that is the fault of the hotel contracted by the operator, he/she can sue the operator in the UK.
2. Operators can be sued for breach of contract if they do not deliver the holiday promised in brochures.
3. Operators must give advice and financial assistance of up to £5000 to clients seeking redress against a supplier that does not perform part of the package but against whom they have a claim because of an accident or illness suffered during the holiday.
4. Tour operators must reply to complaints within 14 days and resolve the matter within 8 weeks.
5. There will be automatic fines for breaches of the code – the minimum fine being £250.

These initiatives are good news for consumers. This trend will persist and will serve to improve standards and quality in destinations across the globe. The increasing protection of travel and tourism consumers is a critical frame condition in the spread of new tourism.

4.9. Summary

A new flexible tourism is on the horizon. The new tourism is driven by consumers on the demand side and by technology on the supply side. Five key forces give rise to the new tourism: (i) changes in the industry's frame conditions; (ii) new consumers, (iii) new technologies; (iv) new production practices; and (v) new management techniques.

In many cases, the conditions giving rise to the new tourism are a complete reversal of the old – from a disposable society to the greening of consumers, from sun-lust to sun-plus tourists, from security in numbers to wanting to be different, from predictable behaviour to spontaneity, from stand-alone to integrated technologies, from mass production to mass customization, from maximizing capacity to managing yield.

Some of the most important factors generating the new tourism come from radically altered frame conditions – from regulation to deregulation, from seemingly unlimited economic growth to restructuring, from uncontrolled growth to limits to growth.

It is difficult to put an exact date on when old tourism ends and when the new begins. The fact is that the old tourism may never completely disappear. The critical issues are not *when* old tourism will end, but rather, the relative rates of growth of old and new tourism. The rate of growth of the new tourism will outspace that of the old.

The challenge is to adopt the new and travel with it. As the new tourism is only just beginning to take hold, the challenge remains to lead and otherwise direct its development. There are tremendous benefits for the early starters – for those who choose to engineer, lead and otherwise shape the industry's new best practice. Which shall it be: the old tourism or the new?

DRIVING FORCES

5

NEW CONSUMERS

5.1. INTRODUCTION

New tourists are the most important driving force in the new tourism. With the old mass tourism, apparently identical tourists were forced by the economics of mass production to consume mass, standardized and rigidly packaged holidays *en masse*. Today, new consumers are dictating the pace and direction of industry changes.

Fundamental changes are characteristic of the new tourists. New tourists are more experienced travellers. They have changed values, particularly with respect to the environment and different cultures. They do things 'just for the fun of it' rather than to be seen doing it. They have changed lifestyles that are brought about by flexible work hours and more free time. Shorter and more frequent breaks, more activity and healthy living are hallmarks of a new lifestyle. New tourists are flexible and more independent – they are hybrid consumers, spontaneous and unpredictable. They want to be in charge. They want to be different from the crowd.

These changes in consumer behaviour and values provide the fundamental driving force for the new tourism. The increased travel experience, flexibility and independent nature of the new tourists are generating demand for better quality, more value for money and greater flexibility in the travel experience.

Demographic changes are also reflected in the new consumers – the population is ageing, household size is decreasing and more income is available per household.

Changing lifestyle and changing demographics of the new tourists are creating demand for more targeted and customized holidays. Families, single-parent households, empty nesters, 'gourmet' babies, couples with double income and no kids (DINKS), young urban upwardly mobile professionals (YUPPIES) and modern introverted luxury keepers

113

(MILKIES) are examples of lifestyle segments. Such segments will become prevalent in tourism and signal the advent of a much more differentiated approach to tourism marketing.

Changing values are also generating demand for a more environmentally conscious and nature-oriented holidays. Suppliers will, therefore, have to pay more attention to psychographics (the way people think, feel and behave) than they have hitherto done.

This chapter will review some of the evidence that suggests that a new tourist is emerging. It will compare and contrast the old tourists with the new. Using the Bahamas as a case in point, the differences in motivation, behaviour, demographic profile and satisfaction levels of old and new tourists will be examined. The Bahamas provides an excellent case study of old and new tourism at work. Since the Bahamas is both a historic and vast tourist destination (encompassing some 1000 miles of ocean with 700 islands and some 2500 cays), old and new tourism exist side by side in the Bahamas – old tourists primarily in Nassau, and new tourists in the Family Islands. A comparison of visitors to both destinations contrasting their attitudes, motives and interests provide fascinating evidence in support of the shift to new tourism.

5.2. THE NEW TOURISTS

The term 'new tourists' refers to consumers who are flexible, independent and experienced travellers, whose values and lifestyles are different from those of the mass tourists. New tourists are fundamentally different from the old.

New tourists are the most important driving force in the new tourism. That is the consumers and not the producers who are driving the new tourism is clearly evident in a statement by Jurgen Bartels, President, Carson Hospitality Group:

> If you believe, as I truly do, in the deep-rooted changes in
> consumers, then you also believe that at least 420 000 guest rooms,
> or approximately 15% of the US offerings have little in common
> with the consumers' desires and will eliminate themselves ...
>
> (Bartels, 1989, p. 145)

Six key attributes are characteristic of the new tourists:

- they are more experienced;
- they have changed values;
- they have changed lifestyles;
- they are products of changing population demographics;
- they are more flexible; and
- they are more independent-minded.

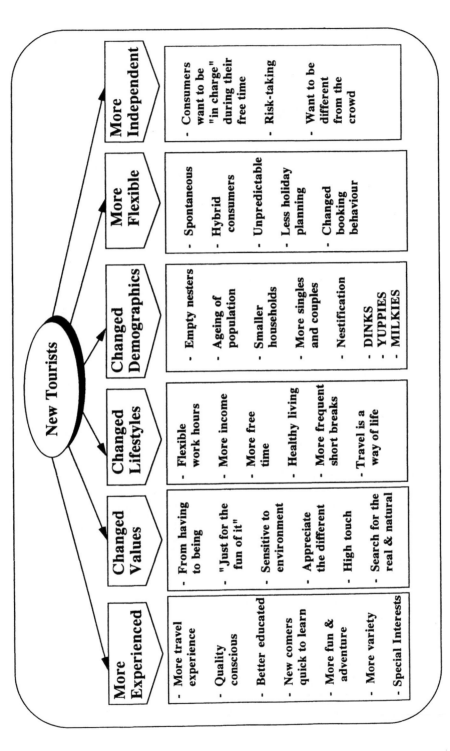

Fig. 5.1. The new consumers.

Figure 5.1 identifies these six key characteristics of the new tourists. The emergence of these six attributes of the new tourist will now be examined.

5.3. MORE EXPERIENCED TRAVELLERS

> The growing number of experienced travellers and the expanding range of their national and cultural backgrounds is challenging traditional patterns of industry service. As travel experience and sophistication continue to develop, travellers will tolerate fewer constraints on international travel and will expect greater choice and flexibility in itinerary.
>
> (*World Travel Overview*, 1988/89)

The growing experience of travellers is one of the most important factors that will change tourist demand. Tourists will be more discerning and will demand quality services as well as choice and flexibility in their travel and tourism consumption (Marriott, 1989; see also p. 101).

5.3.1. More Travel Experience

A look at existing data reveal the increasing sophistication of travellers. It was not until the 1960s that working-class Britons and Germans were able to travel freely more than the distance a train could cover in half a day. It was not until 1964 that ordinary Japanese people were allowed to travel abroad for pleasure and then they were limited to one trip a year (Elliot, 1991). It was not until 1972 that more than half of all Americans had ever flown. By 1987, two-thirds of all Americans had travelled away from home. In 1987, 72% of all Americans had flown at least once, up rom 49% in 1971 and 65% in 1981 (US Travel Data Center, 1989). By 1988, over 70% of British adults had been abroad. In 1990, nearly 70% of all Germans (those in former West Germany) over the age of 14 years took at least one holiday of 5 days or more, up from 57% in 1985 and 41.6% in 1970 (StfT, 1991a; see also Fig. 5.2). By the late 1980s, the Japanese had amassed so huge a trade surplus that the Government was actively encouraging Japanese to travel abroad in order to redress the trade imbalance. The government initiated a *Ten Million Programme* aimed at doubling the number of overseas travellers by 1991. In 1989, the programme was almost complete: an estimated 9.6 million Japanese travelled overseas (Japan Travel Bureau Inc., 1990).

Another key factor in the increased experience level of consumers, is the ageing of the population. As the saying goes: 'Experience comes with

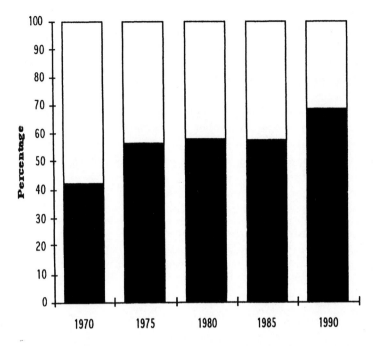

Fig. 5.2. The travel experience of the German population (14 years of age and older) 1970–1990. Nearly 70% of the population have taken at least one trip. Most travellers have taken several trips. Figures exclude Germany's new Eastern States. □ No trip ■ One or more trips.

Source: Reiseanalyse 1990 des Studienkreis für Tourismus.

age!'. According to a recent Mintel survey, one in four of the UK population is in the over-55 age group and this will increase by 3.5% to 15.3 million by 2001. Fenella McCarthy, Mintel's senior leisure analyst, has found that people who are reaching the over-55 age group have become used to taking holidays to more exotic and more expensive destinations than has been the case in the past. Moreover, 'tomorrow's over-65-year-olds will be more experienced and more demanding holiday consumers' (*Travel Trade Gazette*, 1991b, p. 25).

Indications are that the travel and leisure experience curve will continue upward. With increased travel experience comes a growing demand for quality. Value for money is increasingly a premium. The hotel industry now provides a number of up-scale services and special amenities to cater to its increasingly quality conscious clientele. Plaza club floors, concierge services, amenities baskets, bathrobes, hairdryers, bathroom television and telephones, complementary breakfast and afternoon *hors d'oevres*, fruit baskets, flowers, champagne, in-room bar and cable TV, reflect the

hospitality industry's efforts to keep pace with the increasingly sophisticated customers.

5.3.2. Quality and Value for Money

Tourists of old were more taken up with the novelty of travel and their
anticipation of lying in the sun, rather than with the quality of the services
they received. Old tourists were not discerning about the places they
visited, once two basic conditions held: (i) it was affordable; and (ii) it was
'somewhere' in the sun.

The more experienced new tourists are more quality conscious and
more value-conscious. This is a natural consequence of the following:

1. Many already travel extensively for business.
2. They are more experienced holiday-makers.
3. There are growing concerns over airline safety and airport congestion.
[A survey of Americans found that 34% of respondents were 'seriously
concerned' about airline safety and 54% believed congestion to be a 'very
serious' problem (US Travel Data Center, 1989)].
4. There are more destinations to chose from – including China and the
Eastern Block countries and, in particular, the Confederation of Independent States (CIS) formally the Union of Soviet Socialist Republics, and
in the Caribbean, Cuba.
5. Time is of the essence. Many Americans today are 'much more time-
sensitive than price-sensitive' (US Travel Data Center, 1989).
6. Travellers have more information from a variety of media.
7. They are more educated.
8. Many travellers make return visits and, as a result, are more know-
ledgeable about destinations they visit.
9. They expect to do far more than just lie in the sun.

For all of these reasons, holiday-makers are becoming more discerning. It
is not surprising therefore that consumers are willing to pay more for extra
service. A recent international study of the travelling public conducted in
the US, West Germany, United Kingdom and Japan found that, on
average, travellers are cost-conscious, but are willing to spend more to get
special attention. A total of 73% of German travellers, 69% of UK
travellers and 62% of USA travellers agreed with the statement: 'It's worth
paying extra to get the special attention I want when I travel.' (American
Express Global Travel Survey, 1990). These travellers place a premium on
value. The same survey found that the Japanese were less inclined to agree
with paying more for special attention – only 34% of the surveyed
Japanese people agreed with the above statement. With relatively less travel
experience than their Western counterparts, the Japanese tourists may still

tend to be relatively more cost-conscious than quality-conscious.

The growing emphasis on quality and value is a reflection of a broader trend in the USA, Europe and other parts of the world. This trend is related to the declining importance of consumption as a way to express status and individuality. Products and services are wanted and appreciated for their intrinsic qualities and less for their show appeal. Coates summarized this trend as follows:

> We are a mass-educated, prosperous, middle-class society – a society no longer needing to show that we are making it, by sharply creased trousers and shiny shoes or the latest haircut. We are as a society, a population that has made it. There is less need to demonstrate that we have made it with the superficially impressive. The movement is from mere quantity and throw-away goods to high quality and durability. We have moved away from the showy to the stable.
>
> (Coates, 1986, pp.77–78)

It is argued, moreover, that

> tinsel and junk are not limited to the things that we wear, drive in, or surround ourselves with. There is a long-time trend to pseudo-places, pseudo-events, pseudo-festivals and pseudo-authenticity. But the nation is moving in a different direction: it wants the real stuff, the authentic, not the simulated that so often marks the appeal in current advertising for travel and recreation
>
> (Coates, 1986, p.78)

5.3.3. More Personal Attention

Another trend among the new consumers is the increased desire for communication and personal attention on holiday. The personalized holiday is in. 'Europeans are asking for much more communication; they want to be right in the centre of it' (Personal communication, Rolf Freitag, Executive Director, European Travel Data Center, Munich, May 1991). He continues, 'we need waiters with the human touch. And we need guides who act like modern tellers of fairy tales'.

The growing demand for the personal touch ('high touch') is one of the ten trends identified as transforming American society (Naisbitt, 1984). 'High-tech, high touch' refers to the need for human service and the personal touch in our high-tech homes, our high-tech workplace and our high-tech existence, in order to create balance in our daily lives. 'The more we create technology, the more we create compensatory human balance in order to handle it. The more technology, the more people want to gather together' (Naisbitt, 1984, p.64).

Naisbitt argues, for example, that:

> high tech, high touch is responsible for the success of all those
> upscale hotels we are seeing all over the place, because in the
> tremendously high-tech society, the high touch is personal service.
> *High touch translates into service, service, service*
> (Naisbitt, 1984, p.64, emphasis added).

This partially explains why in Europe there is a big boom in the upper-class
hotel business (Personal communication, Rolf Freitag, European Travel
Data Center, May 1991) and why in the Caribbean, boutique hotels,
employing as many as three or four persons for every guest room continue
to 'command top dollars' (Caribbean Futures, 1991a).

The implications of high tech, high touch for travel and tourism can be
tremendous. It could mean, for example, that the humanizing balance of
high touch cannot be met by technology-intensive vacations. It could mean
that there will be the need for more natural, more authentic and 'down-to-
earth' vacations. There can also be the need for more flexibility, better
quality and more service-oriented hotels. Moreover, vacations need to be
more than just escape mechanisms: there will be a need to *be*, rather than
to merely *exist*, and demand will be generated for true re-creation possibilities.

The need for more quality vacations and a more human touch in the
provision of services is a critical driving force in the new tourism. Travel
and leisure suppliers will increasingly have to adopt competitive strategies
that reflect this growing emphasis on quality service and high touch.
Specifically, hotels that now view labour merely as a *costs of production*
will have to re-think their approaches to human resources. In the future,
workers in hotels and other service establishments will have to be viewed as
human beings who hold the key to the delivery of high-quality, high-touch,
personalized services (see Chapter 8).

5.3.4. More Choice

The need for greater variety and choice is another key feature of the new
tourism. In their daily lives, consumers are not content with one TV
station, one newspaper or even one kind of cornflakes. In their leisure lives,
they are no different. Consumers are no longer prepared to go to the same
destinations as their friends and relatives, far less to use the same mode of
transport, stay in the same kinds of hotels, lie on the same beaches, take the
same kind of photographs and buy the same kinds of souvenirs! The
demand for variety, choice and individuality in travel and holiday-making
is definitely on the increase.

The transformation from limited choice ('either/or') to more choice
and variety is another of the ten trends that Naisbitt identified as changing
American society. According to Naisbitt, personal choices for Americans

remained rather narrow and limited from the post-war period through much of the 1960s. There were a few decisions to make; it was an 'either/ or' world: 'either we got married or we did not, either we worked nine to five (or other regular full-time hours) or we didn't work, period' (Naisbitt, 1984, p. 231). Naisbitt argues that this limited either/or option is giving way to a more flexible multiple-optioned society, and that the 1980s was a decade of unprecedented diversity. 'In a relatively short time, the unified mass society has fractionalized into many diverse groups of people with a wide array of differing tastes and values.' (Naisbitt, 1984, p. 232)

5.3.5. More Fun, More Adventure

Another important trend emerging among new consumers is the need to be more active on a holiday. More and more tourists look for things to do on holiday. For many, the vacation is an extension of their normal lives as they take the time to leisurely do the things that they normally do at home but wish they had more time for – playing tennis, golf, scuba diving, dining out, having sex, reading and much more. A Hyatt Travel Futures Project found that:

> Not only do many executives become more sexually-free (55%), but many agree that their sex life improves dramatically when they're on vacation (60%).

> (Hyatt, 1991, p. 15)

Table 5.1 Purpose of Japanese overseas trips

Travel motive	Percentage (%)
To enjoy nature and scenery	72
To see famous tourist attractions	56
To taste food and try delicacies of the country	48
To enjoy shopping	43
To rest and relax	38
To experience a different culture	36
To visit museums	31
To stay in famous hotels	22
To ski and do other winter sports	10
To enjoy water sports (e.g. windsurfing, scuba diving)	10
To go to concerts and other musical events	10
To enjoy land sports (e.g. tennis, golf)	10
To experience the latest world fashions and trends	8
To gamble at casinos and see shows	8

Source: Japan Travel Bureau Inc., 1990.

Many tourists also see a vacation as an opportunity to try their hand at new activities, be it sports, sightseeing or experiencing cultural events. All of these factors contribute to an increasing trend toward more activity on holidays.

In this regard, the Japanese travel and leisure patterns are very interesting because they reveal an activity intensive orientation. Of the 14 reasons the Japanese identified for travelling abroad, only one hinted at rest and relaxation, which ranked at number five. When travelling, the Japanese also look forward to seeing famous attractions, tasting food and delicacies of other countries, shopping, experiencing a different culture, visiting museums, skiing or other winter sports, enjoying water sports (e.g. scuba diving, windsurfing), going to concerts and other musical events, enjoying land sports (e.g. golf, tennis), experiencing the latest world fashions and trends, gambling at casinos and seeing shows (see Table 5.1). With such a hectic travel menu, no wonder there is no time for lying idle in the sun.

5.4. CHANGED VALUES

> In the industrial society, values of being have been crowded out by values of having: possession, property, wealth, consumption, egoism are ranked above community, tolerance, contentment, modesty, meaning, honesty.... The environment is treated and exploited as if resources were inexhaustible and infinite.
>
> (Krippendorf, 1986)

The arrival of the jet age, paid holidays and growing affluence have made travel and leisure an integral part of daily life in developed and developing societies. Emerging changes in the values of industrial societies – from the obsession with having to the fulfilment of being, the pursuit of happiness and healthy lifestyles, the growing consciousness of nature and things natural – will affect the ways in which travel and leisure are bought and consumed. It will compel suppliers to re-think the manner in which they package and deliver the holiday experience. Increasingly, leisure will not be an escape from daily life, but will be an extension of daily life and its packaging will need to reflect these changing values.

5.4.1. Search for the Real and Authentic

Values of conservation, health and nature are spilling over to travel and tourism in a major way. One of the most important trends identified by the European Travel Data Center is that European travellers want nature to be more prominent in their vacations. The trend is vividly demonstrated in the travel motives of German travellers. Nearly 60% of all Germans said that the experience of nature was the most important reason for their main holiday trip in 1990, up from 40% a mere 2 years before (Table 5.2).

The importance of nature and things natural in a holiday cannot be overemphasized. One suspects that just as *sun* was the single common reason for the spread of mass tourism in the 1960s, 1970s and 1980s, nature will become the common denominator in future travel and leisure pursuits. It will mean that destinations and services will increasingly have to improve the quality and quantity of the nature component of their travel and tourism product – not just the quality of the sun, sand and sea but beauty and intact nature of the environment, the aesthetics of buildings, natural parks and protected areas, nature trails and a whole lot more.

However, it must be noted that while authenticity is desired, the tourist, for the most part, is unwilling to pay for it through inconvenience (Opaschowski, 1991). The challenge for individual suppliers is to develop it: sun versus total experience.

5.4.2. Newcomers Are Quick to Learn

The more experienced travellers, because of their own background as former full- or partial-mass tourists, are likely to be in the forefront of the

Table 5.2 Travel motives of German holiday-makers, 1990[a]

Travel motives	Former West Germany	New Eastern States
Experience of nature	57.0	65.5
Good food	55.1	43.7
Time for family, partners, friends	54.7	66.8
Excitement, distractions	47.8	55.4
Sun, escape from bad weather	47.7	26.7
New impressions, different experiences	46.1	64.9
Relax, do nothing	45.1	25.7
Be spoilt, enjoy	43.7	35.0
Drive around, be on the move	33.5	50.5
Broaden the mind, culture, education	31.0	38.7
Improve beauty, get sun tan	30.2	21.1
Improve health, prevent illness	27.0	35.5
Meet relatives and friends	25.0	42.9
Sports and fitness	18.0	9.8
Flirt	11.0	12.4

Source: Studienkreis für Tourismus, 1991b.

[a]N.B.: Since multiple replies possible, columns do not add to 100.

new tourism. At the same time, one wonders if tourists from the formerly closed Eastern European countries or even the Japanese, will first have to be mass tourists before they convert to the new. It is clear that travel novelty, affordability and the search for the sun will continue to be important factors in vacation choice. There are, however, fundamental differences in these new markets, which will limit the spread of the old mass tourism. Some of the key reasons that cheap sun holidays will not be the sole driving force for travel among the new Eastern European consumers and among the Japanese can be identified as follows:

1. The search for the sun is not a very important motive in the newly opened Eastern European countries. Rather, visiting friends and relatives takes priority. (From Table 5.2, it can be seen that visiting friends and relatives has a ranking of 43%, while the desire to escape the bad weather is less than half as important, at 26.7%.)

2. The Japanese are not sun-worshippers as their Western counterparts tended to be. Rather, sport, shopping and sightseeing are more dominant travel and leisure motives.

3. For the Japanese, the most important reason for travel is to enjoy nature and scenery – 72% listed this as a key part of the reason they travel overseas (Japan Travel Bureau Inc., 1990). Refer to Table 5.1.

4. Package tours in Japan are being personalized and custom-made to meet client needs. This means that the Japanese are skipping to the new flexible tourism concept. According to the 1990 report of the Japan Travel Bureau: 'Skeleton type tours that offer 'free time' are flourishing'.

5. There is evidence that Eastern European consumers are also quick learners. The experience of nature is an even stronger travel motive among former East Germans (65.5%) than among their more experienced Western neighbours (old Germany) (57%). Refer to Table 5.2.

5.4.3. The Sun Sets on Tourism

The fashion for the sun has gone full circle. Through recent history and up to the 1920s, any deliberate cultivation of a sun tan was avoided like the plague. It savoured too much identification with the lower classes and the coloured subject peoples. However, by the 1920s, the sun was an element of high fashion. A suntan became a status symbol – a visible indication of those who could afford to escape to the southern sun during cold northern winters. An *Observer* article reported in 1987 that:

> Pale skin, for so many centuries regarded as a status symbol came to
> be associated with the sorry souls who could not afford a
> Mediterranean holiday. For the last 50 years tans have been linked

with health, wealth, sex and hedonism, and in the West,
sun-worshipping has reached obsessive proportions.

(*Observer*, 14 June, 1987)

Today, however, there are growing signs that this fashion for the sun is beginning to fade.

In the UK, for example, a fiercely competitive tour operator and travel market has served to depress the prices of travel to such an extent that a sun vacation is now common. The sun is no longer as viable a status symbol because with the increase means and declining cost of travel it is easily available to 'commoners' as well. In an attempt to reclaim their individuality and to be different from the crowd, there may be a growing tendency on the part of the upper classes to refrain from deliberately cultivating a suntan.

This sociopsychological desire on the part of many travellers is given an additional boost by medical reports that increasingly link cancer and ageing of the skin with exposure to the sun. In the UK, the anti-sun syndrome has been given medical support by a Royal College of Physicians Report (1987). This argued that sun 'can cause accelerated wrinkling, scaling, pigmentation irregularities and skin cancer'. The report warned that white people should avoid lengthy persistent exposure to the sun.

Another source, the *New Scientist* (1987), warned about the dangers of destruction of the ozone layer of the stratosphere. Ozone absorbs and shields us from the ultraviolet light. It is estimated that some 3% of the ozone stratosphere has disappeared since 1970. It means, among other things, that the phytoplankton in polar seas that produces a lot of the oxygen we breathe will start dying. With the depletion of the ozone layer and the growing threat to our oxygen supply, life in the sun is fast becoming very risky. For tourism, and for traditional sun destinations, the danger is that 'anyone who does not have a very black skin will run a high risk of contracting cancer' (*New Scientist*, May 1987, p. 17).

These developments could have untold consequences for certain destinations in the Asia/Pacific area, the Caribbean, Latin America, and the Mediterranean, which have traditionally held comparative 'S advantages' (sun, sand and sea). At the same time it could also open new opportunities for marketing culture (e.g. reggae, calypso, soca, steel band, carnival), cuisine (e.g. Indian, African, Chinese), nature (e.g. rain forests, swamplands, waterfalls, lagoons, flora, fauna), archaeological sites, and a whole lot more.

It is fast becoming clear, therefore that, while still necessary, the sun is no longer sufficient to build a viable and sustainable tourism industry. Destinations have to begin to offer 'sun-plus' holidays such as sun plus spas, plus nature, plus fishing.

5.4.4. Search for the Different

The search for the different is on: the new traveller wants to experience the unexperienced, see the unexpected, gain impressions of new cultures and new horizons.

Among the new tourists of the developed world, the West Germans express the most confidence (82%) in their ability to explore new cities on their own (USA 70%, UK 70%, Japanese 25%) and Germans are least likely to rely on maps and guide books for travel. West Germans also express the highest interest in experiencing different cultures; 84% of Germans say they prefer destinations where the language and culture differ from their own (American Express Global Travel Survey, 1990).

A detailed examination of German travel motives, shows that nearly half (46.1%) of tourists in the former West Germany travel in order to gain new impressions and have different experiences. Very interestingly, two-thirds of the citizens in Germany's new Eastern states travel for this reason (see Table 5.2). It can also be observed that the search for new impressions among German travellers is on the increase (Fig. 5.3). In contrast, Americans are least interested in exploring places with different languages and cultures – only 44% indicated that they travel to seek out new experiences (American Express Global Travel Survey, 1990).

5.4.5. From Escape to Fulfilment

tourism in the 1960s, 1970s and 1980s was mainly used as an instrument of escape from work, routine, stress and urban ugliness at home. According to one observer:

> People leave because they no longer feel at ease where they are,
> where they work and where they live. They feel an urgent need to rid
> themselves temporarily of the burdens imposed by the everyday
> work, home and leisure scene, in order to be in a fit state to pick up
> the burden again. Their work is more and more mechanized,
> bureaucratized, and determined without regard to their wishes. *Deep
> inside*, they feel the monotony of the ordinary, the cold rationality of
> factories, offices, apartment buildings and the highway infrastructure,
> the impoverishment of human contact, the repression of feelings, the
> degradation of nature, and the loss of nature ... *one leaves in order
> to survive.*
>
>   (Krippendorf, 1986, 1987b, emphasis added)

Due to these developments in the major tourist generating countries – countries that are responsible for 80% of all international visits – it is argued that 'the deficiency that one feels in daily life cannot

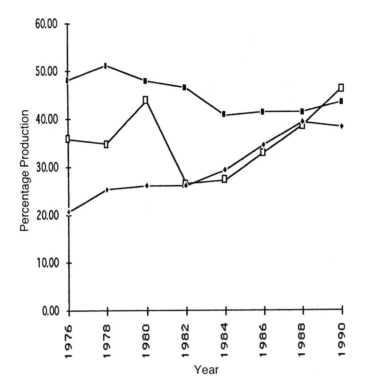

Fig. 5.3. German travel characteristics. A growing number of travellers seek new impressions. The period 1988–1990 shows the first signs of decline in package-tour usage. —■— First-time destinations. —□— New impressions. —◆— Package tour.

Source: Studienkreis für Tourismus, 1990, and FVW, Germany.

be compensated for by a few brief moments of freedom, of creative leisure, of happiness and of self-determination during one's free time and vacation'. The solution, Krippendorf argues, lies in *humanizing the habitat*. If one succeeds in humanizing the habit, there will be profound implications for tourism:

> Such a humanizing of daily life, working conditions, surroundings and leisure activities will also change the nature of tourism. Tourism, in so far as it will exist in its present forms, will no longer be an escape from daily routine into an artificial world of fleeting change, but may well become again a true discovery, a place of experiences and learning, a means of human enrichment, a stimulus for a better reality and a better society.
>
> (Krippendorf, 1986, 1987b)

There is tremendous growth in the number of persons for whom the polarization of everyday life and leisure has already been considerably reduced. Krippendorf estimates that this group of people who seek a unity of everyday life will be the largest leisure segment by the year 2000 (see Section 5.5).

Humanizing the habitat is a necessary condition for the future sustainability of the travel and tourism industry. After all, how can visitors be expected to have integrity towards foreign environments if, at home, they do not care about their own? How can tourists be expected to appreciate and understand a different culture if, at home, they do not speak with their neighbours? How can one possibly hope to eliminate child prostitution in places like Bali, when, in the developed countries, economic, social, psychological and other conditions create a roaring demand for this illicit trade?

5.5. CHANGED LIFESTYLES

There are a number of changes in people's lifestyles that have a profound impact on travel. One observer argues that society has moved through three key phases between the industrial era and the present – first, from one in which people lived to work to one in which they worked to live; and today, to one in which there is a new unity of everyday life. In the third phase, the polarity of work and leisure is reduced (Krippendorf, 1986, 1987b). Travel and leisure have become an integral part of daily life. These changes in the role of travel and leisure in society as well as changes in the workplace and the practice of more healthy living, all have implications for the travel and tourism industry.

5.5.1. People Who Live to Work

In the industrial era, tourists were drawn from a population that '*lived to work*'. Their vacation motivations were simple:

- to recover;
- to recuperate;
- to rest;
- to be served;
- to switch off;
- to have no duties;
- to have no worries; and
- to have no problems.

By the year 2000, it is estimated that only 10% of individuals in tourist-generating countries will belong to this group.

5.5.2. People Who Work to Live

Today, tourists are increasingly drawn from post-industrial societies where people '*work to live*' – leisure is seen as a counterpart to everyday life. The vacation motives of this group are:

- to experience something different;
- to explore;
- to have a change;
- to have fun;
- to increase enjoyment;
- to play;
- to be active;
- to be together with others;
- to relax without stress;
- to do as one pleases; and
- to enjoy proximity to nature and intact environment.

By the year 2000, it is estimated that 45–60% of the population in the developed world will belong to this category.

5.5.3. People Who Live

There is a third lifestyle group, described as those seeking to experience '*the new unity of everyday life*'. Persons belonging to this group want to reduce the polarity between work and leisure and are looking for fulfilment throughout all sectors of life – during working time through humanized working conditions, and at home through habitable cities – and in a more colourful everyday life. The vacation motivations of this group include:

- to broaden their horizon;
- to learn something new;
- to encourage introspection and communication with other people;
- to discover the simpler things in life and nature;
- to foster creativity, open-mindedness; and
- to experiment, take personal risks.

By the year 2000, this group's share of the population of developed countries will rise to about 30–40% compared with 20–30% in 1986. This group has the biggest potential for growth in the 21st Century (Krippendorf, 1986, 1987b).

5.5.4. The Japanese go on Holiday to Work

It is interesting to examine where on the 'work/live' spectrum the Japanese are currently located. It is clear that they are only just beginning to live – to really enjoy life to the fullest. One suspects, however, that there are still large proportions of the Japanese population who live to work, although the proportion of those working to live is increasing.

The development of resort offices, a phenomenon unique to Japan, is indeed a reflection of how intimately intertwined leisure and work have become in this 'high-tech' society.

Resort offices are hotels that provide sophisticated communications so that employees can work at their jobs for periods of 2–3 weeks in pleasant locations with a variety of sports and leisure activities. These offices are peculiar to Japan where people take fewer holidays, the idea being that 'people will work harder if they go on holiday to work' (Gann, 1991).

5.5.5. Travel as a Way of Life

That travel is increasingly becoming a way of life is clearly evident in survey findings. Substantial proportions of travellers (Japanese 67%, West Germans 49%, USA 42% and UK 38% feel that they have to travel in order to enjoy life fully (American Global Travel Survey, 1990). This survey found that in each country, at least three-quarters of all travellers (West Germany 84%, USA 84%, UK 74%, Japan 74% agree with the statement, 'I'm always thinking of new places I'd like to visit'. The holiday is no longer an appendix to working life but has become a focal point of life (Opaschowski, 1991). As leisure becomes an important component of everyday life, the relaxation part of the holiday is no longer sufficient to make the holiday worthwhile. Holidays increasingly have to offer the individual a unique experience (Opaschowski, 1991).

5.5.6. Healthy Living

Good health and a healthy lifestyle are increasingly in vogue. The focus on healthy living manifests itself both in the intake of food and in the care of the physique. This can be observed by the proliferation of health spas, fitness centres, and health-food shops the world over. A 1980s California slogan sums up the phenomenon this way: 'It does not matter if you win or lose, it is how you look'.

This health fad relates to the broader yearning for things natural. It is a reflection of society's needs to balance itself – the need to balance pollution, rapid urbanization, societal perversions and environmental destruction, with a more humane and conscious approach to human *being*. Many observers currently believe that this focus on health is just a fad, like bell-bottom jeans. However, cast in the light of the current environmental renaissance, interest in health looks as permanent an institution as democracy.

The practice of healthy living reflects itself in holiday and tourism lifestyles and is responsible for the proliferation of health spas, saunas, fitness centres, 'fat farms', gyms, massage therapy, shiatsu, and other such additions to many hotels and resorts. At the Ramada Grand in Budapest, for example complementary dental examination is included in the price of the room.

At the same time, however, regular exercise is the norm for only about one-third of the American population. Only 23% of Americans are within range of what health authorities consider to be acceptable weight and most Americans report experiencing stress on a regular basis (US Travel Data Center, 1989). This is an indication of the gap in the market that remains to be filled.

5.5.7. Changing Workplace and Workstyle

The changing nature of work and the workplace are largely due to changes brought about by the increasing use of microelectronics. Two trends can be identified with respect to the impact on travel: (i) a reduction in the amount of people-to-people contact in the workplace; and (ii) the movement towards flexible schedules and computer commuting.

New information technologies, by virtue of their ability to transmit, store, process and manipulate information, as well as to distribute it to areas where it is needed, can minimize the need for personal contact. Witness the number of managers and CEOs (chief executive officers) who have 'personal' computers. If a manager needs to know, for example, the production or efficiency levels within the plant on a particular day, there is no need to contact the floor supervisor, to conduct lengthy discussions over the matter or to even discuss the issue over lunch. The information is readily available to the manager at his/her computer fingertips.

The increasing alienation of person from person in the workplace, as well as the increasing de-personalization and computerization of the environment, will reinforce people's desire for people contact. This is likely to be the trend no matter how user-friendly the man/machine interface becomes. One can observe, for example, the increasing use of music and plants in offices, in an attempt to humanize and naturalize the workplace.

This desire for personal contact is having an effect in travel: since travel is an *experience* – a service that has to be 'lived' to be enjoyed – it is likely to be positively affected by these developments because travel provides opportunities for more interpersonal dealings and contact with nature. No technology can substitute for the travel experience. Technological toys such as electronic games can, at most, be a complement to travel, not a substitute.

Flexible schedules, flexible free time and computer commuting will also have important implications for the types of travel that are possible in the future. For example, flexible work schedules allow more frequent, shorter vacations – a trend that is rapidly taking off in the USA and Europe.

5.5.8. More Free Time

The potential for more free time, especially in America and Japan, is enormous. Japan, for example, is slowly making its way to the 5-day working week. However, while the number of paid holidays received in Japan is around 15 days, the actual number of days taken for holidays has been 8, with the average moving to 7 (Japan Travel Bureau Inc., 1990). Moreover, only 8% of Japanese travelled outside Japan in 1989. This compares with 96% for the Swiss, 51% for the UK, and 32% for Germany (Japan Travel Bureau Inc., 1990). In the USA, 2 weeks of annual paid vacation is still largely the norm. In Europe, by contrast, paid vacation leave is phenomenal. This is particularly true in Germany, where 6 weeks of annual paid vacation plus holiday pay (a 13th salary) are common.

In 1961, 97% of all manual workers in Britain had only 2 weeks' paid holiday leave and by 1981, at least 86% had basic holiday entitlements of 4 weeks or more. In 1982, 38% of all West German workers had 6 weeks' holiday. The trend globally is towards more holiday entitlements. The USA and Japan, perhaps more slowly, are likely to move toward the European standard and the rest of Europe will increasingly catch up with the standard in Germany.

5.5.9. More Incomes

At the end of the day, consumers may want flexible holidays and information technologies could enable suppliers to produce more flexible services. However, these two powerful supply-and-demand imperatives may be insufficient to foster a new tourism. For, in the market place, it is not sufficient to desire or want something. Desires and wants must be effectively backed by purchasing power. Purchasing power in turn will depend, among other things, upon the levels of income that consumers have at their disposal. Hence, in the future, the adoption of a new tourism will depend upon future levels of income.

It is difficult to predict how much spending power (real or plastic) consumers will have in the future. Three factors should be taken into account when considering it:

1. The regions in the world that generate wealth could be different from those of the past decades.

2. The industries that generate income could also be very different.

3. There is likely to be some disturbance in income levels as the world economy adjusts to these new realities.

The fact that new centres of wealth are emerging is evident both in Asia, primarily in Japan, and in Europe. The rate of growth of the Japanese economy in the last decade and a half has been phenomenal, with the Japanese emerging as the highest leisure spenders. Per capita, Japanese travelling abroad spent the most money (US$2219) compared with travellers from other nations. The Italians spent the second most per capita after the Japanese (US$1691), followed by Germans, French, Swiss, and then by the USA, UK and Canada (Japan Travel Bureau Inc., 1990).

In Europe, it is estimated that the total economic advantage of the single European market over the next 5 years could be in the vicinity of US$325 billion.

Wealth is also being generated by non-traditional industries – particularly those in the information and service areas, for example computing and telecommunications. These are increasingly replacing the smoke-stack industries such as coal, iron and steel, as is wealth generated by new regions such as Silicon Valley, the Third Italy, South East Asia and Latin America. This new wealth will have important spill-over effects to the travel and leisure sector.

Table 5.3 Dominant demographic groups in the USA

Group	Born	Dominant decade*	Age in 1992
Baby boomlet	1977–1988	The 1990s	4–15
Baby bust	1965–1976	The 1980s	16–27
Late baby boom	1955–1964	The 1970s	28–37
Early baby boom	1946–1954	The 1960s	38–46
Second World War babies	1935–1945	The 1950s	47–57
Depression babies	1924–1934	The 1940s	58–67
First World War babies	1923 and earlier	The 1930s	69+

Source: US Travel Data Center, 1989.

*The decade in which an influence in consumerism was felt.

5.6. CHANGING DEMOGRAPHICS

Population demographics in the tourism-generating countries are changing. In particular, there are some broad demographic parallels between Europe and the USA, which significantly influence the type of tourist and the tourism demand the industry can anticipate. Although there may be differences among the occidental developed countries in social and cultural attitudes, the shared post-war history has created significant parallels in lifestyles.

The key trend is that the population is ageing. The late baby-boom generation – those born between 1955 and 1964 and currently between 28 and 37 years old – have moved to childbearing (Table 5.3). This same generation, which gave us the YUPPIES (the thing everybody immediately recognized but no one admitted to being), will probably generate the latest specimen created by marketeering acronymania the 'MILKIES' (modern introverted luxury keepers). In other words, the trend towards more mature consumption attitudes is supported by both value changes and a change in the age structure of the population. As the population ages, the demand for quality will be more important than ever before.

5.6.1. The Ageing of the Population

There are two key factors in the ageing of the population in Western countries. The first is that modern medicine allows people to live longer. This leads to a growth in the age group of persons 75 years and older. Between 1986 and 2000, the 75+ age group will grow by 45.6%, the

Table 5.4 Development of demographic groups in the USA

Age group (years)	Percentage change between 1986 and 2000 (%)	Share in 1986 (%)	Share in 2000 (%)
Under 13	+7.3	20.0	19.4
14–17	+4.0	6.1	5.7
18–24	−19.9	11.5	9.2
25–34	−15.3	17.8	13.6
35–44	+32.0	13.7	16.3
45–54	+62.6	9.5	13.9
55–64	+6.9	9.2	8.9
65–74	+2.0	7.3	6.6
75+	+45.6	4.9	6.4

Source: US Travel Data Center, 1989.

second fastest growing population segment next to persons aged 45–54 years (Table 5.4).

The second factor contributing to the ageing of the population is a reduced birth rate. The baby bust of the mid-1960s and mid-1970s was caused by the delayed childbearing of the early baby boomers (those born between 1946 and 1954). The coming of age of this generation brought with it a decline in the relative importance of family values and a greater work-and-career orientation of women. The latter change in attitude is likely to stay and produce an ongoing practice of delayed childbearing, although family values are gaining in importance again.

The baby bust phenomenon is clearly visible in Table 5.4. The age groups 18–24 and 25–34 years are expected to experience significant negative growth (−20% and −15% respectively) to become a smaller share of the population by the year 2000.

This all leads to an ageing of the population, quite in contrast to the youthful Mexican immigrant, for example, whose average age in 1986 was 15 years – half the age of his American counterpart in the same year (Coates, 1986, pp. 75–76).

5.6.2. The Importance of Older Age Groups

The coming of age of the 'baby boomers' and the 'baby bust' will lead to different age distributions in tourist-generating countries. From Table 5.4, it can be seen that the population share of the 35–44 and the 45–54 year age groups in the US will increase dramatically (by 32% and 63%, respectively) and will increase their share of the total population to 16% and 14% respectively by the year 2000.

The entrance of 'late baby boomers' (those who are between 28 and 37 years in 1992) into later life cycles not only leads to an increase in the relative importance of these age groups but also to change in behaviour. Unlike their predecessors, the baby boomers do their buying with extremely discerning and critical eyes. Baby boomers (those currently in their late 20s through their early 40s) take wealth for granted and have higher expectations of the products and services they buy. Moreover, they are more likely to buy products and services for their intrinsic qualities rather than for status reasons. They expect to be listened to by the key companies competing for their discretionary spending. This more careful approach to spending on real goods and services rather than on flashy status symbols is creating hybrid consumers (see Section 5.7.1.).

The 'baby boom' generation is also likely to be wealthier than its predecessors. In Europe, significant wealth is being inherited for the first time since the Second World War, leading to a higher net worth of middle-age households, particularly the 'early baby boomers' who will be in their

Table 5.5 Dominant demographic groups in the USA and implications for travel and tourism*

Group	Age in 2000 (years)	Share in 2000* (%)	Early influences	Implications for travel and tourism to 2000
Baby boomlet	12–23	15	– Travelled extensively as kids	– Preference for visiting friends and relatives, camping, weekend trips, foreign travel – Limited travel resources in 2000
Baby bust	24–35	15	– Travel with and without parents – International travel is common – Deregulation/discounted fares – Hotel market segments prevalent	– Constraints of discretionary income and time – Preference for independent travel and sport breaks – Active in business travel – Increase in travel by air – Growth in family and children-only holidays – Market to decline; a highly competitive market
Late baby boom	36–45	20	– Growth in hotel/motel industry – Usable interstate highway system – Disney World opens 1971 – Beginning of cruise industry – Deregulation (1978) – Travel as a way of life	– Age group will increase by 32% – Very active business travel market – A good market for incentive travel – Growing interest in specialist travel – Impetus to family vacation travel – Multiple and varied vacation trips year-round

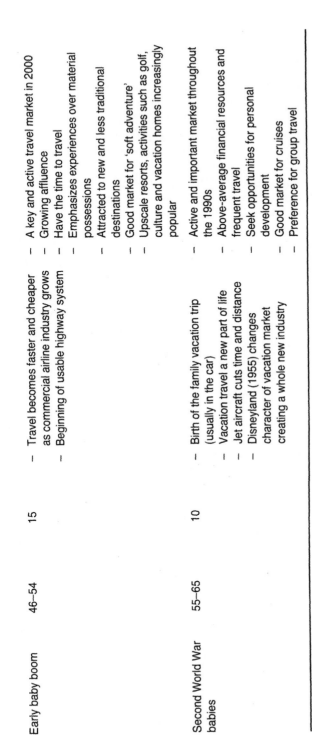

Early baby boom	46–54	15	– Travel becomes faster and cheaper as commercial airline industry grows – Beginning of usable highway system	– A key and active travel market in 2000 – Growing affluence – Have the time to travel – Emphasizes experiences over material possessions – Attracted to new and less traditional destinations – Good market for 'soft adventure' – Upscale resorts, activities such as golf, culture and vacation homes increasingly popular
Second World War babies	55–65	10	– Birth of the family vacation trip (usually in the car) – Vacation travel a new part of life – Jet aircraft cuts time and distance – Disneyland (1955) changes character of vacation market creating a whole new industry	– Active and important market throughout the 1990s – Above-average financial resources and frequent travel – Seek opportunities for personal development – Good market for cruises – Preference for group travel

Source: US Travel Data Center, 1989.

*Author's estimate of percentage share of population.

late 40s and early 50s by the year 2000. Those 'early baby boomers' who will already have raised their children, will have considerable free time and discretionary spending capacity. They will be a very challenging group for travel and leisure activities. They will be experienced tourists for whom well-established destinations have few mysteries. This generation will not be easy to please, nor will they be satisfied with the old tourism products. A tremendous deal of imagination will have to be used in order to please this group of wealthy, discretionary, spenders.

Another new group emerging is the 'late baby boomers'. They will be, perhaps, financially less well-off than their slightly older counterparts, as they will be in the process of raising children. Though this might not deter some of them from acquiring wealth in this new era of economic prosperity. Yet they will have collected extensive travel experience during their 'yuppie' years. They will have to be comparatively careful with respect to their discretionary spending, but they will have holiday expectations formed during the booming 1980s. This group will be looking for holidays that provide value for money, which cater to their new lifestyle and represent an interesting option for families with young children.

The generation of 'late baby boomers' will be similarly discerning and may be even more so than the 'early baby boomers'. To satisfy this group, careful market research will be required. These consumers are hybrid. They combine high expectations with budget-conscious spending behaviour to a greater extent than any other group has done before. Therefore they will only want to spend money on those services and elements of a holiday they really want. Thus offering them different price categories alone will not do. The challenge in attracting this group will be to package holidays creatively and flexibly, such that the customers are capable of discerning in detail on which components they want to spend their money.

Younger groups are more open to travel than ever. Although the young group of the 18–34-year-olds will constitute a declining share of the population, they will remain an important part of the market. They would have gathered significant travel experience at an early age and will take the yearly and more frequent holidays even more for granted than did their elders.

5.6.3. Implications of Demographic Trends

The ageing of the population in the developed countries goes hand in hand with the change in values described above. In general, consumers, will be more mature in planning their holidays, and they will not be so easily satisfied as were their former counterparts. They will listen more carefully to their inner selves and to their pocketbooks to determine what they really need and can afford. To the most important groups, travel will no longer offer the excitement of the new. Instead, they will be looking for the different and for the enjoyable. They will want to be surer and surer that their holidays will be both pleasurable and worthwhile.

There are generational groups emerging that are of tremendous importance to the travel and tourism industry. Yet these groups will be much more difficult to please than groups have been in the past. They will have more clearly defined expectations with respect to their holidays. It will be up to the travel and tourism industry to cater to these expectations.

A summary of the dominant demographic groups in the USA in the post-war era together with an indication of their age and relative importance by the year 2000 is provided in Table 5.5. This table also provides a summary of the early travel influences of each group and the implications for the travel and tourism industry to the year 2000.

5.7. MORE FLEXIBLE CONSUMERS

There are two main characteristics of flexible consumers:

1. They are hybrid in nature, consuming along non-predictable lines, often purchasing in different price categories for the same trip.
2. They are more spontaneous, with a lower level of pre-planning before the trip.

5.7.1. Hybrid Consumers

The emergence of hybrid consumers is a very important trend in the travel and leisure industry. By purchasing services in different price categories, it is more difficult to target the needs of this consumer. Some consumers may not travel first class, but will stay in first-class accommodation. Other consumers may take a charter flight, stay in very modest accommodation and partake in some of the most expensive sporting activities at the destination (e.g. scuba diving and bone fishing). The hybrid nature of consumers is a growing international trend that is not specific to the travel and leisure segment of the industry.

It is not uncommon for hybrid consumers to shop at discount houses (e.g. Wal Mart in the USA or Aldi in Germany) and at the same time buy certain items at the delicatessan counter. As a result of the increased hybrid nature of customers, travel and leisure providers will have to be much more sophisticated in satisfying their consumers. Traditional stereotypical categories of rich, poor or middle-income people are no longer sufficient criteria to segment vacation markets. Travel and tourism suppliers will have to pay far more attention to the psychographics of their consumers. In other words, they will have to cater to the way their consumers think, feel and behave.

5.7.2. Spontaneous and Unplanned

Another characteristic of the new consumer is their casual nature, their drive to do what comes on the spur of the moment and have not been planned out. Consumers are changing the way in which they plan and choose their holidays. There are shorter and shorter lead times before booking and paying for a holiday. The spontaneous and unplanned nature of consumers is partially responsible for the growing numbers of shorter and more frequent breaks.

5.8. MORE INDEPENDENT CONSUMERS

There are two key characteristics of the independent consumer: (i) the need to be in control and to take more risks; and (ii) the need to confirm individuality.

5.8.1. The Need to be in Control

A very important element in the widespread marketability and success of conventional package holidays is the level of risk reduction that the tour operator is able to offer customers. With almost all elements of the vacation pre-paid and pre-arranged, with the creditability of the tour operator well-known; and with insurance coverage and a familiar face at the destination, the vacation was made near-perfectly safe.

The existence of risks in the travel business cannot be overstressed. There are both environmental and man-made risks with which to contend. The dangers and risks involved in travel are evident. Cases of terrorists threats in 1985–1986, for example, and also the consequent withdrawal of American travel from the European markets clearly demonstrate the importance of safety and security. Today, with this evident risk, there is an increasing tendency for consumers to become risk-takers when on vacation. The 1991 Hyatt Futures Project found that: 'many executives become wilder and less inhibited: they describe themselves as "more devilish" (55%) and "more a risk-taker" (53%)' (Hyatt, 1991, p. 15).

The attitude toward risk-taking on the part of tourists is also demonstrated in the case of British travel to Greece where, in spite of a record hot summer (45°C) and thousands of Greeks dying from dehydration and heart attacks, this did not stop British travellers. Many tourists were plainly 'not worried' (BBC News Report, 26–30 July, 1987). According to Coates, 'quite clearly, education and prosperity are moving us to an experimental society, which we see in the explosive growth of such sports as hang-gliding and sailing' (Coates, 1986).

This risk-taking attitude seems to be associated with risks taken at a *personal* level where the individual is in control of situations. As Coates observes, a great irony is that America is simultaneously moving toward both less risk-taking and more risk-taking: 'We want safer everything, safer food, (safer sex), safer travel, safer airlines. On the other hand, we are risk-embracing in our personal attitudes where we have a sense of being in control' (Coates, 1986, p. 81).

This change in consumer perceptions and requirements can have tremendous spill-over effects for travel. One sure thing is that rigidly designed package tours where clients are divorced from the real world and protected in their fantasy island, may no longer be sufficient to satisfy future consumers.

5.8.2. Need to Confirm Individuality

The increasing assertion of individuality on the part of consumers is largely responsible for the growing trend toward more flexible and custom-made travel and leisure options and the decline of the traditional package tour.

A key factor in the spread of old tourism was the existence of a large number of people who, at the time, were willing to sacrifice their individuality for cheap holidays in the Mediterranean sun. Many tourists in the past somehow did not mind following the crowd, or being like everyone else. This trend is changing. People want *to be*, to be different from the crowd, unique, yet nameless and unencumbered.

5.9. OLD AND NEW TOURISM AT WORK

It is very interesting to examine the differences in the motivation of old and new tourists. One of the best ways of doing this is by examining the revealed preferences of visitors. In other words, one needs to answer the questions: Why did visitors go to a particular destination? Did they go to lie in the sun or to be active? Did they go on a package or did they travel independently? How satisfied were they with the destination? Will they return? How pleased were they with the attitudes of the locals and the levels of service at the destination? More importantly, do these values differ among visitors to old and new tourism destinations?

Some of the answers to these questions can be found in the Bahamas. The Bahamas provides a brilliant example of old and new tourism at work for the following reasons:

1. The Bahamas is a unique destination where old and new tourism exist side by side.

2. The Bahamas is an archipelago of approximately 700 islands and nearly 2500 small islets and cays. As a consequence of the vast territory, the level of development of each island is different. The Family Islands provide a good example of *new tourism.*

3. The island of New Providence containing Nassau, is one of the first English speaking islands to develop tourism in a major way. *Old tourism* is prevalent there.

4. The Bahamas has one of the most sophisticated systems of tracking visitor motivation and expenditure through its regular biannual exit survey where a substantial amount of visitors are polled annually. The results of the 1991 survey provides a good basis for comparing the behaviour of old and new tourists.

The Commonwealth of the Bahamas is a young nation democracy that gained independence from the British Crown in 1973. The islands of New Providence (containing the capital, Nassau) and Grand Bahama (containing Freeport) are distinguished from the other islands, collectively known as the Family Islands (now referred to by their traditional name, Out Islands). With a coast length of some 3540 km and numerous islands and cays scattered over 100 000 miles of ocean, the Bahamas islands have enormous potential for the development of tourism. It has a gross domestic product (GDP) currently at US$2.2 billion. With a population estimated at 250 000, the per capita income of this commonwealth of islands ranks it among the top 25 countries in the world – just four points below the UK.

The Bahamas has the largest tourism industry in the English-speaking Caribbean. In 1991 the Bahamas welcomed a total of 3.6 million visitors who collectively spent US$1.3 billion in the local economy. The country takes one-quarter of the Caribbean's cruise arrivals and 13% of stop-over visitors and 15% of visitor expenditure (Bahamas Ministry of Tourism, 1992).

5.9.1. Old Tourism – New Providence (Nassau)

In the Bahamas, New Providence provides a good example of old tourism. Nassau has several high-rise, large-scale Americanized and air-conditionized beach resorts (some of its hotels with an accommodation capacity of over 1000 rooms). The emphasis is on riviera-style casino gambling, shopping, cabaret shows, glitz, fancy restaurants and organized ground tours. Visitors, 90% of whom are American, come on package tours, usually on short breaks of 3–4 nights, usually to bask in the sun.

5.9.2. New Tourism – The Family Islands

The Family Islands contrast sharply with Nassau. These islands have a small-scale indigenous type of tourism. It is very 'laid-back' with a number of family-operated establishments. In 1990, the Family Islands had just over 2000 guest rooms. The majority of hotels/guest houses in the Family Islands (nearly 80% of all establishments) are extra small (having less than 25 rooms). It is a completely different world in the Family Islands when compared with Nassau. When in the Family Islands, it is unbelievable to think that one is still in the Bahamas – so close, and yet so far from the old tourism. In fact, many visitors who have 'discovered' the Family Islands cannot understand how tourists could still go to Nassau for a vacation. The Family Islands are unique and distinct – each one different from the other in its own right. The following paragraphs describe the attributes of some of these islands and provide a flavour of the Family Islands destination:

Andros is one of the largest Family Islands. It is fringed with what is possibly the third longest barrier reef in the world, running parallel along the length of the island. It provides some of the most exciting scuba diving and snorkelling found anywhere. The natural bites of Andros make for excellent bone fishing.

In *the Abacos*, the tourism industry is based largely on boating. Many of the towns on the cays remain very traditional and there is excellent opportunity for good sightseeing by boat. Green Turtle Cay, for example, retains much of its loyalist tradition. The protected waters to the west of the Abacos have been hailed as some of the finest yacht cruising areas in the world.

Due to their proximity (only 47 miles from Miami), *the Biminis* is one of the most popular ports of entry for the Bahamas and has become well-known for big game fishing.

Eleuthera, meaning freedom, is a 100-mile long boomerang-shaped island that has become famous for its pink sand beaches, coves, dramatic cliffs, sweet pineapple, reef diving and snorkelling just off the beach.

Harbour Island is the home of friendly people and pink-sanded beaches. It is the location of Dunmore Town, one of the oldest settlements in the Bahamas and its original capital. Century-old and well-preserved churches, trees and houses, and with roads sufficient to take bicycle traffic, are set amidst tropical ambience and scenery. Harbour Island has managed to cultivate an island elegance and sophistication without the obvious signs of 'development'.

San Salvador (known as Guanahani to the native Indians) is the spot where Christopher Columbus supposedly first set foot in the New World. The island is roughly 12 miles long and 6 miles wide. After Andros, San Salvador is probably the most water-logged island in the Bahamas with lakes of many sizes dotting the landscape. The diving is exceptional in San

Salvador. A quaint town, Cockburn, with a population of 500 inhabitants, rich biodiversity and home of the Bahamas Field Station, is dedicated to the study of the natural environment.

5.10. OLD AND NEW TOURISTS COMPARED

Having described and differentiated New Providence as an old destination and the Family Islands as a new destination, it is important to compare the visitor profiles to each of these destinations. The results are most interesting. The behaviour patterns of visitors to the Family Islands reflect very much the attitude of the new tourists and the behaviour patterns of those in New Providence reflect those of old tourists.

It is useful first to review some of the generic characteristics of old and new tourists (Fig. 5.4). The motivations of the old tourists are different from those of the new. For the old tourists, travel was a novelty. Travel was almost an end in itself. It mattered not where the old tourists went, once they got to a warm destination and could show others that they had been. Quality of services was relatively unimportant. Vacation was an escape from work and from home. For the new tourists, vacation is an extension of life. Vacations are taken for the fun of it. New tourists go on vacation not just to see and do the things that they are used to at home, but also to experience something different. For the new tourists, quality and value for money are a premium.

Old tourists tended to be homogeneous and predictable. If they went first class, they went first class all the way. They felt secure by travelling in numbers. They took vacations where everything was pre-paid and pre-arranged. New tourists, on the other hand, are not like their predecessors, rather, they are spontaneous and unpredictable. They are hybrid in nature and no longer consume along linear predictable lines. The hybrid consumer may want to purchase different tourism services in different price categories for the same trip (e.g. travel tourist class and stay in a five-star hotel). These new, hybrid consumers want to be different from the crowd. They want to affirm their individuality and they want to be in control. They want to make decisions for themselves.

The attitudes of the new tourists are also different from those of the old. Among the old tourists there was an acceptance of waste and destruction and a lack of concern for the environment and cultures of the host countries they visited. They also imposed their values on the receiving destinations with a 'West is best' attitude. In contrast, today there is a 'see and enjoy, but do not destroy' attitude among new tourists. Today, there is greater appreciation for the different as travellers are better educated and informed about destinations they visit.

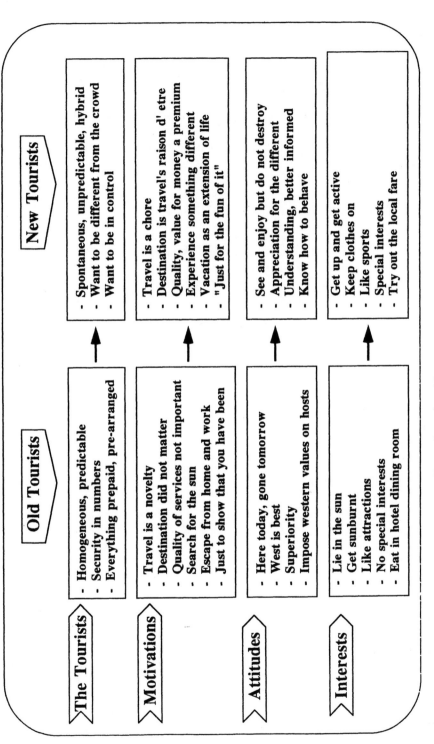

Old Tourists

New Tourists

The Tourists

Old Tourists:
- Homogeneous, predictable
- Security in numbers
- Everything prepaid, pre-arranged

New Tourists:
- Spontaneous, unpredictable, hybrid
- Want to be different from the crowd
- Want to be in control

Motivations

Old Tourists:
- Travel is a novelty
- Destination did not matter
- Quality of services not important
- Search for the sun
- Escape from home and work
- Just to show that you have been

New Tourists:
- Travel is a chore
- Destination is travel's raison d' etre
- Quality, value for money a premium
- Experience something different
- Vacation as an extension of life
- "Just for the fun of it"

Attitudes

Old Tourists:
- Here today, gone tomorrow
- West is best
- Superiority
- Impose western values on hosts

New Tourists:
- See and enjoy but do not destroy
- Appreciation for the different
- Understanding, better informed
- Know how to behave

Interests

Old Tourists:
- Lie in the sun
- Get sunburnt
- Like attractions
- No special interests
- Eat in hotel dining room

New Tourists:
- Get up and get active
- Keep clothes on
- Like sports
- Special interests
- Try out the local fare

Fig. 5.4. How new tourists are fundamentally different from the old.

Old tourists were content to lie in the sun and get sunburnt. They were interested in visiting attractions, had no special interests and ate in the hotel dining room. For the new tourists, the sun is still a necessary factor in the vacation pursuit; while necessary, however, it is no longer sufficient to satisfy the new tourists. They have special interests that stem a wide variety of activities. The new tourists are adventurous (soft, medium and hard). They are also concerned about the effects of overexposure to the sun and its link with cancer.

5.11. NEW TOURISTS IN THE FAMILY ISLANDS

Visitors to the Family Islands can certainly be considered new tourists. The behaviour of tourists in the Family Islands provides some very important insights into the motivation and characteristics of the new tourist. The Bahamas data produces strong evidence to support the following:

- new tourists are sports-oriented;
- new tourists are independent;
- new tourists are more educated;
- new tourists are wealthier;
- new tourists are more satisfied; and
- new tourists are loyal.

These attributes of the new tourists of the Family Islands are examined below.

5.11.1. New Tourists are Sports-oriented

Nearly one-third (30%) of all visitors to the Family Islands claimed that they were attracted to the islands by sporting activities. Sports have become as important an attraction as the beaches in the Family Islands. Visitors to the Family Islands are definitely not the old tourists who come to lie in the sun. In the old tourism destination of New Providence, by contrast, visitors claim to be attracted mainly by the climate and beaches (Fig. 5.5).

5.11.2. New Tourists are Independent

In the Family Islands, most of the visitors arrive as independent travellers seeking to express their individuality – a mere 19% of all visitors come on a package. In New Providence, by contrast, 79% of all visitors use a package (Fig. 5.6). Based on the figures there is a definite pattern in the type of tourists who frequent these alternative destinations.

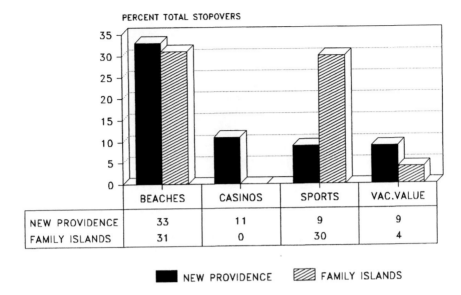

PERCENT TOTAL STOPOVERS

	BEACHES	CASINOS	SPORTS	VAC.VALUE
NEW PROVIDENCE	33	11	9	9
FAMILY ISLANDS	31	0	30	4

■ NEW PROVIDENCE   ▨ FAMILY ISLANDS

Fig. 5.5 Main reason for visit: Family Islands verus New Providence.

Source: Bahamas Ministry of Tourism 1991 Stopover Exit Survey.

5.11.3. New Tourists Stay Longer

The Family Islands have consistently achieved higher lengths of visitors' stay that in New Providence. Visitors to the Family Islands stay between 1 and 2 nights more than do visitors to New Providence (Fig. 5.7).

5.11.4. New Tourists are More Educated

The Family Islands attract more educated clients. About 66% of all visitors to the Family Islands are college or university graduates, compared with about 50% for Grand Bahama and New Providence. Nearly 30% of all stopover visitors to the Family Islands are postgraduates, while for the rest of the Bahamas, it is 17%. About 20% of all visitors to New Providence and Grand Bahama have high-school education, while for the Family Islands only 11% of its visitors graduated only to high-school level (Fig. 5.8).

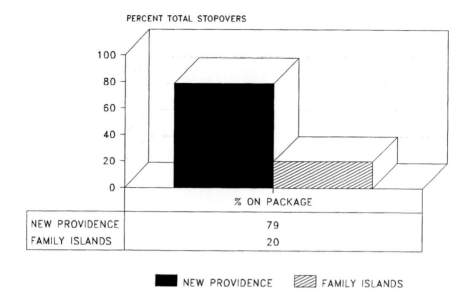

PERCENT TOTAL STOPOVERS

	% ON PACKAGE
NEW PROVIDENCE	79
FAMILY ISLANDS	20

■ NEW PROVIDENCE   ▨ FAMILY ISLANDS

Fig. 5.6. Stopover visitors' use of packages. Family Islands versus New Providence.

Source: Bahamas Ministry of Tourism 1991 Stopover Exit Survey.

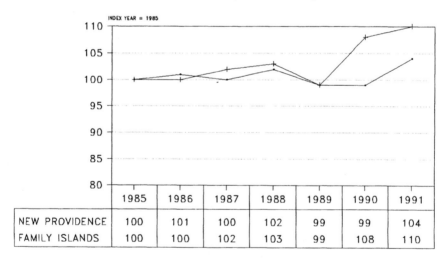

INDEX YEAR = 1985

	1985	1986	1987	1988	1989	1990	1991
NEW PROVIDENCE	100	101	100	102	99	99	104
FAMILY ISLANDS	100	100	102	103	99	108	110

•— NEW PROVIDENCE   +— FAMILY ISLANDS

Fig. 5.7. Visitors to Family Islands stay longer.

Source: Bahamas Ministry of Tourism 1991 Visitor Statistics.

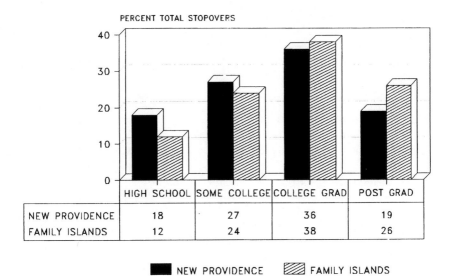

PERCENT TOTAL STOPOVERS

	HIGH SCHOOL	SOME COLLEGE	COLLEGE GRAD	POST GRAD
NEW PROVIDENCE	18	27	36	19
FAMILY ISLANDS	12	24	38	26

■ NEW PROVIDENCE ▨ FAMILY ISLANDS

Fig. 5.8. Education level of stopover visitors.

Source: Bahamas Ministry of Tourism 1991 Stopover Exit Survey.

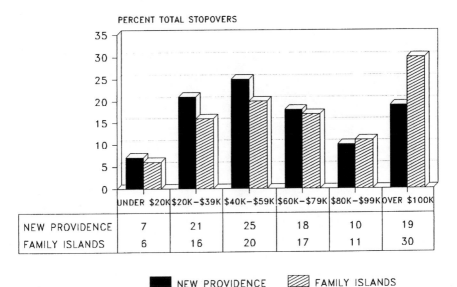

PERCENT TOTAL STOPOVERS

	UNDER $20K	$20K–$39K	$40K–$59K	$60K–$79K	$80K–$99K	OVER $100K
NEW PROVIDENCE	7	21	25	18	10	19
FAMILY ISLANDS	6	16	20	17	11	30

■ NEW PROVIDENCE ▨ FAMILY ISLANDS

Fig. 5.9. Household income of stopover visitors.

Source: Bahamas Ministry of Tourism 1991 Stopover Exit Survey.

5.11.5. New Tourists are Wealthier

A larger number of persons (30% of total stopovers) with a household income of US$100000 or more visited the Family Islands than they did New Providence (19%; Fig. 5.9).

5.11.6. New Tourists are More Satisfied

The Family Islands have a higher level of guest satisfaction compared with New Providence. Visitors to the Family Islands find these islands superior to New Providence in key areas of value for money, attitude (Fig. 5.10), sports, service at restaurants, hotel value and hotel service.

5.11.7. New Tourists are Loyal

Loyalty in the tourist involves the return to the destination of former vacationing. Of all visitors to the Family Islands, 70% are very likely to return. By contrast, only 47% of visitors are very likely to return to New Providence and Grand Bahama (Fig. 5.11). In addition, over 60% of visitors to the Family Islands are repeat visitors, compared with 40% for the rest of the Bahamas. In addition, visitors to the Family Islands are most

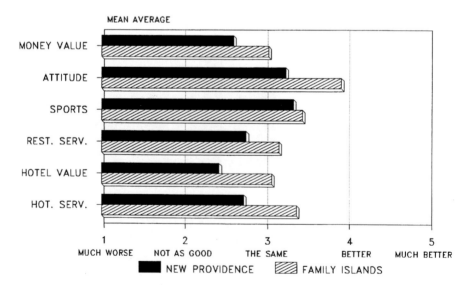

Fig. 5.10. Attitude of the visitors.

Source: Bahamas Ministry of Tourism 1991 Stopover Exit Survey.

likely to be on their third visit, compared with those of the rest of the Bahamas who are likely to be on their first or second visit.

5.12. OLD AND NEW TOURISM IN THE BAHAMAS

The comparison between the old and new tourism in the Bahamas is very informative. It demonstrates the superiority of developing new tourism products for new tourists. It is not surprising that visitors to the Family Islands encounter far better attitudes of the local population than in New Providence (see Fig. 5.10). It is also not surprising that visitors to the Family Islands are better educated, stay longer, are more satisfied and are very likely to return than are visitors to Nassau. This is the stuff that the new tourists are made of. The Bahamas provides a very important example for destinations still contemplating a future between the old and new tourism.

5.13. SUMMARY

Changes in consumer behaviour and values are fundamentally shaping the new tourism. The increased travel experience of the new tourists and a new

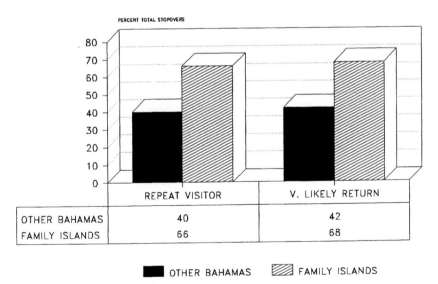

	REPEAT VISITOR	V. LIKELY RETURN
OTHER BAHAMAS	40	42
FAMILY ISLANDS	66	68

■ OTHER BAHAMAS   ▨ FAMILY ISLANDS

Fig. 5.11. Satisfaction of stopover visitors.

Source: Bahamas Ministry of Tourism 1991 Stopover Exit Survey.

'leisure consciousness' are generating demand for better quality, value for money and more flexibility in travel and leisure services. Changing life-styles and new demographics are also supporting this trend towards more targeted and customized holidays catering to specific demographic and psychographic characteristics. Couples, families, single-parent households, empty nesters, couples with double income and no kids (DINKS), young urban upwardly mobile professionals (YUPPIES) and modern introverted luxury keepers (MILKIES) are examples of stereotypical segment classifi-cations. Their emergence in the tourism literature signals the advent of a much more differentiated approach to tourism marketing.

Yet by themselves such segment classifications are unlikely to help tourism managers in providing their customers with what they want. The attitude of the consumer toward the tourism product is extremely complex and personal. Any successful marketing strategy of the future will therefore have to come to terms with the *individual* and not just with market segments. The coming of age of the individual tourist goes hand in hand with a change in values, higher expectations and the decline of the holiday myth. Therefore the entire experience of the holiday will have to be managed to satisfy the modern consumer, and a holistic approach to resorts, destinations and travel services is called for within the travel and tourism industry.

Tourism suppliers are responding to the demands of the new tourists by producing more flexible, segmented and nature-oriented holidays as is evident in the Family Islands of the Bahamas. These new holiday products are made possible through flexible production, mass customization and, most importantly, new technologies.

6

TECHNOLOGY CHANGES TOURISM

6.1. INTRODUCTION

On the demand side, consumer preferences for flexible travel and leisure services provide a strong impetus for the new tourism. On the supply side, technology plays an important complementary role in engineering the new tourism. The applications of technology to the travel and tourism industry allow producers to supply new and flexible services that are cost-competitive with mass, standardized and rigidly packaged options. Technology gives suppliers the flexibility to move with the market and the capacity to diagonally integrate with other suppliers to provide new combinations of services and improve cost effectiveness.

A whole system of information technologies is being rapidly diffused throughout the tourism industry. And no player will escape its impact. Technologies will have the impact of increasing efficiency of production, increasing the quality of services delivered to consumers and generating completely new services – even flexible holidays.

This chapter examines the information-intensive nature of the tourism industry and identifies the technologies being adopted by industry players. The rate of diffusion of information technologies and their impact on the travel and tourism industry are also examined. Finally, the impact of technology in changing the whole new best practice of the tourism industry is considered.

6.2. AN INFORMATION-INTENSIVE INDUSTRY

The information-intensity of travel and tourism is a key driving force in the rapid diffusion of technology in the industry. No player in the tourism industry will be untouched by information technology.

Tourism is a very information-intensive activity. In few other areas of activity are the generation, gathering, processing, application and communication of information as important for day-to-day operations as they are for the travel and tourism industry. Unlike consumer durables and industrial goods, the intangible tourism service cannot be physically displayed or inspected at the point of sale. Travel and tourism services are normally bought well before the time of its use and away from the place of consumption. In the marketplace, tourism is almost completely dependent upon representations and descriptions (information) in printed and audio-visual forms. Thus communications and information transmission tools are indispensable to the tourist trade.

Tourism involves the movement, accommodation, entertainment and general servicing of clients from one geographial loation, in another. These activities must be combined differently, integrated and 'packaged' to suit complex and rapidly changing consumer requirements. Services such as hotel bed nights, car rental, package tours and airline seats are not physically transferred to travel agents who in turn stock them until sold to customers. Rather, it is information about availability, price, quality, location and convenience of these services that is communicated and processed. Similarly, actual moneys (payments or revenues) are not transferred from travel agents to the travel suppliers or commissions from the travel suppliers to travel agents. Rather, in the balancing of accounts, it is mainly information in the form of debits and credits that are transferred through plastic cards and other electronic payment systems.

Nevertheless, information is the cement that holds together the different producers within the travel industry – namely airlines, tour operators, travel agencies, hotels, car rental, cruise lines and other suppliers. The links between and among tourism producers are provided not by goods, but by the flow of information. These information flows are represented, not only by data but also by flows of services and payments (Fig. 6.1).

From Figure 6.1, it can be seen that the relationship between airlines and travel agents is governed by flows of information. Information on flights, service availability, tariffs, schedule and route changes, confirmations and commissions flows from airlines to travel agencies. A return stream of information in the form of bookings and revenues flows from travel agents to airlines. In the case of consumers (not shown in the figure), information in the form of airline tickets, hotel and car rental bookings, travel counselling, and holiday guarantees are received from suppliers. A matching information transaction (payment) flows from consumers to suppliers.

Information in the form of regulation, incentives, advertising, promotion and taxation, plays an important role in linking the tourism suppliers with each other. Airline deregulation in the USA has led to the prolifer-

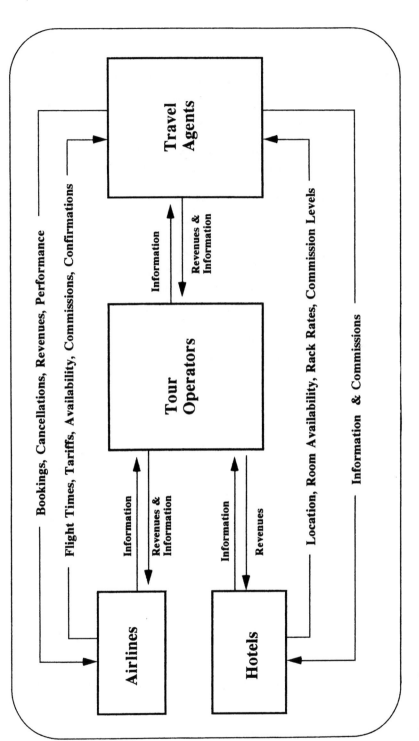

Fig. 6.1. Information – the vital cement of the tourist trade.

ation of endless new information that has become an important driving force in the development of CRSs.

Tourism's critical dependence on information flows can be gleaned from a brief look at the information needs of a company such as American Express – a company that supplies significant services in the travel and tourism industry. In 1986, Peter Alan, head of telecommunications at American Express Travel Related Services, estimated that the company needed rapid, unimpeded global communications to carry out the following transactions:

1. The authorization of more than half a million American Express card transactions every day all over the world, with an average response time of less than 5 s, with the number of transaction authorizations increasing at a rate of 25–35% annually.
2. To verify and speedily replace lost or stolen Travellers' Cheques sold by over 100 000 banks around the world.
3. To access reservation systems and travel-related service databases from offices in over 125 countries (Personal communication, Peter Alan, September 1986, Brighton, UK).

Such is the nature of today's tourism industry that its information-intensity makes it an ideal candidate for the rapid and widespread diffusion of information technologies.

6.3. A SYSTEM OF INFORMATION TECHNOLOGY

In the travel and tourism industry, it is not merely a computer *or* telephone *or* video brochure *or* teleconferencing that is being diffused, but a *whole system* of interrelated computer and communication technologies.

The components of the system of information technologies (SIT) can be seen in Figure 6.2. SIT can be seen to consist of computerized reservation systems, teleconferencing, videotext, videos, video brochures, computers, management information systems, airline electronic information systems, electronic funds transfer systems, digital telephone networks, smart cards, satellite printers and mobile communications.

Each technology identified in the SIT (e.g. computers) is capable of full integration with others – and usually is fully integrated. For example, computer-to-computer communications allow hotels to integrate their front office, back office and food and beverage operations. This internal management system of hotels can, in turn, be fully integrated with a digital telephone network. Together this provides the basis for linkage with hotel reservation systems – systems that can in turn be accessed by travel agents through their computerized reservations terminals (CRTs). Although it is a

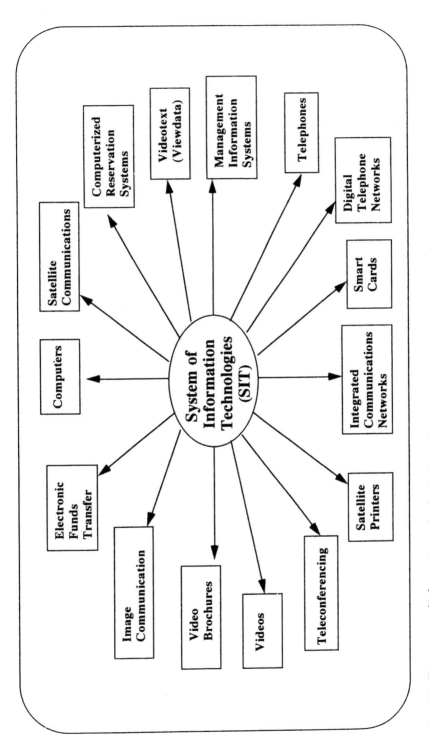

Fig. 6.2. The system of information technologies in tourism.

whole system of information technologies that is diffusing throughout the travel and tourism industry, *computerized reservations systems have emerged as the dominant technology.*

6.4. ADOPTION IS SYSTEM-WIDE

Technology usage in the travel and tourism industry cannot be understood in relation to a single producer, but for the industry as a whole.

The diffusion of information technologies in the travel and tourism industry is system-wide. The system of information technologies is not being adopted by travel agents *or* hotels *or* airlines *or* car rental *or* cruise ship companies *or* charter boat companies *or* tour operations, but by *all* of them. The use of information technologies by each player will affect all other players. To give a simple example: the use of a toll-free number by a hotel must require a travel agent's use of a telephone to make a room reservation for that hotel. This ability to call at will, and at times without paying (toll free), can improve the business of both players. Today, it is altogether commonplace for travel agents to have telephones. Indeed, the same analogy holds for the use of computers: an airline can use computerized reservations systems to store routes, schedules, tariffs and *availabilities* and to facilitate the booking of airline seats; however, it is useless for airlines to develop computerized reservation systems without travel agents having computer reservations terminals (CRTs) to access their services, make reservations and coin a sale.

For competitive reasons, the use of technology by one segment of the industry will serve to foster the use of technology by all other segments. Although all travel and tourism suppliers are users of information technologies, *airlines have emerged as clear technology leaders in the industry.*

6.5. RAPID DIFFUSION OF TECHNOLOGY

The diffusion of technology in the travel and tourism industry is very rapid. The experience of CRSs and travel agencies in the USA provides clear evidence of the speed of diffusion of distribution technology. The development and diffusion of CRSs in the travel and tourism industry is largely a product of the deregulation era. By 1988, a mere 10 years after deregulation, 96% of travel agencies in the USA were automated (Fig. 6.3).

Travel agency automation in the USA has now reached a plateau. In the US, all but 4% of agencies are automated. Those that are not automated are 'either newcomers and have not had the time to install the equipment or those that, because of their market niche or office size, have

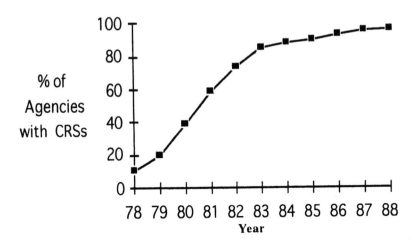

Fig. 6.3. The rapid diffusion of CRSs in US travel agencies.

Source: *Travel Weekly*, 1989.

chosen not to install systems' (*Travel Weekly*, US Travel Agency Survey, 1990d, p. 112). The rapid growth of automation in the travel and tourism industry has been such that 1991 was the first year that CRS vendors in the USA did not claim an increase in the number of agencies using their systems. In 1991, there were 41 120 installations and 180 900 booking units installed in travel agencies in the USA and more than half (53.2%) of these installations were personal computers (*Travel Weekly*, 1991e).

From 1990, 25% of the 7775 travel agencies in the UK were automated with Travicom and Galileo systems; 58% of France's 4150 travel agencies were automated with Esteril; 61% of Germany's 7200 travel agncies were automated with Start; and 58% of Swiss travel agents were automated with Traviswiss. The fact that Europe lags behind the USA in the diffusion of CRSs terminals in travel agencies is related to the fact that the wind of deregulation is blowing across the Atlantic 'painfully slow' (see Chapter 4). In Europe, there is clear evidence, however, that the technology is far more advanced than the prevailing socioinstitutional framework (airline regulations). It is clear that the absence of a good 'match' between the technology, on the one hand, and the institutional framework, on the other, slows down the rate of diffusion of technology in Europe. Table 6.1 summarizes data on the levels of automation for the USA and selected European countries.

The slow diffusion of CRSs in UK travel agencies is due to some peculiar conditions in that market (Hitchins, 1991):

Table 6.1 US travel agents record highest levels of automation in 1990*

Country	Number of travel agents	Percentage automated	Systems used
USA	40281	96	Sabre, Apollo, PARS, System 1, DATAS II
Scandinavia	1105	88	Smart
Germany	7200	61	Start
UK	7775	25	Travicom/Galileo
France	4150	58	Esterel
Switzerland	1270	58	Traviswiss
Spain	4300	36	Savia
Italy	4298	32	Sisma
Austria	1001	31	Traviaustria

Source: Travel Weekly, 2 April 1990d.

*The European Statistics do not take into account the number of agencies automated by a system other than sponsored by their national carriers. Overall automation by national systems was 40%. Other installations were estimated to bring that total to 44%.

1. The UK market is dominated by package tours that are currently distributed through tour-operator systems based on view-data technology. On average, travel agents depend on leisure travel (especially package tours) for over 70% of their sales.
2. There is a polarization of business and leisure travel agencies with the business segment being more automated (more dependent on bookings on scheduled services) compared with leisure agents (where the air service is already packaged by the tour operator). There are 5790 leisure agents in the UK which account for 72% of all agencies. The others are business travel agencies.

The rapid diffusion of technology is not only evident in travel agencies but also in airlines. The rapid development and adoption of CRS technologies in the USA and even in Europe has also been phenomenal. Southwest Airlines is the only significant carrier that does not sell tickets through a CRS. By 1990, Pan Am was the only national trunk carrier that was not a partner in a CRS, and that airline has since shut down. In Europe, all major airlines are now affiliated either with the Amadeus or Galileo systems. In Japan and in Canada, the main airlines have CRSs. And in Asia, airlines such as Singapore Airlines, Malaysian Airlines and Philippine Airlines are part-owners of Abacus (see Chapter 7 and Table 7.1, for a listing of airline affiliations to computerized reservation systems). Nowadays, very few major international airlines are not affiliated with a reservation system.

6.6. TECHNOLOGY IMPACTS IN TOURISM

The rapid diffusion of a system of information technologies throughout the travel and tourism industry has four key impacts:

1. It will improve the efficiency of production.
2. It will improve the quality of services provided to consumers.
3. It will lead to the generation of new services.
4. It will engineer the spread of a whole new industry 'best practice'.

These impacts are consistent with the findings of several authors analysing other sectors of the economy (Schumpeter, 1928, 1976; Barras, 1986; Freeman and Perez, 1986). The impacts of the system of information technology on the travel and tourism industry are summarized in Figure 6.4.

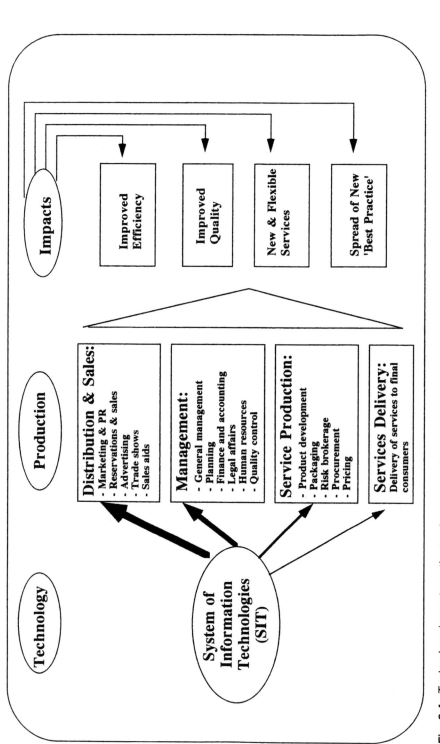

Fig. 6.4. Technology impacts on the tourism production system.

6.7. INCREASED EFFICIENCY

In a very real sense, consumers have always been 'unique, unprecedented and unrepeatable'. That the mass-production paradigm was allowed to flourish in tourism, was due fundamentally to the powerful price benefits that mass production provided. Consumers found it worthwhile to substitute some amount of their individuality and uniqueness because mass-produced holiday packages were darn cheap! Today mass production is still considered to be the most (and indeed the only) cost-effective formula by many industry players.

However, this old best practice of mass production is being superseded by a new best practice, one that incorporates the concepts of quality, flexibility, market segmentation and customization. These are creating a new, flexible package holiday – one that replaces, and even *un-packages*, the old traditionally packaged holiday – to suit the needs of the individual tourist. The use of new technologies and their inherent flexibility can make flexible production cost-competitive with mass-produced holidays.

The cost-reducing potential of information technology is evident in the use of CRSs. CRSs have been identified as highly efficient means for exchanging information between an airline and a customer, with a travel agent as an intermediary. Internal airline studies estimated that CRSs reduced the cost to an owning airline of making a reservation from approximately US$7.50 to US$0.50 (Guerin-Calvert and Noll, 1991, p. 3). A survey of travel agents reported that installing a CRS raised their productivity by 42% and as a result, the direct social costs of airline reservation and ticketing have fallen drastically – as much as 80% (Guerin-Calvert and Noll, 1991, p. 3).

The cost-reducing potential and increased efficiency are not only evident in airlines. UK tour operators such as Thomsons and Horizon (now merged with Thomsons) experienced similar efficiencies. Horizon plugged into a more powerful computer system in September 1986, claiming that the £1.5 million spent on its system enhancements would save travel agents time and money. Horizon sales director, Keith Purdom, claimed that

> the call length will be shorter because information will be more quickly available with average call time reducing from 6 to 4 minutes and the price of making a booking going from 45p to 10p
>
> (*Travel News*, 5 September 1987b, p. 6)

When it is considered that Horizon offered about 200 000 vacations on the market (*Travel News*, September 1987, p. 43), potential savings to agencies are significant.

It is also noteworthy that travel agents' links to the computerized reservation databases of their suppliers via viewdata terminals located in their offices are connected through telephone lines that allow them to access their suppliers at the cost of a local call. This tremendously reduces long-distance telephone charges (and time) that travel agents would otherwise have to spend in the absence of computerization.

6.8. IMPROVED QUALITY

By quality is meant a set standard of acceptable non-static values. Quality, therefore has two fundamental attributes, namely: (i) it is non-static; and (ii) it implies continuous improvements to goods, services and processes to meet the changing requirements of consumers. Quality refers both to the intrinsic value of the goods or service as well as the use-value to the consumers.

One of the most difficult aspects of measurement is quality. Very little information exists to date that allows quality to be consistently quantified. The impact of technology on quality depends upon how different technologies are conceived and whether they are strategically used to render competitive advantages. One hotel may use computers simply as a tool to lay off workers and to reduce wage costs. Another hotel may use technology to improve efficiency and to release valuable human hours to add a 'high-touch' element to the services offered. In the latter case, technology adoption will have the effect of improving the quality and 'human touch' of the services offered. A travel agency may have access to the most sophisticated reservations system, which could tremendously increase its efficiency. With this tool, the travel agency may place its own objectives of selling higher-prices seats or obtaining override commissions above the interest of the consumer. In this case, the actual quality of services delivered could be reduced.

Quality is a critical ingredient for competitive success. The potential of information technology to improve the quality of travel and tourism services is currently under-exploited. The Japanese experience with 'kaizen' (quality) in the automobile industry holds important lessons for the travel and tourism industry. This issue of product quality will be examined in detail in Chapter 9 where being a leader in quality is identified as one of the key principles of competitive strategies for industry players. Chapter 7 also addresses the role of quality-control systems in travel agencies.

6.9. NEW SERVICES

According to Jim Harris of British Airways, 'technology is expensive, but it provides scope for flexibility; the trick will be to move with the techno-

logical changes but maintain the flexibility to move with the market'
(*Travel Trade Gazette*, 3 July 1986, p. 21).

The generation of new and flexible services is one of the most
important areas of impact of technology in tourism. New technologies have
made possible the development of CRSs, frequent-flyer programmes,
satellite ticket printers, automatic ticket vending machines, travel agency
back-office systems, teleconferencing, boat and sky phones and image
communication. In addition, the widespread availability of technology is
making possible the creation of flexible holidays and facilitates such
developments as time-share vacations. Some of these new services are
described below.

6.9.1. Satellite Ticket Printers

In the USA, travel agents are using satellite ticket printers (STPs) at
corporate offices in order to issue tickets directly at the point of demand.
The Airlines Reporting Corporation (ARC) approved the right of travel
agents to operate ticket printers on customer's premises (*Travel Weekly*,
31 May, 1985b, p. 100). Since it costs more than US$2.50 to otherwise
deliver a ticket, satellite printers could save costs and fleets of delivery
vehicles and place tickets in travellers' hands much quicker. It is estimated
that 12% of travel agencies in the USA have satellite printers installed at
some of their clients' premises (*Travel Weekly*, US Travel Agency Survey,
1990d, p. 71).

6.9.2. Automated Ticket Machines

Interactive automated ticket machines (ATMs) consist of a computer with
an attached printer that permits passengers to research schedules and fares,
make reservations, purchase and receive tickets and boarding passes
without the intercession of a human agent. ATMs are located at airports
and city centres in the USA so that tickets can be purchased with payments
directly deducted from credit cards. Smart cards – credit cards with internal
microchip memories – will provide the key to the next generation of ticket
automation. With this technology, passengers (particularly in the US) now
have the ability to obtain tickets and boarding passes with their bank
accounts debited directly.

Initially introduced to sell one-way tickets in high-volume shuttle-type
markets, the capability of these machines has outstripped their use by
airlines. The reason for the limited use of the capacity of these machines is
summed up as follows:

The airlines fail to market this technology because it would compete with travel agents, upon whom they depend to book the overwhelming majority of their tickets, and because certain travel agency organizations have threatened to boycott any airline that relies on self-ticketing machines.

(US Department of Transportation, 1988)

6.9.3. Time Share

'Time share', as its name implies, refers to the purchase of vacation time at a specified tourist resort. It amounts, for example, to owning time (usually 1 week) of one apartment/hotel room in a resort apartment, for a number of years (spanning the life of the unit). The concept of time share is about 20 years old. In 1982, there were about 450 time-share projects and about 250000 owners (Ragatz, 1981, p.183). The very concept of time share – without technology – is inflexible. It would mean that a retired couple (for example) could be limited to spending their vacation in the same room, in the same resort, in the same country, for the rest of their lives. However, information technologies have come to the rescue. Information technologies play a major role in the rapid development of time-share vacations. Through the use of computers and communication technologies, it is possible to facilitate the exchange of time among time-sharing vacationers. For example, assuming that the correct matches can be made, it is possible for a couple who owns a week in a villa in Spain, to exchange it for a week in Jamaica. Information technologies have thus increased the flexibility, choice and variety with which time-share vacations can be produced, marketed and consumed.

6.9.4. CardLink

CardLink, introduced at around 1984, is a service offered jointly by American Express, Barclays Card and Diners Club. It provides security and convenience to merchants and travel suppliers as card transactions can be handled with one authorization telephone. By 'wiping' a card through the magnetic stripe reader on the telephone and entering the value of the transaction, CardLink connects automatically with the appropriate card company's computers so that the card-holders' data remain confidential to each card-issuer and card-holder.

The CardLink service eliminates the need to dial an authorization centre and quote merchant's name, card number and purchase amount. References to lost or stolen cards need no longer be posted in merchants' offices as transactions are checked automatically. The service saves customers' time and it enables the card companies to avoid unnecessary duplication of development and other costs. Additionally, it improves companies' control over fraud and credit loss. This CardLink service is not only available to the travel and tourism trade, but across the whole retailing industry where it has created a virtual revolution in retailing.

6.9.5. Teleconferencing

Teleconferencing is yet another service that has been made possible by computer and communications technologies. Teleconferencing involves the communication between people who are not physically in the same place, with an electronic device or medium being used to link them. The medium is a combination of telephone, television and satellite systems installed at several locations for that purpose (Fein, 1983, p. 279). Teleconferencing generally facilitates the conduct of business (meetings and conferences) among two or more persons or groups from remote or distant locations. It is a service currently on offer by hotels.

6.9.6. Image Communication

Communication technologies have advanced so rapidly that it is not only possible for clients to find out the price, availability and location of their future vacation spot. It is now possible for clients to have to a complete tour of the hotel that they may visit and preview the type of beds they will sleep in, the beaches, proximity to the airport, convention facilities, a map of the area and a lot more. Sabre, a leader in this field, is developing this technology in its SabreVision. SabreVision was created to help travel agencies increase hotel bookings on the Sabre's CRS, and this technology is being presented to the agencies as a productivity and profitability tool. It requires additional equipment and Sabre agents subscribe to this feature as an optional supplement to the standard Sabre reservation service. Jaguar (a division of the Reed Travel Group) claims to be the world's first electronic directory located at the point of sale. Jaguar's database, used as part of SabreVision product, contains hundreds of fields of information including full-colour photos of rooms, exterior, conference facilities and visual maps, resorts, hotels, destinations and other services and facilities (Personal communication, Bradley Miller (Jaguar's regional sales representative) Caribbean Hotel Industry Conference, Puerto Rico, June 1991).

6.10. FLEXIBLE HOLIDAYS

As described above, computerized reservation systems are used by the travel trade to make information more widely available and to increase the efficiency with which travel agents search for information and confirm bookings. Consumers are also able to obtain better information and cheaper vacations through 'late availability' information from suppliers. Tour operators and airlines, for example, can 'announce' late availabilities, at a moment's notice, which can immediately reach all agencies via their computerized reservations terminals. Consumers are thus better able to catch the bargains, and suppliers can increase their chances of selling their entire output while managing yield.

There are tremendous possibilities for creating and combining new and more flexible travel services. This is because of the more widely available information, and the technology with which to gather, analyse and manipulate it. Airline Farebank, of the UK, is an electronic information system that specializes in supplying the trade with airline fares. The system is price-driven, and will have an important impact on the generation of flexible and independent holidays. Airline Farebank offers low-cost and fully commissionable scheduled air fares on a no fees, no subscriptions, no time-based charges basis and is available on Istel and Prestel videotext systems 24 hours a day. One of the major constraints to the growth of independent holidays is price.

Normally, travel agents who do not purchase large volumes of airline seats and bed nights are unable to obtain commission levels and discounts as for tour operators. However, with the proliferation of electronic information systems and the increased trend toward consolidation (discounting), there are growing possibilities for travel agents to package independent itineraries competitively.

Consolidating or discounting is a growing practice in the travel and tourism industry – especially in the UK travel market. The twin objectives of yield management and high load factors underlie consolidation. Airlines block off certain seats, which must be sold at stipulated high prices. Consolidation allows airlines to distribute other highly discounted seats through discount houses. Consolidation makes it possible for travel agencies to offer competitively priced packages because fare-driven electronic systems, such as Farebanks', allow agents to simultaneously search a number of airline databases for the cheapest possible fare. Farebank is soon to add hotel rooms, car rentals and other services to its offerings (Farebank system demonstration, World Travel Market, London, November, 1991). With systems such as Farebank, it could be possible for travel agencies to tailor-make holiday packages at prices that are competitive with tour operators standard brochure offering. It is also possible for tour operators to offer their service to travel agents on a 'mix and match' or un-packaged basis.

6.11. A NEW INDUSTRY BEST PRACTICE

As has been stated in Chapter 3, it is not just technology being diffused but potentially a whole new industry best practice – a change in the organizational and managerial common sense for best productivity and most profitable practice for all industries. Consider the following:

1. It is not a single, stand-alone technology, that is being adopted by tourism suppliers, but a whole system of information technologies (SIT).

2. It is not airlines alone or travel agencies or tour operators that are adopting the system of information technologies, but all of them – no supplier will remain untouched by this technology.

3. The use of technology by one supplier requires technology adoption by other suppliers in order to stay competitive. All suppliers will have to be users of technology to be competitive.

4. These technologies are not incremental additions to the travel and tourism landscape having only marginal effects; rather, these technologies introduce radical changes. Information technology is changing the rules of the industry blowing 'gales of destruction' in its wake: IT will have profound and widespread impacts – IT will increase efficiency, improve quality and generate new services.

5. A proliferation of new technologies and services is being developed and marketed: frequent-flyer programmes, satellite printers, image communications, smart cards, smart buildings, teleconferencing and flexible holidays.

6. Technologies have become the latest competitive weapon and alter the rules of the game in the industry. Products of technology – frequent-flyer programmes, yield managements, virtual nesting, halo effect, architectural bias and super-normal incremental revenues – have become powerful competitive weapons in the industry (see Chapter 7). Regulation has found it difficult to cope with these complex weapons.

7. Technologies are radically altering the process of wealth creation in the travel and tourism industry. Information has become a factor of production comparable in magnitude with land, labour and capital resources. The generation, distribution, control and application of information in the tourism industry all create wealth. CRSs have become systems of wealth creation in themselves. A few airlines are making more money from their CRSs than from their 'main' activity of transporting passengers.

Consider moreover, that:

8. It is not just the travel and tourism sector that is rapidly adopting new technologies. *Manufacturers* use information technologies in the form of robots, flexible manufacturing systems, computer-aided design and computer-aided manufacture (CAD/CAM). *Banks* use automated teller machines, computerized databases, CardLink and other sophisticated communications networks. *Supermarkets* use electronic point of sale (EPOS) equipment to expedite the tallying of customers' purchases. *Schools* use computers and audiovisual equipment of education and training. Intelligent cars and washing machines, high-resolution televisions, microwave ovens are prevalent in *homes* and children *play* with computer games and intelligent toys.

9. Microelectronics lies at the heart of these myriad technologies that affect every aspect of our daily lives: microelectronics is as important and powerful today as cotton, coal, steel and oil of the decades and centuries past (Freeman and Perez, 1986).

10. Although the travel and tourism industry adopted the principles of mass production rather late (the 1960s and 1970s) compared with the automobile industry where Ford developed his Model T in 1908, mass production was short-lived in the travel and tourism industry – but signs of a new, flexible tourism are apparent in the 1990s.

11. On the other hand, travel and tourism, a service industry by nature and very close to the heart of consumers, will be a lead sector in the adoption of the new paradigm of flexibile production.

12. The demands of the new consumers provide the necessary incentive for industry players to adopt the new industry best practice.

13. The future growth and development of the travel and tourism industry is taking place within the context of new socioinstitutional frame conditions (e.g. limits to growth, environmental consciousness, deregulation, consumer protection, more planning and development of 'green' or 'soft' tourism services and facilities). These frame conditions create an excellent match with current technology for the diffusion of a new tourism.

For all of these reasons, therefore, it is not just a system of information technologies that is being diffused in tourism but potentially a whole new industry 'best practice' or 'common sense'. That this new best practice is already diffusing in the travel and tourism industry is beyond question. The handwriting is on the wall: (i) the demand for independent holidays is growing; (ii) the demand for choice and flexibility is greater than it has ever been; (iii) the rate of growth of the traditional sun-package tour business is declining; (iv) there is increasing environmental planning and control of tourism in destination countries; (v) there is increasing segmentation of vacation markets that cater to lifestyle characteristics; (vi) the travel behaviour and motivation of tourists are changing; and (vii) population demographics and work patterns are changing. In addition, as we will see in Chapters 9 and 10, new competitive strategies of product quality, market segmentation, mass customization, diagonal integration and human resource development are increasingly being adopted.

The extent and rate of diffusion of this new best practice, however, will very much depend on the actions of all players in the industry – the consumers, the producers, host countries and governments, as well as the industry's overall frame conditions (e.g. airline deregulation and environmental limits to growth). Exactly who will benefit from this new best practice will depend on who will be first to adopt it and the speed and extent to which other industry players take it on board. The winners, of course, will be the leaders.

6.12. CONCLUSIONS

In tourism, it is not travel agents or hotels or airlines that are using technology, but all of them. The technology is so comprehensive and intertwined that it is not only videotext or CRSs or satellite printers or smart cards that are being used, but a whole system of radically new information technologies. Airlines have emerged as the technology leaders among participants and CRSs have emerged as the dominant technology.

The rapid diffusion of a system of information technologies has four key impacts:

- it will improve the efficiency of production;
- it will improve the quality of services;
- it will lead to the generation of new services (image communication, satellite printers, flexible holidays); and
- it will lead to the spread of a whole new industry best practice.

The new best practice will change the organizational and managerial common sense for best productivity and most profitable practice in the travel and tourism industry. As such, therefore, it is not just technology that is being diffused throughout the travel and tourism industry but a whole new industry common sense – a new tourism. Industry players will do well to play a leadership role in the new tourism (Chapter 8 will examine this).

7

TECHNOLOGY IN ACTION

7.1. INTRODUCTION

A whole system of information technologies is being adopted by all segments of the travel and tourism industry. No player in the travel and tourism industry will escape the impacts of information technology. There is clear technology leadership on the part of airlines and a dominant technology in the form computerized reservations systems (CRSs).

This chapter introduces the concept of the tourist production system (TPS), a tool that helps to determine in which areas of production (e.g. sales, marketing) information technology is being applied. It is found that technology will not affect the human content of tourism. Rather, it will affect the core information-intensive areas of production – general management, marketing, distribution, reservations and sales. The imperatives of distribution of travel and tourism services will dictate the pace of technology adoption.

The technologies being used by industry players – airlines, travel agents, tour operators and hotels – are also considered in this chapter, as well as their impacts on each industry player.

7.2. THE TOURISM PRODUCTION SYSTEM (TPS)

Tourism suppliers possess dual production systems. Their production systems are dual because they comprise *services* and *information*. Suppliers provide the services of hotel bed-nights, airline seats and package tours. However, they must also produce and distribute information with respect to price, special promotions, location, availability, conditions of purchase, arrival/departure times, connecting flights, quality and convenience of their services.

The dissemination of travel and tourism information is of tremendous importance to the tourist trade for tourism services are not capable of display or physical inspection at the point of sale. Information provides the key to product quality and availability. As such, the provision and distribution of information becomes as important to the competitiveness of industry players as is the provision of the services themselves.

The dual production system (service + information) of tourism producers can be simplified into four categories as follows: (i) service production; (ii) management; (iii) marketing, distribution and sales; and (iv) service delivery. In practice, it is very difficult to differentiate among these four elements of the tourism production system (TPS) since the production of travel and tourism services is a very integrated process. However, the identification of the TPS and its subdivision into four parts provide a very useful tool for understanding the diffusion and impacts of the SIT in tourism.

Service provision and service delivery can be considered as service-oriented elements, while management, marketing, discounting and sales are the core information functions of travel and leisure suppliers. The four components of the TPS are identified in Figure 7.1 and described below.

Services produced by the industry include air, sea and land transportation, hotel bed-nights, packaged tours, travel information and other destination services. A number of wealth-creating activities are undertaken in the production of these services. These include packaging, procurement, risk brokerage, familiarization trips, travel agency training, product development, systems and technology development.

Management of the travel and tourism industry involves the following functions: general management; planning, finance and accounting; quality control; human resources development; legal affairs and other activities supporting the production process.

Marketing, distribution and sales activities in this field include advertising, promotions, reservations, public relations, trade show participation and cooperative advertising.

Service delivery refers to the actual provision of travel and tourism related services to the final consumer and includes customer service, consumer satisfaction and complaint management.

7.3. TECHNOLOGY IN PRODUCTION

The impact of technology on travel and tourism operations will depend on the information and human-intensity of the activities to which technologies

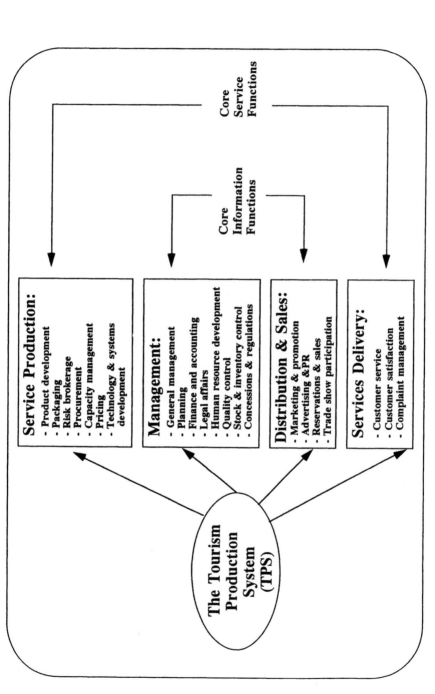

Fig. 7.1. The tourism production system.

are applied. The more information-intensive the activity, the greater will be the impact of technology. On the other hand, the more human-intensive the activity the lesser will be the impact of technology. Technology will have the least impact on highly human-intensive areas of service supply and delivery and the greatest impact on the two information-intensive areas of management and distribution. The imperatives of distribution of travel and tourism services will dictate the pace of technology adoption.

7.3.1. Technology in Service Production

Activities involved in producing travel and tourism services include procurement, product development, quality control, technology development, risk brokerage, capacity management, tour packaging, pricing, development of new markets, negotiations with suppliers and information provision. A number of information technology tools are used to assist industry players in producing services of ground, sea and air transportation, hotel bed-nights, packaged tours and information.

Airlines, for example, use information technologies to aid in the organization, management and control of their operations. Electronic management and information systems aid airlines in: (i) route and schedule planning; (ii) schedule generation; (iii) flight planning, control, departure and analysis; (iv) engineering; (v) crew management; (vi) catering; (vii) accounting; and (viii) future planning (Brown *et al.*, 1983). Systems that help to carry out these operations include: the ARNIC Communication Addressing and Reporting System (ACARS); Aircraft Satellite Data and Relay System (ASDAR); Inertial Navigation Systems (INS); Air Traffic Control (ATC), and Microwave Landing Systems (MLS).

Value-creating activities involved in producing travel- and tourism-related services are intelligence-driven. The decision to offer a new destination, create a second hub, buy an airline, diversify into pleasure boats, develop a new holiday idea, end services to a destination, supply the adventure niche in the holiday market or negotiate discounts with suppliers usually requires human beings with foresight and initiative to carry them out. Information technology is merely a facilitator at this stage of production. Information technology is used to provide reliable, timely and up-to-date information with which to make decisions. *Information technology will therefore not have a great deal of impact on this 'production' area of the TPS.* However, it will be the key facilitator of decisive decision-making.

7.3.2. Technology in Management

Management is an information-intensive area in the provision of travel and tourism services. A number of computers and communications technologies currently aid airlines, tour operators, hotels, travel agencies, cruise lines and car rental companies in carrying out their *internal management* functions. Computers are used to generate, process, analyse and store information for airlines, hotels, travel agencies, tour operators and other suppliers. Communication technologies facilitate various levels of *communication*: for example, among members of staff within an airline; from one department in a hotel to another; among suppliers of travel services; between travel agent and client; and between industry players and their marketing, distribution and sales agents.

Computers are also helpful in the field of *management*. In the management of an airline, for example, important decisions have to be made regarding the purchase, leasing and other contractual arrangements involved in organizing, procuring, managing and controlling the various components of the air transportation service (e.g. aircraft leasing and catering).

These core management functions constitute the internal information functions of the tourism production system and will be a very important area of technology applications.

7.3.3. Technology in Marketing and Sales

By far the most important area of impact of technology will be the areas of marketing, distribution and sales. This can be seen by the extent of development of computerized reservations systems for the distribution of travel and tourism-related services and the extent of their adoption by the industry.

As shown in Chapter 6, almost all airlines in the USA are affiliated with a CRS and nearly all travel agencies have computerized reservation terminals. Product distribution represents the most critical as well as information-intensive area of the TPS. Although linked to the internal information functions of management, planning and financial control, one can view marketing, distribution and product packaging as the external information-intensive areas of the TPS. These are the areas where suppliers must forge links with distributors, agents and one another.

In the tourism industry, each supplier can choose various technological modes and intensities with which to organize and manage their internal affairs. Such choices can be determined independently of what other suppliers are doing. However, at the end of the day, it is the effective sale of output that generates revenues and profits. The effective sale of output requires access to distribution networks and market information. Access to these networks depends critically upon standardization and compatibility of computer and communications networks among suppliers and distributors. It means, therefore, that a minimum level of technology adoption among travel suppliers is necessary for marketing, distribution and industry linkages. Moreover, with the increased diffusion of distribution systems such as CRSs, representation on these systems (through ownership, direct representation or, indirectly, through a marketing link, e.g. a franchise, which is accessed through a CRS) has become a necessary requirement for competitive success for many industry players.

Computerized reservation systems developed by airlines are the main tools used by the industry to distribute travel and tourism services across the globe (refer to Section 7.4 – Airline CRSs). Other technologies adopted by the travel trade to facilitate distribution are videos and video brochures; digital telephone networks; satellite printers; automated ticket vending machines at airports and supermarkets; freephones (e.g. Link Line in the UK); and image communications (e.g. SabreVision).

Electronic funds transfer is another important technology that will be increasingly adopted by the travel trade. This reflects the critical role that payments play in the travel trade. In 1986, Thomson, the largest tour operator in the UK announced the installation of electronic funds transfer, which would allow automatic debiting of travel agency accounts.

The imperatives of marketing, distribution and sales will dictate the pace of the adoption of IT in tourism. These are the areas in which technology will have its greatest impacts. It is therefore not surprising that it is CRSs that have become the dominant technology in the travel and tourism industry and not robot-guided tours or back-office accounting systems.

7.3.4. Technology in Service Delivery

By service delivery, one means the final 'visible' services that are delivered to customers. In the airline industry, it would mean the services of check-in, seating, entertainment and transportation to and from required destinations. The objective of an airline is not to produce an aircraft or even the paper on which airline tickets are printed. It is the delivery of the final transportation, in-flight entertainment, baggage handling, reservations and other related services that are the prime motivation of travel suppliers. The rendering of such services is labour-intensive. For it is people – reservation staff, pilots and in-flight attendants, baggage handlers, airline representatives – who deliver airline services to other people.

Of all elements of the tourism industry, airlines are perhaps the most dependent on information for the safe delivery of their services. For example, electronic information is centrally important in departure control, in systems that could navigate worldwide with exceptional accuracy, and in air-traffic control systems.

Most travel services, however, are delivered by human beings – from airline cabin attendants and pleasure-boat captains to waiters at hotels in this highly human-intense service industry. Information technology is not likely to have much impact here. However, a number of communications technologies are used by industry players to provide:

1. Entertainment and information in the form of stereos, videos, cable television and direct satellite broadcasting of international events such as the Olympic Games, the World Cup, cricket, Super Bowl, Wimbledon.
2. Client information and awareness stimulation from view-data terminals and video brochures at travel agencies, trade fairs and in the hotel room.
3. The facilities to conduct business through teleconferencing.
4. Mobile communications such as boat 'phones and sky 'phones, which allow tourists and passengers the facility to call from anywhere in the world to any part of the world.

The application of IT to the delivery of travel services will increase the safety, quality, flexibility and individuality of travel services rather than alter their manifest human content. Technology will have the least impact on the actual delivery of services by the tourism industry.

7.3.5. Technology Diffuses Unevenly

Information technology will diffuse very unevenly through the four elements of the TPS. Technology will have its greatest impact on the information-intensive areas of tourism production and lesser impact on the service and labour-intensive areas. From Figure 7.2, one can visualize the intensity of the impact of SIT on the four components of the tourism production system. The intensity of impact is indicated by the boldness of the lines that flow from the SIT to each of the four elements of the tourism production system. The area of marketing and distribution will receive the greatest impact of information technology followed by management, services production and, finally, service delivery.

7.4. AIRLINE CRSs

Computerized reservation systems (CRSs) have emerged as the dominant technology in the travel and tourism industry. Airlines have also emerged as the technology leaders. That airlines now control the dominant technology of the travel and tourism industry is due to airline deregulation and the strategic moves made by airlines as well as the continued rapid developments in information technologies. Airline deregulation in the USA provided the framework to facilitate the rapid development and diffusion of computerized reservation systems. Meanwhile, continued rapid developments in

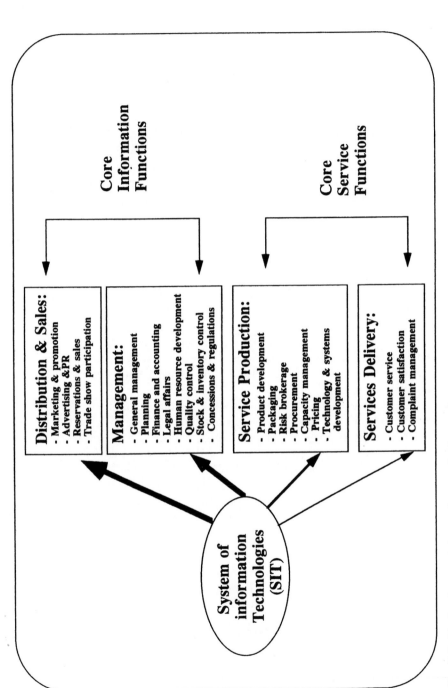

Fig. 7.2. Technology and the tourism production system.

microelectronics, computers and communications technology provided an increasingly sophisticated technological base to spawn CRSs.

A computerized reservation system consists of 'a periodically updated central database that is accessed by subscribers through computer terminals' (US Department of Transportation, 1988, p. 8). CRSs provide subscribers with up-to-date information on air fares and services and permit users to book, change and cancel reservations and to issue tickets. Travel agencies are the main subscribers to CRSs while airlines are the owners, developers, hosts or vendors of the American CRSs. While CRSs were designed primarily to provide travel agents with information on airline services, they now display information for a range of travel and leisure services and permit reservations to be made for hotels, car rentals, cruises, railways, tours, boat charters, theatre and sporting events, as well as issue travellers cheques, exchange currency, validate credit cards, write insurance policies and order flowers (US Department of Transportation, 1990).

CRSs also store and retrieve information on consumers – their airline, ticket class, seating and dietary preferences as well as their addresses, telephone, credit-card numbers and buying patterns of related services (e.g. travellers cheques, insurance). CRSs also store and retrieve information on airlines and other suppliers' services, such as hotels and car-rental companies that distribute their services through CRSs. The intelligent use and manipulation of this information have become a powerful resource for wealth creation. CRSs themselves have evolved into complete travel information systems.

CRSs have become powerful wealth-creating tools in the travel and tourism industry and have become profit centres in their own right. It is not surprising that Bob Crandall, head of American Airlines and its sister company Sabre, when asked whether, if it came to the crunch, he would sell the airline or the CRS, he replied: 'The airline!' (Smith, 1989). Another company, TWA, once referred to the PARS as the 'crown jewel' of its airline empire, but has since sold shares in that treasure.

7.4.1. The Technology is Well Developed

Institutional innovations often tend to lag behind technology. The ideal climate for technology diffusion is provided when there is a good 'match' between the technology on the one hand and the socioinstitutional environment on the other (Perez, 1985). Airline deregulation in 1978 certainly provided the socioinstitutional match for the rapid development and diffusion of airline CRSs. Three clear phases of CRS development in the airline industry are evident. Together they reveal a highly developed technological capability (Fig. 7.3).

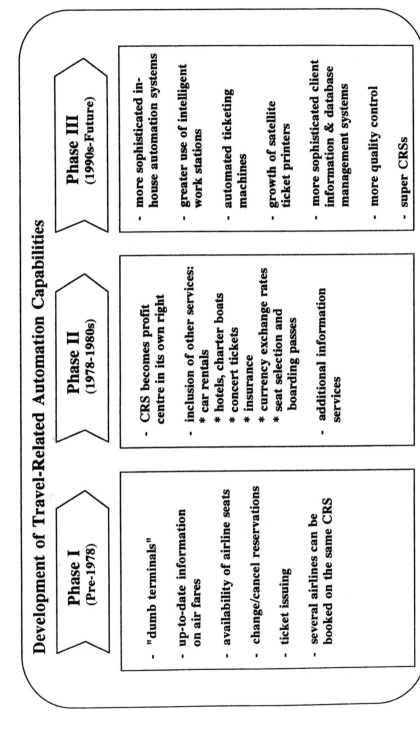

Development of Travel-Related Automation Capabilities

Phase I (Pre-1978)	Phase II (1978-1980s)	Phase III (1990s-Future)

- "dumb terminals"
- up-to-date information on air fares
- availability of airline seats
- change/cancel reservations
- ticket issuing
- several airlines can be booked on the same CRS
	- CRS becomes profit centre in its own right
	- inclusion of other services:
	  * car rentals
	  * hotels, charter boats
	  * concert tickets
	  * insurance
	  * currency exchange rates
	  * seat selection and boarding passes
	- additional information services
		- more sophisticated in-house automation systems
		- greater use of intelligent work stations
		- automated ticketing machines
		- growth of satellite ticket printers
		- more sophisticated client information & database management systems
		- more quality control
		- super CRSs

Fig. 7.3. Development of travel-related automation capabilities.

Before 1976, airlines developed reservation systems that were specific to their own needs and which could hardly 'talk' to other airlines. Their use was limited to the owning airline. The systems had limited capabilities and could display availability of seats and print tickets. In 1976 – the year that the first CRSs were installed in US travel agencies, particularly after deregulation in 1978 – travel agencies became the major factor in airline distribution strategies. Services other than airline seats began to be distributed through CRSs, while the CRSs themselves were becoming profit centres in their own right. The 1990s are witnessing the development of more sophisticated office-management systems, for example: (i) the greater use of intelligent workstations for travel agencies; (ii) the expanded use of fare auditing and quality control programmes in travel agencies; (iii) the development and diffusion of self-service ticketing machines at airports and other remote locations; (iv) an increase in commercial information networks available to the public; and (v) global cooperation and networking particularly among the world's major CRSs (see Figure 7.3).

7.4.2. High Development Costs and Entry Barriers

One of the characteristics of CRSs, indeed of much of the IT infrastructure, is the high cost of development and the long gestation period necessary before profits are realized. Galileo has spent £250 million on the development of its CRS since it was formed in 1979 (Hitchins, 1991). Amadeus claims that its operation has taken £300 million to develop from start to finish (*Travel Trade Gazette*, UK and Ireland, 19 December 1991b, p. 6). Between 1975 and 1986, the five CRS systems in the USA – Apollo, Sabre, DATAS II, PARS and System One – had negative net cash flows of over US$750 million in developing their systems (US Department of Transportation, 1988). At the end of 1986, the total non-recoverable investment made by the five CRS vendors was US$581 million and the ongoing outlays of Sabre and Apollo to enhance the capacity and performance of their CRSs each exceeded US$150 million annually (US Department of Transportation, 1988).

The huge costs of developing CRSs create barriers to entry in the industry. Barriers to entry in the CRS industry are also caused by:

1. The fact that the software for CRSs has been spawned from the airlines' internal reservations systems. A non-airline entrant would have to incur substantial costs in developing and testing the software and marketing the system.

2. Economies of scale and scope in the provision of CRSs with the larger systems such as Sabre realizing a lower unit cost per booking (US$1.62) compared with a smaller system such as DATAS II (US$2.64). This significant cost advantage makes it difficult for new entrants to compete since

they will have to match the prices of long-standing lower-cost competitors.
3. Contractual relationships between CRS suppliers and travel agencies
that make it difficult for a new entrant to capture market share without
incurring the substantial costs of buying out existing agency CRS contracts.
4. Heavy reliance of airlines on incremental revenues as a primary source
of CRS revenues. In other words, the established large CRSs can afford to
add subscribers who pay low or no leasing fees but a new small entrant
would be hard pressed to do the same.

These barriers to entry are largely responsible for the heavily concentrated
structure of the CRS industry.

7.4.3. Industry Concentration

In 1983, the three largest airlines in the USA were responsible for 90% of
the CRSs at travel agency locations: American Airlines, United, and
Trans-World Airlines accounted for 39%, 37% and 14%, respectively, of
the CRSs terminals supplied to travel agents (US Congressional Hearings,
First Session, 1983, p. 101). The concentrated nature of the CRS industry
has not changed significantly since then. Concentration levels are even
higher at the regional level. American Airlines' Sabre is still in the lead,
commanding 34% of all automated agency locations in the US (14000)
and 38.2% of booking terminals (69000); Apollo has 28% of all automated agency locations (11500) and 44000 booking terminals; Worldspan
(a merger of PARS and DATAS II) has a market share of 20.7% for
locations and 21% for terminals; and System One has 17.3% share for
locations and 16.5% share for terminals (*Travel Weekly*, 1991e, p. 41).
Similar levels of concentration in the CRS industry are evident in
Europe. Lufthansa has a 25% stake in the Start reservation system, which,
in 1990, was installed in 4392 travel agency locations (61% of all agencies
in Germany), and Smart, 75% owned by Scandinavian Airways, as of 1990
represented 88% of all agency locations in Scandinavia (refer to Table 6.1
in Chapter 6). By 1986, British Airways increased its share in Travicom
from 55% to 82%, with British Caledonian holding the remaining share
(*Travel Trade Gazette*, 1986d, p. 4). With the merger of British Airways
and British Caledonia in 1988, British Airways fully owns Travicom.
In 1990, Travicom was installed in 25% of the 7775 agencies in the
UK. In 1987, Lufthansa, Iberia, Scandinavian Airways System (SAS)
and Air France concluded a preliminary agreement for the development of
a joint reservation system. Amadeus, with each having a 25% stake,
although SAS has since sold its share to its partners. Galileo was first
formed in 1987 by British Airways, Alitalia, Swissair, KLM and United.
Other airlines such as Aer Lingus, Austrian Airlines, Olympic Airways,
Sabena, and TAP Air Portugal have also joined forces to develop Galileo

Table 7.1 Ownership and affiliations of the world's major agency CRSs

Airline CRS	Owning airlines	Affiliations
Abacus Based in Singapore	All Nippon Airways, Cathay Pacific, China Airlines, Malaysian Airlines, Philippine Airlines, Royal Brunei, Singapore Airlines and Tradewinds (a Singapore subsidiary)	Technology based on Worldspan's PARS; 5% owned by Worldspan and owns 5% of Worldspan; also holds 40% of Infini; has technological partnership agreement with Amadeus
Amadeus Based in Madrid, Spain	Founding partners: Air France, Iberia, Lufthansa	Technology based on System One; has technological partnership with agreement with ABACUS; similar partnership with Sabre collapsed in 1991 before implementation; new technological partnership with System One
Apollo Based in Chicago, Illinois, USA	Covia Partners: Air Canada, Alitalia, British Airways, KLM, Swissair, United Airlines and USAIR	United is a shareholder with Alitalia, BA, KLM and Swissair in Galileo; Covia one-third holder of, Covia, Galileo to be merged to form Galileo International
Axess Based in Tokyo, Japan	Japan Airlines	None
Fantasia Based in Sydney, Australia	Quantas	Technology based on Sabre; distribution company in Australia merged with Galileo distributor there
Galileo Based in Swindon, England	Founding partners: Alitalia, British Airways, KLM, Swiss Air, United Airlines	Technology based on Apollo; all partners are shareholders in Covia, which provides Gemini Affiliation; Covia, Galileo to be merged to form Galileo International
Gemini Based in Toronto, Ontario, Canada	Air Canada and Canadian Airlines	Technology based on Apollo; one-third owned by Covia; Covia, Galileo to be merged to form Galileo International

GETS Based in Atlanta, Georgia, USA	33 Airlines including Aeroflot, LOT, Kenya Airways, Luxair, Manx Airlines and Variag; also one non-airline travel company	Technology based on SITA Gabriel II system
Infini Based in Japan	All Nippon Airways	Plus 40% held by Abacus, by extension making Worldspan a 2% shareholder
Sabre Based in Dallas, Texas, USA	American Airlines	Marketed by local partners in Asia/Pacific region; Amadeus technological partnership failed in 1991, before implementation
System One Based in Houston, Texas, USA	Continental, common ownership	Has technological partnership agreement with Amadeus
Worldspan	Delta, Northwest, TWA	Created by a merger of PARS and DATAS II; 5% owned by Abacus and owns 5% of Abacus, thus giving it a share in Infini

Source: Guerin-Calvert and Noll, 1991; US Department of Transportation, 1990; Wheatcroft, 1990; Travel Weekly, 1991c.

in Europe. These and other European carriers, in order to provide upgraded CRSs in their home countries and to fend off competition from US vendors, opted to create multinational multi-carrier systems – with the expectation of converting users of their local systems to the mega-CRSs with which they are affiliated. For this reason, BA, for example, is now converting Travicom agencies to Galileo.

A summary of the CRS systems available in the travel and tourism industry globally, as well as the various airlines associated with these systems, is provided in Table 7.1. From Table 7.1, the strategic alliances of CRS vendors across the globe are identified. Sabre has interests in systems in the Asia/Pacific region and, until its split with Amadeus in 1991, was actively involved in the development of a pan-European system. Covia is half owned by four European airlines and USAir, with Air Canada having a 1% share. United is a shareholder in Galileo, and Covia is a partner in Canada's Gemini system. After the split of Sabre and Amadeus, Amadeus formed a new technological partnership with System One in May 1992.

7.4.4. CRSs Become Profit Centres

Some CRSs have become profit centres in their own right. Some airlines now make more money from their CRSs than from their 'principal' function of transporting passengers. For those, the high costs of development of airline CRSs are justified by the profitability of the systems. Apollo showed a positive net cash flow of US$21.6 million in 1985 and doubled this figure in 1986. Sabre was the first CRS to turn a profit in 1983, starting with US$5.5 million in that year, reaching US$84 million in 1986 and projected to reach US$150 million in 1992 (Fig. 7.4). It is understandable therefore that, there are those who, like Bob Crandall feels that 'if the company wanted to make more profits on each dollar invested it should give up flying planes and just concentrate on the CRS' (Smith, 1989).

Due to the nature of the CRS infrastructure and the huge fixed investment costs associated with its development, once these telecommunications highways are in place, the wealth-creating possibilities of these systems have proven enormous. This is particularly the case for the large CRSs that were developed at an early date.

With fixed costs, and declining marginal costs, each additional participating industry supplier or travel agency linked to the CRS becomes a potential profit centre. It is estimated that 80% of incremental airline revenues from CRSs accrue to profits and that the major CRS systems are 'extremely profitable' (US Department of Transportation, 1990, p. 93). Incremental revenues refer to the extra income earned by an airline resulting from an increase in the number of passengers who travel on its flights as a result of travel agents' use of its reservation system.

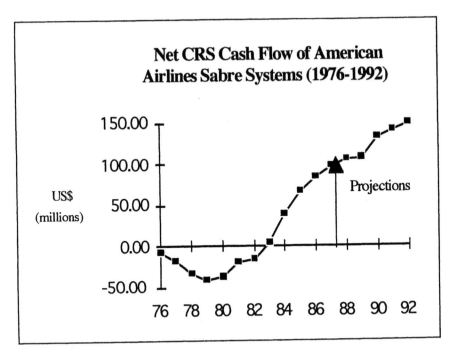

Fig. 7.4. Graph showing how American Airlines' Sabre system has become a profit centre in its own right.
– Sabre was the first CRS to generate positive cash flow.
– High initial investments justified by competitive advantages realized through CRSs.
– Barriers to entry are high due to learning effects, scale and scope economies, contractual relationships with travel agents and incremental revenues.
– Competitive advantage in the airline industry no longer derived from CRS ownership but from its intelligent use.

Source: US Department of Transportation, 1988.

The 1988 net incremental revenues for the five CRS-owning airlines that founded CRSs were estimated at between US$40 million and US$707.8 million. When it is considered that the influence of CRS affiliation on travel agency bookings are commonly between 20% and 30%, the aggregate gross incremental revenues for 1988 could lie between US$2 billion and US$3 billion (US Department of Transportation, 1990, p. 59–73).

CRSs are therefore used as a key tool to capture new clients and to keep a passenger within the airline's network so long as possible. This is achieved not only through the information provided through CRSs, but also by the airlines' computerized capability to manage frequent-flyer programmes aimed at achieving passenger loyalty.

7.4.5. CRSs – The New Competitive Weapon

CRSs themselves have become a very powerful competitive weapon of the travel industry. The competitive significance of CRSs stems from *strategic* as well as *cost* imperatives.

Strategically, CRSs are a very important marketing tool for airlines. They generate invaluable information on: (i) the performance of their services; (ii) on the performance of travel agents who market their services; (iii) on the performance of competitors that are co-hosts on their systems; and (iv) on profiles of the clients of their agency subscribers. CRSs allow their owning airlines to develop and manage frequent-flyer programmes. Large CRS vendors also claim that they are better able to coordinate their yield-management programmes and thus their inventory through their CRS systems. Sabre, for example, allows American Airlines to perform 'virtual nesting' – saving the seats on a flight segment for long-haul passengers and denying them to local passengers in the same class (US Department of Transportation, 1990, pp. 70–71). The strategic importance of CRS ownership also stems from the capacity of owning airlines to generate the incremental revenues from additional bookings as described above. Before the CAB began regulating agency CRSs in 1984, incremental revenues were obtained by explicit bias against rival carriers in data entry and display ranking. Although the rules have succeeded in eliminating display bias, incremental revenues continue to be obtained through 'architectural bias' (refer to Section 7.4.6 on fair competition) and from the relationship between vendor airline and travel agencies that foster travel agency loyalty to the vendor airline.

The cost imperatives of CRSs are also overwhelming. Having developed these computerized reservations networks, their owners can increase the number of suppliers (co-hosts) and users (travel agents) of their systems, with little or no marginal costs. Because users and co-hosts pay market prices rather than marginal cost prices, CRSs have become very important profit centres for the big players who got there early. In addition, since marginal costs – the cost of transporting an additional passenger – are low, CRSs can afford to install computerized reservations terminals (CRTs) in agency locations at very competitive prices. CRTs at agency locations are key to maximizing revenues and passenger bookings on airline CRSs because the incremental revenues obtained from transporting an additional passenger on a flight far exceed the cost of transporting that passenger.

This explains why CRSs are fiercely competing with each other to expand their offerings and distributorship, madly trying to attract co-hosts (e.g. hotels and car-rental companies) and travel agents alike. Airlines therefore compete not only on the basis of cabin service, arrival/departure times, connections, leg room, shiatsu massages, food and price, but also, since deregulation, through their affiliated CRSs. Many airlines were forced to respond to the moves of the early and most successful CRS developers. With the entry of American's Sabre and United's Apollo into the UK market, for example, British Airways Travicom was forced to respond competitively by slashing prices, enhancing the number of lines to travel agencies and introducing an automated data system (President) to link with reservations. The development of Galileo and Amadeus is also a competitive response by European airlines to the aggressive entry of US systems, particularly Sabre, in the European market. Even airlines in the USA have joined major CRSs for competitive reasons. Northwest, for example, became a partner in PARS 'for defensive purposes' (US Department of Transportation, 1990, p. 47).

7.4.6. Fair Competition

CRSs have become a very controversial addition to the travel and tourism landscape. They have been blamed for several anti-competitive practices. The nature of these anti-competitive practices is reflected in the rules that were implemented by the US Civil Aeronautics Board in 1984 to redress display bias, discriminatory booking fees, denial to participating carriers of access to marketing data and restrictive travel agency contracts. Some industry observers believe the following anti-competitive practices still exist:

1. Architectural bias – that make it easier and more reliable for an agent to book a traveller on a CRS vendor airline than on another carrier. This creates the natural tendency of agents to book flights on their CRS vendor airline rather than those of competing airlines and results in substantial incremental revenues accruing to the airline that owns the CRS (the halo effect). Further to this, CRS enhancements that tend to favour the vendor's owning carrier, together with delays in loading information on changes in fares and schedules of competitor airlines, enhance the halo effect.
2. The practice of restrictive provisions in travel agency contracts that make it difficult for agents to change CRSs. Smaller vendors tend to view the contracts as still too restrictive while major CRSs, as the beneficiaries, are more satisfied with the status quo.
3. Many co-hosts complain of an ongoing problem in checking the accuracy of booking fee bills received from vendors and assuring the timeliness and accuracy of marketing data provided by CRS vendors.

4. Owning airlines can use their market power to charge 'supra-competitive' booking fees, which in turn can be passed on to consumers in the form of higher prices (US Department of Transportation, 1991, p. 9).

The post-regulation period up to 1990 witnessed a series of private litigations and a renewed look at regulation. It is believed that the solution to the complex and seemingly intractable problems ushered in by CRSs lies primarily in the field of regulation or legislation that would 'impose striking and substantial changes in the structure and operating practices of CRS' (Guerin-Calvert and Noll, 1991).

The US Department of Transportation's view is that 'stronger rules appear necessary to enhance competition in the airline and CRS industries' (Guerin-Calvert and Noll, 1991). So in May 1991, the US Department of Transportation issued proposals for new rules that could open doors for multi-CRS access, allowing agencies to use one terminal for access to more than one or all the CRSs and could facilitate the use of third-party equipment and software in conjunction with a CRS. With these options, agents could more easily reconfigure the information provided by the CRSs so that it better met their needs. A revision of CRS rules was done in October 1992.

7.5. TECHNOLOGY IN TRAVEL AGENCIES

Travel agents are a vital link in the travel and tourism chain. With the rapid diffusion of computerized reservations terminals (CRTs) in US travel agencies, the agency share of airline ticket sales rose from 57% to 87% shortly after deregulation, and the agency commission rate rose from 8.3% to 10% (Hitchins, 1991, p. 91). By 1990, US travel agencies were selling about 80% of all airline tickets and they used CRSs to make 92% of their domestic airline bookings (US Department of Transportation, 1990, p. 44).

In 1990, travel agencies in the UK accounted for about 85% of package tour sales. Without the agencies and without their interface with the customer, the travel and tourism industry would not have witnessed the tremendous growth that it has over the past two decades. Initial fears that the travel agency's days were numbered as a result of the airlines' development of CRSs proved to be short-lived. Travel agents now play a more important role in the industry than they ever did. The increased importance of the travel agent is related both to the need for 'high touch' to complement an increasingly technology oriented industry and the need for human intelligence to sift the incredible volume of information and services that technology, deregulation and competition now make possible.

Travel agency use of information technology can be divided into three areas: (i) front-office automation; (ii) back-office systems; and (iii) middle-office automation.

Front-office automation refers to systems used to confirm the sale of travel products electronically. *Back-office systems* refer to those computer programs that agents use to gather and manipulate data for record-keeping, analysis and marketing. Included here are accounting systems, programs used to prepare reports for corporate customers, programs that analyse agency's internal operations (e.g. monitoring productivity of staff, tracking commissions, identifying most profitable products, etc.), database management and other software used to track customers' travel patterns in order to market more effectively to them.

Middle-office automation – a third and new category – essentially focuses on quality control issues and involves services typically implemented between the time a booking is made and the time the traveller departs. One system in this category relies on frequent automated queries to a CRS in an attempt to accomplish any or all of the following: (i) identifying better air fares that clients can use for travel on the same itinerary; (ii) getting a wait-listed client on his/her preferred flight; (iii) and/or obtaining the airline seat assignment that the client wants. Another type of quality control system focuses on such things as whether the booking record itself is logical (e.g. whether the hotel night arranged for the date that the traveller will be out of town). Quality control systems also determine whether the booking record has all the information required by the agency for accounting purposes and if the booking itself is in accordance with the client's personal travel preference or the corporate travel policy of the traveller's employer, if travelling on business.

The use of information technology by travel agents also confirms the view that it is the imperative of distribution that will dictate the pace of technology adoption. Technology adoption for travel agency back-office functions continues to lag behind that of the front office.

In 1991, approximately 96% of 40000 US travel agencies were automated with computerized reservations terminals. However, only 59% of US travel agencies had automated accounting systems. In 1985, when 90% of the travel agencies approved by the Airlines Reporting Corporations were automated in the front office, only 25% had automated accounting (*Travel Weekly*, 1991f, p. 1) and the automated systems for the middle office were largely non-existent. Fare-auditing systems first appeared in 1986.

Travel agencies in Europe are also users of CRSs, although the level of usage is far less impressive. As from Spring 1990, national airlines in Western Europe had automated about 40% of IATA-approved agencies in those national carriers' home countries. Allowing for some installations by other vendors, about 44% of agencies had CRSs. Those statistics varied widely from country to country: for example, only 25% of UK-based travel agencies were automated with airline-installed reservations terminals although 90% use videotext. In Germany, 61% of agencies were automated, while in Switzerland it was 58%. Table 6.1 in Chapter 6 shows data for selected European countries on the extent to which national carriers had automated agencies in their own countries.

The evidence from the USA to date is that travel agencies are 'very glad' that they have automated their functions, so much so that 'the question is no longer whether to install computers; it's how best to use them' (*Travel Weekly*, US Travel Agency Survey, 1990d, p. 112). Of course, there are some drawbacks to automation, but the back-office products elicit more criticism than CRSs. In particular, built-in limitations inhibit the development of better accounting systems; often agencies must input the same data several times because of difficulty of downloading information to off-the-shelf programmes, and many systems have little or no analysis capability, churning out numbers with no interpretation to assist agents or their customers in understanding them (*Travel Weekly*, 1990d, p. 23).

In an effort to solve these problems, and/or provide better or unique services to clients, agents have, from 1986, developed or purchased the middle-office quality control products discussed above. The next phase in the development of these systems will involve implementing most of these quality control checks while the sale is actually being made. Of course, some supplemental fare checking, waiting-list clearing and seat booking would still have to be done post-booking because options can become available between booking and travel.

In addition a new category of products, called 'platform products' or 'workstation systems', has emerged – although they are seldom seen in US travel agencies. Their creators, for the most part, are awaiting new CRS rules (due before the end of 1992) that are expected to give the agents more freedom to use third-party hardware and software when accessing CRSs and to use a single personal computer to access multiple CRSs. These rules came into effect in October 1992. About a dozen vendors of such 'platform products' have indicated interest in marketing in the US. Their software would typically allow agencies to: (i) connect with one or more CRSs; (ii) access and search other data-bases at the agency or off premises, possibly including those of cruise lines or tour operators; (iii) speed up the booking process; (iv) simplify staff training with user-friendly formats; and (v) integrate a variety of office functions running the 'gamut' from booking trips to letter-writing, accounting and other chores (speech by Nadine Godwin, *Travel Weekly*'s Managing Editor, 6 April, 1992, Universal Federation of Travel Agents Associations, Automation Seminar, New Delhi, India).

In addition to technology usage by travel agencies to manage their reservations and back-office accounting and to control quality, the technology is also available to alter the mode of distribution of travel-agency services. Developments in the fields of telebooking and interactive automated ticketing machines that promise to dispense with the human interface, together with satellite ticket printers at corporate offices and interactive databases accessible to consumers, via their personal computers at home, will increasingly alter the relationship between the travel agent and the final consumer. This means that travel transactions can take place from comfortable as well as remote locations such as at home (via personal computers) or at work (via satellite printers) or at airport terminals (via airline ticket-dispensing machines, using smart cards) rather than through personal contact with the neighbourhood travel agent. A number of these technologies are diffusing into the travel industry and are increasing efficiency and quality of services offered by travel agents. One suspects, however, that these technologies will not alter the manifest human content of neighbourhood travel agency services.

7.6. TECHNOLOGY IN TOUR OPERATIONS

We have seen in Chapter 2 that the role and importance of tour operators in the travel and tourism industry differs between the USA and Europe. The role of the tour operator is considerably greater in Europe than in the USA. In Europe, tour operators play an important role in the development and introduction of computerized bookings of tour packages themselves. Within the UK, Thomson, the largest tour operator has been very active in the development of technology since the early 1980s. Thomson provides a good example of the role of UK tour operators in automating the distribution of holidays.

Thomson was the first tour operator in the UK to develop its own private viewdata system – Thomson Open-line Programme (TOP) – which, until recently, was unavailable on any other network. Thomson began using videotext in 1982 and the company has, since then, established the largest private videotext system in the world (*Guardian*, 15 September, 1986, p. 7). Thomson claimed that 99% of all its bookings were supplied by travel agents, 85% of which were handled by the computer. Similarly, 80% of Horizon's bookings (Horizon has now merged with Thomsons) come through viewdata (*Financial Weekly*, 7 August 1986, pp. 28–33).

In December 1986, Thomson went a step further by becoming the first tour operator to make bookings available to travel agents by interactive videotext and stopped all reservations via the telephone. If travel agents had not invested in the technology, they could not book Thomson holidays.

UK tour operators are very happy that they invested in automation. Thomson claims that its £20 million investment in information technology over the past 10 years has paid off in productivity terms. The company estimated that labour productivity for 1986 was three times higher than that for 1978 (*Datalink*, 1986). Thomson expanded its services to its customers, carrying 2.5 million passengers in 1986, triple the amount it carried in 1979, but with no increase in staff (*Guardian*, 15 September, 1986). Thomson claims that its holidays can be offered more cheaply because of the computerized booking system linked directly to travel agents. This means that Skytours, its greatly expanded sister company, can be run by just 4 people, compared with the 1000 who would be needed to operate a tour company in the absence of such a computerized system (*Financial Times*, 1985).

In the UK, most packaged holidays can only be accessed through on-line viewdata terminals developed and provided by the major tour operators. This is because UK tour operators have invested in the development of their own viewdata technology, while other suppliers have become partners or co-hosts in airline CRSs, and still others (particularly the small operators) chose not to automate – using conventional telephone calls as the main vehicle for bookings.

In Germany, by contrast, only 5% of holidays are booked through viewdata terminals (Hitchins, 1991). With the exception of Germany, tour operators have not been so active as airlines in the development of CRSs and, today, none of the major CRSs are tour-operator-dominated. Touristic Union International (TUI), which controls a quarter of all package-tour sales in Germany, has a 25% stake in 'Start', Germany's national reservation service (Drexl, 1987). In addition to TUI, other smaller tour operators sell through to the system.

7.7. TECHNOLOGY IN HOTELS

The ability of computers to store, process, manipulate and distribute information has greatly improved the efficiency of hotels. By releasing staff time from the mundane paper-pushing functions within the hotel, computers can greatly enhance the opportunities for staff utilization in the hospitality, service and guest-contact points of the hotel. By so doing, the quality of service that hotels offer their guests can be greatly improved.

Image communication is also revolutionizing the way in which hotel bed-nights and other services, such as conference facilities, are sold.

Hotels use computers in their core-information processing centres of marketing and distribution, front-office, back-office and food and beverage control (American Hotel and Motel Association, 1983; Sheldon, 1984; and Bruce, 1984). Information technologies are diffusing in eight key areas of hotel operations:

- marketing, distribution, reservations and sales;
- telecommunications;
- guest accounting;

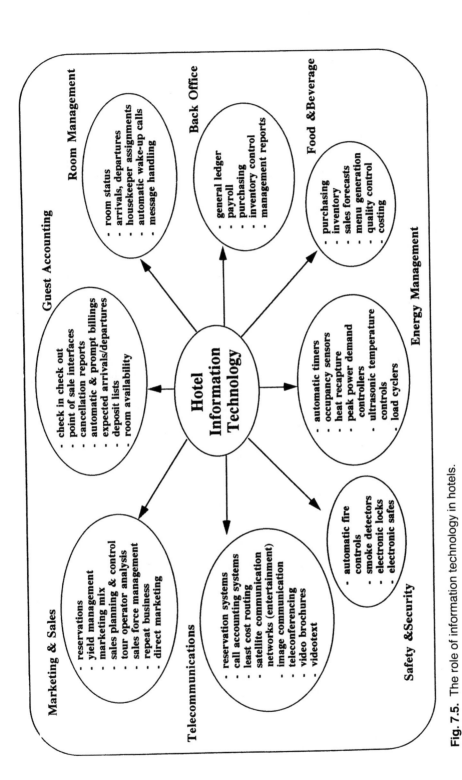

Fig. 7.5. The role of information technology in hotels.

Source: Sheldon, 1984; Poon, 1987a.

- room management;
- back office;
- food and beverage control;
- energy management; and
- safety and security.

Figure 7.5 summarizes the areas of the hotel operations in which technologies are diffusing.

7.7.1. Marketing, Distribution and Sales

Product distribution is a critically important function of hotels. Information technologies, such as computerized reservations systems and video brochures, assist hotels in marketing and distributing their bed-nights. For hotels, the employment of information technologies to link together their front-office, back-office and food and beverage departments may be necessary for the efficient and cost-effective delivery of their services. However, it will not be sufficient to guarantee the sale of hotel bed-nights. Without links to international marketing and distribution networks, hotel bed-nights cannot be sold. The case of hotels in the Caribbean clearly highlights this fact. It is commonplace for many of them to be non-users of computer technologies in their internal management functions but, at the same time, to be externally linked to international computerized reservation networks (Poon, 1987a). Similarly, the major technological flagships of the Holiday Corporation are its reservations and communications systems (Holidex 1, Holidex 11 and Hi-Net), which are in the distribution, marketing and product-packaging areas of the hotel company's production system. In 1986 Hi-Net was the largest privately owned satellite communications network in the world.

Reservations are a key to the sale of hotel bed-nights. Reservation systems, depending on the software and sophistication, contain information and generate reports on: (i) rooms available by type each day; (ii) the numbers of guests expected to arrive and depart each day; (iii) reservations that have changes made to them on a particular day; (iv) cancellations by day; (v) deposits by guests; (vi) numbers; and (vii) date of arrival. In addition, the database can generate forecasts on expected arrivals, departures and rooms sold. Information contained in, and generated by, hotel reservation systems is an invaluable source of marketing information and can generate mailing lists, client profiles and preferences. It can also monitor hotel performance through the development and processing of guest questionnaires. Reservation systems also allow hotels to carry out travel-agency and tour-operator analyses in order to determine which agencies and operators consistently generate business for the hotels.

7.7.2. Communications

There are two principal areas in which information technologies are helping hotels to improve their communications: (i) in their internal inter-departmental communications; and (ii) in their external links with agents, suppliers, reservation systems and data networks. The internal interdepart-mental links of the hotel are facilitated by computers and communications technologies, which serve to integrate the front-office, back-office and food-and-beverage operations. This is facilitated through computer-to-computer communications. The external hotel communication links are necessary between hotel and head office, between hotels and their marketing/distribution agents and between hotel guests and the inter-national environment, for example, entertainment and/or stock-market information.

Communications technologies used by hotels include digital telephone systems, teleconferencing, satellite broadcasting, videotext and audiovisual information tools, image communications and various communication networks for reservations and communications.

Telephone systems used in hotels have been substantially improved to incorporate features such as call accounting systems. These systems can automatically track calls made by guests so that they can be promptly identified and billed. Least-cost routing options automatically send each call over the cheapest transmission networks. The use of these systems has substantially reduced the need for telephone operators. Automatic call-accounting systems now help hotels to transform their telephone calls into an important profit centre of the hotel (Personal communication, Chervenak, August 1985). As a marketing technique, for example, hotels can offer long-distance telephone calls at discount rates to their guests and still find it profitable.

Teleconferencing involves the transmission of both voice and video via telecommunications technology. It allows conferences and meetings to be held where participants are in different locations. Teleconferencing requires the use of earth stations and satellite transpondents, which are both very costly. Two types of teleconferencing facilities are available: interactive (which allows two-way transmission and receipt of both voice and video at one or more locations) and receive-only (where information flows in only one direction). This technology makes it possible for a hotel's conference room to become a lecture theatre for delegates on conferences where the main speaker might be elsewhere. It also allows for closer association among hotels situated at different locations.

Satellite communications are also important entertainment tools for the hotel industry. This is especially the case where hotels can increase services to their guests by transmitting live sporting events such as the World cup, Wimbledon, the Olympic Games and Super Bowl.

In the guest rooms, videotext terminals are connected to the television screen and to the telephone (via a modem) so travellers can gain access to distant information sources. On these terminals, hotel guests can access information on travel and schedules, news reports, updates on stock prices, and many other subjects depending on the networks to which the hotel is connected.

7.7.3. Guest Accounting

Guest-accounting systems are often contained within the reservation system. They keep track of individual guest charges and can be interfaced with point-of-sale terminals in restaurants, bars and shops throughout the hotel. This greatly increases efficiency and saves potential loss of revenue through unrecorded transactions. The guest history file enables frequent guests to be identified for special attention as it can store data on special requests from previous visits. This could help to encourage repeat business through the provision of special services.

7.7.4. Room Management

Room-management systems can give updated information on room occupancy and status and they assist in scheduling housekeeper duties for maximum efficiency. Rooming lists, arrivals, stay-overs, extended stays, departures and room preferences can all be handled by room-management systems. Automatic wake-up calls and message handling are also possible with these systems.

7.7.5. Back Office

The back-office procedures in a hotel are similar to general business applications and include general ledger, payroll, purchasing, inventory control, cash flow and revenue control and management reports. Technology makes the workload easier in the back-office by automating many of the frequent repetitive, data entry and processing functions. And, by extension, while technology saves on labour, it releases valuable human hours for guest contacts.

7.7.6. Food and Beverage

Food-and-beverage systems allow the hotel to better plan and manage inventory, costing and sales forecasting of its food and beverages. Meals can be better planned and coordinated, and interfaces with guest accounting and back-office systems can increase efficiency. Other technologies available to assist hotels in controlling costs and minimizing theft include electronically controlled drink dispensing machines and robot bars (electronically controlled bars available in guest rooms); while point-of-sale interfaces are important in effectively tracking guest purchases at bars and restaurants.

7.7.7. Energy Management

Another important area of technology impact, particularly since the quadrupling of the price of oil in the 1973–1974 oil boom period, is energy control. Hotels are large consumers of energy. Electronic control systems that help them control energy consumption include water-flow restrictors, automatic timer clocks, load cycles or programmable controllers, automatic lighting controls, room-occupancy sensors, and solar heating.

7.7.8. Safety and Security

In the field of safety and security, electronic devices and systems have been developed in order to aid hotel management in better protecting lives and properties. Among the systems and devices developed are automatic fire control, electronic locks, intrusion detectors (e.g. closed-circuit television, seismic detectors, infra-red beams, radio frequency fields, etc.), employee identification systems, forced entry alarms and watchman tour systems.

7.7.9. Stages of Technology Adoption

There are three clearly identifiable stages in the adoption of information technology in hotels: (i) the clerical stage; (ii) the administrative stage; and (iii) the tactical stage – each having different impacts on hotel operations (Gamble, 1991). The differences among these stages can be gleaned from Table 7.2, which identifies the nature of technology usage and the types of impacts on hotels. In the clerical stage, the main impacts are labour displacement and improved efficiency and control. In the administrative stage, computers assist hotels in carrying out a number of functions including reservations, accounting, cash-flow management, inventory control and guest history. The tactical stage is marked by the full integration of front office, back office and food and beverage departments into a total information system. Use of computers to carry out tactical functions in hotels result in the optimization of yield and sales, better rates of return and more effective direct selling.

Table 7.2 Stages of technology usage in hotels

Stages	Main functions	Impacts
I: Clerical	Stock control Reservation records Payroll Accounting	Labour displacement Better control Improved efficiency
II: Administrative	Reservations Accounting Cash-flow control Planned maintenance Dynamic inventory control True food and beverage control Word processing Automatic guest history	Better customer service Lower labour turnover Lower working capital Better materials management Increased revenues
III: Tactical	Determination of marketing mix Financial management Personnel and industrial relations Bidding strategy for banqueting Food production, management and scheduling Materials management Room management	Improved sales planning and control Optimization of yield Optimum selection of sales and advertising budgets Improved negotiating position with suppliers and tour operators Better rate of return More effective direct selling Better forecasting and planning

Source: Gamble, 1991.

7.7.10. A Total Information System

The integration of computers and communication technologies allows hotels to control their internal operations (e.g. front office, back office and food and beverage departments) and external operations (e.g. reservation systems, marketing, distribution and links to external data sources) from a single integrated management system. This comprehensive system of information management can become a very powerful tool for wealth creation for the hotel industry. With a comprehensive system in place, all levels of management are supposed to be involved in it and to depend on it to inform most decision-making. There is also integration of the internal computer and communications capabilities of the hotel with external data sources.

7.7.11. Smart Buildings and Resort Offices

Technology's role in hotels is not limited to its impact on the information-intensive aspects of operations. It also has an important role in the construction of infrastructure in the tourism industry. As such, the design, development and function of buildings are greatly affected by information technologies. This is evident in the development of *'smart' buildings* and *resort offices* in Japan. Today, the development of intelligent buildings – buildings incorporating automated digital telecommunications, office-automation systems and building management systems – plays as important a role in improving efficiency of office workers as automation has played on the shop-floor of manufacturing industry (Gann, 1991, p.469). These all-electronic 'smart' buildings are not limited to offices, but are diffusing at a rapid rate in Japan in the area of resort offices (Personal Communication, David Gann, Science Policy Research Unit, Sussex University, December 1991).

Resort offices are hotels providing advanced communications to permit short periods of telecommuting of 1–3 weeks in pleasant locations providing sports and leisure activities such as golf. Resort offices are peculiar to Japan where people take fewer holidays – the idea behind the concept being that 'people will work harder if they go on holiday to work.' (Gann, 1991, p.469). Resort offices were found to be suitable for project-group work and brainstorming activities in the areas of 'R&D' design and planning, report writing and software programming. The development of resort offices is occurring faster in Japan than anywhere else in the world. It is too early to tell whether the trend will take off elsewhere. What is certain, however, is that the diffusion will be far more rapid in the business and related segments of the tourism industry than in the pure leisure segment of the industry. So far, all-electronic, 'humanless', hotels that are already operating in Japan and London have had a negligible impact on the leisure segment of the travel industry. It is worth noting that the competitive advantage of Asian hotels and the superior performance of Singapore Airlines, for example, are human- rather than technology-driven.

7.8. CONCLUSIONS

In tourism, it is not travel agents or hotels or airlines that are adopting IT, but all of them. Airlines have emerged as the technology leaders in the arena of participants and CRSs have emerged as the dominant technology.

The imperatives of distribution will dictate the pace of technology adoption in the travel and tourism industry. The rapid diffusion of a system of information technologies throughout the tourism industry has four key impacts:

- it will improve the efficiency of production;
- it will improve the quality of services;
- it will lead to the generation of new services (image communication, satellite printers, flexible holidays); and
- it will lead to the spread of a whole new industry best practice.

It is not just technology that is being diffused throughout the travel and tourism industry, but a whole new industry common sense or 'best practice'. The new best practice will change the organizational and managerial common sense for best productivity and most profitable practice in the travel and tourism industry.

These radical changes in the travel and tourism industry warrant competitive strategies for long-term survival and competitiveness.

IV
COMPETITIVE STRATEGIES

8

COMPETITIVE SCENARIO

8.1. INTRODUCTION

The boundaries within the tourism industry, and between this industry and others, are becoming increasingly blurred. Players are crossing each others' borders more than ever before: banks move into travel agencies; insurance companies acquire hotel interests; airlines provide credit cards; department stores operate travel agencies; and pleasure-boat companies move into hotels. Diagonal integration – a process where firms use information technologies to logically combine services for best productivity and most profitability – will be one of the most significant developments in the travel and leisure industry. This chapter introduces the concept of diagonal integration and compares it with other forms of integration, namely vertical integration, horizontal integration and diversification.

Diagonal integration will become a key tool for controlling the process of value creation in the tourism industry. It will continue to blur the boundaries among industry players and make the travel and tourism industry an engine of wealth creation. The industry's borders will be increasingly re-defined. The industry will become more *systems-like* in nature. One of the key implications of the trend towards diagonal integration is that competitors will increasingly come from outside the industry. Equally, diagonal integration will offer opportunities for travel and tourism players to move into other industries.

This chapter also introduces the value chain – an important tool for tracing the process of value creation in the tourism industry. An analysis of the industry's value chain is the key to determining how each player creates value. It is also key to understanding why and how each players' position could change as the rules of the game change.

New tourism will alter the process of value creation in the travel and tourism industry. It will change the relative positions of different players in the industry. Players that are closest to the consumers and those that can most efficiently control the production, manipulation and distribution of the industry's information, are expected to gain. Travel agents, airlines and suppliers on site are all expected to increase their influence on the industry's wealth-creating process. The role of tour operators is expected to decline. Airlines will continue to dominate the industry's value chain. Some activities will take on added importance in the industry's wealth-creating process, for example, human-resources development, retail distribution, product development, service delivery, customer service and client management.

8.2. THE TOURISM SYSTEM

The travel and leisure experience is a living experience. Almost everything one would normally do at home, one does on holiday, and more; such as eating, drinking, sleeping, playing, shopping, travelling, driving, renting a car, making telephone calls, having sex, taking beauty treatments (e.g. hair cuts, hair braids, massages), working, swimming, sunbathing, attending shows and live performances, 'play mas' and paying bills. Together, all of these elements of the leisure experience make up an industry with enormous wealth-creating potential.

Nine players make up the tourism industry. These core industry players are organized in a systemic flow of production, the tourism system, as represented in Figure 8.1. Eight of those players – airlines, holiday-makers, hotels, on-site service providers, incoming agents, tour operators, financial services suppliers and travel agents – are the *producers* of travel and tourism services. These players are organized to deliver services to the ninth player – tourists and passengers – who are the *consumers* of the industry's output.

The services of airlines (e.g. transportation, baggage handling), hotels (e.g. bed-nights, check in, food and drink) and other suppliers on site (e.g. trains, taxis, car rentals, villas, guest houses, restaurants, pleasure boats, sports and entertainment) constitute the main 'products' of the tourism industry. In the delivery of these products, the distribution channels of the industry are of fundamental importance. This is so because the products of the tourism industry are invisible services, incapable of feel, smell, touch and inspection at the point of sale.

Travel agents and tour operators perform the main distribution function for the tourism industry, although airlines and other suppliers sell directly to the passengers and tourists too. CRSs have become the dominant channel for the distribution of travel and leisure products. Financial services suppliers facilitate payment transactions for services bought from suppliers (e.g. airlines and hotels) and services (e.g. package tours, airline tickets, hotel bed-nights, sightseeing tours) sold to consumers.

'*Holiday-makers*' is the catch-all term introduced here to describe

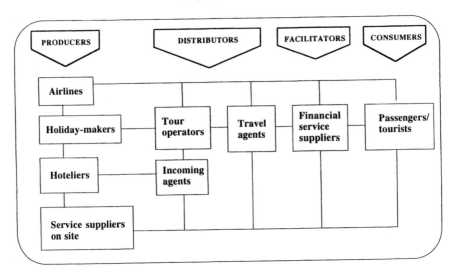

Fig. 8.1. The tourism system.

companies and corporate entities whose business it is to create and deliver holidays. Holiday-makers include cruise ships (e.g. Carnival, Princess, Royal Caribbean), all-inclusive resorts (e.g. Club Med, Sandals, Super-Club, Robinson Club), theme parks (e.g. Disneyland, Centerparcs), boating companies (e.g. The Moorings, Stevens Yachts, Go Vacations). Holiday-makers differ from conventional hotels and airlines because the output of the holiday-maker is not a hotel bed-night or an airline seat, but a total experience. Holiday-makers differ from conventional tour operators because their objectives are not simply to package and sell a holiday. The key distinguishing characteristic of holiday-makers is the fact that they *make* as well as *deliver* the holiday experience. Holiday-makers are to the travel and tourism industry what the Japanese are to the automobile industry (see Chapter 3). Both focus on quality and value for money. They are very close to their consumers and have the flexibility to respond to the changing needs of the marketplace. Holiday-makers have been and will continue to be one of the most resilient and fast-growing sectors of the travel and tourism industry.

Incoming agents play a special role in the tourism industry. Destination-based, these agents act as the intermediaries between tour operators and their clients, and between local suppliers and tour operators. Incoming agents attend to visitors' needs and ensure that tour operators deliver the promise made in their brochures. Incoming agents could play a greater role in the value creation process of the industry as consumer protection laws tighten and as tour operators strive for greater quality control throughout the vacation.

Marketing and promotion agencies also play an important role in the tourism industry. They market and promote the destination in the market-place, develop marketing strategies, design and implement marketing campaigns, collateral materials (e.g. brochures, videos) on behalf of tourist destinations, airlines, hotel groups and other suppliers. *Hotel representatives* also represent hotels and resorts in the marketplace. They play the role of 'middle men' for hotels, acting on their behalf in negotiations and communications with tour operators and consumers. Some hotel representatives even handle the reservations on behalf of hotels. Finally, government-supported tourist boards represent and promote the destination in the marketplace.

Financial services suppliers are important facilitators in the travel and tourism value chain. They not only provide travellers cheques, charge cards, credit cards and currency exchange, but also travel insurance services, travel payment systems (e.g. Citicorp, USA) and even tour-operator and travel-agency services (e.g. Midland Bank, UK, which owned the Thomas Cook travel-agency chain and was since sold for UK £200 million to the German LTU group in June 1992). Financial services suppliers are increasingly crossing their borders and diagonally integrating into the travel and tourism industry. Companies, like American Express, are even moving beyond the financial services and traditional travel and leisure activities, and now provide the services of complementary airport lounges to their Gold Card members in Argentina, Barbados, Brazil, Ecuador, Mexico, Miami and Puerto Rico.

Consumers constitute the final, but by no means the least important, element of the tourism system. As we have seen in Chapter 5, consumers are no longer passive acceptors of mass, standardized and rigidly packaged holidays. They are more mature, more experienced, more 'green', more flexible and infinitely more independent. Consumers are the most important link in the tourism wealth-creating system. The travel and leisure industry will be more consumer- rather than producer-driven. For those who can anticipate and cater to the needs of the new consumers, the prospects for creating wealth are enormous. As we will see in Chapter 9, putting consumers first is one of the key principles for competitive success in the travel and leisure industry.

8.3. THE INDUSTRY VALUE CHAIN

A value chain is an analytical tool developed for tracing the process of value-creation in an industry (Porter, 1987). Understanding how an industry creates value is key to understanding the role of each player in the industry. It is also key to understanding why and how each players' position

Value-creating activities such as route and yield management, marketing and public relations, tour guiding, advice and counselling, purchase of airline and hotel capacity, destination representation, risk brokerage, distribution, information gathering, bookings, confirmations, packaging and selling, are all information-driven activities. Some of these activities will take on increased importance as industry players strive to stay ahead of the game; these include human-resources development, retail distribution, product development, service delivery, customer service and client management.

Industry players will attempt to control as many of the industry's value-creation activities as possible. *It is no longer relevant whether a company is an airline, a travel agent, hotel or tour operator. As the boundaries among players are re-defined, what becomes more relevant are the activities along the value chain that they control.* New tourism will change the value chain in two areas:

1. Those players in control of the manipulation and distribution of the industry's *information* will increase their share of the industry's value. Airlines already have a head start in this area.

2. Those players closest to the *consumer* will also gain. Travel agencies and suppliers on site (such as hotels, cruise ships and resorts) are therefore expected to increase their importance in the industry.

In Section 8.6 some of the strategic moves that industry players will need to make in order to stay ahead of the game will be considered. We turn now to explore the concept of diagonal integration – a tool that will give industry players the capacity to control the industry's value-creation process.

8.5. DIAGONAL INTEGRATION

Diagonal integration will become the key vehicle for controlling the value-creation process of the travel and tourism industry. As the industry is increasingly driven by information and consumers, firms can diagonally integrate to control the more lucrative areas of value creation. The purpose of diagonal integration is not to produce a single service and market it to a supermarket of clients. Rather, the objective is to produce a range of services and to sell them to a target group of consumers. The consumers targeted are expected to consume simultaneously these services at regular intervals over their lifetime (e.g. travel + insurance + holiday + personal banking).

The essence of diagonal integration is that: $2 + 2 = 5$. In other words, the benefits of integrating activities are greater than providing each activity separately. Diagonal integration is created by new information technologies. It is the process by which firms use information technologies to logically combine services (e.g. financial services and travel agencies) for best productivity and most profits. One of the key attractions to firms in diagonally integrating is the lower costs of production associated with it. This is made possible through the *synergies, systems gains* and *scope economies* firms reap when they integrate diagonally.

Firms, such as American Express, are diagonally integrated to produce a whole package of services including financial services, investment services and travel-related services. The economics of diagonal integration is leading to the cross-fertilization of many unconventional services. This will have tremendous implications for travel and tourism suppliers: competitors will increasingly come from outside the industry and industry players will have increased opportunities to enter other industries.

Diagonal integration is a distinct and unprecedented development in the travel and leisure industry. It defies conventional typologies of vertical and horizontal integration as well as diversification. In what follows, it will be shown how diagonal integration differs from other types of integration and why this strategy will grow in importance for industry players.

8.5.1. Vertical Integration

Firms integrate vertically to control different stages of production. They do this in order to defend themselves against shortages of important raw materials and unreliable delivery times. Vertical integration has been a common practice among manufacturing firms, such as automobile manufacturers. Typically, an automobile manufacturer would vertically integrate to control iron and steel production, component and parts manufacture, as well as the assembly, marketing and distribution of cars.

Some of the representative activities into which an automobile manufacture can vertically integrate are contained in Figure 8.4. From this figure two types of vertical integration are evident: (i) backward integration and (ii) forward integration. By integrating backwards, a firm attempts to control the *inputs* and raw material supplies that are vital to its production process. By integrating forward, a firm attempts to control the *market* for its output. Control of the market has been a very important area of activity for automobile suppliers. Automobile manufacturers entered the financial services sector in order to provide loans to consumers to purchase their cars. Toyota dealers in the UK, for example, offer car buyers special insurance deals in order to encourage purchase of their cars.

Vertical integration is not so pervasive in the travel and tourism industry as it is in the manufacturing sector. This is so because travel and leisure suppliers focus on the delivery of finished services. They do not focus on producing components or the 'raw materials' for their trade. In any event, the raw materials of travel and leisure suppliers are already finished products (e.g. cars, beds, towels, linens, aircrafts and surfboards).

Airlines, for example, do not attempt to manufacture aircraft. Even in the development of computerized reservations systems (CRSs), the emphasis has always been on the development of software rather than on the production of computers and telecommunications hardware. From Figure 8.5, it can be seen that airlines mainly integrate forward into charter flights, holiday packaging, retail distribution and sales. This is done in order to control the marketing, distribution and sales of their services. British Airways, for example, is vertically integrated in the areas of charter operations, tour operations and travel agencies. British Airways owns a charter subsidiary, Caledonian Airways, which controls 7.8% of the UK charter market. Four Corners, a travel agency chain, is also owned and operated by British Airways. In addition the airline owns two tour-operating companies – BA Holidays and Overseas Air Travel Limited and has 50% and 51% share in Redwing and Alta Holidays, respectively (EIU, Travel and Tourism Analyst, No. 1., 1990). Some airlines are also involved in hotels. Lufthansa (Germany), for example, operates the Penta and Kempinski hotel chains through one of its companies, Lufthansa Hotel GmbH.

Hotels also focus on the management and delivery of hotel bed-nights rather than developing construction companies to build hotels. Hotels do not vertically integrate to produce linens, cutlery, pots and pans for their trade. However, they engage in several associations (e.g. franchises, consortia) in order to obtain competitive prices for goods and services they must buy. Hotels undertake only limited levels of forward integration. Even the large hotel chains only indirectly control the marketing, distribution and sale of their products (via reservation systems, brochures and toll-free numbers). The Carson Hospitality Group is one of the few enterprises that has major controlling interests in hotels (Radisson) as well as travel agencies (Carson Travel Network, formerly Ask Mr Foster) and cruise ships (Radisson Diamond).

Tour operators are the most vertically integrated of all industry players. Tour operators integrate both backward and forward. From Figure 8.6, it can be seen that tour operators integrate backwards in order to control as many of the elements of the holiday package as possible (e.g. hotel rooms and charter seats). They also integrate in a forward direction in order to control the distribution and sales of their packaged tours. Tour operators in the UK, for example, are heavily involved in travel agency and air-charter operations. The Monopolies and Mergers Commission in the UK found that a complex monopoly existed in the travel-agency/tour-operator market with 70% of travel-agency services in the UK being supplied by tour operators (*Financial Times*, 11 September, 1986, p. 10). Thomsons, the largest tour operator in the UK also owns Lunn Poly, the third largest

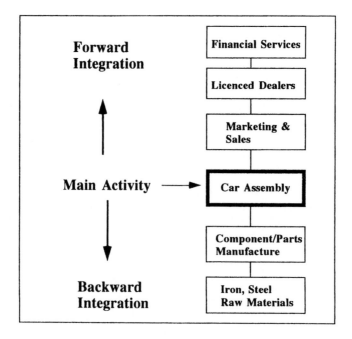

Fig. 8.4. Vertical integration in the automobile industry.
- Automobile manufacturers undertake both backward and forward integration.
- Backward integration allows control of raw material supplies.
- Forward integration is undertaken in order to control markets for finished products.
- The Japanese, for example, developed overseas subsidiaries in order to capture market share in the USA and UK.

travel agency, and is also heavily involved in the air-charter market. Thomsons also operate Britannia Airways, a charter airline.

Particularly as a result of Germany's tough consumer protection laws, German tour operators tend to have more ownership and management interests in hotels as a way to control the service levels in hotels. TUI, the largest tour operator in Germany also owns Club Robinson, a German version of Club Med, while Neckerman and ITS own Club Adiana and Club Calimera, respectively.

8.5.2. Horizontal Integration

Horizontal integration takes place when firms at the same stage of production (e.g. airlines) come together to affect the level of *concentration* within the industry. Firms integrate in this way in order to increase *buying*

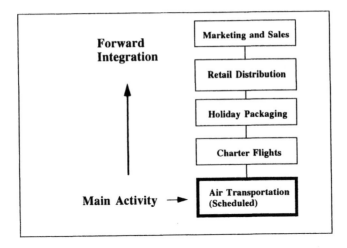

Fig. 8.5. Vertical integration in the tourism industry: airlines
- Airlines pursue strategies of vertical integration in order to control the marketing and distribution of their seats.
- Airlines have charter subsidiaries as well as interests in tour operations and travel agencies (in Europe). They also operate their own ticketing offices.
- Like tour operators airlines are also integrated backwards along the industry's value chain, some having interests in hotels and other services.

power over their suppliers (monopsony power) as well as to control the *distribution and sale* of their product in the marketplace (monopoly power). An extreme case of horizontal integration occurred in the mid-1970s when the oil producing and exporting countries (OPEC) formed a cartel to quadruple the price of oil. They achieved this through controlling the output of each producer, via a quota system.

The travel and leisure industry is characterized by very high levels of concentration – particularly among airlines, tour operators and travel agencies.

8.5.2.1. Airlines

The US airline industry is very concentrated. In 1985, 7 years after deregulation, Texas Air Corporation and American, the two largest airlines in the USA accounted for 32.4% of the airline market (measured by revenue passenger miles). In that year, the top ten airlines in the USA accounted for 94.1% of the revenue passenger miles carried (*Travel Weekly*, 26 March 1987b). In 1988, Air Canada and Canadian Airlines International, together with their affiliated airlines, accounted for 90.6% of all scheduled passengers carried in and out of Canada and 87.2% of all

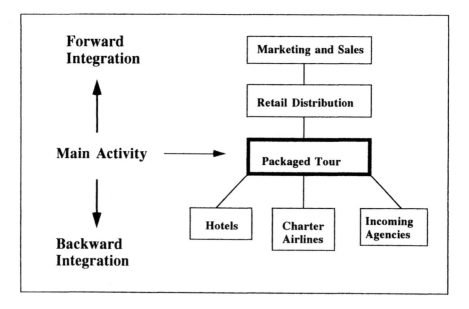

Fig. 8.6. Vertical integration in the travel and tourism industry: tour operators.
- European tour operators are more vertically integrated than other industry players.
- Tour operators are integrated forward into marketing, retail distribution and sales of their packaged holidays.
- Tour operators are also integrated backwards into the ownership and control of package components (e.g. charter flights, hotels and incoming agencies).

scheduled passenger kilometres flown (Economist Intelligence Unit, 1990b). In 1987, British Airways (with a fleet of 163 aircrafts) and British Caledonian (with a fleet of 29) controlled 81% and 11% respectively of all passengers carried on British scheduled airlines (*Daily Telegraph*, 24 April, 1987, p. 30). The £237 million merger between British Caledonian and British Airways in 1987 has created a very concentrated air-transportation market in Britain.

8.5.2.2. Tour operators

In the UK in 1986, Thomson and Intasun, the two largest tour operators through their Britannia and Air Europe charter subsidiaries respectively, controlled 68.11% of the charter seats on offer (*Sunday Times*, 20 July, 1986, p. 6). These 'big three' have virtually squeezed out or taken over all their medium-sized competitors. In 1988, these three operators shared 62% of the market (Euromonitor, 1988). In 1990, Thomsons, the largest tour operator merged with Horizon, the third largest operator. Thomson controlled 32% of the tour operator market in 1990 (*Economist Intelligence Unit, Travel and Tourism Analyst*, No. 1, 1990a). Intasun, a subsidiary of the International Leisure Group is no longer in operation. A proposed Airtours/Owners Abroad merger will make this combined operator the largest in the UK with an estimated 34% of the market in 1993 (*Travel Trade Gazette*, 1993). The 17 top companies in Germany shared 60% of the market; in France the top five companies shared 40% of the market; and in Japan, the top seven companies share only 33% of the market (Euromonitor, 1988). The tour operator industry is also concentrated. In the USA, less than 3% of the independent tour operators controlled 30% of revenues and 37% of the passengers, while operators with over 50000 passengers annually accounted for 68% of the market (United States Tour Operators Association, 1975, p. 5).

Following the surprise purchase of Thomas Cook by the German LTU group, this German operator is poised to become a major player in the pan-European travel market. The 151-year-old Thomas Cook is the world's largest issuer of travellers cheques, has 1800 outlets in 114 countries and in 1991 made a profit of UK £9 million. LTU is one of the most vertically integrated travel companies in Germany. It is Germany's third largest tour operator and owns the second largest airline, behind Lufthansa, with a fleet of 28 aircraft. It also owns Jahn, Tjaereborg and Meiers travel agencies (with incoming agencies in the US, Caribbean and Asia), operates Nile cruises and owns resort hotels. In 1990, LTU announced a 50:50 joint venture with France's Club Mediterranée to launch German-speaking holiday clubs (*Travel Trade Gazette*, 1992b).

8.5.2.3. Travel agencies

High levels of concentration are also evident among travel agencies. As early as the 1980s, it was found that:

> The years between 1981 and 1983 marked the emergence of one of the most profound trends that the travel industry has witnessed in recent times – the tremendous growth of the multi-million dollar agencies and the accelerated concentration of sales in the upper tier of the trade.
>
> (*Travel Weekly*, 1984, p. 4)

According to a recent study of the US travel-agency market, more than 73% of all retail agencies handled over one million dollars in business annually. Together, the million-dollar-plus agencies accounted for 91% of all travel agency sales (*Travel Weekly*, Louis Harris Study, 28 June 1990e).

In 1991, the top 50 agencies in the USA had just under 4000 retail outlets, representing nearly one in eight of the 32000 travel agencies outlets at the end of 1991 (*Travel Weekly*, 1992a). For these 50 agencies, iles for 1001 totalled about US$15 billion, representing nearly one-third of total US agency air sales of US$48 billion (*Travel Weekly*, 1992a).

The higher level of concentration (horizontal integration) in the tourism industry is not limited to travel agencies, but also among airlines and tour operators. Concentration is also evident among cruise lines as mergers, acquisitions and consolidations have created a small number of mega-carriers. The four largest companies – Carnival, Closter Cruises, Royal Caribbean Cruise Lines and Princess Cruises – control more than half of the berths marketed out of the United States (Caribbean Tourism Organization, 1992a).

The travel and tourism industry will continue to be characterized by high levels of concentration and fierce competition. This combination of *concentration* and *competition* in the industry results in a unique mixture of market forces, which create worrying issues for policy-makers: Can the air transportation industry become a stable and profitable oligopoly? Will the interest of the travelling public be adequately served?

8.5.3. Diversification

The concept of diversification applies when a firm undertakes the provision of a new product, without ceasing the production of existing lines. The line into which the firm has diversified need not be related to its former activity. One example is the investment by oil companies in computers and information-based services. No synergies need develop between oil production and the firms' investments in Silicon Valley. Electronics and computers provide the new wave of goods and services, and it is sufficient that these diversified investments provide a good return. An example of a diversified enterprise is British American Tobacco, which produces everything from tobacco to insurance.

Airlines are perhaps the most diversified of all travel-industry players. Several airlines including Aer Lingus and SAS derived over a quarter of their revenues from non-airline activities (Clairmonte and Cavanagh, 1984). Of the 22 major airlines examined by Clairmonte and Cavanagh, 73% were involved in tour operations; 86% had hotel interests; 13% had interests in car rentals; 68% were associated with other airlines and all of them had related interests such as catering, international merchant banking, worldwide aviation insurance and re-insurance.

Virgin Atlantic provides an interesting example of a company that has diversified into the airline business. The founder of Virgin Atlantic, Richard Branson, was involved in the retailing and recording businesses before forming the airline.

Table 8.1 Diagonal integration compared with other forms of integration

Characteristics	Forms of integration			
	Vertical integration	Horizontal integration	Diversification	Diagonal integration
Production focus	Many stages of production	Same stage of production	Many unrelated activities	Many tightly-related services
Objectives of integration	Control over stages of production	Monopoly power/concentration	Spread risks	Get close to the consumer/Lower costs of production
Integration mechanism	Acquisition/start new businesses	Acquisition/collusion	Acquisition/start new activities	Information partnerships / Strategic alliances / Strategic acquisitions
Operationalization	Integrated production and management	Operate as one entity	'Arms length'	Synergistic production/shared networks
Orientation of production	Production-oriented	Supply-oriented	Investment-oriented	Consumer-oriented
Production concept	Economies of scale	Economies of scale	Production unrelated to markets	Economies of scale / Economies of scope / Synergies/systems gains
Examples	Ford (old days)	American Airlines	British American Tobacco (BAT)	American Express / Midland Bank

8.5.4. Diagonal Integration Is Different

The distinguishing feature of diagonal integration is not that firms at the same stage of production come together to affect the concentration levels within the industry (as with horizontal integration) or that they try to control various stages of production (vertical integration) or they enter other activities in order to spread their risks (diversification). The distinguishing feature of diagonal integration is that firms become involved in tightly related activities to reduce costs and to get closer to their consumers. *Diagonal integration is mainly a phenomenon of the services sector and is created by information technology.*

The key objectives of diagonal integration are to get close to the consumers and to reduce costs through economies of scope, system gains and synergies (see Table 8.1, which compares diagonal integration with other forms of integration). By contrast, vertical integration is production-oriented, horizontal integration is supply-oriented, and diversification is investment-oriented. From Table 8.1, it can also be seen that while *economies of scope*, systems gains and synergies are the driving forces of diagonal integration, *economies of scale* dominate vertical and horizontal integration strategies.

Another major difference between diagonal integration and other types of integration is the integration mechanism. Whether it is vertical integration, horizontal integration or diversification, *ownership* tends to be the key mechanism for integration – be it the start-up of a business or take-over. With diagonal integration, by contrast, ownership may not be necessary. In fact, diagonal integration could be achieved through *strategic alliances* and *information partnerships*. With information partnerships, firms can: (i) collaborate to share resources, information and client data-bases; (ii) reduce operating costs; (iii) share the costs of technology development; and (iv) gain bargaining power. *A firm does not necessarily have to own activities along an industry's value chain in order to create value.* More important than ownership is the shared information and networking among different value-creating activities such that synergies, systems gains, scale and scope economies are realized, thereby increasing production efficiency.

The concept of diagonal integration is graphically represented in Figure 8.7. From the figure, is can be seen that information technologies provide a key platform for firms to diagonally integrate. Firms can use information technology to identify their target group of consumers as well as to integrate production of services to satisfy their consumers. Firms, such as American Express, integrate diagonally by tailor-making a number of tightly-related services (e.g. personal banking, credit cards, insurance and travel services) all of which their target consumers are expected to consume at regular intervals over their lifetime. At Amex Europe Ltd, for example,

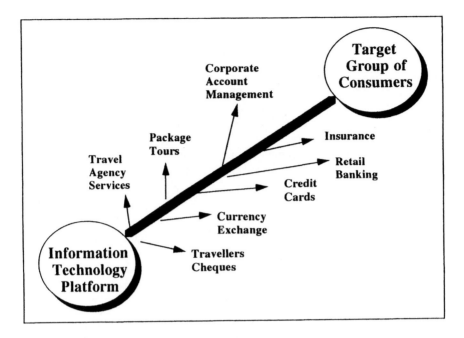

Fig. 8.7. Diagonal integration in the travel and tourism industry.
- Firms integrate diagonally in order to get close to their consumers and to lower production costs.
- Information technology provides the critical platform for diagonal integration.
- Diagonally integrating firms benefit from economies of scope, systems gains and synergies.
- When economies of scope exist, it is cheaper for one firm to produce a combination of services, than for many firms to produce each separately.

one-third of its leisure sales come from American Express credit-card holders (Saltmarsh, 1986).

It is important to consider that travel is not consumed like washing machines, where relatively few purchases fix the need. Travel is regularly purchased over one's lifetime. Travel, moreover, is not purchased by itself. It is usually purchased in combination with a number of other services such as travellers cheques, credit, insurance, investment services and personal banking. The economics of producing a whole range of services to a targeted market is very different from providing the same service to a supermarket of clients. This provides a very powerful impetus for diagonal integration (joint production) of services because of the way in which services are consumed (the purchase of several related products at regular intervals over one's lifetime).

From the technology perspective, the imperatives for diagonal integration are equally compelling. Investment in a telecommunications infrastructure results in diminishing marginal costs with increasing utilization. A computerized reservation system (CRS), for example, can market several travel services including airline and hotel reservations, flower and champagne services, cruises, car rentals and yachting. Once an initial investment is made in a computer and communications infrastructure, several services can be added at little or no marginal cost to the provider. For example, the cost to American Airlines Sabre of representing the 1001st hotel chain is not so high as the cost of representing the first. Given that the 1001st hotel chain pays the going market price (rather than the marginal cost price), profitability to the supplier of the system is very great.

Both from the supply side (technology) and demand side (consumption of several related products at regular intervals), therefore, there are tremendous pressures for the joint production (diagonal integration) of services.

8.5.5. The Basis of Diagonal Integration

The backbone of diagonal integration is the *lower costs of production,* which are made possible by the existence of economies of scope, systems gains and synergies. These are explained below.

8.5.5.1. Economies of scope

Economies of scope refers to the lower costs associated with the joint provision of more than one product or service, rather than producing each separately. Unlike economies of scale where benefits accrue from *volume* production, with economies of scope, production economies accrue from *variety.* Scope economies do not replace scale economies, rather they reinforce them. Players who reap scale and scope economies will be more competitive than those who continue to rely on scale economies alone.

Economies of scope exist over the production of Goods 1 and 2 if:

$$C(q_1,q_2) < C(q_1,0) + C(0,q_2),$$

$$\text{for } q_1 > 0, q_2 > 0$$

where $C(q_1, q_2)$ is the firm's minimized cost of producing q_1 units of Good 1 jointly with q_2 units of Good 2, at given parametric input prices; $C(q_1, 0)$ is the firm's minimized cost of producing q_1 units of Good 1 and zero units of Good 2; and $C(0, q2)$ is the firm's minimized cost of producing q_2 units of Good 2 and zero units of Good 1 (Willig, 1979, p. 346).

With economies of scope, the joint production of two goods by one enterprise is less costly than the combined costs of two firms either producing Good 1 or Good 2. Assuming that scope economies existed in the provision of car rentals and hotel bed-nights, for example, it would mean that the cost to one firm of adding on the provision of car rentals to hotel bed-nights will be cheaper than two companies producing car rentals and hotel bed-nights separately.

Scope economies largely emanate from information, networks, and other resources within a firm, which can be jointly utilized without causing complete congestion. The existence of infinitely renewable information resources that can be used and reused without losing their value, and the existence of a telecommunications network that can spawn an array of services, adding value with little or no marginal costs, create overwhelming new possibilities for scope economies and the diagonal integration of services. Scope economies are reinforced by synergies and systems gains, which also accrue from joint production.

8.5.5.2. Synergies

Synergies are benefits that accrue to the management, operation and organization of interrelated activities, where each activity can generate benefits that reinforce the other activities. Each activity adds value to the other, thereby making the whole output greater than the sum of the discrete parts. Synergies can create scope economies. United Airlines, for example, is able to obtain a great deal of synergy from linking its credit card with its frequent-flyer programme. For every dollar spent on its credit card, users can earn a free mile on United Airlines' frequent-flyer programme.

Similarly, American Airlines has joined forced with Citibank to provide air-mileage credit for every dollar spent on the card. 'American has thus increased the loyalty of its customers, and the credit-card company has gained access to a new and highly credit-worthy customer base for cross marketing' (Konsynski and McFarlan, 1990, p. 114).

8.5.5.3. Systems gains

Systems gains refers to the benefits or economies derived from creating and engineering linkages among different activities. Examples of systems gains are networked activities, where each activity (or subdivision within an organization) can share a common database or pool of knowledge. Systems benefits can occur, for example, when banks use their extensive client information and mailing lists to market different services, such as travel, insurance and real estate to their clients. Systems gains also accrue from the 'systemization' of production, where information-intensive productive organizations link design, management, production, marketing and distribution into one system.

8.5.6. Implications of Diagonal Integration

There are two key implications of diagonal integration:

1. The travel and leisure industry will become a system of wealth-creation, a process that will continue to blur the borders among players.
2. Competitors will come from outside the industry.

Wealth in tourism will increasingly be created through the diagonal and synergistic integration of a number of activities into a total system. This process will continue to blur the boundaries among players within the industry. Competitors will come from outside the travel and leisure industry. Financial-services suppliers will increasingly find it lucrative to enter the travel and leisure industry.

Diagonal integration, however, is a double-edged sword. Not only will financial services suppliers find it lucrative to provide travel and leisure services, but equally, travel and leisure suppliers could find it lucrative to provide financial services. Airlines, for example, provide their own credit cards.

8.6. STRATEGIC RESPONSES FOR INDUSTRY PLAYERS

The changes in the tourism value chain brought about by the rapid development of information technology and the maturing of consumers will require responses from the key actors in the tourism industry. The traditional division of activities among hotels, airlines, tour operators and travel agencies immediately comes into question. Each of these players will have to think about which value-creating activities to focus on and which activities are most sensibly combined.

Hotels will no longer be able to leave their marketing up to tour operators. They will have to get closer to their consumers. This is the only way that hotels will be able to effectively adjust their products to suit their changing clients. Tour operators will have to find ways of better controlling and influencing the product delivered to consumers. Travel agencies will have to flexibly combine various services that can be booked on computerized reservations systems to suit consumer needs. *CRSs will increasingly become the flexible alternative to packaged holidays offered by tour operators.*

These changes imply a radical transformation of the opportunities available to the various players in the tourism industry. New functions and demands will emerge (e.g. quality control, flexible holidays), while at the same time other key activities will become less important (e.g. prepackaged tours). Thus, the position of each player within the value chain will have to be re-thought. In addition, as the rules of the game continue to change, the pressures of cooperation and/or concentration are likely to be more intense.

It is best to analyse a few of the key players within the industry to evaluate how the competitive conditions are likely to evolve and what strategic actions might be recommended. The following analysis will focus on tour operators, hotels and travel agencies.

8.6.1. Tour Operators

Three key factors will affect the role and functions of tour operators. First, the development of CRSs will give travel agencies the flexibility to package exactly what consumers want. Tour operators are not so flexible given that they can only offer what is in their catalogues. Second, the increasing transparency of information will diminish the tour operator's traditional role of risk brokerage. The availability of information technologies will allow hotels to gain direct access to the marketplace and will allow them to better manage their yield. Increasingly, the need to pre-sell rooms at tremendously discounted rack rates will be reduced. Third, the maturity of consumers will lead to a growing demand for more flexible travel and leisure options.

In Table 8.2, the key value-creation activities of tour operators are identified, together with an assessment of their current and future importance. A number of the value-creating activities of tour operators will decline in importance – particularly those of packaging, risk brokerage and distribution. These functions are being increasingly superseded by com-

Table 8.2 Strengthening the strategic position of tour operators

Value-creating activities	Importance now	Future importance	Strategic response
Packaging	++	–	Flexible packaging
Risk brokerage	+	–	Expand information functions
Distribution/marketing	++	–	Product control; link marketing with product development
Incoming business	+	++	Product control; quality control

puterized reservation systems. As seen in Chapter 6 the development of computerized reservations services, such as Farebank in the UK, will provide low fares and prices for individual elements of a holiday, allowing travel agencies to tailor-make packages that are cost-competitive with rigidly-packaged tour-operator options. The risk brokerage function of tour operators will become less important as individual hotels improve quality, increase repeat visitors, gain direct access to computerized reservation systems and undertake sophisticated yield-management programmes. In the Caribbean, for example, the development of a Caribbean hotel reservations and management system (CHARMS) by the Caribbean Hotel Association, in collaboration with Cable and Wireless (UK) is expected to provide even the smallest guest house with direct distribution through major CRSs in the marketplace.

In response to the declining importance of value-creating activities of packaging, risk brokering and distribution, tour operators will have to take action on a number of fronts. They will have to create more flexibly packaged holidays, they will have to expand their information functions (e.g. provide computerized reservations niches for specific products or destinations), they will have to develop creative relationships with travel agencies (selected agents could have the option of flexibly packaging holidays on-line from the tour operator's portfolio), and they will have to generate more wealth from information and networks. In this latter respect, it is important to note that Saga, a UK tour operator specializing in the mature market, has developed a client mailing list of some two million customers and markets directly to them (Gilbert and Kapur, 1990). Saga has been able to use its database to obtain synergies in marketing, distribution and even in product development. It is certainly a strategy of getting and staying close to its consumers. Tour operators will also have to link more effectively their marketing with product development (see Chapter 9) and seek to control the delivery of the holiday experience at all levels.

Quality control at all key phases in the delivery of the holiday will become a key source of competitive advantage for tour operators. For this reason, the role of the incoming businesses will increase in importance. These incoming agencies located on site will have a greater role to play in ensuring that standards are met and their guests are satisfied. Tour operators will have to become more involved in controlling different elements of the holiday (e.g. managing hotels) and ensuring that they 'deliver the promise' as contained in their pretty brochures. With the increased focus on consumer protection, particularly in Europe, tour operators will also have to take steps to toughen standards at all points in the delivery of the holiday. Thomson's (UK) introduction of a holiday services division in early 1993 covering quality control, overseas staff and customer services is certainly a step in the right direction (*Travel Trade Gazette*, 1993).

Tour operators will equally have to take a far broader view of the holiday they deliver. They will have to realize that their holiday does not end at the hotel but involves the entire destination. Control of as many of the areas that affect the quality and enjoyment of their clients' holidays will be key to their future success. Tour operators will need to develop alliances and collaborate with tourism authorities in the destination to achieve joint objectives – particularly with regard to the environment, standards at hotel establishments, as well as the general well-being of visitors to a destination.

8.6.2. Travel Agencies

The role of travel agencies is expected to grow in importance for three reasons:

1. Travel agencies are very close to the industry's consumers and often play a key role in determining the type of travel and leisure services that is consumed.
2. Travel agencies are key to the diffusion of computerized reservations systems. Without computerized reservations terminals at the point of sale (in travel agencies), airline CRSs will have little value.
3. There are tremendous opportunities for the CRSs to flexibly package holidays.

If travel agencies can creatively respond to these opportunities, their prospects for increased wealth-creation will be enormous. From Table 8.3, it can be seen that the role of travel agencies in three of its core value-creating activities is expected to increase.

Table 8.3 Strengthening the strategic position of travel agencies

Value-creating activities	Importance now	Future importance	Strategic responses
Reservations	+	++	Creatively use CRSs
Ticketing	+	++	Creatively use CRSs
Client advice	+	++	Seek to provide unbiased information
Packaging	–	+	Use CRSs to package holidays flexibly
Greater representation of services other than tour operators and airlines	–	+	Increase buying power through cooperation

The importance of reservations, ticketing and client advice is expected to grow. Already travel agencies handle a large and growing proportion of airline bookings. In creating more value from these activities, travel agencies will have to use their CRSs creatively and provide the information that consumers want. With the incentives provided by airlines for travel agencies to increase bookings on their carriers, there is always the possibility that the interests of the airlines could be placed before those of consumers. For example, a travel agent could route a passenger on a flight with an inconvenient stop in order to gain an extra commission on a preferred carrier, rather than provide the client with a more convenient direct flight. Also, with increased interlining among major international airlines, regional and small commuter airlines, inadequate detailed knowledge of the services of airlines could cause passengers to be routed on what may appear to be a through flight on the major airline, only to find that at the transfer point, it is a small unknown carrier that picks up the tail end of the journey. Another direct option provided by a competitor airline, would probably better serve the interest of the passengers – though it must be stated that the draw of extra air miles in a frequent-flyer programme could cause passengers to opt for the inconvenient flight, just to add to their air-miles credit on a particular carrier.

It is the satisfaction of the travel consumers that agencies must give priority to in order to ensure their own long-term survival and competitiveness. *The ability of travel agents to acquire, provide and transmit unbiased information in a courteous, efficient and timely manner will be key to their competitive success.* Indeed, a competitor agency will be able to copy a convenient 'high street' location, subscribe to the same airline reservation system and place satellite printers in their corporate clients' offices. However, a competitor will have tremendous difficulty in copying travel agency personnel who place the interest of the consumers first, causing them to be loyal.

New opportunities for travel agencies to create value will emerge in the areas of packaging and in the representation of services other than those of tour operators. Travel agencies will have the information at their fingertips to provide flexible itineraries. Strategically, through cooperation with other agencies, agents can increase buying power with airlines and other suppliers in order to obtain competitive prices for package components. This will allow travel agencies the avenue to provide competitively priced flexible holiday packages that can be cost-competitive with the rigidly-packaged options of tour operators. Travel agents – particularly the multiples – will also find it lucrative to develop their own brands and build brand loyalty as well as to creatively re-package holidays. Travel agencies will also find it profitable to represent other services such as cruise ships, pleasure boats, car-rental companies, spas and other segments that will grow in importance in the travel and leisure industry. This does not simply mean calling up and selling services that happen to be represented on computerized reservations terminals (CRTs). What is implied here is true representation, detailed knowledge of, and even first-hand experiences with, the products they sell. Here, niche strategies for travel agencies will need to be developed. In this regard, travel agencies may need to develop expertise on the sale of specific holiday experiences (e.g. boutique hotels in the Caribbean, all-inclusive hotels, speciality cruises, crewed yachts in the Virgin Islands, student travel, cheap flights and last-minute deals).

8.6.3. Hotels

With the inexperience of earlier travellers and the historic importance of tour operators, many hotels have focused narrowly on delivering services within the confines of their property. This was common sense at a time when travellers were undemanding and tour operators did the packaging, marketing, distribution and risk brokerage for them. In other words, tour operators removed from hoteliers the worry of whether their bed-nights would be sold or not. Hotels thus had limited control over who their clients were, where they came from, or the marketing of their products. Hotels were extremely specialized in delivering services within their four walls. Many hotels do not even provide airport transfers, tours or interpreters for their guests. These are left to tour operators and their incoming agencies on site.

Being close to consumers and supplying the experiences they want have become so important that hotels can no longer simply sit back and wait for tour operators to fill their rooms. One of the key ingredients in the success of Sandals and SuperClub all-inclusive hotels in the Caribbean is the strong links they have established with the travel trade and with travel agents in particular. Nothing is left to chance. Sandals and SuperClub employ sales agents in the marketplace whose business it is to travel the length and breadth of the USA (and increasingly the European) market to educate travel agents about their product – to inform them of special deals and new services and experiences being offered. Getting close to their consumers through travel agents – the closest link to the consumer in the marketplace – has paid handsome dividends to these Caribbean all-inclusive operators.

Hotels will also have to work more closely with their guests, listen to them and modify their services to meet the new demands. Hotels will also have to identify market niches, segment the market and provide the experiences that consumers want and for which they are willing to pay. What motivated their clients to visit? What did their guests like or dislike? Why do they defect to competitors or other destinations? These are some of the questions that they will have to ask and answer. Hotels focusing on satisfying holiday segments will increasingly have to realize that they are

Table 8.4 Strengthening the strategic position of hotels

Value-creating activities	Importance now	Future importance	Strategic response
Service at hotels	+	++	Put consumers first
Product development	–	+	Be a leader in quality
Packaging	+	++	Develop improved links with CRSs and travel agencies
Risk brokerage	–	+	Use technology; manage yield
Marketing and sales	+	++	Link marketing with production development
Client management	–	+	Listen to consumers; aim at 'zero defections'

not only competing with hotels on their own destinations, but also with other destinations. For competitiveness hotels will have to:

- get closer to their consumers;
- control more activities within the value chain; and
- maximize bargaining power through cooperation.

From Table 8.4, it can be seen that hotels currently focus on delivering services in the hotels. Important value-creation activities such as product development, systems development, packaging, marketing, distribution, sales and client management have been very marginal. In the future, all of these activities will become more important. Even the traditional concentration on services in hotels will have to be re-thought in order to put consumers first. Hotels will have to be leaders in quality, they will have to develop management styles to accommodate change, and they will have to empower their front line. Most critically, hotels will have to re-invest in and refurbish their most valuable and most neglected asset – their employees!

8.7. SUMMARY

Diagonal integration will become a key tool for controlling the process of value-creation in the tourism industry. It will continue to blur the boundaries among industry players and make the travel and tourism industry a system of wealth-creation. The industry's borders will be increasingly re-defined. It is no longer relevant whether a company is an airline, a travel agent, hotel or tour operator. What becomes more relevant are the *activities along the value chain that they control.*

New tourism will alter the process of value-creation in the travel and tourism industry. It will change the relative positions of different players in the industry. Players that are closest to the consumers and those that can most efficiently control the production, manipulation and distribution of the industry's information are expected to gain. Travel agents, airlines and suppliers on site are all expected to increase their influence on the industry's wealth-creating process. The role of tour operators is expected to decline. Airlines will continue to dominate the industry's value chain.

Hotels will no longer be able to leave their marketing up to tour operators. They will have to get closer to their consumers and to travel agents in the marketplace. This is the only way that hotels will be able to effectively adjust their products to suit their changing clients. Tour operators will have to find ways of better controlling and influencing the product delivered to consumers. Travel agencies will have to flexibly combine various services that can be booked on computerized reservations systems to suit consumer needs. *CRSs will increasingly become the flexible alternative to packaged holidays offered by tour operators.*

In the next chapter, we will examine four key principles for the competitive success of industry players. Adopting these strategies will allow them to stay ahead of the game.

9

COMPETITIVE STRATEGIES FOR INDUSTRY PLAYERS

9.1. INTRODUCTION

The notion of competitive strategies has grown in importance and popularity in tourism industry. Competitive strategies, however, have not been specifically designed or developed for tourism; rather, they are based upon the application of concepts borrowed from the manufacturing sector. Unfortunately, they continue to leave 'many questions unanswered' (Olsen, 1991). This book represents the first major attempt to develop systematically competitive strategies for industry players and to tackle some of these unanswered questions.

New tourism changes the rules of the game in the industry and calls for new strategies to ensure competitive success. Four key principles of competitive success are identified: (i) put consumers first; (ii) be a leader in quality; (iii) develop radical innovations; and (iv) strengthen the player's strategic position within the industry's value chain.

Those players that can most efficiently implement one or more of these strategies will be sucessful. The question here is no longer whether to be a low-budget, up-market or a 'differentiated' hotel, resort or cruise ship – it is too easy for competitors to imitate one another. The question is: 'How do players implement either or all of these strategies more efficiently than their competitors?'.

9.2. COMPETITIVE STRATEGIES

A strategy is a set of principles developed by an organization to give it direction and to allow it to continuously adapt to its changing environment. The more rapid the changes in the firm's environment, the more important becomes conscious strategy formulation and implementation. The travel and tourism industry is undergoing rapid and radical transformation.

Therefore, competitive strategies are more important than ever for the survival and competitiveness of industry players.

The objective of strategy is to enable a company to defend itself, to enjoy a long life, to grow and to be strong and profitable. Such strategies may be explicit or implicit. Strategy may be implicit in the way some companies operate, for example, running a lean organization. On the other hand, strategies can be consciously and explicitly developed – for example, the development of CRS to control the distribution of airline seats. This latter process of conscious strategy formulation is what is commonly referred to as *strategic planning*.

Competitive strategies refer to the broad formulae that determine how a business is to compete, what its goals should be and what policies will be needed to carry out these goals (Porter, 1980). Competitive strategies are conscious policies and procedures developed by companies in order to 'strategically align themselves with the turbulent environment and select appropriate strategies to create defensible competitive positions' (Tse and Olsen, 1991). Competitive strategies are therefore reflected in the targets, goals and objectives set for an organization. In turn, they influence the allocation of resources, policies toward human resources, division of responsibilities and even corporate culture.

Some examples of competitive strategies that help companies to defend themselves, to grow and to be profitable include: (i) being first to the market with a radically new product or service (IBM computers); (ii) producing at lower costs than the competition (e.g. discount stores such as Wal-Mart in the USA and Aldi in Germany); (iii) producing top quality at top prices (e.g. Mercedes Benz, Swiss watches); (iv) producing high quality at relatively low prices (Toyota); (v) running a lean, 'no-frills' organization (Southwestern Airlines); (vi) focusing on satisfying a particular niche (Porsche); (vii) emphasising specialization and flexibility (Benetton); (viii) differentiating oneself from the competition (Swept Away, the all-inclusive, cash-less, couples-only holidays for health enthusiasts in Negril, Jamaica).

There are two key building blocks in the formulation of competitive strategy:

1. Assessment of the environment in which the firm is operating.
2. Assessment of the internal operating conditions of the firm.

The first building block – analysis of the firm's environment – tells the firm: (i) what moves competitors are making into a new market; it (ii) anticipates the threat of a substitute product (e.g. plastic cards); (iii) warns of the threat of new entrants (e.g. Peoples Express); and (iv) assesses how the regulatory framework (e.g. airline deregulation, CRS rules) will affect the firm. An assessment of the competitive environment helps the firm to determine what it will take for the firm to survive, grow and prosper. For example, with the rapid development and diffusion of technology industry wide, those who fail to adopt technology are likely to be left behind.

The second building block – internal company assessment – helps the firm to assess its own strengths and weaknesses. This is done with a view to determining the capacity of the firm to respond to its continuously changing environment and to the moves being made by competitors. An assessment of the internal operating conditions of the company will determine the extent to which they hinder or facilitate the organization's response to changing competitive conditions. For example, poorly trained employees, outdated management practices and the absence of a capacity for continuous innovation could severely weaken an airline, a hotel, or travel agency's responses to changing technologies and the new competition.

9.2.1. Generic Competitive Strategies

The notion of competitive strategies grew in importance in the 1970s and the 1980s as firms needed to defend themselves against their rapidly changing environment over which they had no control – for example, the oil crisis of 1973–1974, recession in the early 1980s and early 1990s and increasing competition from Japan and the Asian 'tigers'. Competitive strategies were developed and applied almost exclusively to the manufacturing sector. Three generic competitive strategies have been developed (Porter, 1980):

- overall cost leadership;
- differentiation; and
- focus.

Overall cost leadership, a common strategy of the 1970s, is achieved in an industry through several policies specifically targeted at reducing costs, namely: (i) the aggressive construction of efficient scale facilities; (ii) tightened cost and overhead control; (iii) relocation of plants (in Asia and elsewhere) to take advantage of cheap labour; (iv) cost minimization in areas such as research and development (R&D), service, sales force, and advertising; and (v) the overwhelming tendency toward large-scale production of standardized items in order to reap lower unit costs (economies of scale).

Differentiation refers to creating something that is perceived industrywide as being unique. There are many areas in which a firm can differentiate itself, including design (e.g. Bang and Olufson), operating systems (e.g. Apple computers), brand image (e.g. Coca Cola, McDonalds), product/service features (e.g. Virgin Atlantic's head-and-neck massages aboard its transatlantic flights), distribution network (e.g.

Thomson's Top videotext system, airline CRSs) and other dimensions.

Focus, the third generic strategy, is built around satisfying a particular target market very well. Focus strategies can be developed by focusing on a particular buyer group (e.g. independent travellers), a particular geographic region (e.g. Central America); catering to a particular segment of the market (e.g. Carnival 'fun' cruises to the Caribbean), or to specific niches in the market (e.g. sport fishing, diving, study tours).

9.2.2. Limitations of the Generic Strategies

These generic strategies developed by Porter, although relevant, are inadequate tools to explore competitive success for travel and tourism players. Porter's analysis is more applicable to the manufacturing sector than to services. A recent attempt to apply Porter's analysis to restaurant firms in the USA proved unsuccessful because of the existence of 'fundamental differences in manufacturing and service' and because of 'the relatively short life cycle of an innovative product or service' in the restaurant business (Tse and Olsen, 1991).

Porter's three generic strategies are not only more appropriate to the manfuacturing than the services sector but they are more appropriate in a static environment and during the maturity stage of a product. Thus Porter's strategies are less applicable in a dynamic environment where learning and radical changes are taking place (Personal Communication, Professor Keith Pavitt and Dr Roy Rothwell, Science Policy Research Unit, Sussex University, UK, December 1991). Cost leadership, for example, is far less important when an industry is in transition and new products and services are emerging.

Even with cost leadership, a unique product, or superior focus, the producers of typewriters would have limited success in face of the rapid diffusion and declining cost of computers. In this case, innovation – the introduction of new and unprecedented products to the market – is far more important than low cost, differentiation or focus.

For these reasons Porter's generic strategies have little value in today's tourism industry, for they cannot create defensible competitive advantages in the unstable tourism environment where competitors can easily imitate one another.

9.2.3. Competitive Strategies for Tourism

Mindful of the limitations of Porter's generic strategies, competitive strategies for the tourism industry have to take account of several key realities of the industry: (i) the service-orientation of the industry and its need to focus on *quality* and the development of human resources; (ii) the sophistication of travel and leisure consumers who require producers to put them first; (iii) the industry-wide diffusion of information technology, which alters the rules of the game and forces firms to re-position themselves strategically; and (iv) the radical transformation of the travel and tourism industry, which demands continuous innovation for competitive success.

As stated earlier, travel and tourism players will have to follow a number of principles in order to compete successfully in today's tourism market place. These are as follows:

- put consumers first;
- be a leader in quality;
- develop radical innovations; and
- strengthen the firm's strategic position within the industry's value chain.

Those companies that develop the capability to implement these strategies most efficiently will be successful. Figure 9.1 shows the principles of competitive success.

9.3. PUT CONSUMERS FIRST

The maturing of travel and leisure consumers make for an increasingly demanding and 'hard-to-please' clientele. Profitably satisfying this market requires suppliers to get even closer to their consumers – to understand and monitor their behaviour, to listen to them and to provide them with what they want. Profitability and success will come to those who can create the best match between their own products and services, and the effective demands of the marketplace.

There are three strategies associated with putting consumers first. These are:

- link marketing with product development;
- satisfy the consumer; and
- develop a holistic approach to the holiday experience.

These strategies are summarized in Figure 9.2 and explained below.

9.3.1. Link Marketing with Product Development

A travel and leisure company will succeed only if it completely understands its markets and the people who decide whether to buy its services or not. In linking marketing with product development and delivery, one of the key objectives is to ensure that the product reflects as closely as possible the

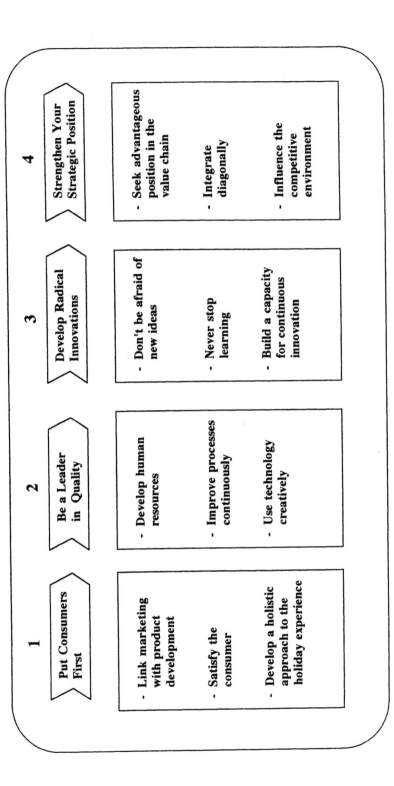

1	2	3	4
Put Consumers First	**Be a Leader in Quality**	**Develop Radical Innovations**	**Strengthen Your Strategic Position**
- Link marketing with product development	- Develop human resources	- Don't be afraid of new ideas	- Seek advantageous position in the value chain
- Satisfy the consumer	- Improve processes continuously	- Never stop learning	- Integrate diagonally
- Develop a holistic approach to the holiday experience	- Use technology creatively	- Build a capacity for continuous innovation	- Influence the competitive environment

Fig. 9.1. Four principles of competitive success in travel and tourism.

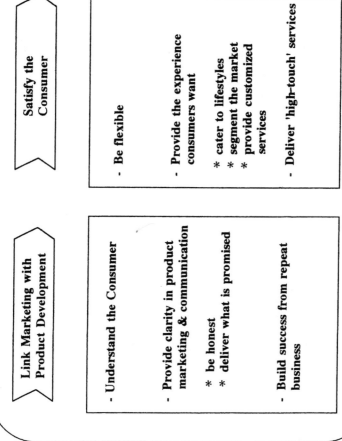

Fig. 9.2. Principle 1: Put consumers first.

Link Marketing with Product Development

- Understand the Consumer

- Provide clarity in product marketing & communication

  * be honest
  * deliver what is promised

- Build success from repeat business

Satisfy the Consumer

- Be flexible

- Provide the experience consumers want

  * cater to lifestyles
  * segment the market
  * provide customized services

- Deliver 'high-touch' services

Develop a Holistic Approach to the Holiday Experience

- Influence the image and development of the entire destination

- Collaborate with the public sector

- Control service delivery at all levels:

  * customs and immigration
  * tours & attractions
  * own services
  * third-party services

needs of the people who make the 'buy-or-don't-buy' decisions. Few organizations have formal channels that feed information from the market-place directly into the product development and delivery functions of the organization. As a result, the products, services and experiences delivered to consumers often do not adequately reflect their needs. To be of great use, 'customer information must move beyond the market research, sales and marketing functions and permeate every corporate function' (Shapiro, 1988, p. 120).

Success, therefore, will not stem from collecting costly market-intelligence data. Success will come from translating vital consumer statistics into product features and services for which consumers are willing to pay.

9.3.1.1. Understand the consumer

Travel and leisure suppliers will have to pay far more attention to under-standing the consumer than they have hitherto done. The importance of understanding the consumers cannot be overstated. Misunderstanding consumers can be a major source of product failure. This is clearly evident in the failure of American Express' Optima card. American Express launched its Optima card in 1987 as a revolving charge card in response to Visa and Mastercard, which had successfully turned credit cards into a consumer lending vehicle. Prior to this, American Express had issued only charge cards and employed a billing approach that required full payment each month. Optima was supposed to be a well-targeted card, never to be offered to a mass clientele, but offered 'only to its existing customers who were presumably good credit risks' (*Times International*, 21 October, 1991a, p. 54). However, many Amex clients, although accustomed to paying in full each month, 'proved much less disciplined in their approach to the Optima card' (*Times International*, 1991a, p. 54). The result is that Optima card members (more than three million) defaulted at much higher rates than expected. The result: US$155 million in Optima write-offs during the third quarter of 1991 were expected to produce a loss – the first ever – of between US$50 million and US$75 million for the company's Travel Related Services division. According to Amex chairman, James Robinson, 'we thought we had better demographics and experience with our customers' (*Times International*, 1991a, p. 55).

The need to better understand consumers is important at all levels of the industry – even for those firms with sterling reputations such as American Express.

9.3.1.2. Provide clarity in marketing

Another key aspect of linking marketing with product development is to provide a clear and clean message about the products and services offered for sale. Consumers can no longer be taken for a ride. Honesty is not just the best policy – it is fast becoming the most profitable policy. Thus product clarity must transcend the advertising, marketing, public relations and promotion strategies of travel and leisure suppliers. More importantly, suppliers have to develop and maintain a capacity to deliver exactly what is promised (refer to Section 9.4 on quality).

9.3.1.3. Build success from repeat business

One of the best barometers for measuring the success of a company is the extent to which consumers remain loyal to it. Since companies do not hold their customers captive, the only way they can know if their customers are satisfied is if they keep on buying. If customers are not satisfied, they vote with their feet and take their business elsewhere. In other words, they defect. Understanding why customers defect to the competition will direct management attention to the specific things that are causing consumers to leave. A key tool for improving quality in services is to aim at '*zero defections*', that is, learning how to keep customers and track the ones you lose (Reichheld and Sasser, 1990).

Companies have to develop the art of keeping their customers. Keeping customer defection to a minimum will show up in the profit margins of the company over time; for it often costs more to attract a new customer than to retain a seasoned one. Indeed, research has shown that the cost of retaining a loyal customer is only one-fifth of attracting a new one (Heskett *et al.*, 1990b). For example, it costs less to service a repeat visitor – repeat visitors to an all-inclusive resort would need less orientation, would know what to expect (e.g. tipping not allowed), would know the role they are expected to play and how to play it and are likely to make less calls to the front desk.

Companies with long-time customers can often charge more for their products or services. Many people will pay more to stay in a quality hotel they know, or to go to a doctor they trust, rather than to take a chance on a less-expensive, unknown, competitor. The fact is that customer loyalty and profitability go hand in hand. It was found that if a credit-card company increased its repeat visitors by 5%, this could increase its profits by 125%. Similarly, a 5% increase in client-retention rates could lead to a 35% increase in profit for software companies; a 40% increase in profits for office business management companies; and 28% increase in profit for car-service chains (Heskett *et al.*, 1990b, pp. 33–34).

9.3.2. Satisfy the Consumer

The next important component of putting consumers first is to satisfy them. This means providing consumers with the experience they want. It means providing flexibility in the services offered. It means catering to specific needs of the market and delivering 'high-touch' services. Travel and leisure suppliers always have to retain sight of their *raison d'être* – satisfying their clients, thereby causing them to be loyal and ensuring that they do not defect.

9.3.2.1. Be flexible

As we have seen in Chapter 5, travellers no longer consume vacations along linear predictable lines. They want flexibility. Being flexible involves listening to consumers, interpreting their wants and modifying products, processes and services to satisfy their needs. One attempt to provide the experience consumers want is the concept of *exchange dining* – a concept introduced by selected hotels in the Caribbean and around the world to give consumers variety and flexibility.

Exchange dining allows hotel guests to dine at other hotel/restaurants in the destination they visit. This is a significant development in the leisure industry. When buying a holiday package, guests sometimes pre-pay for a number of their meals (e.g. in a Modified American Plan, breakfast and dinner are usually pre-paid) or for all meals (e.g. in an all-inclusive plan). As a result, there is reluctance on the part of hotel guests to dine around and experience other cuisine, and share in the atmospheres outside the hotel. The dine-around concept, by contrast, allows hotel guests the freedom and flexibility to experience more fully the hotel and tourism experience of the whole destination, without forfeiting pre-paid meals.

Dining around has always been a common practice of many tourists: indicated by the number of quality, independent restaurants that have sprung up to service the tourist trade. It is only within recent times, however, that exchange dining has become a *conscious* and *organized* initiative on the part of some hoteliers. Some hotels have gone a step further in the pursuit of flexibility in satisfying the needs of their clients. Thus hotels that belong to the same group or chain, for example, Elegant Resorts of Jamaica, allow their clients the flexibility to sleep and eat around at participating properties. Sandals, for example, offer their guests the flexibility to 'sleep at one and play at five' of its resorts in Jamaica.

9.3.2.2. Segment the market

Another tactic for satisfying the consumer is to segment the market. Market segmentation is a process by which firms attempt to identify their markets as precisely as possible and tailor their services to suit the section of the market chosen. The better and the more profound the understanding of the consumer, the better will suppliers be able to satisfy their needs. There are two main types of market segmentation:

1. Demographic segmentation (e.g. age, income, education, location).
2. Psychographic segmentation (e.g. the way people think, feel and behave).

Segmenting the market along *demographic* lines simply means that consumers are identified, defined and categorized by their age, income, educational attainment and where they live. Services are provided to satisfy the segment of the market targeted (e.g. young, single travellers in search of sun, sex and hedonism). Suppliers also reach their target markets based on demographic profile of their market (e.g. they may advertise in a magazine read by persons with an income of over US$50000.00 per year). Segmenting the market along *psychographic* lines means that consumers are defined and categorized by how they think, feel and behave. Psychographic segmentation allows suppliers to get even closer to their consumers. With psychographic segmentation, a supplier could target empty nesters (parents whose children have already grown up and left home), offering them a chance to be active (through dancing, walking, biking), while being personally fulfilled (e.g. where learning how to use computers, to speak another language, or to prepare local dishes is part of the holiday experience). Although infinitely more complex and difficult to measure, psychographic segmentation is rapidly gaining ground and offers key challenges and opportunities for industry players.

In the travel and tourism industry, as indeed in other industries, it has been common practice to segment the market along the demographic lines. The approach to segmenting the market during much of the 1960s and 1970s remained limited in focus: either you stayed in a down-town business hotel or at a roadside motel; either you travelled first class or economy class.

With the hotel overbuilding, recession in the early 1980s, and the increasing recognition of the maturity of their clients, many hotels turned to market segmentation. Market segmentation was seen as a vehicle to get ahead of competitors and to get closer to their consumers. Suddenly, market segmentation was seen to be the formula for success. Hotels in the USA embarked on a market segmentation spree.

By the early 1980s, the hotel industry in the USA was hit by 'market-segmentation mania'. In confirmation of this, an Economic Survey of the Travel Industry observed that:

> Hotel segmentation reached epidemic proportions in 1984, as one chain after the other announced it would expand from a well-established base market and develop different types of properties for different types of people.
>
> (*Travel Weekly*, 1987a, p. 158)

Between 1983 and 1984, a total of 50 new brands or concepts were introduced by the hotel industry (Bush, 1984a, p. 7). Still, this market segmentation rush by American hotel chains remained limited in focus. It was driven mainly by a business clientele and was largely *supply-driven*. As such, markets continued to be defined by limited characteristics: the price of the rooms (e.g. budget, middle-price, luxury); physical structure (e.g. all-suite, mega-hotels), contents (e.g. hair dryers, bathrobes and amenities baskets in rooms), and facilities (e.g. teleconferencing, in-room entertainment, executive floors, automatic check out, meeting rooms).

Segmentation in today's leisure travel environment is unique, unprecedented and infinitely more complex. Today, the mass market in tourism is splitting apart. One of the profound changes in the travel marketplace comes from the tourists themselves. Tourists no longer want a standardized and rigidly packaged product. They never did. Tourists were simply forced by the economics of mass production, to consume standardized and rigidly packaged holidays *en masse*. Today, new technologies, coupled with diagonal integration, are making it possible to produce flexible and segmented vacations, which are *cost-competitive* with mass, standardized holidays.

Today, therefore, one has to be much more sophisticated in defining markets. Specifically, hotels must cater not only to the demographics but also to the psychographics of the new consumers. In other words, they have to cater to the income and education levels of the new consumers as well as their lifestyles and thought patterns. In this regard, *cluster segments* of the vacation market must be catered to – that is, segments based on clusters of needs and consumer lifestyles. This means that the choice is not between sun *or* fun holidays, young *or* old clients, male *or* female travellers but, rather, the choice is creative holiday combinations that incorporate a *cluster* of requirements reflecting the lifestyle and behaviour of the new tourists. For example, vacations could be provided to cater to couples with 'double income no kids' (DINKS), from the sunbelt region of the USA who seek sun *plus* windsurfing, *plus* bird watching *plus* fresh air *plus* good food. Similarly, vacations might be tailored to the over-50s couples, who may seek sun *plus* sailing *plus* educational tours *plus* healthy foods. The key challenge for travel suppliers is to understand the components and composition of these cluster segments and to determine in which of these clusters they can gain a competitive advantage.

The real innovation in market segmentation in the travel and tourism industry comes from the *leisure* segment of the industry – a phenomenon that is more marked in Jamaica than elsewhere. Innovative Jamaican hoteliers have moved beyond defining their markets based on physical buildings, location and price. They have moved into segmenting holidays based on *lifestyle* characteristics of the new consumers. These segments take account of a variety of consumer attributes: (i) where people live; (ii) their age, sex, wealth and education; (iii) how they think, feel and behave; (iv) their perceived risks; (v) what services they want, where and at what price; (vi) why they want these services; and (vii) how they want them delivered.

All-inclusive hotels in the Caribbean now cater exclusively to families, couples, hedonists, health enthusiasts and other segments. In addition, they offer a completely cash-less, all-inclusive experience where even tipping is forbidden. The Sandals hotel group of Jamaica, for example, caters strictly to couples – couples of all ages and types are welcome at Sandals. The SuperClub hotel chain caters exclusively to different segments of the market in its five properties in Jamaica: from couples-only at its Couples resort; families-only, at Boscobel; to persons who want to 'be wicked for a week' at Hedonism, Negril; to those with a focus on health, nature, sport and a 'touch of Jamaica' at Runaway Bay; and guests who want grand luxury at Grand Lido.

Other properties have targeted travellers who combine three specific characteristic and/or product requirements. For example, Frank Rance FDR resorts are all-inclusive, all-suite properties catering only to families; while Swept Away, Negril, is an all-inclusive, all-couple, health-and-fitness resort. These tiers of segmentation are all in addition to the traditional doses of tropical sun that they all offer on their own secluded beaches. Their success demonstrates that sun, sand and sea are no longer sufficient market-segmentation criteria. Sun, sand and sea have become *necessary* conditions for success in sun destinations as are 'creature comforts' for the business segment. Competitiveness lies in fulfilling the *sufficient* conditions – providing friendly, flexible and quality services for which consumers are willing to pay.

The section of the travel and tourism industry that is perhaps the most segmented is the cruise industry. Already one of the fastest growing segments of the leisure market, with a predicted three-fold increase in passengers carried worldwide by the year 2000, market segmentation is a common practice among cruise lines: Club Med, Star Quest and Windstar offer romance under sail; Renaissance, Crystal and Seabourne offer sophistication; Lindbar and Frontier offer adventure; Windjammer Barefoot offers active holidays; Carnival offers fun and entertainment; Radisson Diamond offers business and incentive travel; and Ocean Quest specializes in diving (Caribbean Tourism Organization, 1992b).

Not only hotels and cruise ships but several tour operators increasingly segment their markets, creating specialist packages that emphasize golfing, skiing, dining tours, history and archaeology, adventure and ecotourism. Suppliers are diversifying their products and attempting to make them more flexible. With the ageing of the population, programmes have been developed for the over-55 holiday market. Saga Holidays, in the UK, has been one of the most successful over-55 holiday operators – having succeeded in developing sophisticated marketing programmes involving regular contact with customers and building on brand loyalty. A large number of other companies have also launched over-55 packages – including Thomson (Young at Heart), Horizon (Home for Home), Global (Golden Circle) and Yugotours (Golden Age), and Enterprise (Leisure Days). Within these 'grey market' segments operators such as Thomson and Enterprise, however, offer holidays for single holiday-makers, bowling competitions, sequence-dancing competitions, and walking.

Success of travel and tourism suppliers will increasingly depend on how closely they reflect the needs of their market. This will mean that industry players have to redefine their markets and find innovative ways of satisfying these segments better and more efficiently than the competition. A word of caution, however: by itself, market segmentation is no panacea to success. It is altogether the capacity to put consumers first, to supply them with exactly what they want, to be a leader in quality, to innovate continuously – and to do all of these better than the competition – that will determine the winners.

9.3.2.3. Deliver 'high-touch' services

The delivery of 'high-touch' services is another important element in satisfying consumers. In societies increasingly characterized by dirty skies and cluttered streets, anonymous high-rise flats, social attitudes that are more concerned with things than with people, the search for self-fulfilment and high-touch services is critically important. In Europe, one of the main trends uncovered by the European Travel Data Centre is the need for personal attention and more communication during the holiday. Consumers want more than just to be served a meal. They want to be served by people whom they can talk to. They may ask about the ingredients used to prepare their meals or about the local flora and fauna. They want waiters and service personnel who can answer these and other questions correctly, responsively and with a human touch.

Singapore Airlines clearly understand the need for personal service. In a world of anonymity where one tends to be referred to by a seat or room number, Singapore Airlines provides that extra special attention to their first-class and business-class passengers. All flight attendants take the time to know the names of all the passengers they serve and, at every point of service, passengers are courteously addressed by their name. It is this attention to detail, partially made possible by the power of information technology, that provides the personal touch that travellers appreciate and for which they will continue to pay and patronize.

Boutique hotels have also understood the need for 'personal touch' and provide high-quality, high-touch services. Boutique hotels are typically small (less than 50 rooms) and are not the conventional franchised hotels that one finds at every crossroad. They are different. One of the main differences between boutique and ordinary hotels is the superior quality and quantity of its employees. In order to pamper their guests, boutique hotels in the Caribbean tend to employ deliberately more persons per room than ordinary hotels. There is also a great deal of training to provide the perfect host. By their very difference and superiority, boutique hotels are able to command a premium rate – US$500–800 per night during the winter season (Caribbean Hotel Association, 1991). Caribbean hotels that are classified as boutique hotels include: Curtin Bluff (Antigua); Petit St Vincent (Grenadines); Little Dix Bay (British Virgin Islands); Malliouhana (Anguilla); Young Island (St Vincent); Treasure Beach (Barbados); Bitter End Yacht Club (Virgin Gorda, British Virgin Islands); Peter Island Resort and Yacht Harbour (British Virgin Islands). Boutique hotels are likely to grow in importance and significance in the hotel sector – they can continue to add value, variety, flexibility and quality to the current hotel offerings. In addition, they are very well positioned to capture a growing share of the luxury cruise yacht market as clients tend to spend their first and last nights in a hotel and expect similar levels of luxury to those found aboard their luxury yachts.

The focus on offering high-touch services and cultivating a staff who can deliver high quality will be a key source of competitive success in the future. Suppliers will increasingly realize that, eventually, many of their innovations (e.g. providing all-inclusive holidays, building all-suite hotels and targeting the mature market) will be copied and that the only asset that cannot be copied is the staff. The most significant factor in competitive success in the hospitality industry is the quality of its human resource – a factor whose quality will have to be improved in order to ensure competitiveness through leadership in quality.

9.3.3. Develop a Holistic Approach to the Holiday

The third strategy for putting consumers first is to develop a holistic approach to the holiday experience. The holiday experience is not simply the bed-nights at a hotel, villa or guest house. The holiday experience begins at the travel agency and, at the destination, it begins on arrival.

The actions of customs and immigration officers and the attitudes of taxi drivers and others who meet, greet, transfer and brief arriving guests are all key aspects of the holiday experience. At the destination, the critical factors in making the holiday experience include: the quality of the food; the ambience in the restaurants; the drug pushers on the beach; the muggers; 'smartmen' and beggars on city streets; harassment by 'boat people'; garbage on the roads; the quality of the fast-food outlets; the availability of water-sports equipment; the quality of instructors and the competence of the tour guides.

Travel agent Bob McMullen, former president of the American Society of Travel Agents, noted that during any successful trip there are 285 identifiable points at which something can go wrong that will destroy the entire experience for the traveller. Controlling as many of the elements of a holiday experience as possible is key to producing and delivering a successful holiday.

Traditionally, travel- and tourism-related establishments have narrowly concentrated on their physical space and let God and the government handle the rest. The success of holiday-makers – those who create and deliver holiday experiences (e.g. Disneyland, Center Parcs, Club Med, cruise ships, Sandals and SuperClubs) – is due precisely because they have taken a holistic approach to the holiday experience. All of them seek to control as many of the elements of the holiday experience as possible.

To successfully develop a holistic approach to the holiday experience and to succeed in delivering quality services, travel and tourism suppliers must:

- influence the image and development of the destination;
- collaborate with the public sector; and
- control the service delivery process.

These three principles of competitive success and their subcomponents are explained below.

9.3.3.1. Influence the destination's image

Travel and tourism suppliers have to play a much greater role in influencing the development and positioning of the entire destination. They should lobby governments more effectively to take an approach to the industry's development that is in the interest not only of the hotel, airline or cruise ship but of the entire destination. The absence of pavements, the dumping of sewage at sea, the location of rubbish dumps, dirty streets, dilapidated and run-down buildings, historic buildings in need of restoration and unemployed youths on the streets affect everyone in the community and will affect each visitor's holiday or business trip. The quality of the environment is not just a government responsibility. It is increasingly the responsibility of all those who live by it – especially travel and tourism suppliers. They must therefore take a more active approach in influencing what happens to the entire destination – and that includes the environment!

The competitive advantage of an upmarket hotel such as Raffles in Singapore will depend as much on the quality and image of the destination as on the quality of the hotel's staff. The fact that Singapore is a super-clean, super-safe and super-efficient destination reinforces the positioning of this upmarket hotel. Business and incentive travellers, as well as families and shoppers, thrive in Singapore. Similarly, hotels and other suppliers worldwide have to reinforce and support efforts by the government to upgrade the skills of the industry, to improve the quality of its attractions, and to upgrade the entire destination.

9.3.3.2. Collaborate with the public sector

Collaborating with the public sector is key to influencing the whole holiday experience. Public-sector collaboration allows suppliers to control the nature, pace and direction of development of the destination. In the travel and tourism industry, a very high level of public- and private-sector collaboration is already evident. For example, the management of tourism-development authorities and boards of tourism is made up of public- and private-sector members. This takes place at the broad level of policy-making. However, much more collaboration is needed in projects aimed at conserving the environment, restoring old buildings, historic sites and city markets. In addition, programmes aimed at educating and training youths – to keep them off the streets, thereby preventing them from harassing visitors – are as important for the success of a hotel as is a hair dryer or sewing kit in the guest room. Hotels must therefore take a much more active role in working with the public sector; and they must also play a more active role in suggesting, developing and designing programmes for the development and enhancement of the whole destination. Equally, they must be active in lobbying effectively for more resources for the sector.

The importance of this 'greater' role for the travel and tourism sector is also evident in the formation of the World Travel and Tourism Council (WTTC) – funded by the international travel and tourism private sector. It is the explicit aim of WTTC to further the interest of the industry on a global level (Personal communication, Geoffery Lipman, Director, WTTC, London, 1991). As an institution, WTTC is unique and unprecedented in that its focus is much broader than traditional industry interest groups. For example, WTTC is a main force behind the development of the World Travel and Tourism Environment Research Center (WTTERC) to foster the development of responsible tourism. Seed funding for this project has been provided by American Express, British Airways, the British Tourism Authority, Stigenberger Hotels and Thomas Cook. According to WTTC, one of its major priorities is to foster growth that is compatible with protecting the environment. It is pursuing this goal through the following activities:

1. By developing environmental audit and impact assessment principles for application at the individual country level.
2. By cooperating with governments to improve understanding of industry actions aimed at environmentally sensitive growth.

3. By working to improve industry practices in respect of environmentally sensitive growth.
4. By tracking the implementation of travel and tourism environmental programmes.

Hotels and other industry associations will do well to emulate the example of this 'greater' and 'greener' role that WTTC has set.

9.3.3.3. Control the service delivery process

The third strategy associated with developing a holistic approach to the holiday experience involves controlling the service delivery process at all levels. This begins by controlling the quality of services delivered at all service points of the travel supplier's own operation – from reservations, to service at restaurants, and entertainment in hotels. However, it does not end here. A greater effort has to be made to control services delivered by third parties, both at the travel suppliers' own premises and beyond. This can be achieved through better control of third-party services, for example, by establishing standards and instilling tougher competition among firms that travel suppliers do business with.

In attempting to control the services delivery process, certain questions must be asked: Why are competitor hotels always full? Why do clients return to the destination but stay elsewhere? Why do customers defect? Are there better ways of satisfying clients? Does the hotel recommend the worst restaurants to guests so that they will continue to patronize the hotel's dining room for the rest of their stay? Or does the hotel try to provide the experience for which its guests are looking? Does a hotel just advertise for any tenant to operate its beauty parlour? Or does it hand pick an operator because it fits the image and needs of the clients being attracted to the hotel? These are key issues that must be addressed in controlling the service delivery process and satisfying customers.

The importance of service and control over the service delivery process in travel and tourism establishments is highlighted by American Airlines Chief Executive Officer, Bob Crandall, when he stated that:

> ... a person travelling almost anywhere in the world is more likely to meet a surly bar tender than a terrorist. He is more likely to lose a bag than encounter a machine gun, more likely to feel held for ransom by a fancy hotel or an over-priced restaurant, than by a kidnapper.
>
> (Farrell, 1989, p. 147)

9.4. BE A LEADER IN QUALITY

Quality is perhaps the most important principle for competitiveness in the travel and tourism industry. If the last three decades of world development was led by price and large-scale production, it can be said that quality and flexibility will lead the next three. The drive towards quality and flexibility (lean production) was perfected by the Japanese in the automobile industry (Womack *et al.*, 1990). Leadership through quality does not hold only for the automobile industry. It has become a dominant trend globally and has important implications for the travel and tourism industry. As the novelty of driving a car and going on holiday have worn off, consumers have become far more discerning. They increasingly vote for *quality*, *flexibility* and *value for money*.

The drive for quality goes far beyond the inherent features of a car or holiday (be it a first-class seat on an airplane or a Mercedes Benz). Quality increasingly is defined by consumer values, that is, how well-suited the goods or services are to the needs of the *consumer*. During 1973–1974, when oil prices quadrupled, consumers were more interested in saving on fuel consumption and saving Planet Earth. Their preference was for smaller cars. It was not that the quality of large American cars was poor or that standards of production had fallen. It was simply that American cars no longer suited the needs of their buyers. Small, fuel-efficient and environmental friendly cars supplied by the Japanese won over increasing market share from the USA and UK manufacturers. Japanese cars competed not just because they were small but because small also came to be associated with high-quality and sensitivity to the environment – a car did not have to be big to be better. This fact is well supported by surveys done in the USA in the 1970s and 1980s where it was found that: 'in 1973, 12% of US consumers felt that Japanese cars were of better quality than US ones, but by 1983 that figure had risen to 40%' (Bessant, 1991, p. 235).

Nor is it that consumers simply got up one day and decided that they wanted quality and flexibility. It was Japanese ingenuity that inspired them; for in attempting to compete in the automobile industry, the Japanese adopted the concept of kaizen (continuous improvement) as their guiding philosophy (see Chapter 3). This made their goods both price and quality competitive and resulted in lower prices and better value for money to customers. This concept of kaizen is one of the roots of Japanese success. It explains why the Japanese automobile producers have won increasing market share over their USA and European counterparts. The growing Japanese competition in the USA automobile industry is largely responsible for the increasingly poor performance of a company such as General Motors. In 1990, the annual revenue for General Motors was US$127 billion and the company had a workforce of 395000. The 1991 Christmas

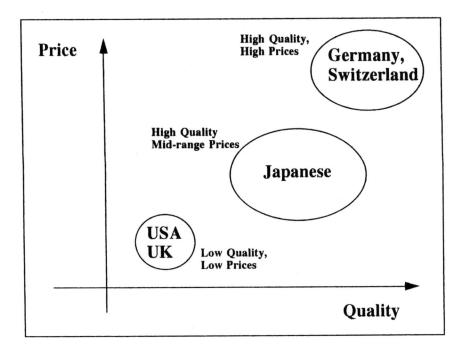

Fig. 9.3. Competition through high quality at lower prices.
- The ballgame has shifted from price to quality competition.
- Many producers in the USA and UK compete through low prices and low quality.
- Many producers in Germany and Switzerland compete with high quality and high prices.
- The Japanese filled the quality gap by producing high quality at mid-range prices.

Source: Personal communication, Dr Roy Rothwell, Science Policy Research Unit, Sussex University, December 1991.

address by Robert Stempel, Chairman of General Motors, announced that the company would close 25 North American plants and reduce its workforce by 74000 (nearly 20%) and would 'abandon for the foreseeable future its hope to regain its lost share of the US market', which had fallen in the last decade from 45% to 35%, is clear testimony to the competition provided by Japanese suppliers. According to Stempel, 'the rules of the game have changed overnight' (*Times International*, 30 December 1991b).

Indeed, the rules of the game have changed, but not only has it changed for automobile manufacturers but also for travel and tourism suppliers. The drive for mass production, endless supplies and standardized services is giving way to *quality* rather than *quantity* competition. Consumers in many industries are maturing – and they demand quality. As producers begin to compete on quality, consumers are expected to get better quality at all prices that they pay. Producers will be able to produce better quality at lower prices by taking advantage of new technologies and economies of scale and scope where they apply.

Low price and large-scale production have traditionally been the main determinants of competitiveness – the lower the price, the greater the quantity consumed; the greater the demand, the more a company could produce; the lower the unit cost of production, the greater the economies of scale and the greater the profit. Indeed, this price/quantity relationship has been the guiding philosophy of production and consumption during much of the post-Second World War period leading up to the 1980s. However, the 1990s is witnessing the dawn of a new era where the new emphasis is on quality. Frigenbaum reports that 'in the late 1970s only 40% of US buyers ranked quality as being at least as important as price in their decisions, but that the 1990s figure is over 80% and rising' (cited in Bessant, 1991). Today, there is little doubt that *quality* is replacing *quantity* as the major pillar of competitive success.

It is interesting to compare the competitive approaches of selected countries and see how they have positioned themselves along the price/ quality spectrum. From Figure 9.3, it can be seen that many manufacturers in the USA and UK focused on the production of low-quality goods at low prices. Volume production and mass consumers were key to the success of this low-price, low-quality strategy. In Germany and Switzerland, by contrast, manufacturers competed on the basis of high quality and high prices (e.g. Swiss watches, BMW, Porsches, Mercedez Benz). This high-price, high-quality strategy survived through target marketing, the exploitation of niche markets and meticulous attention to detail. This strategy is also marked by continuous improvements in the production processes and product quality. The Japanese, by contrast, came in between these two extremes and filled the *quality gap*. The Japanese produced good quality at mid-range prices.

The Japanese example is an important one for the travel and tourism industry. The question it poses to the industry, the question the travel and tourism industry must be continually asking, is this: 'How do we produce better and better quality services at more and more reasonable prices?' Here, holiday-makers provide an important key.

The 'Japanese equivalents' in the travel and tourism industry are holiday-makers – companies whose business it is to make, market, distribute and deliver holiday experiences. Holiday-makers include cruise ships, Disneyland (and other similarly-themed entertainment complexes) and all-inclusive establishments such as Club Med (France), SuperClub (Jamaica) and Sandals (Jamaica). The drive towards continuous quality improvement

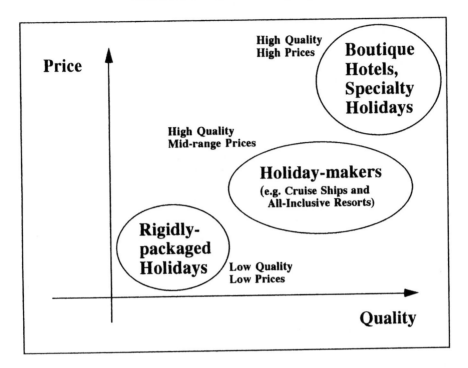

Fig. 9.4. Price and quality competition in the travel and tourism industry.
– Rigidly packaged holidays are offered at low prices to mass clientele.
– At the other extreme are boutique hotels and suppliers of speciality holidays, who command high prices for the unique experiences they provide.
– Like Japanese car manufacturers, holiday-makers fill the quality gap.
– It is not surprising that holiday-makers are the most resilient in today's fiercely competitive and turbulent environment.

and flexible production is being adopted by holiday-makers and is largely responsible for their tremendous success compared with other industry players. Like the Japanese, it can be seen that holiday-makers increasingly fill the quality gap in the travel and tourism industry. They produce quality holiday experiences at mid-range prices.

The role of holiday-makers in the travel and tourism industry and their positioning on the price/quality spectrum is illustrated in Figure 9.4. Also represented in the figure are suppliers providing low quality at low prices (e.g. mass, packaged holidays) as well as suppliers who provide exclusive 'boutique' experiences (e.g. on crewed yachts or at boutique hotels) or cater to very specialized interests (e.g. bird watching in the Amazon, study tours to the Mexican ruins, diving on the Great Barrier Reef).

While quality is a key determinant of competitive success in the travel and tourism industry, *the key to quality in the travel and tourism industry is its human resources.* Being a leader in the travel and tourism industry involves empowering, redirecting and rewarding the industry's most valuable asset – its human resources. Thus it might be concluded: the key to quality is quality labour. Such labour is an invaluable asset in the process of production. In this respect, human beings are unmatchable, since it is they who determine the quality of services delivered throughout the travel and tourism value chain.

While one recognizes the need to focus on quality, there are no well-established techniques or principles for measuring quality in the services sector. One of the most difficult aspects in delivering quality travel and tourism services is the fleeting nature of the product. This makes it very difficult to use traditional manufacturing tools to inspect it before it is delivered. The fact is that 'employees create it and then it disappears' (Armstrong and Symonds, 1991).

In what follows, three important conditions of becoming a leader in quality will be explored:

- developing human resources;
- improving processes continuously; and
- using technology creatively.

In Figure 9.5, the various subcomponents of the quality leadership strategy are delineated; these are explained in detail in the following section.

9.4.1. Develop Human Resources

Unlike goods in the manufacturing sector, 'a service transaction cannot be halted, examined and re-cycled' (Heskett *et al.*, 1990a, p. 122). Quality must be produced right from the beginning. The key to quality service is the human beings who deliver them.

It seems paradoxical that employees hold the key to competitive success in an industry that has traditionally viewed labour as a cost of production, a replaceable item, an item to dispose of in the low season, an item that can be hired and fired at will. Yet, for those companies that have stayed on top of the heap – from Disneyland to the Marriotts to Singapore Airlines – it is the unending drive toward quality and investment in human resources that has made the difference.

Leadership through quality involves creative recruitment and personnel management practices, investing in education and training and motivating, empowering, leading and rewarding employees.

Usually, low-paid, young and inexperienced, the customer–contact employee in most travel companies spends more time with the customer than any other person in the organization (Farrell, 1989, p. 150). The finest

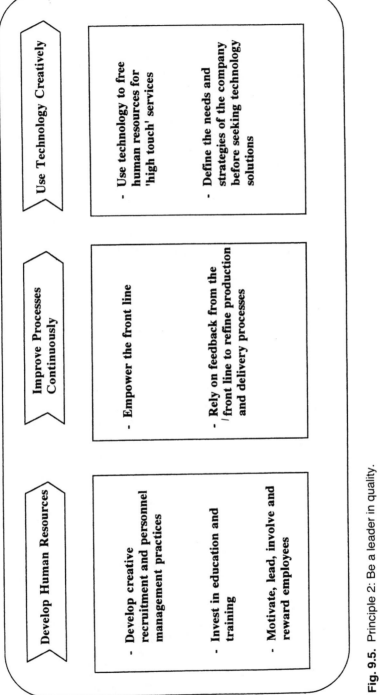

Fig. 9.5. Principle 2: Be a leader in quality.

The figure contains three headed sections:

Develop Human Resources

- Develop creative recruitment and personnel management practices
- Invest in education and training
- Motivate, lead, involve and reward employees

Improve Processes Continuously

- Empower the front line
- Rely on feedback from the front line to refine production and delivery processes

Use Technology Creatively

- Use technology to free human resources for 'high touch' services
- Define the needs and strategies of the company before seeking technology solutions

china or the most beautifully designed rooms cannot compensate for an unfriendly employee who ill treats a customer. Travel suppliers have to make every effort to ensure that their frontline customer-contact employees have the skills and interests to respond professionally to customers. This point is clearly understood by some of the leading players in the industry. In the USA cruise industry, for example, the most important consideration in hiring potential employees is their *attitudes*. According to James Godsman, President of the Cruise Lines Industry Association of America, cruise lines hire employees based on their attitudes. Once the attitudes to service and to clients are right, then the skills to carry out the specific duties aboard the ship can be acquired. The logic is this: a skill can be acquired, not an attitude.

The challenge for many travel and tourism players is to develop their most neglected asset – human beings. This process begins with the selecting and hiring of the right employee, training them on the job, and empowering, motivating, leading and rewarding them in their duties.

9.4.1.1. Develop creative personnel practices

Hiring, training and keeping the right kind of employees is the key to success in the travel and tourism industry. Companies such as Disneyland and Four Seasons Hotels understand only too well the value of the people they employ. Thus they invest a great deal of time and effort in selecting the right kind of employees. At the Toronto-based Four Seasons Hotels, it takes four or five rigorous interviews to sort out applicants with a friendly nature and a sense of teamwork. When the chain opened its Los Angeles Hotel in 1987, it interviewed 14000 candidates for 350 slots (Armstrong and Symonds, 1991, p.59).

At the Disney Company, 'where everything happens like magic', management interviews prospective employees or 'cast members' in groups of three so it can watch how they interact: do they show respect for example, by paying attention when the others speak? (Armstrong and Symonds, 1991, p.59). Disney prides itself in the quality of its products and its employees who make it all happen. The philosophy of the Disney management is to 'create programs that are done right or not done at all' (Elrod, 1989, p.120). Hence according to Thomas R. Elrod, Disney's Vice President of marketing:

> The park's cleanliness is no by-product. It is a conscious effort that all employees take pride in participating in. Streets and sidewalks are squeaky clean, hosed down every night. If they see a scrap of discarded paper, they pick it up. Attractions are 'rehabbed', cleaned and painted on a regular basis. Flower gardens are meticulously cleaned. It becomes a different world. Employees are as

well-groomed as the gardens. No long hair or moustaches are
allowed. No excessive make-up or jewelry. Employees both look and
act the part of friendly helpful members of the cast, each of whom
continuously attends the Disney University for stimulating and
inspirational programs designed to educate and motivate them into
better understanding the company's philosophy of doing business
and giving them a sense of their importance in it.

(Elrod, 1989, p. 120)

This 'magic touch' to product quality has paid off for Disney. By 1989,
at least 230 million visits had been made to Walt Disney World in Florida
since it opened in 1971. Results of Disney's regular price/value guest
surveys reveal that, although more expensive than other parks, 'people are
willing to pay for outstanding value they receive on their visit' (Elrod,
1989, p. 120). The company has expanded its base outside the USA,
opening Tokyo Disneyland in 1984 and, more recently, EuroDisney in 1992.

9.4.1.2. Invest in education and training

The education and training of employees is an essential part of the
building block of any business: it is they who shoulder the daily responsibility of satisfying clients. The quality of the service produced is reflected in
employee performance. This, in turn, is a reflection of the quality of their
education, experience and training acquired before and on the job. Travel
and tourism players who understand this and take their time to educate and
train their workforce are the ones most likely to succeed.

An excellent example of training employees for the purpose of
improving quality of service is provided by Sandals, the all-inclusive,
couples-only hotel chain of Jamaica. Reports are that in the opening of the
newest Sandals property – Sandal's Dunn's River, Jamaica – the entire staff
was employed and paid full time for a period of 3 months prior to the
opening of the hotel, an investment in training to the tune of hundreds of
thousands of US dollars just to get the product right. It is not surprising
that Butch Stewart, Chairman and CEO of Sandals could claim that:
'Sandals offers quality with the ease of the all-inclusive vacation without
sacrificing service or style.' (Travel Agent, 1992, p. 1). Sandals also boasts of a
ratio of three staff members to every guest and has a number of playmakers on
its payroll.

Although the role of the employees is vital to the efficient running of
the organization, for many travel and tourism establishments employees
are still seen as an unnecessary evil, a cost of production. Many of these
players have not yet understood that employees are the key to quality and
profit. As a result, millions of dollars are spent on physical plant and
equipment, room refurbishment, lawns and gardens, marble floors and the

like, but, at the same time, little is spent on training, re-training and upgrading the workforce. Yet, at every successful tourism establishment, it is the employees that stand out.

The question some unenlightened employer might ask is this: 'Why incur additional cost to educate the employee?'. The answer is simple – the employee is not a cost but an asset whose efficiency is multiplied with increased education and training. Hence the development of staff will go a long way in improving the communication skills and creative thinking necessary to respond professionally to all consumers, including irate ones. Training, when focused properly on teaching employees to make and take decisions and to develop an awareness for customer concerns, will help to enhance the quality of the service and encourage guests to come back. In the services industries, a quick considerate response is often better than a letter of apology or clarification from the hotel manager 2 weeks later.

In the training of the 'new employee' in the pursuit of excellence, one must bear in mind that the type of training necessary today is different from what was best practice a few decades ago. There is the need for a kind of training for employees that prepares them to serve a new generation of travellers. Workers need to be trained not only in a specialized skill, they must be trained to be loyal, flexible, tolerant, amiable and responsible. This will allow employees to act responsibly in any situation while doing so with an air of natural pleasantness. Training should be so organized as to increasingly give trainees a sense of the whole organization – a sense of their own role and importance in the smooth and efficient running of the whole. According to some observers:

> Extreme specialization of tasks gives operators tunnel vision, which makes it difficult to see problems in the making. A worker who understands the entire service-delivery process is more likely to understand the 'inter-connectedness' of the system and find a quick solution.
>
> (Hart *et al.*, 1990, p. 154)

The need for high quality and flexible staff is well recognized by Thai Airways International. Thus the quality and versatility of its air hostesses was the main focus of its recent advertisements. Thai Airway's 2-page ad' appearing in *Time International* (European edition) features an air hostess on the right side of the page, while the left side had the caption:

> She's a child psychologist
> a Maître'd
> a diplomat
> a multi-linguist
> an accomplished pianist and a
> mean mixer of margaritas
>
> (*Times International*, 6 April 1992, pp. 2–3)

9.4.1.3. *Motivate, lead, involve and reward employees*

In the pursuit of quality, it is important that workers are motivated and made to feel a part of the whole organization. Motivating employees to the point where they feel committed to the delivery of a whole experience and not just their job description is a key challenge for industry players. Without happy, motivated and satisfied employees, quality service cannot be delivered. One of the key objectives, then, is to keep employees happy and satisfied in the fulfilment of the greater aim – that of keeping the guests satisfied and loyal. For the key to keeping guests happy is in ensuring that the *employees* are happy, satisfied and loyal. Travel and leisure providers have to develop a number of innovative ways to motivate, involve and reward employees, knowing that once properly motivated, employees will deliver quality service.

A good example of creativity in rewarding, motivating and involving employees is that provided by Ciboney, a Radisson villa, spa and beach resort in Jamaica. Ciboney no longer employs maids or waiters. These categories of employment are obsolete – the concept is no longer in keeping with the quality product that the hotel delivers. Ciboney trains and hires *hosts* who have the responsibility and authority to look after the well-being of the guests – responsibilities spanning from making beds to serving breakfast, preparing meals, looking after their guests' children and providing information. These hosts are assigned to each of 196 well-appointed villa suites. This makes for an extremely flexible, very personal-ized and high-quality service. The personal host, for example, can prepare breakfast and make the bed at any time convenient to the guests. Moreover meals can be prepared for guests, taking into account dietary preferences while, at the same time, children can have a nanny while parents are at play.

While Ciboney is innovating, not far away, two leading hotel chains, Sandals and SuperClub are taking gigantic steps in motivating and rewarding employees, through the development of housing schemes for their workers. This project is being undertaken with the collaboration of the Jamaica Ministry of Tourism and the Environment.

9.4.2. Improve Processes Continuously

Another important aspect of being a leader in quality is to improve processes continuously. It is not enough to bring a new idea or service to the marketplace. The delivery of the services and the processes by which they are produced are as important as bringing a new product or service to the marketplace. Success in the travel and tourism industry is no longer a matter of providing 'unlimited warranties and smile training' (Kanter,

1991, p. 10). The process of delivering services to final consumers has to be continuously improved. Employees are the obvious starting-point in the process of continuous performance improvement because they are the ones who deliver the services. In the pursuit of continuous improvement travel and leisure suppliers have to:

- empower the front line; and
- rely on feedback from the front line to continuously improve processes.

These are explained below.

9.4.2.1. Empower the front line

Responsibility means the obligation to act. Authority, on the other hand, means having the power to act. In the efficient running of an organization these two always go hand-in-hand. People with the responsibility to work must also be given the authority to make legitimate decisions. Some measure of authority must be vested in those given the responsibility to serve the consumer directly on the front line. According to James A. McEleny, Vice President for Corporate Quality Improvement at the Chicago and Northwestern Transportation Company, 'what management needs to understand is that it isn't in charge of customer satisfaction. It is the employees who talk to the customer' (Armstrong and Symonds, 1991, p. 58). For this reason, front-line employees having been given the responsibility to look after the needs of the guests must also be given the authority and incentives to recognize, care about and respond to consumer needs.

It is not enough to delegate more responsibility to the front line. Rather, it is critically important to give employees *authority* to fix and otherwise modify the process in the interest of the final consumers. The authority to act refers to the set of resources employees have access to and the decisions they are permitted to make. In most travel and tourism companies, this authority is reserved only for managers – especially the authority to spend money or otherwise make things happen. Organizations that empower workers make it clear that they are permitted to use their judgement to make, among other things, 'phone calls, credit amounts or send flowers in the fulfilment of expressed goals. At the Minneapolis Marriott City Center, for example, management authorizes employees to spend $10.00 at their discretion to satisfy guests (Hart *et al.*, 1990).

A fine example of success resulting from employee empowerment is provided by Satisfaction Guaranteed Eateries in the USA. At Satisfaction Guaranteed Eateries, employees are empowered to do virtually anything to keep the customers happy:

> In the event of an error or delay, any employee right down to the

busboy can provide complementary wine or desserts, or pick up the entire tab if necessary

(Firnstahl, 1989, p. 29)

9.4.2.2. Rely on feedback from the front line

Feedback from the front line is always crucial in developing successful strategies. Employees are a key element of the service improvement process because they are closest to the customer. It is on them that management must rely for feedback to improve quality. The development of systems to convert feedback from employees into process improvements will help suppliers to better satisfy their customers. For example, the Stouffers Oakbrook Hotel near Chicago promises 'breakfast in 20 minutes – or it's free'! It is through delivering the promise to customers that a hotel may find that too many breakfasts are being given away, thus uncovering a number of system failures that should be fixed.

Timothy Firnstahl, founder and Chief Executive of Satisfaction Guaranteed Eateries found that the cost of keeping the company's promise is the cost of *system failure*. He found that honouring the guarantee of satisfaction uncovered a number of system failures (e.g. the kitchen turning out the wrong orders, workers punching in wrong orders, failure to double-check orders, inadequate training and other inefficiencies). System failures pointed to the need for new training, new procedures, recipe and menu changes, restaurant re-design, equipment purchases and whatever else it takes to put things right. In the long run, the guarantee works only if it reduces system failure costs and increases customer satisfaction.

9.4.3. Use Technology Creatively

Creatively used, technology can become a powerful competitive weapon. With labour viewed as a cost of production and a replaceable item, technology has often been viewed as a substitute for labour – as a tool for reducing labour costs. In the hotel sector, for example, the effectiveness of technology adoption has often been measured by how much labour it replaces. On the other hand, attention is rarely focused on developing strategies to utilize the valuable human hours that have been released from mundane paper-pushing functions to satisfying guests. It may well be that the utilization of these valuable human hours to deliver 'high-touch' services to the consumer will render competitive advantages to travel and leisure suppliers.

By itself, technology cannot create competitive advantages. Technology cannot substitute for decisive strategies or for efficient employees, rather, it can complement them. Information technologies, as used in the travel and tourism industry, are tools that make information functions such as billings, payroll and communications more efficient.

As such, technologies are a vehicle, a means to an end, a tool creatively at use in furthering efficiency and quality – the true creators are happy, satisfied and loyal employees. Therefore, it is a complement to labour, not its replacement. The needs, objectives and strategies of the corporation must first be clearly defined. Only then comes the technology (refer to Chapters 6 and 7). Using technology creatively, that is, using it in such a way that it enhances the efficiency of labour without unduly threatening the workforce, is the way to go.

9.5. DEVELOP RADICAL INNOVATIONS

Innovation is the essence of being creative and bringing new goods and services to the marketplace. According to Schumpeter, innovation is the first commercial transaction involving: *new goods* (e.g. computers, microwave ovens, portable CDs), *new services* (e.g. flexible holiday packages on-line, teleconferencing, direct satellite broadcasting, inflight telephone services), *new markets* (e.g. Eastern Europe), *new methods of production* (e.g. just in time, flexible specialization), *new organization forms* (e.g. flatter hierarchies), and/or *new sources of raw material* (e.g. information) (Schumpeter, 1965).

Two types of innovations are relevant for industry players:

1. *Incremental innovation* involves day-to-day improvements and modifications to existing know-how; for example, new ways of rewarding and empowering employees.
2. *Radical innovation* involves sudden, revolutionary, leaps in product or process technology; for example, plastic, personal computers, the jet aircraft, the club holiday and the package tour.

Although incremental innovations are necessary they are not sufficient to keep ahead of the game; change is happening at a tremendous pace. According to Alan Fredericks, Vice President and Editor-in-Chief of *Travel Weekly*, '… if you've tried to figure out what tomorrow's fares will be, you will identify with that.' (*Travel Weekly*, 18 June 1992b, p. 10). In the world of dynamic change it is important to move beyond day-to-day improvements. It is necessary to innovate radically.

When a mature product (e.g. typewriters or mass tourism) is being replaced by a new product (e.g. computers or flexible tourism), cost-cutting and incremental innovations, for example, adding memory to typewriters, are no longer sufficient to ensure competitive success. Many of those who once thought, and possibly still think, that typewriters and mass tourism were indispensable will increasingly discover that this is not the case.

Innovation holds an important key to success, opening new opportunities.

To innovate for competitive success, firms must be first to the market. They must also be quick to follow those who have invented the idea. They must also learn from their employees, their customers, their competitors as well as from their own experience.

New innovations must be discovered, put into practice and continuously improved upon to create a competitive edge. Three basic rules are associated with developing radical innovations for competitive success. These are as follows:

- don't be afraid of new ideas;
- build a capacity for continuous innovation; and
- never stop learning.

The subcomponents of these competitive principles are detailed in Figure 9.6 and elaborated in the following sections.

9.5.1. Don't Be Afraid of New Ideas

New ideas are the seeds that ferment change. They create change by virtually willing it into being; but wherever change is in motion, uncertainty arises. Now where uncertainties emerge there is sure to exist an element of risk, and where risk is visibly involved, many are understandably afraid. Radically new ideas (e.g. cruises to nowhere, one way sails, midnight golf, wedding and vow-renewal cruises) are creating waves in the travel and tourism industry and, understandably, uncertainties abound.

As a result of changes in today's tourism marketplace, industry players virtually have to be masters of innovation in order to survive. Industry players have to be innovative in order to stay ahead of the game. In a sea of change, where innovative sharks are gobbling up small and big fishes alike, players have to use their ingenuity to survive. Innovation is definitely the way to go. Indeed, a number of travel and leisure companies have gained the competitive edge mainly because of their innovativeness and willingness to dare. Examples of innovative travel and leisure suppliers who were not afraid of change are: Club Med (with the club holiday); American Airlines (with frequent-flyer programmes and Sabre computerized reservation system); the Disney Company (with creative leisure activities for the entire family in a crime-free, controlled environment); Sandals (with all-inclusive holidays for couples only); and Carnival and other cruise lines (with affordable, all-inclusive, flexible holidays to multiple destinations). Although many of these innovations have been copied by others, it has given some inventors sufficient lead-time, experience and economic rent (monopoly profit) to stay ahead of the competition. The future of the travel and leisure industry will lie in more innovation.

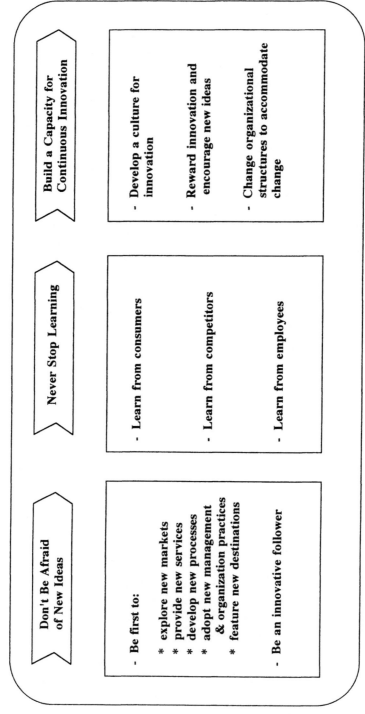

Fig. 9.6. Principle 3: Develop radical innovations.

9.5.1.1. Be first to the market

Being first to the market is the essence of innovation. It involves being first to bring a new product and service to the market. Being first to the market is a risky business. However, being first offers key economic advantages for first movers. They can charge monopoly prices virtually at will since consumers have nothing to compare with and they can gain an important lead, in terms of time, that it will take followers to catch up.

New product/service innovations in tourism include the opening up of new destinations (e.g. China, Eastern Europe), the packaging of multi-destinations (e.g. Miami and the Bahamas), the development of new market segments (e.g. disabled persons, grandparents travelling with grandchildren, non-smokers, vegetarian homosexuals, female business travellers, divers, bone fishers). Other innovations in tourism include: (i) new organizational forms (e.g. the movement of boating companies into the hotel business); (ii) new systems (e.g. automatic checkout at hotels) and (iii) new procedures (e.g. empowering employees) – and there are many others yet to be invented.

Several travel and leisure suppliers have been particularly innovative. Virgin Atlantic is one such supplier in that category. According to one market observer, 'innovations have kept Virgin flying high on the competitive North Atlantic stage' (*Travel Trade Gazette*, UK and Ireland, 1992a, p. 44). Virgin Atlantic has been a leader in innovation with such features as Shiatsu and Swedish head and neck massages aboard trans-Atlantic flights, personal video sets, heart defibrillators and child safety seats. The concept of added value has always been one of the airline's watchwords in its attempt to win passengers and keep them loyal. Its frequent-flyer programme, Freeway, relied heavily on leisure-based prizes such as hang gliding, skiing or photo safaris rather than on free flights or points. With increased competition, however, Virgin has had to respond more competitively. The airline has made a more direct appeal to its trans-Atlantic frequent flyers with two free economy tickets with every round-trip upper-class (first-class) journey (*Travel Trade Gazette*, UK and Ireland, 19 March 1992a, p. 44).

The pleasure boating industry is also innovative in responding to the changing needs of its clientele. In an attempt to control as many aspects of the vacation as possible, boating companies are diversifying into hotels. Club Mariner, The Moorings Hotel brand, for example, positions itself as 'the cure to the common vacation'. The Moorings already has Club Mariner hotels in the British Virgin Islands and Grenada. Entry into the hotel sector allows The Moorings to directly influence the quality experience that their clients receive both on land and at sea. Also reflecting the growing maturity and sophistication of their clients, charter boats are getting larger and more comfortable, with more creature comforts aboard.

'Sail and fly' and 'stay and sail' programmes have also been introduced to offer flexibility to their clients. In the Grenadines, for example, sail and fly programmes are growing in popularity as clients like the pleasure of sailing down-wind but like the flexibility of being able to fly back, avoiding the slightly more challenging return journey up-wind (Caribbean Tourism Organization, 1991a).

Club Mediterranée is another innovator. Beginning with tents and straw huts in the 1950s, 'Club Med' built its first permanent purpose-built and permanent bungalow village at Agadir in Morocco in 1965. In being first to the market it became the leader in the club/village holidays worldwide. Club Med pioneered a vacation experience that emphasized sports and the pleasures of the table. It provided an all-inclusive holiday programme in which one price included all on-property sports, all meals and unlimited wine. Only the bar made charges. This recipe allowed Club Med to grow at a tremendous rate. By the 1980s, Club Med was the leader in all-inclusive club holidays. In 1987, Club Med had 213 hotels with 55 152 rooms in over 30 countries. It was the 12th largest hotel chain in the world. Today it has grown into an empire whose primal claim to success is that it was first to the market.

9.5.1.2. Be an innovative follower

Sometimes being quick to follow can be as important as being first to the market, for it places one next in line; and, with continuous improvements, sometimes at the side of competitors – at times even ahead. Whether it is a frequent-flyer programme, a focus on ecotourism or the development of all-inclusive holidays, it is important to follow the market, feel its pulse and understand its behaviour. In following, however, it is important that the innovation is not copied wholesale but improved upon.

Sandals and SuperClub, like the Japanese approach to technology transfer from the West, are clear examples of innovative followers. They followed the market, saw innovations, learned, copied and improved on them. They have brilliantly copied the Club Med formula, Caribbeanized it, and in some areas, have gone on to be even more innovative than Club Med. Today, these Jamaican-owned and managed hotel chains are fast becoming market leaders in all-inclusive holidays in the Caribbean.

For years, Club Med was the standard by which one judged an all-inclusive holiday. By the 1980s, however, Club Med's clients still had to pay for drinks and cigarettes – and beads adorned the necks of their clientele in order to pay for these items. The idea of including bar drinks, cigarettes, airport transfers and tips in the price of the holiday was success-fully pioneered in 1978 by SuperClub at its Couples property in Jamaica, when the proprietor, John Issa, decided that everything a guest ate, drank, and did should be included in the pre-paid price. The idea was to provide adult couples with the ideal environment for a romantic yet fun-filled holiday. Eliminating the use of money removed any potential for embarrassment or conflict that the spending of money could generate. Since this successful experiment, SuperClub now has seven properties located on the Caribbean islands of Jamaica, St Lucia and Cuba. These properties as well as other all-inclusive hotel chains, such as Sandals and Club St Lucia, are the most successful hotels in the Caribbean today. Year-round occupancy rates of over 90% are the norm for these chains. In fact, all-inclusive hotels consistently out-performed standard hotels in Jamaica. In 1990, standard non-all-inclusive hotels achieved an average yearly occupancy rate of 55% compared with 83% for all-inclusive hotels (Jamaica Ministry of Tourism, *Annual Travel Statistics*, 1990, p. 72).

The Sandals and SuperClub hotels in Jamaica have not only successfully copied and Caribbeanized Club Med's all-inclusive (one price includes everything) concept. These two hotel chains have gone beyond Club Med, having begun to exploit some innovative market niches. Sandals, for example, caters only to couples, while the SuperClub hotel chain caters to a different market segment at each property. Sandals and SuperClub have managed to secure some very important market niches at a time when Club Med is beginning to battle with 'demographic obsolescence', attempting to mature with its market, turning to families in a major way.

While Club Med's marketing in the USA 'has tended to neglect, even offend travel agents who book 85% of its packages', the Sandals and SuperClub hotel chains have succeeded in establishing successful alliances with US travel agencies (Forbes, 1989). In addition, being Caribbean-based and focusing on its human resources, SuperClub and Sandals have succeeded in cultivating strong and loyal links with their employees. As a result, they produce satisfied guests.

9.5.2. Never Stop Learning

Learning is a key component of competitive success. Learning refers to conscious decisions, procedures and methods adopted by an organization to allow it to learn from doing business. Three key aspects of learning are important: learning from consumers, competitors and workers. It is also important that firms learn from their own experience – for there is no greater teacher than experience.

Learning provides players with a critical source of competitive advantage – time. Since learning is a time-consuming process, firms accumulate tremendous knowledge and experience only over a period of time. While a competitor may be able to copy innovations, it will not be easy to copy the time and effort invested in learning because learning provides players with a tool to be continuously innovative. If a player continues to learn, then by the time an invention is imitated, the player would have jumped ahead of the game.

9.5.2.1. Learn from consumers

Perhaps the most important source of learning is learning from consumers, for consumers are always right – after all, they are the ones who are paying. Travel consumers today know the world of travel. Their collective experience is a source of tremendous wealth; their collective desires are a source of tremendous information for those seeking to satisfy them.

In satisfying their clients, travel and leisure suppliers have to learn from their consumers and grow with their market – it is the only way that they, the suppliers, will survive. Learning from the consumers can become a very important means of bringing new products and services to the marketplace.

With the ageing of the population in the major tourist-generating economies, several companies are finding it important to respond accordingly. The Body Shop in the UK, for example, has introduced a line of baby products to grow with its clients who have become parents – an attempt, one might say, for Body Shop to grow while the babies grow.

In the travel and leisure industry, Club Med is a good example of a company attempting to change with its market. Club Med is finding it increasingly more important to move away from its swinging singles image and to cater to families. The ageing, more family-oriented America is outgrowing the sexy formula that made the club offering successful in the 1970s. Its clients, who once descended on their villages for sun, sex and self-indulgence have progressed to parenthood. Club Med is out to trash its old image as the place for endless partying or a global singles bar. According to one Club Med marketing official, 'we also want the fat rich guy who just wants to eat all day' (Forbes, 1989, p. 137). Club Med introduced baby and mini-clubs to cater to the children of their maturing clients and has launched Club Med I and II, sailing and motor vessels that are currently the world's largest sailing ships. According to one observer, 'the new Club Med is taking a much wider aim – at couples, families, corporate seminar and incentive business, and the elderly – but still not trying to turn off the young and sex-starved' (Forbes, 1989, p. 137). Whether and to what extent Club Med will be able to successfully mature with its clients will depend on how well it understands its clientele and how innovative the company is in responding to their needs. Club Med's success has traditionally been its innovativeness. With its holiday villages Club Med virtually created a new holiday lifestyle – a lifestyle that has been fashionable and highly desirable. Can Club Med develop new innovations that will continue to sustain it in the years ahead? The time has changed and consumers have changed. A whole new formula is necessary to satisfy the new consumers. Just as the Club holiday filled a niche in the 1960s, 1970s and 1980s, a radically new concept seems to be necessary for the decades to come. Whether Club Med will be the one to invent this new concept for the new tourism remains to be seen.

9.5.2.2. Learn from competitors

Many smart players consciously learn from their competitors. One of the keys to good strategic planning is to know the competition. As J.W. Marriott Jr., Chairman of Marriott Corporation puts it: 'I stay at competitive hotels three or four times a year to learn about new things plus to see what they could do better and to think about those things we can do better' (Marriott, 1989, p.291). Learning is not only important for laggards. Learning is important for any and everyone to stay ahead of the game – even for those who are already in the lead.

9.5.2.3. Learn from employees

It is also important to learn from one's own employees – for these are the ones who are in touch with the pulse of the consumer and the day-to-day running of the organization. One hotel chain, the Canada Pacific Hotel and Resorts (CPH&R) took the initiative to learn from their employees. This they did by soliciting their employees' views on a planned policy to begin to consciously think green (Canadian Pacific Hotels and Resorts, 1991, p.1). Environmental questionnaires were distributed to all employees. The findings are very revealing:

- 95% of employees see the environment as a critical issue;
- 89% want to know more about what they can do to help;
- 82% would volunteer extra time and effort to help;
- 92% agree the CPH&R efforts will help our planet; and
- 88% will take more pride in jobs with a 'green' CPH&R.

It will not at all be surprising that CPH&R have total support for thinking green.

9.5.3. Build a Capacity for Continuous Innovation

Innovation must not only be total, it must also be continuous. A company cannot hope to develop a single innovation and expect it to provide a competitive edge forever. The innovation itself has to be sustained and, if possible, it must be allowed to evolve into new strains of innovation. For with innovation, *sustainability usually requires more innovation.*

For success, innovations sometimes need to be coupled together. For example, the introduction of a new technology may necessitate organization and staff changes in a company. It is necessary, therefore, to be totally innovative in many areas at the same time – not just in marketing or in the development of new vacation concepts but also in other areas, such as technology adoption or the development of new markets or market niches and new organizational forms. A stand-alone or de-linked innovation is not likely to be so potent as a cluster of innovations related to different spheres of a firm's operation. This will make it more difficult for competitors to copy. It is therefore important to be innovative in as many areas as possible. In building a capacity for continuous innovation, players must:

- develop a culture of innovation; and
- change organizational structures to accommodate change.

These are explained below.

9.5.3.1. Develop a culture of innovation

As stated before, neither can a firm afford to innovate and rest, for to rest is to be left behind. In the travel and leisure industry, it is too easy for firms to imitate one another. Firms have to build a capacity for continuous innovation. Innovations do not fall from the heavens but are usually embodied in human beings. Employees have to be motivated and encouraged to propose and implement new ideas. This can be done in an environment in which innovation becomes a way of life and a vital part of the corporate culture of an enterprise.

Some of the best examples of making innovation a fundamental principle come from the Japanese, where *kaizen* (continuous improvement) has become a way of life. Employees are continuously encouraged to develop new ways of improving systems and procedures in the company. According to Eiji Toyota, Chairman of Toyota Motors: 'Our workers provide 1.5 million suggestions a year, and 95% of them are put to practical use' (Imai, 1986, p.15). The suggestion system has become very important. According to Imai, the main subjects for suggestions in Japanese companies' suggestion systems include:

- improvements in one's own work;
- saving in energy, material, and other resources;
- improvements in the working environment;
- improvements in machines and processes;
- improvements in jigs and tools;
- improvements in office work;
- improvements in product quality;
- ideas for new products; and

- improvements in consumer services and consumer relations.

In 1985, Matsushita topped the list of all Japanese companies in number of suggestions with over 6 million suggestions, and the most suggestions made at one company in 1 year by an individual was 16 821 (Imai, 1986, p. 112).

It is not enough to encourage new ideas and foster a culture of innovation. It is also important to develop mechanisms such as bonuses, prizes and praise that reward creativity. This will ensure that the incentive is there to continuously innovate.

9.5.3.2. Change organizational structures

Finally, players will often find that the current and historical patterns of the organization cannot accommodate change – its structure suffers from outdated plant and equipment to outdated management styles and employees who are set in their ways. These obstacles often prevent a company from taking on board new ideas and innovations. There is often a mismatch between the new innovations and the organizational form in which they are supposed to take hold. This reality is borne out by research that has shown that the biggest constraint to innovation is not the lack of creativity or technology but the absence of social, organizational and management structures that will allow new ideas to take hold and to reach the marketplace. In other words, there may be a mismatch between the technology and the organization adopting it.

Players will have to change their organizational forms to accommodate change. One of the biggest changes will have to come in the way labour is organized in the production process. Front-line, customer-contact, employees will need to become more involved in shaping services and the delivery systems. Firms will need to adopt flatter hierarchies and will have to develop the organizational flexibility to accommodate change.

9.6. STRENGTHEN YOUR STRATEGIC POSITION

In Chapter 8, we saw that profound changes in the value chain of the industry are expected. Some players will lose while others will gain. Three main changes were identified:

1. The relative positions of different players in the industry will change. Players that are closest to the consumer as well as those that can most efficiently control the industry's value creation, are expected to gain. Travel agents, airlines and suppliers on site are all expected to increase their influence on the industry's wealth-creating process. The role of the tour operator is expected to decline. Airlines, with their global CRSs, will continue to dominate the tourism industry.

2. The tourism industry will become more diagonally integrated. The industry will become an engine of growth and a system of wealth-creation – a process that will continue to blur the boundaries among industry players. **3.** Competitors will increasingly come from outside the industry.

In order for industry players to respond competitively to these changes, it is necessary for them to take action on three fronts:

- seek an advantageous position in the industry's value chain;
- integrate diagonally; and
- influence the competitive environment.

These three rules for competitive success are explained in Figure 9.7 and elaborated below.

9.6.1. Seek Advantageous Position in the Value Chain

Chapter 8 considered some of the strategic responses that tour operators, travel agencies and hotels should make in order to respond competitively to the changes taking place in the industry. Tour operators, for example, will need to produce more flexible holiday packages. They will need to expand their information functions, link product development with marketing and control the delivery of the holiday experience at all stages. Travel agencies need to use CRSs to create flexible holiday packages and to provide unbiased information. They need to increase their buying power through cooperation and they need to shift their emphasis from tour operators to the actual service providers. For hotels that have not been innovative or forward-thinking, there will be the need to put the consumers first – to listen to their customers and aim at 'zero defections'. They will also have to be leaders in quality. They will have to continue the process of improving their electronic links to the marketplace while, at the same time, improve the skill and quality of their employees. They will also need to develop creative relationships with travel agencies as they strive to become more actively involved in the marketing of their bed-nights.

Whether it is a hotel, a travel agent or an airline, two basic principles are necessary in order to gain an advantageous position in the industry's value chain. There will be the need to:

- influence the process of wealth-creation; and
- build strategic alliances.

9.6.1.1. *Influence the process of wealth-creation*

Influencing the process of wealth creation requires control over the two key agents of wealth generation – information and consumers. In the

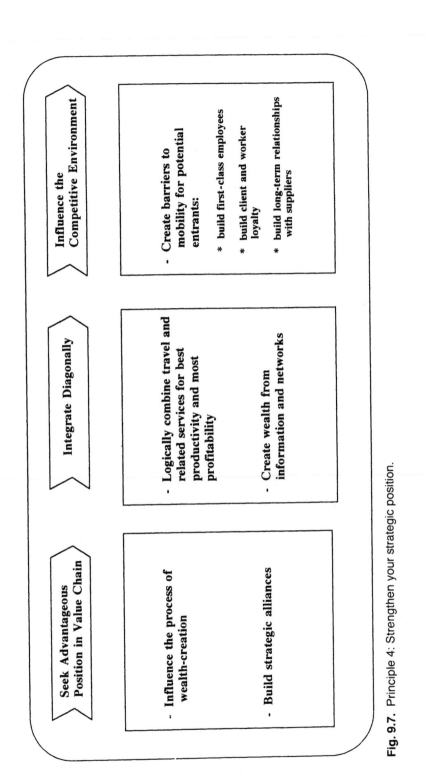

Fig. 9.7. Principle 4: Strengthen your strategic position.

analysis of the travel and leisure value chain in Chapter 8, it became clear that wealth is created through a number of information-driven activities that industry players perform – from yield management, marketing and public relations, to customer service at hotels, bars and restaurants. Influencing the process of wealth-creation invariably means generating, controlling and manipulating the industry's most important raw material – *information*. However, information is not desired for its own sake. Rather, it is the means to understand the consumer, the vehicle to produce goods and services that satisfy their needs and the distribution channel to reach their target markets.

Another key avenue for influencing the process of wealth-creation is to influence *consumers*. As already stated, getting close to consumers, understanding them and providing them with the experience they want, are also important for competitive success for all industry players (see Section 9.3).

9.6.1.2. Build strategic alliances

Strategic alliances refer to agreements made among industry players that allow them to mutually benefit from cooperation through marketing, purchasing, jointly supplying markets and other areas. Strategic alliances extend the operating arms of those participating in it, affording them economies not possible to players operating on their own. Such alliances abound in the travel and tourism industry. In the airline industry, for example, 43 of the 50 top regional carriers in the US have code-sharing agreements with the major airlines (Economist Intelligence Unit, 1990c). Car-rental companies strategically align themselves with airline frequent-flyer programmes and other cooperative advertising initiatives in order to secure markets that, on their own, may be difficult to command. Hotels band together in order to benefit from joint marketing programmes for the same reason – one such example of an alliance is the Elegant Resorts grouping in Barbados and Jamaica and the Outrigger Hotel chain in Hawaii.

9.6.2. Integrate Diagonally

As have been seen in Chapter 8, diagonal integration has become one of the key vehicles for controlling the process of value creation in the travel and leisure industry. As the industry becomes more information-and-consumer driven, firms can diagonally integrate to control the more lucrative areas of value creation. The process of diagonal integration will continue to blur the boundaries among players within the industry. *Whether the company is a hotel, a travel agency or an airline will no longer be relevant. What will become more relevant is the activities along the industry's value chain that it controls.*

Diagonal integration is one of the key strategic moves for the success of industry players in the new environment. When diagonally integrating, firms must:

- logically combine travel and related services for best productivity and most profitability; and
- create wealth from information and networks.

9.6.2.1. Logically combine services

When players diagonally integrate they are, in effect, combining services. A company that has successfully combined the production of services for best productivity and most profitability is American Express. American Express is diagonally integrated in four distinct yet complementary spheres of activity. These include:

- travel, finance and communications;
- international banking;
- insurance; and
- investment and asset management services.

American Express is involved in these four core activities, making a broad range of services available to its individual and corporate clients. The key to American Express' success and their underlying philosophy is its ability to work as 'one enterprise'. American Express claims that each of the four major business segments interact with one another to blend products, services, distribution and expertise to meet the demands of sophisticated consumers and add to their convenience and satisfaction.

American Express can enjoy a high level of synergies and can benefit from scope economies by integrating in this way. The company also claims that it does not intend to be the financial supermarket of the world. It has therefore targeted its choice of services to a specific consumer segment. The company can supply the broad range of travel, insurance, banking and investment services to this targeted group of consumers. The economies of scope involved in selling a single consumer an entire range of services is very different from the economies of scale associated with the selling of a single service to a broad range of consumers.

While American Express with its 'one enterprise' vision is a case study of success, this does not mean that all firms are going the diagonal integration route or that all who have tried have succeeded.

Many difficulties lie ahead for many travel and leisure suppliers. The difficulties are associated with the inherent diversity of the travel and leisure industry. Just about any combination of services (e.g. fast food, theme parks, real estate, portfolio management) appear to blend together.

In addition, technologies are already available to allow suppliers to produce these services jointly.

However, the joint production of these services may not always be viable. This is exactly what United Airlines managers found when they formed the Allegis Corporation and acquired the Hertz Corporation in the hope of creating an integrated travel company. Together with Westin Hotels, which they already owned, the idea of combining air transportation, car rentals and hotels seemed logical at the time. Nobody speaks of Allegis today without adding the word 'fiasco' to it.

One of the key lessons from the failure of Allegis is that ownership of various activities in the travel and leisure value chain is not necessarily the route to strategically positioning a firm within the industry's value chain. Systems gains, synergies and even economies of scope can be derived from partnerships and strategic alliances (such as the American Airlines/ Citicorp partnership tying credit cards to a frequent-flier programme) and need not be based on ownership.

Tremendous opportunities are provided by the maturing of the industry's consumers and the sophisticated technologies available to industry players. Key to taking advantage of these opportunities are:

- matching the resources of the firm with the opportunities of the marketplace; and
- understanding that partnerships and alliances engineered by information systems need not be based on ownership.

A company will be best able to take advantage of opportunities provided by building on the strengths that the company has already acquired. Firms should avoid ownership and management of activities in which they have no knowledge or experience. They should focus instead on developing synergies among related activities (even if these activities are owned and operated by other companies). They should invent creative ways of building information partnerships and strategic alliances with other suppliers in order to reap production and marketing synergies. Opportunities for partnerships and for entry into new markets must also be based on the firm's established strengths and capabilities (e.g. loyal customers, CRSs, a good workforce, an innovative holiday concept).

9.6.2.2. Create wealth from networks

With over 20 000 outlets, banks and building societies in the UK are diagonally integrating into travel and travel-related services in order to take advantage of their branch networks. These institutions have already established consumer goodwill by providing financial services over a period of time; they have a ready segmented market at their disposal; they have details of consumer requirements, based on their history of purchases of investment, banking, travel and insurance services. The economics of tapping this ready market for these multiple services is promising. This is particularly the case when it is considered that services are jointly consumed at regular intervals over one's lifetime. The wealth-creating potential of this market is enormous.

9.6.3. Influence the Competitive Environment

Another strategy for competitiveness is to influence the competitive environment. This can be achieved by creating barriers to mobility that would hinder the growth and success of a prospective competitor. In other words, firms have to make their strategies as difficult as possible to imitate. In the travel and leisure industry, it is nearly impossible to prevent a new firm from entering the industry. Unlike other industries where barriers to entry are created by high start-up costs (e.g. oil drilling) or huge investments in plant and equipment (e.g. iron and steel), or by sophisticated technology (e.g. super computers), in the travel and leisure industry, these barriers to entry are not so significant. Computerized reservations systems is probably one of the few areas in the industry where barriers to entry have been created because of high investment outlays (see Chapter 7). This being the case, it is more appropriate for industry players to create barriers that make it difficult for competitors to enter its industry and be a success.

Barriers to mobility in the travel and tourism industry are intangible. They are related to the skills, quality, goodwill and experience that a company has accumulated over time; for example, the knowledge and experience of a company on a particular destination; a niche in a market that has been built up over years; competent and professional staff who deliver the services for which consumers are looking; the negotiating skills of tour operators; knowledge of consumers and tourism generating markets. In order for a player to make it as difficult as possible for competitors to enter this market segment and be as profitable, three strategies are recommended:

1. Develop first class employees.
2. Build client and worker loyalty.
3. Forge long-term relationships with suppliers.

Travel and leisure suppliers will increasingly find that nearly every aspect of their strategies can be copied (from a focus on green tourism and budget hotels to 'sail and stay' holidays). *The only asset that a company has that cannot be copied is its employees.* Firms therefore have to invest in adding value to their human resources, empowering them, keeping them happy, and ensuring that they do not defect.

It is also important for firms to build loyalty among their workers. While it will be difficult to copy the experience that a firm has accumulated in a particular area of the travel industry, it must be remembered that this experience is usually embodied in human beings. When employees defect, they take this experience with them. More often than not, they take their clients with them as well. Keeping clients and employees loyal will help firms to stay always ahead of the game.

Building long-term relationships with suppliers also contributes to success. The closer a company is to its suppliers, the more readily suppliers can respond to the changing needs of their clients. Travel and tourism players can also work closely with suppliers in the development of products (e.g. flight menus, passenger seats, and the use of recycled paper for hotel stationery) that suit the changing needs of consumers. Once industry players can work with their suppliers to deliver quality to their clients, they will stay ahead of the game and ahead of their consumers.

9.7. SUMMARY

To be better and more efficient than competitors, travel and leisure suppliers have to *put consumers first.* Consumers are more experienced and harder to please than ever before. They vote both with their pocketbook and with their feet. If they are not satisfied, not only do they not buy, they take their business elsewhere. Industry players have to learn to keep their customers and track the ones who never come back. This is the challenge that faces them. The fact is that consumers are changing and it is not sufficient to keep up with them – one must be ahead of them. Being ahead of the game means being ahead of the consumers – understanding them, anticipating their needs and supplying them with what they want.

Quality will be the most significant factor for competitive success among industry players. Success in the travel and leisure industry is no longer a matter of providing unlimited warranties and smile training. As the novelty of driving a car and going on holiday has worn off, consumers have become far more demanding. They want quality, flexibility and value for money. Unlike a manufactured item, when there is a defect in a service transaction, it cannot be halted, examined or recycled. With travel and tourism services, quality must be produced right from the beginning. The key to quality is empowering, redirecting and regarding the industry's most valuable asset – its human beings. In this regard, the Japanese successes with lean production and kaizen (continuous improvements) in the automobile industry have some very important lessons for travel and leisure suppliers.

In a highly competitive and rapidly changing industry where one virtually has to run in order to stand still, firms have to *introduce radical innovations.* Being first to the market, however, is not enough. One cannot afford to innovate and rest. Companies always have to find new markets, develop new products, feature new destinations and modify their organization to accommodate change. Industry players also have to develop a capacity to learn from their consumers, suppliers, competitors and employees. The development of capacities for learning and for continuous innovation are key ingredients or competitive success.

As the value chain changes, players will also have to *strengthen their strategic positions within the industry.* They will have to build strategic alliances and diagonally integrate for best productivity and most profits. Firms will have to create barriers to mobility and ensure that competitors do not enter their market segments and become as successful as they.

V
THE FUTURE

10

STRATEGIES FOR TOURISM DESTINATIONS

10.1. INTRODUCTION

Tourism is a double-edged sword – it can be a potential blessing and it can be a blight. Many tourism destinations benefit from the flows of tourists and the hard currencies they bring. However, they have not completely avoided some of tourism's negative consequences – prostitution, crime, deviance, commercialization of culture and changing social norms and values.

The tourism industry is the largest in the world and it will continue to grow – as it grows, it will offer enormous opportunities for creating wealth. Already countries and destinations such as the Caribbean, Latin America, Australia, Spain, Britain, Switzerland, Mexico and the USA derive substantial revenues from tourism. With the decline of traditional exports such as sugar, coffee, cocoa, bananas, bauxite, spices and citrus, many developing countries will find that they have no choice but to turn to tourism. Even the former Eastern Block countries (e.g. Czechoslovakia, Hungary, Poland, Yugoslavia) and the socialist countries of China and Cuba are attempting to develop tourism in a major way. The fact is that, across the globe, dependence on tourism will increase.

Today, therefore, the issue is not *whether* to develop tourism but rather:

- *how* to develop the industry in such a way that the local communities benefit,
- *how* to use the tourism industry to regenerate other sectors of the economy such as agriculture, manufacturing and services,
- *how* tourism can create a sustainable economic and environmental basis for the future,
- *how* to limit tourism's negative social and cultural impacts,
- *how* tourism destinations can ensure adequate air access in a deregulated air transportation market,

- *how* to cope with the increased dominance of cruise tourism,
- *what* should be the new role of national tourism offices (NTOs) in the marketplace,
- *how* tourism destinations can use technology to enhance their competitiveness,
- *how* to build a dynamic local private sector,
- *how* to encourage the private sector to improve quality continuously.

It is to these issues that this chapter now turns. As tourism destinations begin to address the problems that accompanied old tourism, they will increasingly turn to new tourism. In fact, tourism destinations have a vital role to play in the spread of new tourism; for actions, policies and decisions taken at the destination level can either encourage or hinder its growth.

This chapter will identify competitive strategies that tourism destinations will need to implement in order to foster the development of a new and more sustainable tourism. Such strategies include:

- putting the environment first;
- making tourism a lead sector;
- strengthening distribution channels in the marketplace; and
- building a dynamic private sector.

Successfully implementing these strategies will place tourism destinations firmly in the camp of new tourism – a tourism that is sensitive to the environment and the people of the country; a tourism that is sustainable; a tourism that is able to transform tourism-dependent and vulnerable island economies into viable entities.

This chapter will draw on the experience of the Caribbean – a destination that offers the 'best laboratory' for analysing the effects of tourism in the developing world (*Economist*, 23 March 1991).

10.2. TOURISM – BLESSING OR BLIGHT?

By its very nature, mass tourism 'radically alters the manifest cultural content of local communities, even though local people are peripherally involved' (Pi-Sunyer, 1974). This, it is argued, results from a prevailing perception that tourists must have culture 'on demand', giving rise to 'phony folk culture' (Cohen, 1972, 1973), 'staged authenticity' (Mac-Cannell, 1973), cultural 'commercialization' (Forster, 1964) and 'culture by the pound' (Greenwood, 1978). This occurs, for example, when locals begin to stage religious ceremonies out of time, place and context just to 'put on a show' for tourists.

It is lamented, for example, that whether tourist attractions are natural (e.g. ski slopes) or contrived (e.g. Disneyland), they have to be transformed or manipulated to make them suitable for mass consumption. It is contended, moreover, that tourists are:

> ... supplied with facilities, reconstructed, landscaped, cleansed of unsuitable elements, staged, managed, and otherwise organized. As a result they lose their original flavor and appearance and become isolated from the ordinary flow of life and the natural texture of the host society.
>
> (Cohen, 1972, p. 170)

The consequences of this, is that there is basic uniformity and similarity of tourist experience: countries lose their individuality and become inter-changeable in the minds of tourists.

Other social effects of tourism on host communities include:

1. Increased social deviance (e.g. in some small communities children boycott school to sell T-shirts and post-cards to hordes of arriving cruise passengers).
2. Standardization of roles (locals and tourists know how they are supposed to behave).
3. Increasing impersonality (guests are known by their room number).
4. Tourism fatigue (the society and infrastructure begin to wane under the pressures of tourism demand – poor attitudes and environmental degrada-tion set in).
5. Monetization of relationships (people smile 'on demand', and only if they are rewarded for it).
6. Increased intergenerational conflict (family values and religion are marginalized).
7. The outburst of new diseases (e.g. sexually transmitted diseases such as VD, syphilis, gonorrhoea, AIDS).

Other observers (Hong, 1985; O'Grady, 1981) have raised concerns about prostitution (the 'flesh trade') and disruption of family life as women, men and children enter the industry as maids, waiters and prosti-tutes and sometimes work long hours, even on Sundays, to the neglect of religious and family life.

Negative impacts of tourism are specific not only to developing countries – on the contrary, the confusion and cultural concerns that EuroDisney raised in France, are clear testimony to the more global nature of tourism's cultural impacts. Nor are all cultural impacts negative or caused by tourism. Indeed, the spread of 'ethnic' foods and cultures in London and New York – caused primarily by migration rather than tourism – have become part of the attractiveness of those cities. Addi-tionally, the first Japanese cultural export, Karaoke, as well as Jamaica's reggae and Trinidad and Tobago's steelband and limbo have demonstrated that the business of culture and cultural impacts are neither one-way flows from the West to the rest of the world, nor all negative.

Negative impacts of tourism are also felt in the economic sphere (Bryden, 1973; Turner and Ash, 1975; Belise, 1983). Economically, tourism is seen to bring the benefits of foreign exchange, employment and incomes to communities that have few other prospects of modernization and economic development. However, the beneficial impact of tourism in national economies is seen to be weakened by:

1. The high import content of tourist expenditure (the need to import food, wine, pots and pans to cater to the tourist trade).
2. The demonstration effect (locals abandon their own foods, dress and lifestyle and mimic those of the tourists).
3. Disruption of the agricultural sector (locals prefer to work in hotels, rather than in the hot sun).
4. High seasonality (in the Caribbean, 4 months of feast – December to March – and 8 months of famine – April to November);
5. Sensitivity to income swings (e.g. caused by oil crisis, recession, movements in exchange rates, changes in personal disposable incomes and prices).
6. Domestic and international political conditions (e.g. political unrest in Haiti, the Gulf War).
7. The dominance of short-stay (cruise tourists) over long-stay (hotels) thereby generating less revenue to the local economy. In the Bahamas, it is estimated that it takes 13 cruise ship passengers to compensate for one long-stay visitor (*Caribbean Futures*, 1992).

Tourism is also viewed as 'intrusion' leading to the reinforcement of the historical process of colonialism, imperialism and underdevelopment, loss of control of the direction of development and dominance by multi-national corporations (Matthews, 1977; Nash, 1977; Britton, 1982; Erisman, 1983). It is also argued by some commentators that tourism perpetuates the ties of colonialism and results in the development of 'enclaves', 'mass seduction', 'whorism', 'playground cultures' and 'a new plantation system'. It is argued, for example, that:

> metropolitan promoters of tourism have come to view Third World destinations not as sovereign countries striving to make a place in the world, but rather as socially uninhibited *places* where metropolitan visitors can unwind amid an abundance of sun, sand, sex and servility.
>
> (Matthews, 1977, p. 25 – his emphasis).

The evils of tourism are mainly associated with the old 'mass' forms of tourism that prevailed during much of the 1960s, 1970s and 1980s. So overpowering has been the tendency toward mass tourism that, three decades ago, countries developing tourism had little choice but to go the mass tourism route – only to be host to tourism's backlash at a later date. Today, however, tourism destinations have a choice – the choice is new tourism.

10.3. COMPETITIVE STRATEGIES ARE NECESSARY

In attempting to address the negative impact of old tourism, and to redress three decades of decadence that it has brought in its wake, a completely new tourism is fast emerging to challenge the old. A new tourism with its concern for nature and with an orientation towards what is flexible and individual is fast gaining ground. However, although it has already begun to take shape, new tourism will not just happen – it has to be planned and consciously created. It has to be willed into being. Competitive strategies are therefore critically important for tourism destinations to sail a new tourism course. This is so because:

1. Comparative advantages are no longer natural.
2. Tourism is a volatile, sensitive and fiercely competitive industry.
3. The industry is undergoing rapid and radical transformation – the rules of the game are changing for everyone.
4. What is at stake is not just tourism but the survival of tourism-dependent economies.
5. The future development and viability of tourism-dependent economies will depend not only on tourism, but on the entire service sector.

These are explained below.

Comparative advantages are no longer natural. They are increasingly man-made, brought on by the mastery of science, technology, human intelligence and innovation (Rada, 1980). Competitive strategies – the conscious and creative use of human intelligence, innovation and creativity to create defensible competitive positions – are critically important in order to convert natural advantages into competitive success. Those tourism destinations that believe that they can continue to survive because of their God-given gifts of nature, sun, sand, sea and ski slopes are in for a rude shock. Today, it is not just the whiteness of the sand, the hotness of the sun, the slope of the snow terrain, or the nature of the hotel, that will determine competitive success. More important than the mere existence of natural attributes, is the quality of human beings who deliver services around them (e.g. hotel staff, tour guides, boat operators, customs and immigration officers). Equally important are the protection and conservation of natural assets (e.g. development of national parks and environmentally protected lands); the cleanliness and ambience of the whole destination and not just the resort (e.g. with friendly people, good signposting, clean and safe streets); innovation in product development, packaging and marketing (e.g. the sale of unique experiences and not just a bed-night or a berth-night); and access to distribution channels in the marketplace (e.g. creatively using technologies, travel agencies and promotional offices overseas).

Competitive strategies are also necessitated by the *volatility and sensitivity* of the tourism industry. Tourism is perhaps the only industry that a 'bad press', for example a riot (e.g. Los Angeles), political events (e.g. China's Tiananmen Square massacre), domestic disturbances (e.g. civil war in Dubrovnik, Yugoslavia) and hurricanes (e.g. Gilbert, Hugo and Andrew in the Caribbean), can destroy overnight. Competitive strategies are therefore necessary in order to give tourism destinations the capability to *anticipate* change, the *flexibility* to accommodate change and the *robustness* to weather the storms.

The tourism industry is *fiercely competitive*, and increasingly so. The Caribbean's sun, sand and sea, for example, is in competition with the wildlife of East Africa, the jungles of Latin America, the temples of India, the cathedrals of Europe and the crocodiles of Australia. Competitive strategies are increasingly necessary to stay ahead of the game. Unfortunately, advertisement and promotions in the marketplace and generous incentives to attract foreign investment to build hotels are often considered to be the requirements for success. And despite increased competition and the radical transformation of the industry, tourism in many developing countries is still considered an 'easy', 'laid-back' industry – an industry not requiring much in the way of strategic planning, professional management, or sensitivity to the environment and local cultures.

This recipe may have worked in an environment where paid holidays, the jet aircraft and cheap package tours offered tourists a chance to visit a warm destination – any warm destination! However, as we have seen in Chapters 2 and 6, the tourism industry is radically changing. Traditional best practices are now obsolete. The rules of the game are changing for everyone – for industry players and for governments, for international players and for local suppliers – and for all tourism destinations! Airline deregulation, new technologies and new consumers have profound implications for the travel and tourism industry. No destination will escape their impacts. *Competitive strategies are as necessary for governments and tourism destinations as they are for industry players.*

What is at stake here is not just the survival of *a* tourism industry. What is really at stake is the survival and viability of tourism-dependent economies and the delicate environments on which they, and increasingly the world, depend. *New strategies of development are needed.* Tourism has a key role to play in transforming small island economies into viable entities. Strategies have to be developed to assist destinations to use the presence of a tourism industry to regenerate their agriculture and

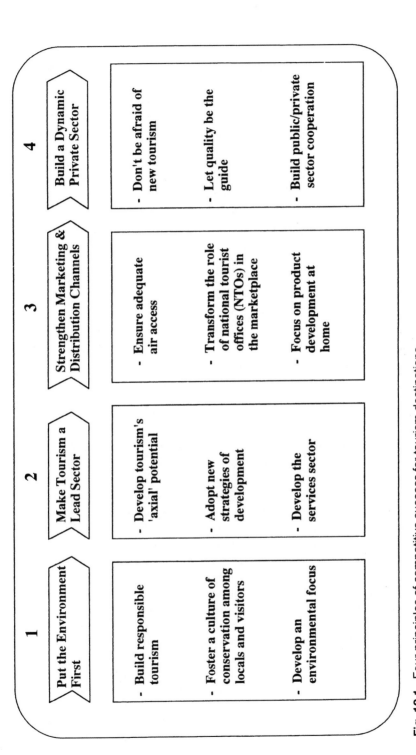

1	2	3	4
Put the Environment First	**Make Tourism a Lead Sector**	**Strengthen Marketing & Distribution Channels**	**Build a Dynamic Private Sector**
- Build responsible tourism	- Develop tourism's 'axial' potential	- Ensure adequate air access	- Don't be afraid of new tourism
- Foster a culture of conservation among locals and visitors	- Adopt new strategies of development	- Transform the role of national tourist offices (NTOs) in the marketplace	- Let quality be the guide
- Develop an environmental focus	- Develop the services sector	- Focus on product development at home	- Build public/private sector cooperation

Fig. 10.1. Four principles of competitive success for tourism destinations.

manufacturing sectors. Old strategies of development based on import substitution are no longer appropriate. Island economies must be developed in a *focused* and *flexible* manner, and be ready to move with changes in the world economy, technology and markets. In other words, they have to become competitive. Once competitiveness is achieved, it is immaterial whether production is geared to local markets (i.e. inward-looking) or export markets (i.e. outward-looking).

Tourism destinations need to develop strategies that allow them to forge linkages with agriculture, manufacturing and, in particular, the wider services sector. Tourism has an important role to play in fuelling growth in the services sector. To make this possible, entirely new strategies of development, based on the concepts of *flexibility, specialization* and *focus* are needed.

To take advantage of the opportunities that the new tourism brings and to stay ahead of the game, competitive strategies are vital. Four crucial strategies for the competitive success of tourism destinations are identified. These strategies are as follows:

1. Put the environment first.
2. Make tourism a lead sector.
3. Strengthen distribution channels in the marketplace.
4. Build a dynamic private sector.

These four basic strategies are summarized in Figure 10.1 and explained in the following sections.

10.4. PUT THE ENVIRONMENT FIRST

The need to redirect the tourism industry, to build a new tourism and to ensure that the industry can play a vital role in sustaining fragile, tourism-dependent, economies and in saving Planet Earth, are the greatest challenges facing the industry. Already there is growing awareness among tourism destinations of the *disadvantages* that tourism brings. This, in turn, is changing the approaches to the way in which the industry is being developed. The emerging trend is toward more planning, monitoring, assessment and a more cautious development of the tourism sector. Tourism destinations are realizing that they have to put their environment first. There are three main principles associated with putting the environment first. These are:

1. Build responsible tourism.
2. Foster a culture of conservation.
3. Develop an environmental focus.

These principles are detailed in Figure 10.2 and explained in the text.

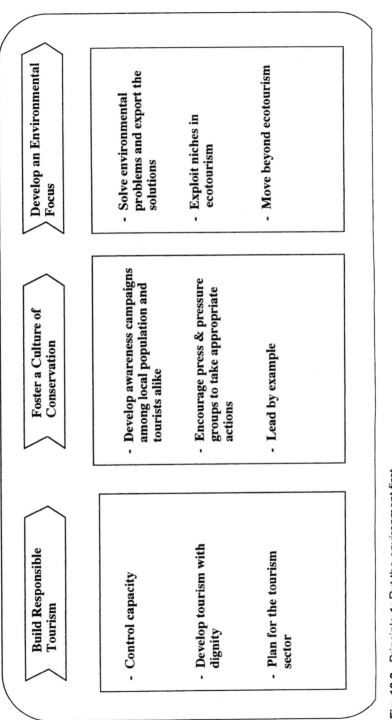

Fig. 10.2. Principle 1: Put the environment first.

Build Responsible Tourism	Foster a Culture of Conservation	Develop an Environmental Focus
- Control capacity - Develop tourism with dignity - Plan for the tourism sector	- Develop awareness campaigns among local population and tourists alike - Encourage press & pressure groups to take appropriate actions - Lead by example	- Solve environmental problems and export the solutions - Exploit niches in ecotourism - Move beyond ecotourism

10.4.1. Build Responsible Tourism

There is growing evidence that tourism destinations are beginning to take serious action to conserve their tourism assets. Some islands have already begun to build a new, environmentally sound and sustainable tourism. They are doing this by careful and integrated planning of their tourism development, through controlling capacity, and through developing tourism with dignity. In what follows, it shall be shown how:

- Bermuda controls capacity; and
- Trinidad and Tobago develops tourism with dignity.

10.4.1.1. Control capacity

Bermuda provides a shining example of a destination that is dedicated to controlling its capacity. With a land area of approximately 21 square miles, Bermuda has taken steps to control tourism so that resorts do not exceed their carrying capacities. Bermuda has refused to grant permission for the building of new hotels on the island for more than a decade. In addition, Bermuda has drawn up a cruise-ship policy for the 1990s that sets out to limit the number of cruise passengers visiting the island and to focus on the upper end of the market (Personal communication, Hon. C.V. 'Jim' Woolridge, JP, MP and Bermuda's Ministry of Tourism in Cancun, Mexico, June 1991). This policy specifically sets out to:

1. Maintain Bermuda's image as a quality destination.
2. Reduce the demand on the infrastructure – particularly on the capital city of Hamilton.
3. Retain the quality of life as a result of the reduced pressure on the infrastructure and by allowing for a common day of rest (Sunday).
4. Limit cruise passenger arrivals to 120000 during the May–October period to four regularly scheduled vessels, all catering to the up-scale market, and a maximum of 12 occasional ships.
5. Spread cruise arrivals throughout the year – particularly in the off-peak season. In 1989, cruise passenger arrivals to Bermuda reached a record 159, 277 of which only 6342 (4%) visited outside the May–October period.
6. Prohibit weekend cruise calls.

It is, therefore, not at all surprising that the port charges and passenger taxes payable in Bermuda are much higher than other countries in the region. Their $40.00 passenger tax was introduced in April 1990 (up from $30.00) and increased to $60.00 per passenger from April 1991. By contrast, cruise passengers pay as little as US$2.00 per head in St Lucia and US$3.00 per head in Barbados (Caribbean Tourism Organization, September, 1990a).

10.4.1.2. Develop tourism with dignity

Another destination, Trinidad and Tobago, is building responsible tourism. Having neglected the tourism sector for nearly three decades, the twin-islands Republic of Trinidad and Tobago is fast becoming a player in the Caribbean tourism industry. She is, however, emerging as a player with a difference – a player that is set on developing its own brand of new tourism. Trinidad and Tobago, lying just 7 miles off the coast of Venezuela, has one of the most innovative tourism policies that aims at developing 'tourism with dignity'. This policy places emphasis on the country's cultural heritage, natural resources and history. The idea is not merely to perpetuate the image of sea, sun and sand but to keep intact the rich cultural heritage of the twin island republic (Government of the Republic of Trinidad and Tobago, 1988). The Government of Trinidad and Tobago is therefore committed to the development of the industry in a manner that will:

1. Preserve the national pride and dignity of the peoples of Trinidad and Tobago, while simultaneously encouraging foreigners to visit and experience the Trinidad and Tobago way of life.
2. Take into account the need to stimulate the expansion of *domestic tourism* in harmony with the drive to increase international tourism.
3. Pursue a policy of exploiting the tourism market selectively, stressing to the various target groups the uniqueness of the tourism product.
4. Not encourage the creation of enclaves that exclude nationals on the grounds of race, colour, religion and sex.
5. Not permit the establishment of gambling casinos and/or any similar activities that are likely to have undesirable consequences for the society.

Viewing these policies of the twin island state of Trinidad and Tobago, it can be deduced that the explicit intention of the Republic is to avoid mass tourism. In the words of one of the Trinidad and Tobago Tourism Development Authority (TDA) officials, 'hotels above the nearest palm tree are illegal ... we are not prepared to denude our hills or beaches simply to put up a concrete jungle and say it's tourism' (*Travel Trade Gazette*, 21 November 1991c, p.96). In addition, the twin-island state also has a very powerful conservation lobby, a very active Town and Country Planning Agency and a vibrant Institute of Marine Affairs. So stringent are the regulations governing the development of tourism facilities, often requiring the conduct of an environmental impact assessment (EIA) before building plans are approved, that these agencies are often criticized for keeping back development.

Indications are, however, that these conservation efforts are beginning to pay off as conscious investors appreciate and applaud these efforts and cite them as a very important reason for considering investments in

Tobago. According to John Jefferis, recipient of the Caribbean Hotel Association's 1990 'Caribbean Hotellier of The Year' Award, who is renovating and re-opening the 115-room Crown Reef Hotel in Tobago: 'the conservation focus of the government and its careful attitude toward the planning of its development is a definite plus for the country and for his investments in Tobago' (Personal communication, John Jefferis, Bermuda, May 1991).

The preliminary plan for tourism in Trinidad and Tobago, funded by the InterAmerican Development Bank (IDB) and completed in 1990, is an attempt by the government of the Republic to put into operation its tourism policy. This plan, based on extensive consultations with the local population, proposes a *network* approach to tourism development, identifying eight foci of development (*Caribbean Futures*, 1991b). The plan, which included a preliminary environment impact assessment (EIA), concluded, among other things, that:

1. Tourism will grow and develop only if the natural environment is alive and healthy.
2. Trinidad and Tobago are different islands – development on the islands must reinforce and reflect this diversity.
3. The quality of manpower will determine the quality of the product.

The redevelopment of the city of Port of Spain and its positioning as the *cultural capital of the Caribbean* is seen as *key* to the success of tourism in Trinidad. The focus on minimizing tourism's negative impacts on Tobago's environment, the avoidance of large-scale cruise tourism and the attraction of appropriate investors are seen as *keys* to the prosperity of tourism in Tobago (*Caribbean Futures*, 1991b).

10.4.2. Foster a Culture of Conservation

A sustainable approach to the development of tourism can only be achieved if the government, private sector and the local population work hand-in-hand to achieve this goal. To build this strong partnership, conservation must become a way of life – it must become an essential part of the society and culture of the country. If a strong partnership exists locally and pervades the culture and orientation of the country, then visitors can be encouraged to fall in line – to 'see and enjoy but do not destroy' the environment. A visitor, however, will be hard-pressed to fall in line with conservation if streets are dirty, or if the local population is careless, or if there is no appropriate infrastructure for environmental conservation (e.g. legislation and its enforcement, incentives, appropriately located receptacles for rubbish and recyclable materials). The development of a culture of conservation can be achieved through *creating awareness* of environmental problems and opportunities; through *encouraging the Press and pressure groups to take appropriate action,* and through *leading by example.*

10.4.2.1. Create awareness

A fundamental part of cultivating a culture of conservation is developing awareness of the environment among the local population the business community and among incoming tourists. This can begin at schools, through awareness campaigns, competitions, incentives and through the work of community groups, non-governmental organizations (NGOs), environmental pressure groups and the Press. The Press and pressure groups have a particularly important role to play in creating awareness of the environment.

Environmental conservation can also become an important pillar in attracting tourists. If the governments of a region could establish at least one significant protected area in each destination, and implement a coordinated environmental mandate, this could have important consequences for the future of tourism in that region. The action could help to generate awareness at the marketplace, and among potential visitors and investors, of the conservation efforts of the region. Positioned as an ecozone, and complemented by a rich culture and a tolerant and flexible way of life, the Caribbean, for example, can become *the* place on earth where one will want to live, work, play and be. Imagine the economic impact that this positioning will have in such areas as tourism, health, financial, professional, business and environmental services.

10.4.2.2. Encourage press to take appropriate actions

Pressure groups and the press have particularly important roles to play in preparing people for new tourism. They can develop awareness of the negative impacts of old tourism and the positive gains that some have made in building the new tourism.

While the press and many a pressure group have made brilliant strides in the creating an awareness of the ills of the old tourism, they still lag behind in the role of creating an equally explicit awareness of the positive role the new tourism can play – and is playing. Perhaps, this lack of enthusiasm on their part stems from the verity that while the ill-effects of tourism make for 'juicy' headlines and have been widely publicised as a result, the 'green initiatives' taken by conscious governments and suppliers have not been given the attention they deserve – perhaps because they are less juicy. While one recognizes the need to be critical of tourism, failure to give coverage to the positive examples deprives the tourism community of learning from the examples that others have set. This could delay the spread of new tourism and lead to the deterioration of host countries and the environment.

In this regard, it is critically important that the Press maintains integrity and is not sidetracked from covering the real issues. For example, apart for the degree of 'spice' in the news, the Press might not be inclined to cover the negative environmental impacts of certain industry segments or destinations because of the amount of advertising revenues they generate. In this regard, it could be quite probable that, due to the tremendous amount of advertising undertaken by cruise ships, there is not enough coverage of the environmental damages that they have wrought in the Caribbean. Caribbean governments have taken a firm stand on cruise tourism and are attempting to redress the negative environmental and other impacts (e.g. limited economic impacts) of the cruise tourism sector. Cruise ships are increasingly being asked to pay their fair share. From January 1993, St Lucia will impose a minimum cruise tax of US$10.00 per passenger.

10.4.2.3. Lead by example

It is not enough to talk about the environment and wish that the problems would just go away. It is important that governments lead by example, that is to ensure that their own actions, polices and expenditure patterns are conservation-conscious.

Many Caribbean economies depend on a dominant export for their sustenance, for example, oil (e.g. Trinidad and Tobago), bauxite (e.g. Jamaica) and bananas (e.g. Dominica and St Lucia). The benefits derived from these major export industries usually accrue to the local economy in the form of government revenues through taxation and government participation in investment. This means that the government is usually forced to play a major role in the economy – sometimes creating over half of the employment in the country.

In playing such a major role, it is important that governments ensure that their own expenditures and activities are environmentally sensitive. For example, governments' use of recycled paper for all ministries and public organizations (as is the practice in Germany) ought to become a permanent governmental practice. In addition, when attracting foreign investors to establish operations in the Caribbean, governments must not only ensure that economic targets (e.g. employment, incomes, foreign exchange) are met; they must insure that environmental targets also are met. This latter policy is critically important in a climate where manufacturers and even cruise lines in the USA are legally forced to avoid disposal of hazardous and other wastes on their shores. The temptation to engage in environmentally unfriendly activities for short-term profit, must be avoided.

As a key part of leading by example, it is important that governments develop and implement environmental mandates. This can be done through the development of an appropriate frame of regulations and action, which could include:

1. The development of environmental standards and laws.
2. Development of a system of policing parks and protected areas.
3. The development of tax incentives and other measures to encourage firms, for example, to recycle paper and to encourage others to adopt production technologies that are more friendly to the environment, even if initially they may be more costly.
4. The phasing out of environmentally destructive industries (e.g. sand mining).
5. The development and management of natural parks and other protected zones.
6. The promotion of ecotourism.
7. The development of incentives for companies to maintain and beautify the environment.
8. The development of national history museums, marine parks, protection of rare bird and plant life.

With the best will in the world, however, there remains a big gap between policies and practice. In some destinations, such as the Bahamas, the amount of legislation already in place to protect the environment is amazing. However, implementation falls far short of regulatory intentions. This is a particularly acute problem in geographically dispersed tourism destinations such as the Bahamas, the Virgin Islands and the Grenadines, which require the policing of hundreds of square miles of ocean, islands and cays and which instantly requires a population effort. For these island destinations, conservation is proving to be quite an insurmountable task. It is important, however, that the government and private sector begin to see the environment as a viable industry – an area of opportunity for skills, employment and wealth-creation.

10.4.3. Develop an Environmental Focus

The conservation of the environment is viewed mainly as a problem by those who have not developed a keen vision of its potential. It is not seen as a serious industry capable of generating wealth. As such, the wealth-creating potential of this sector is not realized. Ask any group of high-school students, for example, in the Caribbean what they would like to be when they grow up. If any of them were to say that they would like to be an environmentalist, you will be very fortunate indeed to have received such an answer. This partially summarizes the problem: conservation of the environment is not considered as an economic opportunity – an activity that can create income and wealth. In fact, conserving the environment is now often associated with keeping back development.

Notwithstanding this perception, increasingly the government and the private sector have to see the environment as an opportunity – an opportunity to create wealth and incomes by solving environmental problems and exporting the solutions. In making the environment an opportunity, it is important for governments and tourism destinations to: (i) exploit niches in ecotourism; and (ii) move beyond ecotourism.

10.4.3.1 Exploit niches in ecotourism

Ecotourism – an increasingly popular 'buzz-word' in the tourism industry – refers to the development and promotion of environmental attractions (e.g. national parks) and activities (e.g. catch-and-release fishing, organic agriculture) for the specific purpose of conserving the environment and generating income for its surrounding local communities. The idea behind ecotourism is that local inhabitants can become gainfully employed (e.g. as park wardens, interpreters, park managers, organic farmers, owners and managers of lodges and other professions) in conserving the environment, rather than engaging in environmentally disruptive practices (e.g. slash-and-burn farming).

Already, the evidence is that ecotourism could pay off in economic terms. The travelling public's interest in nature and adventure travel is at an all-time high and still growing. Destinations that offer visitors a look at rain forests, rare species or pristine landscape are in more demand than ever before. A recent World Wildlife Foundation (WWF) study explored the subject of ecotourism in Mexico (5.4 million visitors annually), Costa Rica and Ecuador (260000 visitors annually), Belize (55000 annually) and Dominica (30000). In a random airport exit survey in these countries, it was found that almost half (46% of the 436 visitors surveyed) said that protected areas were the 'main reason' or 'very important' in their decision to visit the country (World Wildlife Foundation, 1990). Of the 436 people polled at airports in Belize, Costa Rica, Dominica, Ecuador and Mexico, more than half visited at least one national or ecological site.

Of the travellers surveyed who listed parks and protected areas as their main reason for visiting the country, the average length of stay was 13 days and the average expenditure US$2588. For those who listed them as not important, the average length of stay was 14.7 days and the total US expenditure was $1531. *At a differential of more than $1000 per visitor, the study gives the first clear indication that it can be profitable to protect the environment and attract ecotourists.*

Ecotourism is an avenue in which destinations can benefit from conserving the environment while encouraging tourism. What it requires is that the growing environmental sustainability be placed first, and that the travel and tourism industry be developed from the perspective of sustainable development.

One such attempt to put the environment first is being undertaken by Belize (formerly British Honduras). Belize is a country that is committed to the idea of conservation and is actively exploiting ecotourism niches.

The government of Belize recognizes the interdependence of Belize and the global community and sees the protection of its forests and wildlife as important for its own existence as well as for the existence of the world's communities. So committed to the environment is Belize that it is the first country to effectively link tourism with the environment, through the development of a Ministry of Tourism and the Environment. (Jamaica has since followed suit.) The commitment of the government to conservation has been described as 'strong and steadfast', by the Hon. Glen Godfrey, Minister of Tourism and the Environment and Attorney General for Belize (Personal communication, Belize, January 1991). As Minister of Tourism, Hon. Godfrey sees it as his duty 'to ensure that tourism development in Belize does not adversely affect the ecology, the social fabric or the future of the land'.

Belize has thus embarked upon several innovative projects geared towards developing ecotourism in the country.

The first jaguar reserve in the world was opened in Belize in 1990. The reserve was extended to 206000 acres by the Hon. Florencio Marin, Deputy Prime Minister and Minister of Industry and Natural Resources, in a very touching ceremony at the Maya Centre, which involved the parents and children of the surrounding village of the jaguar reserve. According to the Belize Audubon Society:

> ... the success of any protected area is integrally dependent on the actions of the people and communities that live around and with it.
> If for this reason alone, the November 6th Ceremony was a definite success
>
> (Belize Tourism Industry Association, 1991)

One of the rationales behind the jaguar reserve is this: if the jaguar is alive and healthy, everything that it feeds on will be alive and healthy.

Belize currently has a total of 17 national parks and protected areas, which represent 37% of the country's entire land mass (see Table 10.1). According to Mr Oscar Renanado, of the Ministry of Industry and Natural Resources, the government is working very closely with the *man and biosphere concept* of the International Union for the Conservation of Nature to declare yet another reserve – the Maya Mountain Biosphere reserve, an area that could be in excess of 500000 acres.

The Belize Audubon Society and the Programme for Belize are two organizations very active in conservation programmes in Belize. The primary goal of these organizations is to respond to the invitation of the

Table 10.1 Belize national parks*

Name of park	Acreage	Interest
Guanacaste National Park	50	Recreation; guanacaste trees
Half Moon Caye	45	2 distinct ecosystems; reptiles
Crooked Tree Wildlife Sanctuary	86	Migratory birds; jabiru stork
Community Baboon Sanctuary	33	Community-based, involving eight villages; black-howler monkey
Cockscomb Basin Wildlife Sanctuary	102 600	Jaguar reserve; watersheds
Society Hall Nature Reserve	6741	Research; mayan presence
Bladen Nature Reserve	97 000	Watershed, primary growth forest
Blue Hole National Park	575	Linked to one of the world's largest underground cave systems
Shipstern Nature Reserve	22 000	Butterfly breeding; jaguars
Hol Chan Marine Reserve	1 sq. mile	Protection of reef ecosystem
Rio Bravo Conservation Area	282 000	Sustainable development

Source: Belize Audubon Society, Belize City, Belize, Central America.

*In addition to these 11 protected areas, there are six other forest reserves. Together, these protected areas represent about 37% of the entire land area of Belize.

Belize government to participate directly in the effort to link development and conservation in ways that advance the objectives of both organizations while building the economy and helping Belizeans to achieve a better standard of living. By acquiring the 282 000-acre Rio Bravo Conservation area, the Programme for Belize intends to demonstrate effectively that the area can be kept intact and still generate significant economic return through the development of long-term research, appropriate agroforestry projects and tourism emphasizing natural history and archaeology.

Ecotourism is taking off primarily in Central America. The concept of joint nation development is being discussed in a number of Central American areas. A fine example of this is *la Ruta Maya*, a project that encompasses hundreds of Mayan ruins throughout five Latin American countries including Mexico, Guatemala, Belize, Honduras and El Salvador. Although still in the theory stages, if this concept is developed and agreed upon by all nations involved, it could provide for a single regional Ruta Maya tourist visa and bus service that would allow passengers to cross country borders at their convenience. 'This regional plan would increase environmentally oriented tourism and sustainable, non-destructive development to provide jobs and money to help pay for preservation.' (*National Geographic*, October 1989).

Another joint project currently being considered is a three-nation *Maya Peace Park*. This park would include the Calakmul Reserve in Mexico, the Maya reserve in Guatemala and the Rio Bravo Conservation and Management area in Belize. If accomplished, and 5 million acres in total, the international park would be twice the size of Yellowstone, the largest National Park in the USA.

In summary, ecotourism offers tremendous opportunities for the development of tourism. Belize and Dominica are exploring carefully this market segment, while Jamaica and Trinidad and Tobago, are taking a special interest in this market segment. The ecotourism possibilities for the Caribbean are vast.

A major natural advantage that the Eastern and Southern Caribbean islands possess in ecotourism is the accessibility of their eco-attractions. In many countries with developed eco-attractions, in Central and South America, for example, it often takes days of air, sea, road, foot and river transportation to access the places of interest to ecotourists. Moreover, limited overnight accommodation is available at many of these sites. In Trinidad, by contrast, one can go bird-watching in the Caroni Swamp and in Dominica one can marvel at the magnificent waterfalls, while benefiting from 'creature comfort' at Fort Young Hotel in Dominica or the Hilton Hotel in Trinidad. The Caribbean can develop a major competitive advantage in the 'soft-adventure' tourism market, taking advantage of the growing trend away from sedentary 'baking-in-the-sun' holidays.

10.4.3.2. Move beyond ecotourism

While it is important for tourism destinations to realize the potential of environmental conservation to generate wealth through ecotourism, it is equally important that they begin to move beyond the narrow confines of the tourism sector. As these destinations will increasingly discover, the development of an environmental focus in the wider spheres of the economy will have important spill-overs for tourism itself.

The development of an environmental focus is not simply the creation of an industry to recycle paper or develop national parks. It goes far deeper than this and involves an entire system of wealth-creating activities – from production activities to government regulation and enforcement. A number of activities can become the focus of an environment industry:

- recycled products such as paper, tin, glass, etc.;
- organically grown agriculture produce;
- ecotourism services and facilities (interpretation centres, tour guides);
- development of spas, stress-management techniques and alternative medicine;
- development and promotion of natural drugs and healing methods;
- international conventions, seminars, meetings on the environment;
- environmental impact assessments (EIAs) for companies and countries;

- environmentally related consultancy services;
- management of national parks and protected areas;
- export of 'know-how' of environmental conservation;
- the development and management of interpretation centres;
- environmental research programmes and other training for export;
- audiovisual programmes on the environment; and
- accommodation and facilitation of visiting professors and researchers.

These are some examples of the ways in which caring for the environment can become an economically profitable venture. To have full impact, however, it is important that many of these productive activities are developed in a focused manner, in a fashion that allows each activity to mutually reinforce the other. For success, it is necessary to build an environmental focus where key efforts, such as research and development, training, marketing, production and regulatory instruments, are targeted in the same direction – the direction of sustainable development.

10.5. MAKE TOURISM A LEAD SECTOR

According to John Bell, the Executive Vice President of the Caribbean Hotel Association: 'It is an undoubted reality that tourism, with all its warts, is the engine that will drive the Caribbean's economy into the 21st Century and beyond' (Bell, 1990, p. 30). The Caribbean Tourism Organization also contends that 'tourism has exhibited sustained growth and vitality over the last 20 years and has been the most reliable engine driving the Caribbean economies' (Caribbean Tourism Organization, 1990a). The President of the Caribbean Development Bank, Sir Neville Nicholls uttered not too dissimilar a sentiment as he stated categorically: 'those economies in which tourism was significant performed consistently better than those in which it was not' (Caribbean Development Bank, 1989). Indeed tourism contributed 85% of the gross domestic product (GDP) of Bermuda; 78% of GDP for Antigua and Barbuda; 53% for the Bahamas and 34% for Barbados (Caribbean Tourism Organization, 1990a).

Despite the importance of tourism to Caribbean island economies, there is still some reluctance to let tourism become its engine of growth. Development is still largely wedded to the physical goods sector – namely agriculture and manufacturing. It was only in February 1992, for example, that the Caribbean heads of government for the first time, convened a meeting to address the specific issues of the tourism sector. The reluctance to make tourism an engine of growth is partially due to associated problems of negative sociocultural impacts and limited economic benefits – problems that have not yet been solved.

The real limiting factor in preventing tourism from playing a lead role in the economic development of the Caribbean, however, is the fact that the view of tourism remains limited – confined to tourists, hotels, sun, sand and sea. The broader 'axial' possibilities that the presence of a tourism industry brings are not fully grasped. Worse yet, the potential of the tourism industry to create linkages with the rest of the economy is still seen to lie in producing locally the things hotels need – linens, towels, food and furniture – in other words, the things one can see and touch.

Tourism is not seen as having the capability to spawn dynamic, flexible and focused industries – be it in field fashion, entertainment, environment or health. The real potential of tourism to regenerate the agriculture and manufacturing sectors, and to render competitive advantages to the services sector, is yet to be realized.

The Caribbean is in a very fortunate situation in that despite its relatively small domestic market size, it is host to a ready market of tourists: 11.8 million long-stay visitors in 1990 and 7.5 million cruise visitors in 1990 (Caribbean Tourism Organization, 1991c). The 250 000-strong population of the Bahamas, for example, receives 14 times as many tourists as inhabitants: in 1991 the Commonwealth was host to 3.6 million long- and short-stay visitors (Bahamas Ministry of Tourism, 1992). The key question remains: 'What is sold to these tourists?'. Is it just souvenirs and T-shirts made in Taiwan, China or the USA?

In order to make a tourism a lead sector, it is important to:

- realize tourism's axial potential;
- adopt new development strategies, and;
- develop the services sector.

These principles are summarized in Figure 10.3 and are explained in the following sections.

10.5.1. Develop Tourism's Axial Potential

One of the major economic curses associated with the spread of tourism in the developing world is the high leakage of tourist expenditure. In other words, although tourists spend locally, a large proportion of this expenditure is 'leaked' back into the economies of the tourist-generation countries, in order to import items to service the tourism trade and to pay for advertising and marketing. This problem is vividly illustrated by the Christian Council of Churches in the chart '*Does Tourism Earn Foreign Exchange?*', which is reproduced in Figure 10.4.

The need to find solutions to this problem of tourism's limited economic benefits for host destinations is a major challenge facing the industry. The concern with leakages in the tourism sector has attracted a great deal of research and analysis. Much of this research, however, has focused on

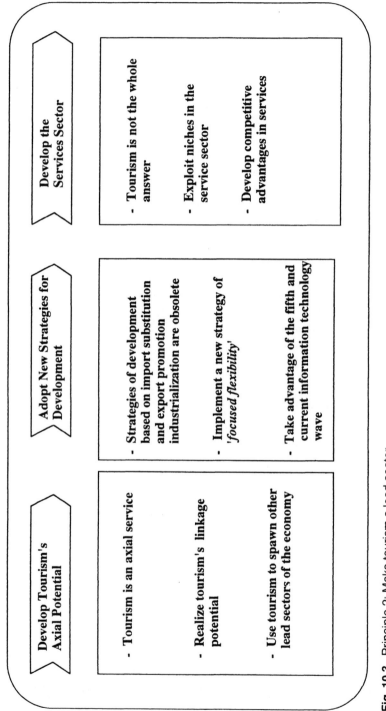

Develop Tourism's Axial Potential

- Tourism is an axial service

- Realize tourism's linkage potential

- Use tourism to spawn other lead sectors of the economy

Adopt New Strategies for Development

- Strategies of development based on import substitution and export promotion industrialization are obsolete

- Implement a new strategy of *'focused flexibility'*

- Take advantage of the fifth and current information technology wave

Develop the Services Sector

- Tourism is not the whole answer

- Exploit niches in the service sector

- Develop competitive advantages in services

Fig. 10.3. Principle 2: Make tourism a lead sector.

Fig. 10.4. Tourism leakages.

Source: O'Grady, 1980.

trying to measure the leakages and multiplier effects, while remaining silent on the question of what is to be done. A recent attempt to tackle the problem of leakage in tourism was made by the West Indian Commission in a study on *Tourism as an Axial Sector – Potential for Linkages and Development of Services,* prepared by *Caribbean Futures.* The report concluded that:

1. Tourism is an 'axial' sector – a sector that produces a domino effect on virtually every other sector of the economy.

2. The axial potential of the tourism sector in the Caribbean is under-exploited.

3. The real potential for linkages in tourism does not lie in agriculture or manufacturing but, rather, in services.

4. New strategies of development – strategies based on flexibility, specialization and focus – are necessary in order to realize tourism's axial potential (the study proposed a strategy of 'focused flexibility' for the Caribbean).

5. A new vision – a vision of leadership in the fifth wave – is necessary in order for the Caribbean to realize the true potential of tourism and indeed other sectors.

Tourism is an axial industry offering key opportunities for wealth-creation. A number of services are directly and indirectly activated by the presence of a tourism industry – from air transportation, ports, insurance, duty free shopping, car rental, marketing and promotions to food and beverages, furniture and fixtures. No other goods, service or activity can replicate the unique opportunities that the tourism sector provides. The wealth-creating effects of the tourism industry go much further than the bed-nights, berth-nights or airline seats that are consumed. One reason for this is that the final touches (value) are added at the destination, be it the basket of fruit or flowers in the room, currency exchange, the unexpected toothache, the guided tour or other services. Tourism, therefore, contrasts very sharply with Caribbean's historical Muscovado-biased production patterns, where the islands were limited to the low-value-adding process, for example the production of sugar in its most unrefined form (muscovado). Perhaps, most importantly, the presence of tourists on the island could lead to impulse shopping and purchases that are increasingly facilitated by plastic money – the credit card. This can lead to the purchase of items greater in value than the price of the holiday package itself.

Equally, unlike other industries, tourism brings consumers to the product. The Caribbean thus becomes the supermarket or boutique to which visitors are attracted – like bees to a honey-pot. Apart from the normal consumption of sun, sand and sea, rum, roti, room and recreation, their presence in the Caribbean allows visitors to inspect other goods and services for sale in the region. In other words, tourism's disadvantages – the invisibility of the tourism experience (its difficulty of inspection at the point of sale, for example) – provides exactly the opposite advantage for goods and services produced in the Caribbean – that is, high visibility and inspection of goods produced by the Caribbean (and also imported items). Bringing visitors to the goods and services also has the advantage of sampling (e.g. food); it provides the leisure time as well as the opportunity to consume services (e.g. business clients who rarely have the time for routine dental check-ups); and it provides an atmosphere in which consumption of items is possible. This means that when tourists buy Caribbean music, rum, food and other items 'back home', they not only purchase the item, they also buy the experience that goes with it.

It is these kinds of possibilities for linkages between tourism and the rest of the economy that are not realized in the Caribbean. The real potential of the tourism industry in the Caribbean does not lie in building more hotels and trying to locally produce the items that these hotels use. The real potential of the tourism sector lies in:

1. Using the presence of a tourism industry to market high-value-adding goods and services.
2. Using the presence of millions of tourists in the Caribbean to overcome the limitations of small market size and distance from the major centres of metropolitan consumption. Tourists present in the Caribbean, can become an important source market for product testing, product launch and marketing. The opportunity must not be missed, for example, to spawn a high-fashion industry based on casual elegance for warm-weather destinations. In fact, the time could be not too far off when an all-inclusive vacation in the Caribbean could allow visitors to come to the Caribbean at a moment's notice and the flexibility to leave their luggage at home with clothes and other paraphernalia included in the price of the holiday.
3. Reversing the historic patterns of imported consumption patterns by encouraging visitors to eat, and buy locally. Possibilities for these are enormous as the trend toward healthy eating and organic consumption could spawn markets for speciality agriculture (e.g. organic agriculture, cut flowers). This could provide an important impetus to diversify the export-oriented agriculture sector, which is largely based on bananas and sugar. In fact, producing organically grown fruits and vegetables for the hotel sector is producing for an export market.

In order to realize the axial potential of the tourism sector, it is necessary to adopt completely new approaches to tourism, to focus on developing the services sector, and to be a leader in the fifth wave.

10.5.2. Adopt New Development Strategies

As governments of many developing economies begin to battle with budget deficits and shortages of foreign exchange, and as they swallow the structural adjustment programmes that the World Bank and the International Monetary Fund (IMF) continue to dish out, there seems to be a complete lack of vision as to where these economies are going – what role they can play in the information age, how the United States of Europe, the increasingly dominant Pacific Rim, and new technologies (e.g. microelectronics, biotechnology) will affect their competitiveness in the decades ahead.

Somehow, despite the rapid changes in the world economy, there continues to be 'business as usual'. There seems to be a belief that what worked in the past will continue to work in the future.

Although there is growing disenchantment with the role of import substitution industrialization, there is no clear idea of what is to replace it. Attention is often drawn to the success of export-oriented approaches of the Asian 'tigers' – Singapore, Hong Kong, Taiwan and South Korea. The implicit belief is that export-oriented industrialization is the way of the future. However, the Asian economic miracle, and indeed that of Japan, was born out of a peculiar cultural environment (e.g. work orientation, the work ethics) and institutional circumstances (e.g. lifetime employment, the role of the Ministry of International Trade and Industry (MITI) in Japan) that cannot easily be replicated in other parts of the world. In addition, the global economic, technological and social and political circumstances that facilitated the rapid take of Japan and the Asian 'tigers' in the 1960s, 1970s and 1980s have changed profoundly.

What seems to be clear, however, is that: *just as Superclub and Sandals hotel chains in Jamaica copied the Club Med recipe, Caribbeanized it, and is now a serious competitor to Club Med, the Caribbean region needs to Caribbeanize the Asian success formula and develop the flexibility and focus necessary to become a leader in the decades ahead.*

Unless a completely new approach to development is taken – an approach based on focus, flexibility and specialization – not only will the tourism sector fail, but entire economies of the Caribbean will fail (*Caribbean Futures*, 1991a). It is necessary therefore to:

- abandon old strategies of import substitution
- implement a new strategy of focused flexibility; and
- be a leader in the fifth wave.

10.5.2.1. Abandon old strategies of development

The realization of the true potential of the tourism sector is inextricably linked to the adoption of radically new approaches to development. The tourism sector is not an island unto itself. Developments in the economy at large (e.g. high import duties, import restrictions, non-competitive domestic manufacturing sector, high cost of finance) severely affect the profitability of tourism. The type of development strategies adopted also affect the tourism sector. Old strategies of development – primarily import substituting industrialization (ISI) – limit the development potential of the tourism sector.

ISI – a strategy adopted by Latin America and to a lesser extent the larger Caribbean islands since the late 1950s – involves the substitution of imports by local production. Within this strategy, cars, consumer durables, and processed foods, for example, would be produced or assembled locally instead of imported. The sustenance of this strategy usually requires a paraphernalia of protection for domestic 'infant' industries, some of which, experience has shown, never grow up.

In the Caribbean, import substitution is still viewed as a strategy that could allow tourism to generate more linkages with the rest of the economy. It is believed that if only one could locally produce the beef, wines, cutlery, pots, pans and elevators for the tourism industry, that all would be well. Unfortunately, this is not likely to be the case.

The real potential of the tourism industry does not lie in attempting to produce locally the items that hotels need. The real potential of the tourism industry lies in exploiting the ready market that tourism brings, in using the presence of a tourism industry to develop niches in manufacturing (e.g. a fashion industry featuring casual wear for the sun), in developing a dynamic agriculture sector (e.g. speciality fruits and vegetables, organic agriculture, cut flowers) and fuelling the services sector (e.g. ecotourism, bone fishing, health tourism, entertainment, adult education).

It is only possible to develop the full potential of the tourism industry through new strategies based on flexibility, specialization and focus. Indeed strategies of flexible specialization, underlie the success of Silicon Valley, Route 128 circling Boston, industrial districts in the 'Third' Italy and even in tourism economies like Cyprus. The old strategy of import substitution should be abandoned and its regulatory trappings dismantled.

10.5.2.2. Implement new strategies

One of the key problems of Caribbean island economies is the fact that they are small. The small size is not conducive to the realization of scale economies in many activities. Services such as design, education, training, research and development operate far below levels that are considered to be economically efficient. In addition there may be one research and development facility that attempts to be all things to everyone, from product testing to market intelligence. Despite this limitation, there continues to be a lack of focus and specialization. As such, the critical mass necessary to achieve economies of scale, systems gains and scope economies is not present. The result is that on many Caribbean islands there may be a handful of first-class fashion designers, artists and furniture manufactures. However, they are in insufficient numbers to make a significant impact, and also they tend to be too small a fraternity to command resources for training, research and development, access to technology, markets, and more.

A new approach to development must be taken – one that is based on the identification of focused sectors, specialization and flexibility. A strategy of focus and flexibility is the essence of developing target sectors, in which the region, or individual island, focuses simultaneously on building and coordinating capabilities in all activities related to the sector in focus. Such related activities include: management, design, production, marketing, networking, a regulatory environment, research and development (R&D) and training. In developing and applying the concepts of focus and flexibility to the agriculture, manufacturing and services sector, the tourism sector can become a very powerful 'axial' partner.

Key to the successful implementation of this strategy are:

- the *selection* of focus sectors (e.g. fashion, health services)
- the *activation* of the eight key sector-related capabilities (e.g. research, development, sourcing of materials)
- the development of *flexible production* capabilities to respond to changing market conditions;
- *networking* locally, regionally and internationally to provide *inter* and *intra* firm dynamics and to source materials, information and market intelligence data; and
- *continuous innovations* to stay always head of the game (see *Caribbean Futures*, 1991a).

10.5.3. Develop the Services Sector

The future of the Caribbean is not only in tourism: it is in services. The services sector offers tremendous opportunities for development. Although countries such as Germany, Japan, the USA and the UK derive over 70% of their wealth, incomes and employment from services, in the Caribbean, development still tends to be wedded to physical goods production – things we can readily see and touch. It is for this reason that the whole quest for linkage-creation between tourism and the rest of the economy invariably tends to be focused on the agriculture and manufacturing sectors.

Contrary to popular opinions, the real potential for linkages in tourism is not in the agriculture and manufacturing sectors – it is in services. Recent empirical findings in the economy of St Lucia bring the traditional agriculture and manufacturing focus of linkage-creation into serious question.

10.5.3.1. Tourism is not the whole answer

In 1991, a pioneering work on the economic impact of tourism in the economy of St Lucia was completed. One of the most important findings of that study was that *the services sector had the greatest potential for linkages – more than the manufacturing and agriculture sectors combined.* The manufacturing sector accounts for only 4.3% of total value creation in the tourism sector, while the agriculture sector accounted for 7.3% of the total wealth generated by the tourism sector. By contrast, 42% of the wealth generated by the tourism sector is generated by the services sector (Fig. 10.5).

Services create over 42% of the total wealth created by the tourism sector in St Lucia. Within the services sector, the construction sector, by far the largest creator of wealth in the economy, accounts for 37% of total value created. 'Miscellaneous services', which include yachting services, domestic tour-operator services, floral services and real estate is the next significant category. The study revealed, for example, that 30% of the revenue of the estate agency sector is linked with tourism. This can be explained by the very dynamic tourism sector in St Lucia. Other significant categories of linkages between the tourism sector and services were

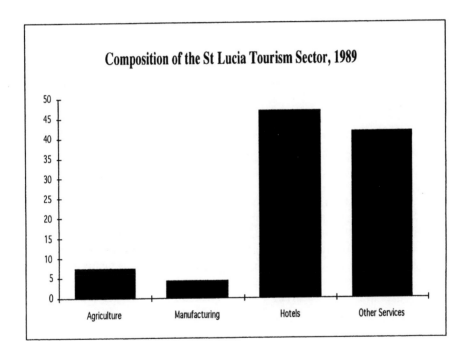

Fig. 10.5. Services offer the greatest opportunities for linkages in tourism.
- The real potential for linkages in tourism is not in the agriculture and manufacturing sectors.
- Manufacturing accounts for 4.3% of the value created by the tourism sector.
- Agriculture accounts for 7.3% of total wealth generated by the tourism sector.
- By contrast the services generate 42% of total wealth created by the tourism sector.

Source: Caribbean Tourism Organization, 1990b.

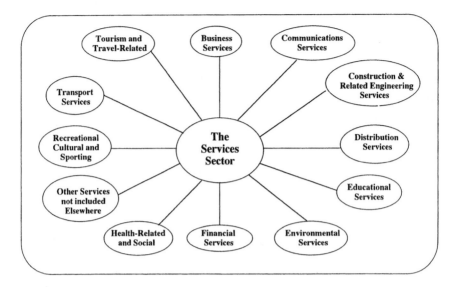

Fig. 10.6. The 12 activities that make up the service sector.

Source: GATT, 1991.

electricity and water, transport and communications. Financial services played a small role in the tourism sector in St Lucia. One suspects, however, that in countries with a more developed financial services sector, such as Jamaica, the linkage coefficient will be greater.

With the services sector generating four times the wealth of the combined agriculture and manufacturing sectors of the tourism industry in St Lucia, and with as yet no clear Caribbean policy towards the services sector, the need to focus attention on the services sector remains an urgent priority. It is not that one should abandon attempts to create linkages in the agriculture and manufacturing sectors. However, far greater focus should be placed on the service sector than has hitherto been the case.

10.5.3.2. Focus on services

It is important that Caribbean economies begin to seek opportunities in this sector. The service sector is made up of a vast array of activities. The General Agreement on Trade and Tariffs (GATT) issued a services sectoral classification list in 1991. Services identified by GATT fall into 12 categories: (i) business services, (ii) communication services; (iii) construction and related engineering services; (iv) distribution services; (v) educational services; (vi) environmental services, financial services; (vii) health and related social services; (viii) tourism and travel-related services; (ix) recreational services; (x) cultural and sporting services; (xi) transport services; and (xii) other services not included elsewhere (General Agreement on Trade and Tariffs, 1991). Figure 10.6 provides a diagrammatic representation of these services. Each of these services are broken down into several other services. Business services, for example are further broken down into:

- professional services;
- computer and related services
- research and development services
- estate agency services
- retail and leasing services; and
- other business services.

The various subcomponents of these services are indicated in Figure 10.7.

Services are a critically important part of an economy and forms a key pillar of development. In the developed countries, the growth and development of the services sector has already outpaced that of the agriculture and manufacturing sectors. Services now account for at least 70% of the employment and national incomes of Japan, France, USA, Germany and the UK. Available estimates for some member countries of the Organization for Economic Cooperation and Development (OECD) show that the telecommunication sector's proportion of GNP is comparable with the share of the steel or the textile sector.

Services were historically seen as unproductive elements of a nation's economy and, until recently, have been the 'stepchild' of economic research. Services are now looked upon as a viable engine of growth and a key source of competitiveness for other sectors of the economy – particularly in the area of producer services (such as accounting, software, marketing, advertising, management consultants) – which are inputs into production in the agriculture and manufacturing sectors.

Services are growing in importance for the following reason:

- technology is diffusing very rapidly in services making them increasingly transportable and tradable;
- the quality, reliability, efficiency and costs of services influence the competitiveness of other sectors of the economy;
- services now account for a sizeable share of the national income and employment of an economy;
- developing countries are now being asked to liberalize their services sectors with few of them really grasping its full implications; and
- tourism is becoming more dynamic when linked with other services (e.g. financial services, health and entertainment).

Developing countries need to focus on the development of their services sector as a matter of urgent priority.

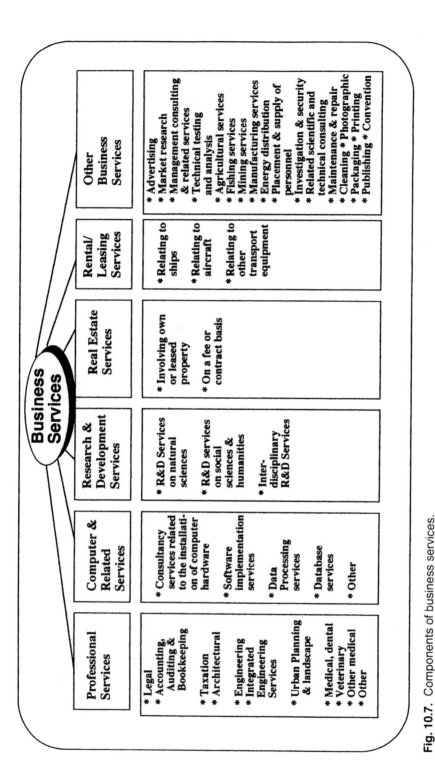

Fig. 10.7. Components of business services.

Source: GATT, Services Sectoral Classification List, July 1991.

10.5.3.3. Develop niches in services

It is clear that due to the vastness of the services sector and the technology intensity of some services, it is not possible to develop a production capability in all services. Niche strategies are more appropriate. Here again, the West Indian Commission Study on tourism sheds some important light. Based on a simple determination of the skills and technology intensity of individual services, several potential services for development have been identified.

Figure 10.8 contains a matrix that indicates the attractiveness of different types of services to the Caribbean. Services most attractive to the Caribbean are those with:

- high-skill and low-technology requirements;
- high-skill and medium-technology requirements;
- medium-skill and medium-technology requirements; and
- low-skill and medium-technology requirements.

Figure 10.9 identifies several services that could be developed in these different categories. Such include:

- software services for tourism;
- hotel design, architecture and renovation services;
- entertainment;
- music and recording;
- education;
- sport;
- health; and
- incentive travel and conference services.

It is important that such areas of new opportunity be exploited. It is only with the development of other dynamic parts of the economy (see Fig. 10.9), that the tourism sector will be relieved of the burden of carrying the rest of the economy and realize its true 'axial potential'.

It should also be considered that services, by their nature, are environmentally clean. They provide an ideal partnership for the tourism industry as they help to conserve the vital base of the tourism industry – the environment.

10.5.3.4. Be a leader in the fifth wave

A final ingredient in making tourism a lead sector, indeed ensuring the viability and sustainability of Caribbean island economies, is the development of a new vision – a vision of Caribbean leadership in the fifth wave.

As we have seen in Chapter 3, the world economy is on the brink of the fifth wave – the information technology wave. It is important that

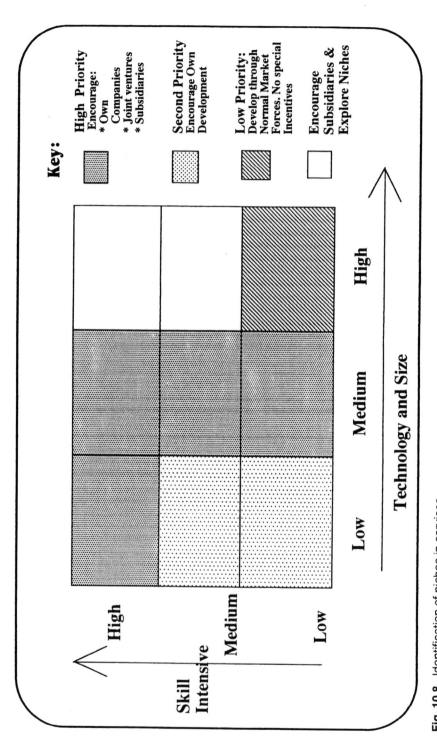

Fig. 10.8. Identification of niches in services.

Source: *Caribbean Futures*, 1991b.

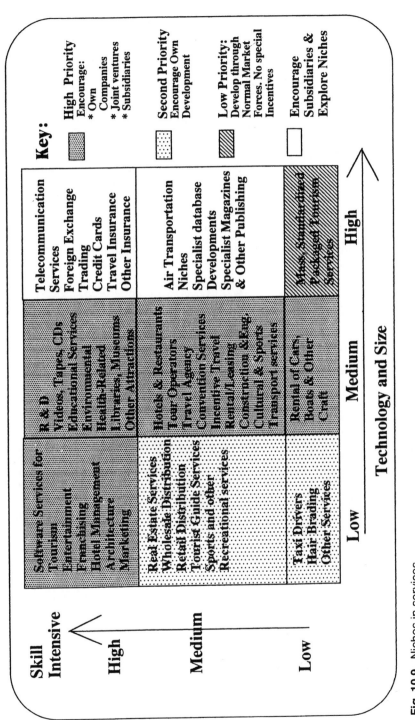

Key:

High Priority
Encourage:
* Own
  Companies
* Joint ventures
* Subsidiaries

Second Priority
Encourage Own
Development

Low Priority:
Develop through
Normal Market
Forces. No special
Incentives

Encourage
Subsidiaries &
Explore Niches

	Low	Medium	High
High	Software Services for Tourism Entertainment Franchising Hotel Management Architecture Marketing	R & D Videos, Tapes, CDs Educational Services Environmental Health-Related Libraries, Museums Other Attractions	Telecommunication Services Foreign Exchange Trading Credit Cards Travel Insurance Other Insurance
Medium	Real Estate Services Wholesale Distribution Retail Distribution Tourist Guide Services Sports and other Recreational services	Hotels & Restaurants Tour Operators Travel Agency Convention Services Incentive Travel Rental/Leasing Construction & Eng. Cultural & Sports Transport services	Air Transportation Niches Specialist database Developments Specialist Magazines & Other Publishing
Low	Taxi Drivers Hair Braiding Other Services	Rental of Cars Boats & Other Craft	Mass Standardized Packaged Tourism Services

Skill Intensive

Technology and Size

Fig. 10.9. Niches in services.

Source: *Caribbean Futures*, 1991b.

Table 10.2 The fifth wave offers new opportunities for the region

Character	Waves				
	First	Second	Third	Fourth	Fifth
Time frame	1770s and 1780s – 1830s and 1840s	1830s and 1840s – 1880s and 1890s	1880s and 1890s – 1930s and 1940s	1930s and 1940s – 1980s and 1990s	1980s and 1990s – 2040s and 2050s?
Description	Early mechanization	Steam power and railway	Electrical and heavy engineering	Fordist mass production	Information and communication technology
Main carrier branches	Textiles Textile machinery	Steam-powered transport	Electrical and heavy engineering industries	Producer and consumer durables petrochemicals tanks, aircraft, etc.	Computers and telecommunications industries services, tourism
Leading resources	Cotton	Coal	Steel	Oil	Microelectronics
Leading countries	Britain	Britain	Germany	USA	Japan
Caribbean's role	Colony	Free peasantry/ indentureship	Trade unions self-government	Independence	Regional integration
Caribbean strategies	Primary commodity production (e.g. sugar, coffee, cocoa) Exploitation of natural and mineral resources (e.g. oil, bauxite) Services (e.g. distributive trades, craft production)			Import substitution	Focused flexibility

Source: *Caribbean Futures*, 1991a and Freeman and Perez, 1988.

tourism-dependent economies view themselves as leaders in this new wave. The first three 'long waves' of development (e.g. early mechanization, steam power and railway, electrical and heavy mechanization) bypassed much of the developing world. The Caribbean, for example, only became marginally involved in the fourth (Fordist mass production) wave. This involvement was through import-substitution strategies and the exploitation of natural resources and tourism. In Table 10.2, it can be seen that the Caribbean was marginalized during the first four waves of economic development – from the industrial revolution in the 1770s and Victorian prosperity in the 1830s to the golden age of full employment in the 1940s. The fifth wave (1980s–2040s?) – the information age, the wave of the future – is driven by information and computer technologies (ICT). It is critical that the Caribbean does not miss this wave.

The key to meaningful participation in the information age is to understand its implications and to develop strategies to respond to them. The Information age offers four key implications for the Caribbean and indeed other economies:

1. Strategies of technology application are more important than manufacturing the hardware. Tourism-dependent economies such as the Caribbean should therefore focus its efforts on applying and using the technologies, rather than trying to manufacture the hardware (e.g. through import substitution).
2. Old strategies of development – import substitution – are obsolete. New strategies based on focus and flexibility must be developed.
3. Services take on a larger share of the value-creation process in all industries and everywhere. A concerted effort should be made to develop the services sector in order to consciously capture the value that services create.
4. The key to unlocking the opportunities of the information age is people – highly skilled and trained people who can identify opportunities, produce new or improved goods and services and who can gather, process, store, retrieve and apply information at all levels of the productive system.

To take advantage of these opportunities, a new vision for the Caribbean region is needed. Figure 10.10 provides some elements that could constitute such a vision.

10.6. STRENGTHEN MARKETING AND DISTRIBUTION CHANNELS

We have seen in Chapter 8 that distribution is one of the activities along the industry's value chain that will take on increasing importance. We have also seen in Chapters 6 and 7 that technology will have the greatest impact

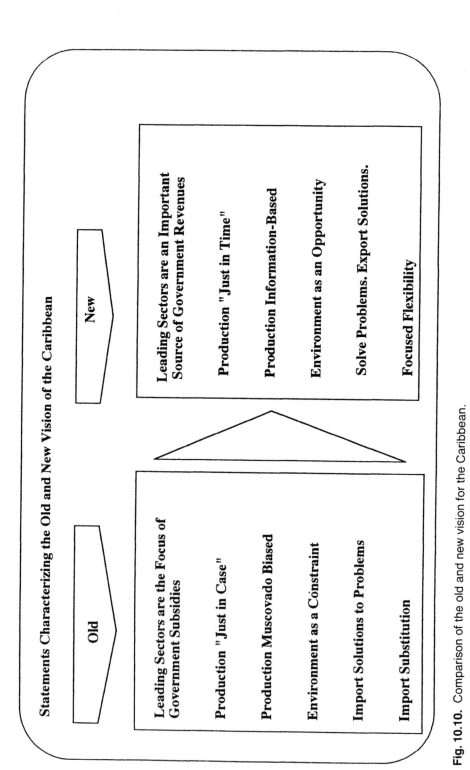

Statements Characterizing the Old and New Vision of the Caribbean

Old

Leading Sectors are the Focus of Government Subsidies

Production "Just in Case"

Production Muscovado Biased

Environment as a Constraint

Import Solutions to Problems

Import Substitution

New

Leading Sectors are an Important Source of Government Revenues

Production "Just in Time"

Production Information-Based

Environment as an Opportunity

Solve Problems. Export Solutions.

Focused Flexibility

Fig. 10.10. Comparison of the old and new vision for the Caribbean.

Source: *Caribbean Futures*, 1991b.

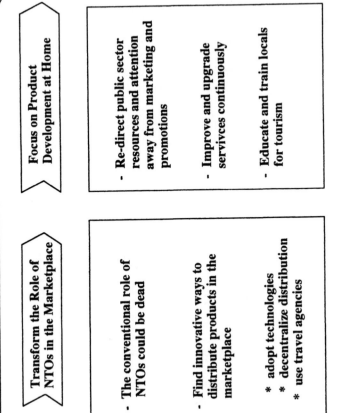

Ensure Adequate Air Access

- Understand the implications of deregulation

- Strengthen national and regional carriers

- Respond strategically

Transform the Role of NTOs in the Marketplace

- The conventional role of NTOs could be dead

- Find innovative ways to distribute products in the marketplace

  * adopt technologies
  * decentralize distribution
  * use travel agencies

Focus on Product Development at Home

- Re-direct public sector resources and attention away from marketing and promotions

- Improve and upgrade servivces continuously

- Educate and train locals for tourism

Fig. 10.11. Principle 3: Strengthen the marketing and distribution channels.

in the areas of distribution. Distribution is the most important activity along the tourism chain. Without adequate air access and product-distribution channels in the marketplace, the best destinations in the world would find it extremely difficult to survive. Two key aspects of distribution are important for tourism destinations: (i) air transportation; and (ii) the role of tourist boards and promotion agencies in the marketplace. When strengthening distribution channels, tourism destinations need to:

- ensure adequate access;
- transform the role of national tourist offices in the marketplace; and
- focus on product development at home.

These strategies are identified in Figure 10.11 and explained below.

10.6.1. Ensure adequate air access

The development of tourism destinations is dependent on reliable air access. A destination can fail or succeed depending on decisions taken by a single airline. The Caribbean has had its share of air transportation problems, with the bankruptcy of carriers such as Eastern Airlines (which ceased operations in 1991). Pan Am, for example, accounted for 14.1% of all passengers to Barbados between January and July 1991 – a major loss in seat capacity when it was shut down. Pan Am also supplied 17.2% of all airline seats to the Bahamas during January to September 1991, and over 60% of all seats into the Turks and Caicos Islands during January and October 1991. For the Turks and Caicos, Pan Am was the only carrier (Caribbean Tourism Organization, 1991b). The demise of these carriers has left many Caribbean islands, without direct scheduled air services from the USA. Flights to many Caribbean islands are now routed through the American Airlines' hub in Puerto Rico. It means that visitors to many islands in the Caribbean, will have to stop and change aircraft in Puerto Rico before arriving at their final destination. The fact is that the Caribbean is really 'small fry' in the context of global activities of international carriers.

Decisions that international airlines make or take to influence their own profitability and competitiveness, sometimes without warning, can severely hurt destinations. The Bahamas, for example, has suffered from the demise of carriers such as Eastern and Pan Am, which provided lift from multiple gateways in the USA. Although these services are being replaced by smaller commuter airlines from gateways in South Florida like Miami, Fort Lauderdale, Orlando and West Palm Beach, with these small commuter airlines there is a constraint to the movement of large-group meetings and conventions. In addition, these commuter airlines have far less marketing clout than the former giants of the airline industry. The Bahamas has also suffered from the decision of British Airways to withdraw its direct flight from London to Nassau, preferring instead to 'beef-up' service directly into the USA in an attempt to become more competitive with US carriers across the Atlantic stage.

It must be recognized that, for tourism destinations, *the logic of operating an airline could sometimes run contrary to the objective of the local tourism industry.* Airlines find it increasingly common sense to manage yield. Managing yield could sometimes be inconsistent with high-load factors. As such, while the airline could benefit by transporting fewer higher-fare-paying business passengers, rather than 'tourist'-class passengers, this could run contrary to the needs of the local hoteliers, guest houses, villa operators, bars and other services that are concerned with maximizing their own occupancy rates and profits. Many on-site suppliers depend on large inflows of tourists for profitability.

To ensure adequate air access to service the local tourism industry, strong local and regional carriers are vitally important. The experience of the Caribbean clearly demonstrates the importance and necessity of a regional carrier that serves the interest of the local tourism industry. The Caribbean's tourism industry benefits significantly from the operations of British West Indian Airways (BWIA), the national airline of the Republic of Trinidad and Tobago, which performs an important service to the Caribbean tourist industry. In fact, the growth impetus from the European market has been fuelled, to a large extent by BWIA, which continues to provide direct weekly scheduled services from many European cities (e.g. London, Frankfurt, Cologne, Munich, Stockholm and Zurich) to Barbados, St Lucia and Trinidad and Tobago, with onward connections to Grenada, St Vincent and other islands. On examination of Figure 10.12, it can be seen that the growth impetus for the Caribbean region over the last 5 years has been and continues to come from the European market. BWIA performs a vitally important role in allowing the Caribbean region to capture business from European markets.

10.6.2. Transform the Role of NTOs in the Marketplace

In the past two to three decades of tourism development, the Caribbean destinations have focused almost exclusively on marketing and promoting their destinations: getting the marketing correct was, and still continues to be, a major pre-occupation of the tourism public sector. It did not matter what was produced or how it was produced, so long as it could be sold. So much so that any problem facing the tourism industry tended to be solved by more marketing and advertising and promotions. Unfortunately, very little attention was paid to the development of the product – not just the hotel and standards for them (which do not exist in the Caribbean) but the total product – the environment, the service at hotels, customs and immi-

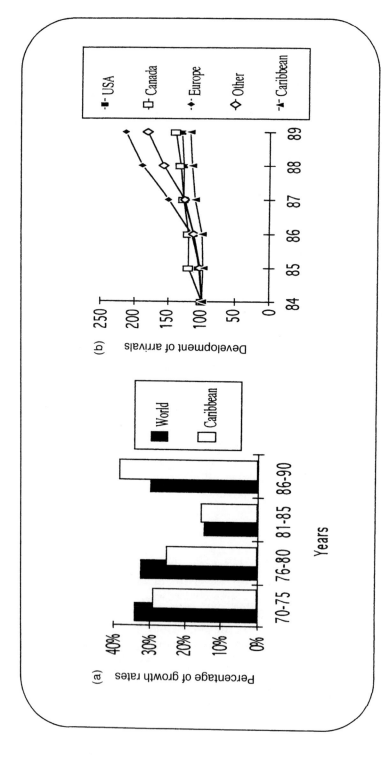

Fig. 10.12. European-fuelled Caribbean tourism in the last decade. (a) 5-year growth rates in World and Caribbean tourism arrivals; (b) development of arrivals in the Caribbean by key tourism-generating regions, 1984–1989, where 1984 = 100.

Source: World Tourism Organization, 1990; Caribbean Tourism Organization, 1990a.

gration, taxi drivers, tours, attractions, roads, road signs, sewage and other infrastructure.

However, 'supply no longer creates its own demand' and 'nothing kills a bad product like good marketing'. Any product put on the market is not guaranteed to be sold. Not even price manipulation and cheaper holidays will help. Clients are more educated, better travelled, more environmentally aware and vote with their pockets. If the product is not right, they simply will not buy, irrespective of price.

Product development is a serious issue because the tourism industry is so multifaceted, covering so many aspects of the economy and country. Yet no single body or agency has responsibility for the health of the whole product. As a result of this situation, it has been convenient and probably seemed common sense in the last decades for tourism authorities and ministries to look after the marketing and 'let God handle the rest'. Today, this approach is no longer optimal. New and innovative ways have to be devised to take the entire tourism product in hand. Collaboration between the public and private sectors is key to creating a better and more competitive tourism product (Holder, 1992b).

10.6.3. Focus on Product Development

Product development relates to the whole state of well-being of the tourism product. In the past, tourism development efforts have mainly focused on marketing. It was implicitly assumed that whatever is produced will be sold. This was an era of cheap holidays and packaged tours – corresponding to the era of standardization and mass production witnessed by manufacturers. Producers called the shots, consumers had little variety and little choice but to buy.

Today, consumers are well travelled, sophisticated and demand quality and value for money. The advertising dollars have to be matched by product development and quality controls. The importance of the product development focus is likely to shift value-creation from the marketing and distribution activities to the product development side (see Chapter 8). However, because of the development and levels of sophistication of the marketing activity, it is very likely that, in the future, the marketing companies will have a larger influence in the product development effort, with many companies integrating the product development and marketing functions.

10.7. BUILD A DYNAMIC PRIVATE SECTOR

For many developing countries, generous incentives to attract foreign investors to bring their franchised hotels and management know-how is

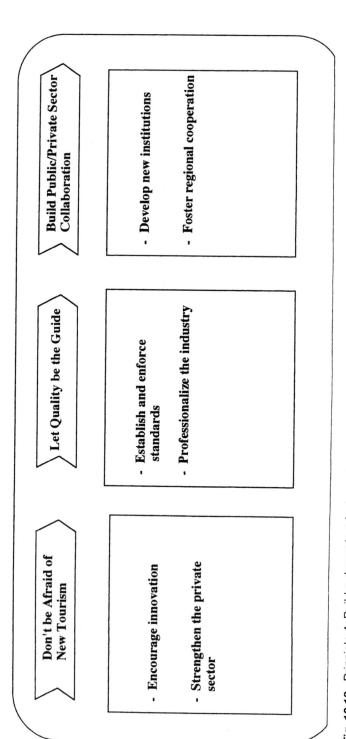

Fig. 10.13. Principle 4: Build a dynamic private sector.

seen as the way – for many, the only way – to develop the tourism industry. While multinational corporations and foreign investors will continue to play an important and *necessary* role in the development of Caribbean tourism, these initiatives will not be *sufficient* to sustain the tourism development over the long term.

True long-term sustainability of the tourism industry will come from the development of an indigenous entrepreneurial class. Jamaica, perhaps more so than any other Caribbean island, demonstrates the importance of indigenous entrepreneurship. Equally, these classes must show the commitment to country. This is certainly the case of Butch Stewart in Jamaica whose actions have come to be known as the 'Butch initiative'. In early 1992, the Jamaican dollar was losing value against the US dollar: the US dollar exchange was slipping from J$23 to J$30. Speculators were having a 'field day' and the government was helpless. The Jamaican hotelier, Butch Stewart, the 1991 Caribbean Hotelier of the Year and Chairman and Chief Executive Officer of the Sandals hotel chain stepped in to sell the government US$1 million per week for several weeks, thereby causing the country's exchange rate to stabilize. This is the sort of commitment to country that helps to develop an entrepreneurial spirit that relies on, and has faith in, the potential of the country. Caribbean entrepreneurs will increasingly find that just as being 'green' means money, commitment to people and country could also be profitable.

The importance of spawning a dynamic private sector locally cannot be underestimated. There is growing evidence in the Caribbean to suggest that the indigenous tourism private sector is coming of age. In tourism, more so than many other industries in the Caribbean, locally-based multinational operators have emerged. The Sandals and SuperClub hotel chains of Jamaica, for example, are involved in properties throughout the Caribbean including St Lucia, St Kitts, Antigua, Cuba and the Bahamas. Involvement takes the form of management contracts, franchises, direct investments and other joint-venture arrangements.

As these regional multinationals continue to spread their wings, one can expect more Jamaican involvement in the rest of the Caribbean tourism industry and other investors in the region to join the fray. This will increasingly mean that the future of tourism in the entire region will depend upon the health of tourism in all the countries of the region.

When building a dynamic private sector, three courses of action are recommended:

● don't be afraid of new tourism;
● let quality be the guide; and
● build public/private sector collaboration (Figure 10.13).

10.7.1. Don't Be Afraid of New Tourism

New tourism offers several new opportunities for tourism-dependent economies. As we have seen in Chapter 5, new consumers are more experienced, more 'green', more adventurous and more quality conscious. They have special interests, a greater appreciation for the different and a taste for the novel. The demands of tourism's new consumers create a good match with the needs and demands of the host communities who are increasingly concerned about preserving the integrity of their own environments, cultures and ways of life. It is important that governments of the Caribbean take the new tourism on board, and as they do this, listen to the locals and to the tourists. They are very likely to find that they are asking for exactly the same things: conservation of the environment, preservation of cultural forms and tourism with dignity. When building a new tourism, it is important for governments to consciously strengthen their private sector.

10.7.1.1. Strengthen the private sector

The tourism industry is already providing a very lucrative opportunity for local private-sector investment in the Caribbean. Many companies involved in other sectors of the economy, primarily in services (e.g. insurance companies, distributive trades, automobile assembly, venture capital and other financial services) now see the tourism sector as a viable avenue for diversification. It is interesting to note that the principal businesses of the Sandals (Butch Stewart) and SuperClub (John Issa) chain of hotels, before entry into tourism, were appliance distribution and automobile sales, respectively. Other enterprises across the Caribbean region are following the Sandals/SuperClub example.

The entry of local insurance companies and even credit unions in the Caribbean tourism industry are a key driving force in the growth of Caribbean tourism. In fact, the growth of the two Caribbean multinational hotel chains (Sandals and SuperClub) is strongly backed by the local financial sector in Jamaica. There are many other examples of companies moving into the tourism sector in a major way (*Caribbean Futures*, 1991a):

1. Life of Jamaica has invested in two all-inclusive properties in Jamaica (Jamaica Jamaica on Runaway Bay and Sandals Dunns River, Ocho Rios) to the tune of J$350 million (about US$35 million), representing about 15% of the company's portfolio.

2. Eagle Merchant Bank has investment interests in Ciboney, Ocho Rios, and has plans of building a health resort, also in Jamaica.

3. Mutual Life of Jamaica has interests in Terra Nova, Trelawny Beach, Hedonism II and Grand Lido.

4. Jamaica's National Commercial Bank owns the Wyndham Hotel in Kingston.

5. The Colonial Life Insurance Company (CLICO), Trinidad, has invested in the 133-room Grand Barbados Beach Resort in Barbados and has plans of extending its interests throughout the region.

6. Dominica Coconut Products has also established the Fort Young Hotel and plans to become more involved in the tourism sector in Dominica and has already invested in the St Lucia tourism industry.

7. In Trinidad, Angostura Trinidad Limited has acquired a 750-acre estate in Tobago for tourism development.

8. Neal and Massy, a Trinidad conglomerate, has also acquired a substantial acreage of land in Tobago for the purpose of developing tourism.

9. Amar, involved in the automobile industry in Trinidad, has also acquired the Pigeon Point estate in Tobago.

10. In Tobago, the famous Mount Irvine Hotel and Golf course has been acquired by Bob Yorke, of York Construction and the Grafton Hotel has been developed by Ish Galbaransingh, also from the construction sector.

One of the most interesting private-sector developments in the Caribbean tourism industry is the Mount Pleasant Credit Union in Tobago. The Mount Pleasant Credit Union represents about 60% of the adult labour force on the island. The Mount Pleasant Credit Union acquired the 350-acre Bon Accord Estate in 1990 with the intention of developing an integrated tourism, homestead farming and residential community, all based upon the idea of sustainable and integrated development. The Credit Union's development of a tourism project of this magnitude represents another key thrust in the direct and widespread local participation in the ownership and development of the regional tourism industry.

The tourism sector in the Caribbean has definitely come of age. Tourism now provides a major source of investment dynamism for the entire region. Investment dynamism comes from the insurance, finance and credit-union sector of the Caribbean, as well as the construction sector and other distributive trades. Tourism has become an important avenue for diversification strategies of companies in the non-traditional sectors and a key source of foreign exchange for its providers. This is the beginning of a very important trend in the region. Much will depend upon how profitable the recent ventures, especially the large-scale investment ventures by the Jamaican finance and insurance sector, turn out to be.

All of these developments augur very well for the future development of tourism at the local and regional levels.

10.7.2. Let Quality be the Guide

Another key component of competitive strategies for the tourism industry is building quality products and services. In this regard, the issues of quality as they relate to the private sector (see Chapter 9) are no different for the public sector. In addition, however, governments must take steps to professionalize the industry and establish and enforce standards.

10.7.3. Build Public–Private-sector Collaboration

The tourism industry is like no other: local suppliers and governments work hand in hand – local suppliers provide visitor accommodation, guided tours, car rental and other services for visitors, while governments assist with the marketing and promotion of the destination as well as providing infrastructure, training and other services (including taxation). Despite this 'hand-in-hand' relationship, there is evidence that the private and public sectors at times work at odds with each other. Private- and public-sector cooperation is key to the success of any tourism destination. When strengthening private and public sector cooperation it is necessary to develop new institutions and to foster cooperation at the regional level.

10.7.3.2. Develop new institutions

It is important that new institutions are developed in order to bring new dimensions to public–private-sector collaboration. Jean Holder, Secretary General of the Caribbean Tourism Organization, believes that 'new institutions are critically important in order to foster a new tourism in the Caribbean'. Some new institutions have already begun to emerge. The establishment of a Ministry of Tourism and the Environment in both Belize and Jamaica is an important example of the development of new institutions to allow the spread of a new tourism. Another important initiative has been taken by Jamaica in the establishment of Tourism Action Plan (TAP) Limited. This particular example holds very important lessons for the rest of the Caribbean.

With the assistance of a United States Agency for International Development (USAID) Jamaica established TAP Limited in February 1988. TAP, comprising a representative group of private- and public-sector members, has four main objectives:

1. To identify and prioritize the areas with potential for enhancing Jamaica's tourism product and to plan, develop and implement all initiatives so as to help ensure and improve Jamaica's competitiveness as a tourism destination.
2. To stimulate investment in tourism and related sectors and foster the

participation of public and private enterprises in the development of the industry.

3. To seek to ensure at all times the best practicable reconciliation of aesthetic, cultural, architectural, economic and environmental considerations, all of which must be taken into account in securing commitment and cooperation from all parties concerned in any specific project.

4. To liaise and cooperate with all other entities, both public and private, in furthering the development of the above-stated objectives.

The idea behind TAP is that a number of important areas of activities critical to tourism development fall outside the control of the tourism sector (e.g. water supply, airport expansion, sewage treatment, road signs, national parks, markets, car parks, streets, renovation of old buildings of historic value). Yet, all of these factors have a critical impact on the tourism product. TAP saw it as necessary that a group like itself should exist to coordinate efforts in these many areas.

Working with the Chambers of Commerce in the different regions of Jamaica, TAP has been able to operate with tremendous success. Since its formation in 1988 the projects completed by TAP (to August, 1991) include:

- institutional strengthening of Chambers of Commerce in four regions;
- provision of architectural services and historic preservationist for the restoration of Properties in the Falmouth area;
- training of 57 persons in Caribbean culinary skills;
- anti-harassment programme (ongoing);
- repair of market;
- re-paving of sidewalks;
- facade improvement, Montego Bay;
- repair and replacement of park benches;
- repair and replacement of street signs;
- construction of four braiding booths;
- repair and renovation of building for library;
- repair and enhancement of park and amphitheatre at Port Antonio;
- restoration of old washroom and kitchen at historic Hanover District Prison to be used as gift shop; and
- others.

The list of projects undertaken is very impressive and definitely 'state-of-the-art'. These actions are in keeping with the new tourism – a recognition that what is being sold is not simply a bed-night, but a way of life. Other Caribbean islands will do well to learn from this example that Jamaica has set.

10.7.3.3. Build cooperation at regional level

Beyond cooperation between the private and public sector at the national level, it is important to take collaboration to the regional level. The Caribbean Tourism Organization and the Caribbean Hotel Association are excellent examples of this (Holder, 1992b).

10.8. SUMMARY

A new tourism is rapidly emerging. The changes brought in its wake are so rapid and so radical that they warrant competitive strategies to ensure success. The key decision for industry players and tourism destinations is not just one of opting for 'new tourism' but, more profoundly, being leaders of the new tourism. Today is not too early to begin.

References and Further Reading

ACP-EEC Courier (1990a) *Special Issue on Tourism.* No. 120, March–April, Dieter Frisch, Belgium.

ACP-EEC Courier (1990b) *Special Issue on the LOME IV Convention.* No. 122, July–August, Dieter Frisch, Belgium.

American Express Global Travel Survey (1990) *An International Study of the Travelling Public Conducted in The United States, West Germany, United Kingdom and Japan 1989/90.* The Gallup Organization Inc., Princeton, New Jersey.

American Hotel and Motel Association (1983) *The State of Technology in the Lodging Industry. An Update of a Multi-billion Dollar Market.* American Hotel and Motel Association, New York.

Archer, E. (1984) Estimating the Relationship Between Tourism and Economic Growth in Barbados, *Journal of Travel Research.* Spring issue.

Armstrong and Symonds (1991) Service strategies, *Business Week*, 2 December, pp. 58–61.

Artus J.R. (1972) An econometric analysis of international travel. *IMF Staff Working Papers* 19(3), 579–614.

ASSET (1985) Foreign exchange earnings prospect for Trinidad and Tobago. *Journal of the Economics and Social Science Teachers of Trinidad and Tobago*, 4(1), whole issue.

Baer, W. and Samuelson, L. (1981) Towards a service-oriented growth strategy, *World Development* 9(6), 499–514.

Bahamas Ministry of Tourism (1992) *Bahamas Tourism Statistical Review*, The Bahamas Ministry of Tourism, Research and Planning Unit, Nassau, Bahamas.

Barbados Hotel Association (1984) *A Report of the Problems Facing the Barbados Tourism Industry with Proposals for Corrective Action with Special Reference to the Hotel Sector.* Paper prepared by a joint committee of major institutional creditors, related government departments and institutions and representatives of the Barbados Hotel Association. Barbados Hotel Association, Christ Church, Barbados.

Bargur, J. and Anva, A. (1975) A comprehensive approach to the planning of the tourist industry, *Annals of Tourism Research*, 14(2), 10–15.

Barras, R. (1986) Towards a theory of innovation in services. *Research Policy* 5(4), 161–178.

Barras, R. and Swan, J. (1983) *Information Technology and the Service Sector — Quality of Service and Quantity of Jobs.* Paper presented at the Brighton Association for the Advancement of Science, Annual Meeting, 22–26 August, Brighton.

Barrett, G. (1990) EEC-Caribbean co-operation on tourism. *ACP-EEC Courier Special Issue on Tourism.* No. 122, July–August, Dieter Frisch, Belgium, p. 80.

Bartels, J. (1989) How we view marketing at Carlson. In: Vladimir, A. (ed.), *The Complete Travel Marketing Handbook.* NTC Business Books, Illinois USA pp. 142–146.

Becheri, E. (1991) Rimini and Co. — the end of a legend. *Tourism Management* September, 12(3), 229–235.

Beckford, G. (1972) *Persistent Poverty.* Oxford University Press, New York.

Belise, F.J. (1983) Tourism and food production in the Caribbean, *Annals of Tourism Research* 10(4), 497–513.

Belize Tourism Industry Association (1991) *Belize Tourism Link*, Vol. 1, First Quarter. BTIA, Belize City, Belize, Central America.

Bell, J. (1990) *Caribbean Tourism in the Year 2000.* Paper prepared for University of the West Indies, Trinidad.

Benett M. and Radburn M. (1991) Information technology in tourism: the impacts on the industry and the supply of holidays. In: Sinclair, M.T. and Stabler, M.J. (eds) *The Tourism Industry — An International Analysis.* CAB International, Wallingford, UK.

Bessant, J. (1991) *Managing Advanced Manufacturing Technology: the Challenge of the Fifth Wave.* Blackwell, Oxford.

Bessant, J. and Cole, S. (1985) *Stacking the Chips: Information Technology and the Distribution of Income.* Frances Pinter, London.

Bessant, J. and Grunt, M. (1985) *Management and Manufacturing Innovation in the United Kingdom and West Germany.* Gower, Aldershot, Hampshire.

Best, L. and Levitt, K. (1975) The character of the Caribbean economy. In: George Beckford (ed.) *Caribbean Economy: Dependence and Backwardness.* Institute of Social and Economic Studies (ISER), Mona, Jamaica, pp. 34–61.

Best, M. (1990) *The New Competition Institutions of Industrial Restructuring.* Polity Press, Oxford, in association with Basil Blackwell, Oxford.

Bevan, D.L. and Soskice, D.W. (1977) Appraising tourism development in a small economy. In: Little, I.M.D. and Scott, M.G. (eds) *Using Shadow Prices.* Heinmann, London, pp. 205–229.

Bhagwati, J.N. (1984) Splintering and disembodiment of services and developing nations. *World Economy*, 7(2), 133–143.

Bishop, M. (1979) Speech delivered to the Regional Conference on: *The Socio-cultural and Environmental Impacts of Tourism in Caribbean Countries.*

Blackman, C.N. (1979) *The Balance of Payments Crisis in the Caribbean: Which Way out?* Paper delivered at an interdisciplinary seminar sponsored by the Guild of Undergraduates, 5th February, University of the West Indies.

Blake, E.W. (1974) Stranger in paradise. *Caribbean Review* 6(2), 8–12.

Boberg, K.B. and Collison, F.M. (1985) Computer reservation systems and airline competition. *Tourism Management* 6(3).

Boodhoo, K.I. (1979) The multinational corporations, external control, and the problem of development — the case of Trinidad and Tobago. In: Millet, R. and Will, W.M. (eds) *The Restless Caribbean: Changing Patterns of International Relations.* Praeger Special Studies, New York, pp. 62–70.

Booth, R. (1990) Dominica, difficult paradise. *National Geographic* 177(6), 100–120.

Brandenberg, M. (1979) Are computers helping the hotel industry? *Accountancy* (UK) 90, 44–48.

Branscombe, A.W. (1985) Global governance of global networks: A survey of transborder data flows in transition, *Vanderbilt Law Review* 36, 985–1043.

Braun, E.T. and Macdonald, S. (1982) *Revolution in Miniature: The History and Impact of Semiconductor Electronics.* Cambridge University Press, Cambridge.

Bressand, A. and Nicolaidis, K. (eds) (1989) *Strategic Trends In Services: An Inquiry into the Global Service Economy.* Harper and Row, New York.

British Tourist Authority (1981) *Technology in the World of Travel.* A report of a seminar held at the 1981 World Travel Market, Olympia, London. The report is produced in conjunction with the European Travel Commission.

Britton, R. (1979) The image of the Third World in tourism marketing. *Annals of Tourism Research* 6(3), 318–329.

Britton, S.G. (1982) The political economy of tourism in the Third World. *Annals of Tourism Research* 9(3), 331–358.

Brower, H. (1983) American Express credits growth to rapid changes in technology. *Travel Weekly* 25th Anniversary Issue: Twenty-five Years of the Jet Age. News America Publishing Inc., New York, p. 284.

Brown, I.L., Colwell, R. and Catt, C.M. (1983) Electronic Information for Airline Operations. *Interdisciplinary Science Reviews* 8(1), 34–44.

Brown, T.E. and Lefever, M.M. (1990) *A 50-Year Renaissance: The Hotel Industry From 1939 to 1989.* The Cornell H.R.A. Quarterly, May 1990, pp. 18–25.

Bruce, M. (1984) Information Technology Changes the Travel Trade. *Tourism Management* 4(4), 290–295.

Bryden, J.M. (1973) *Tourism and development: A case study of the Commonwealth Caribbean.* Cambridge University Press, Cambridge.

Burkart, A.J. and Medlik, S. (1974) *Tourism: Past, Present and Future.* Heinemann, London.

Burn H.P. (1975) Packaging paradise — the environmental costs of international tourism. *Sierra Club Bulletin* 80(5) 25–28.

Burns, A. (ed.) (1984) *New Information Technology.* Ellis Horwood, Chichester.

Burnstein, D. (1984) Singapore's 21st Century dream — a tiny city state hopes that software development will make it the Silicon Valley of the Far East. *Datamation* 155–158.

Bush, M. (1984a) *The Age of Market Segmentation: New Opportunities in Today's Market Place.* A special Presentation at the American Society of Travel Agents World Travel Congress, November 1984. Las Vagas, Nevada.

Bush, M. (1984b) *New Opportunities in Travel After January 1, 1985.* A special presentation of the Association of Retail Travel Agents (ARTA) International Travel Conference, September 1984, Brighton, England.

Bush, M. (Publisher) (1990) The European Travel Market in the 90s. In: *Hotel and Travel Index.* Reed Travel Group, New Jersey.

Business Week (1985) Cover Story, Up, Up and Away? Focus on Peoples Express, 25 November, pp. 58–64.

Business Week (1986a) Cover Story, The Highflier — Frank Lorenzo's Bid for Eastern Airlines is the Latest and Most Daring Move in the Restructuring of the Airline Industry. Will It Work?, 10 March 1986, pp. 46–51.

Business Week (1986b) Cover Story. Is Deregulation Working? 22 December, pp. 48–53.

Business Week (1987) Disney's Magic. Feature on Disneyland's Corporate Strategy, 18 March, pp. 54–59.

Cabinet Office (1985) *Pleasure, Leisure and Jobs: The Business of Tourism.* Cabinet Office, Enterprise Unit, HMSO, London.

Caloghirou, J. (1991) *The Levera National Park in Grenada.* Paper presented at the First Caribbean Conference on Ecotourism, 9–12 July 1991, Belize City, Belize.

Canadian Pacific Hotels and Resorts (1991) *We're thinking green — 12 steps to help create an environmentally friendly setting for our guests, for ourselves and for our future.* CPH and R, Canada.

Canton, I.D. (1984) Learning to love the service economy. *Harvard Business Review* 62(3), 89–97.

Caribbean Development Bank (1988) *Is Tourism a Potential Engine of Growth?* Statement by Sir Neville V. Nicholls, President of the Caribbean Development Bank at the 18th Annual Meeting of the Board of Governors, St. Kitts, 11 and 12 May 1988.

Caribbean Futures (1991a) Tourism as an Axial Product — Potential for Linkages and Development of Services. Report prepared for the West Indian Commission, Barbados.

Caribbean Futures (1991b) Preliminary Plan for Tourism for Trinidad and Tobago. Inter-American Development Bank, Washington, USA, January.

Caribbean Futures (1992) The Bahamas Tourism Sector Study — Focus on the Family Islands. Report prepared for the Inter-American Development Bank Washington DC.

Caribbean Hotel Association (1991) *The Caribbean Gold Book — Caribbean Travel Directory, Winter 1991/1992.* Caribbean Publishing Company, Cayman Islands, 360 pp.

Caribbean Tourism Organization (1990a) *Caribbean Tourism Statistical Report 1989 edn.* CTO, Barbados.

Caribbean Tourism Organization (1990b) *Statistical News.* December, 1990, Issue 4/90, CTO, Barbados.

Caribbean Tourism Organization (1991a) *Boating in the Caribbean — Industry Trends and Development Prospects.* Report prepared by A. Poon. July 1991, 77 pp.

Caribbean Tourism Organization (1991b) *Special Report on the Impact of the Closure of PAN AM on Caribbean Tourism.* September 1991.

Caribbean Tourism Organization (1991c) *Statistical Report.* October 1991, Issue 3/91, CTO, Barbados.

Caribbean Tourism Organization (1992a) *Cruise Tourism.* CTO briefing paper for the First Tourism Meeting of the Caribbean Heads of Government, Kingston, Jamaica 16–18 February, 15 pp.

Caribbean Tourism Organization (1992b) *Statistical News.* March, 1992 Issue 1/92, CTO, Barbados.

Caribbean Tourism Research and Development Center (1979) *The Role of Tourism in Caribbean Tourism or Buying Time with Tourism.* Paper presented by Jean S. Holder at the *Third Annual Caribbean Conference on Trade, Investment and Development*, 28–30 November.

Caribbean Tourism Research and Development Center [and others] (1984a) *Feasibility Study of a Caribbean Hotel Reservation System.* CTRC, Christ Church, Barbados.

Caribbean Tourism Research and Development Center [and others] (1984b) *Feasibility Study of a Caribbean Tour Operator for the European Market.* Study financed by the EEC and prepared by Stokes Kenedy Crowley, Dublin, in conjunction with the Irish Tourist Board. CTRC, Christ Church, Barbados.

Caricom Community Secretariat (1992) Overview of the trends and key issues in world and Caribbean tourism. Document No. CST0 92/1/2 prepared for the *First Caricom Summit on Tourism*, 18 February, 42 pp.

Chervenak, L. (1981) Revolution in telecommunications — newly developed telephone systems turn losses into profits. *Resort Management* 9–13.

Chitty, N. (1984) Third World entry into the electronic age. *Telematics and Infomatics* 1(1), 47–52.

Cimoli, M., Dosi, G. and Soete, L. (1986) *Innovation Diffusion, Institutional Differences and Patterns of Trade: A North-South Model.* SPRU, Sussex University, First draft, February.

Clairmonte and Cavannah (1984) Diversification activities of international airlines, *UNCTAD Trade and Development Review*, No. 5, United Nations Conference on Trade and Development, Geneva.

Cleverdon, R. (1979) *The Economic and Social Impact of Tourism on Developing Countries.* Special Report No 60. Economist Intelligence Unit, London.

Coates, J. (1986) The Next 30 Years in Travel. Paper presented at the US Travel Data Center, *1985–86 Outlook for Travel and Tourism.* US Travel Data Center, Washington, pp. 75–84.

Cockrell, N. (1987) Credit cards, cash and travel vouchers in Europe. *EIU Travel and Tourism Analyst*, No. 5, 33–46.

Cockrell, N. (1991) Outbound markets/market segment studies. *EIU Travel and Tourism Analyst*, No. 4, 38–48.

Cohen, E. (1972) Towards a sociology of international tourism. *Social Research* 39, 164–182.

Cohen, E. (1973) Nomads from affluence: notes on the phenomenon of drifter-tourism. *International Journal of Comparative Sociology* 14, 89–102.

Cohen, E. (1974) Who is a tourist? A conceptual classification. *Sociological Review* 22, 527–555.

Cohen, E. (1982) Thai girls and Farang men: the edge of ambiguity. *Annals of Tourism Research* 9(3), 403–428.

Cooper, C. and Kaplinsky, R. (1989) *Technology and Development in the Third Industrial Revolution.* Frank Cass and Co. Ltd., London.

Creative Computing (1984) Focus on Japan. August, 10(8), whole issue.

Cruise Lines International Association (1992) *The Cruise Industry — An overview.* CLIA, New York, USA, 34 pp.

Cullen, R. (1988) Paying for travel — a dynamic market. *Travel and Tourism Analyst*, No. 1: Economist Intelligence Unit, London.

Curnow, R.C. and Freeman, C. (1978) *Product and Process Change Arising from the Microprocessor Revolution and Some of the Economic and Social Issues*. Keynote address to the Institute of Mechanical Engineers, May.

Curtin, V. and Poon, A. (1988) *Tourist Accommodation in the Caribbean*, Caribbean Tourism Research and Development Center, Barbados, West Indies, 66 pp.

Daily Telegraph (1987) UK, 24 April, p. 30

Datalink (1986) 16 June.

David, P.A. (1986) Technology diffusion, public policy and industrial competitiveness. In: Landau, R. and Rosenberg, N. (eds) *The Positive Sum Strategy — Harnessing Technology for Economic Growth*. National Academy Press, Washington, pp. 373–391.

Davies, S. (1979) *The Diffusion of Process Innovations*. Cambridge University Press, Cambridge.

de Coster (1990) Paying for travel — the role of the Eurocheque. *Travel and Tourism Analyst*, No. 1. Economist Intelligence Unit, London.

Demas, W. (1965) *The Economics of Development in Small Countries with Special Reference to the Caribbean*. McGill University Press, Montreal.

Dixit, K. and Tüting, L. (eds) (1986) *Bikas-Binas? Development-Destruction? The Change in Life and Environment of the Himalayas*. Geobuch, Munich.

Doganis, R. (1985) *Flying Off Course: The Economics of International Airlines*. Allen and Unwin, London.

Dommen, E.C. (1971) Tourism as pollution: a report of uncontrolled growth in tourism in developing countries. *Rural Life* 16(4), 12–17.

Dosi, G. (1982) Technological paradigms and technological trajectories. *Research Policy*, 147–162.

Drexl, C. (1987) Tour operators in West Germany. *EIU Travel and Tourism Analyst*, May, pp. 29–43.

Drucker, P.F. (1984) Our entrepreneurial economy. *Harvard Business Review*, 58–65.

Dubois, R. (1970) *So Human an Animal*. Rupert Hart-Davis, London.

Dunning, J.H. and McQueen M. (1982) Multi-national corporations in the international tourist industry. *Annals of Tourism Research* 9(1), 69–90.

Economist (1991) A Survey of World Travel and Tourism. 23 March, 1991.

Economist Intelligence Unit (1990a) *Travel and Tourism Analyst*, No. 1.

Economist Intelligence Unit (1990b) *Travel and Tourism Analyst*, No. 3.

Economist Intelligence Unit (1990c) *Travel and Tourism Analyst Database* No. 3.

Economist Intelligence Unit (1991) *Competitive Strategies for the International Hotel Industry*; Special Report No. 1180. Business International Limited, London.

Economist Intelligence Unit International Tourism Quarterly (1980) Printed communication tools in destination marketing. Special Report No. 53, 52–56.

Economist Intelligence Unit International Tourism Quarterly (1982) Package tours — Where they have been and where they are going. No. 4, Special Report No. 42, 39–51.

Economist Intelligence Unit International Tourism Quarterly (1984a) The Caribbean as a Tourist Destination. No. 1 Special Report, No. 49, 37–55.

Economist Intelligence Unit International Tourism Quarterly (1984b) Information Technology Applications in Travel and Tourism, No. 3; Special Report No. 47, 37–43.

Economist Intelligence Unit International Tourism Quarterly (1984c) UK. Travel Agents: Who they are and their markets? 2 parts, Nos 2 and 3, 43–56 and 40–56 respectively.

Economist Intelligence Unit International Tourism Quarterly (1984d) The West German Package Holiday Market, No 4, Special Report No. 51, 31–44.

Elkinton, J. and Hailes, J. (1989) *The Green Consumer Supermarket Shopping Guide*. Gollancz, London.

Elliot, M. (1991) *Travel and tourism survey — the pleasure principle*. The *Economist* Survey, 23 March.

Elrod, T.R. (1989) Marketing the magic kingdom. In: Valdimir, A. (ed.). *The Complete Travel Marketing Handbook*, NTC Business Books, Illinois USA pp. 117–131.

English, E.P. (1986) *The Great Escape? An Examination of North-South Tourism*. The North South Institute, Ottawa, Canada.

Erisman, M.H. (1983) Tourism and Cultural dependency in the West Indies. *Annals of Tourism Research*, 10(3).

Esh, T. and Rosenbloom, I. (1975) *Tourism in Developing Countries: Trick or Treat? A Report from The Gambia*. Research Report No. 31. The Scandinavian Institute of African Studies, Uppsala.

Euromonitor (1988) *International Outlook The World Package Holidays Market 1980–1995*. Euromonitor Publications Ltd, London.

Fanon, F. (1968) *The Wretched of the Earth*. Grove Press, New York.

Farber, M.L. (1954) Some hypothesis of the psychology of travel. *The Psychoanalytic Review* 41, 267–271.

Farrell, J. (1989) It's people that build success in hotel marketing. In: Vladimir, A. (ed.) *The Complete Travel Marketing Handbook*, NTC Business Books, Illinois USA pp. 147–152.

Farrell, T.W. (1980) Arthus Lewis and the case for Caribbean industrialization. *Social and Economic Studies* 29(4).

Farrell, T. (1982) *Small Size, Technology and Development Strategy*. Research Paper Studies, Caribbean Technology Policy Studies 2, August.

Farrell, T. (1985) *The Facts about the Trinidad Oil Crisis*. Discussion Paper No. 1, Department of Economics, University of the West Indies, St Augustine, October.

Farris, M.T. and Southern, N. (1981) Airline Deregulation's Effects on Marketing Strategy. Paper in the *Travel and Tourism Research Association, Twelfth Annual Conference Proceedings*, June 7–10, 1981, pp. 257–263.

Fein, C.S. (1983) Teleconferencing and its effects on business travel. *Tourism Management* 4(3), 279–289.

Feldman, J. (1983) The Jet Aircraft was the Catalyst for Prolonged Travel Boom. *Travel Weekly's 25th Anniversary Issue — Twenty-five Years of Jet Age* May 31, 42(46), 124–128.

Feldman, J. (1988) Developing strategies for the world's airlines. *EIU Travel and Tourism Analyst*, London.

Feldman, J. (1989) *The Growth of International Travel Service Companies.* EIU The Economist Intelligence Unit, London, No. 2, 56–69.

Financial Times (1985) UK, 19 October, p. 31.

Financial Times (1986) UK, 11 September, p. 10.

Finney, B.R. and Watson, K.A. (eds) (1977) *A New Kind of Sugar: Tourism in the Pacific: 2nd edn. Honolulu, Hawaii: The East-West Center and Santa Cruz.* Center for South Pacific Studies, California.

Firnstahl, T.W. (1989) My employees are my service guarantee. *Harvard Business Review*, 29–31, 34.

Fleschner (1988) An ongoing process. Editorial. *Travel Weekly* Ten Years of Deregulation 47(87), 30 September, p. 4.

Forbes, A.M. (1977) The Trinidad Hilton: A Cost-Benefit Study of a Luxury Hotel. In: Little, I.M.D. and Scott, M.G. (eds) *Using Shadow Prices.* Heinemann, London, pp. 15–42.

Forbes, A.M. (1989) *I Am Sorry We Have Changed.* Marketing report on Club Med edited by Joshua Levine, 4 September.

Forrester, T. (ed.) (1982) *The Microelectronics Revolution.* Basil Blackwell, Oxford.

Forster, J. (1964) The Sociological Consequences of Tourism. *International Journal of Comparative Sociology* 5, 217–227.

Fredericks, A. (1985) 1985 Outlook for Travel Agents. Paper Presented at the *1985 Outlook for Travel and Tourism.* US Travel Data Center, Washington, pp. 69–77.

Freeman, C. (1974) *The Economics of Industrial Innovation.* Penguin, Harmondsworth, England.

Freeman, C. (1979) Microelectronics and unemployment. In: *Automation and Unemployment: An ANZAAS Symposium.* The Law Book Co. Ltd, Sydney.

Freeman, C. (1982) The economic implications of microelectronics. In: Cohen, C.D. (ed.) *Agenda of Britain: Micro Policy Choices for the 80s.* Philip Alan Ltd, London.

Freeman, C. (ed.) (1984) *Long Waves in the World Economy.* Frances Pinter, London.

Freeman, C. and Perez, C. (1982) The economic implications of microelectronics. In: Cohen, C.D. (ed.) *Agenda of Britain: Micro Policy Choices for the 80s.* Philip Alan Ltd., London.

Freeman, C. and Perez, C. (1986) The diffusion of technical innovations and changes in the techno-economic paradigm. Paper presented for the *Venice Conference on Innovation Diffusion*, 17–22 March, Venice.

Freeman, C. and Perez, C. (1988) Structural crisis of adjustment: Business cycles and investment behaviour. In: Dosi, G., Freeman, C., Nelson, R., Silverberg, G. and Soete, L. (eds) *Technical Change And Economic Theory.* Francis Pinter, London.

Freeman, C., Clark, J. and Soete, L.G. (1982) *Unemployment and Technical Innovation: A Study of Long Waves and Economic Development.* Frances Pinter, London.

Fuchs, V.R. (1968) *The Service Economy.* National Bureau of Economic Research, New York.

Gamble, P. (1991) Innovation in innkeeping. Inaugural lecture. *International*

Journal of Hospitality Management 10(1), 3–23.

Gamble, P.R. and Kipps, M. (1983) The conception and development of a micro-computer-based catering information system, *International Journal of Hospitality Management* 2(3), 141–147.

Gann, D. (1991) Buildings for the Japanese information economy — neighbourhood and resort offices. *Futures* 469–481.

General Agreement on Trade and Tariffs (1991) *Services Sectoral Classifications List.* Note by the Secretariat, 10 July MTN.GNS/W/120 8 pp.

Gershuny, J.I. and Miles, I. (1983) *The New Service Economy: The Transformation of Employment in Industrial Societies.* Praeger, New York.

Getz, D. (1983) Capacity to absorb tourism: concepts and implications for strategic planning. *Annals of Tourism Research* 10(2), 239–263.

Giarini, O. (ed.) (1987) *The Emerging Service Economy.* Peragmon Press, Oxford.

Gilbert, D.C. (1991a) European tourism product purchase methods and systems. *The Service Industries Journal* 10(4), 664–679.

Gilbert, D.C. (1991b) Appropriate Rural Development for Social and Environmental Sustainability. *AIB Environmental Development Conference Presentation,* Dublin, Ireland.

Gilbert, D.C. and Kapur, R. (1990) Strategic marketing planning and the hotel industry. *Hospitality Management* 9(1), 27–43.

Girvan, N. (1973) Dependence and development in the New World and the Old. *Social and Economic Studies* Special Issue, 22(1).

Girvan, N. and Jefferson, O. (1974) *Readings in the Political Economy of the Caribbean,* 3rd edn. New World Group Ltd, Jamaica.

Global Futures Digest (1983) Tourism: A Growing Field. Vol. 2.

Go, F., Ritchie, J.R.B., Swainson, K., Brown, F. and Brown, P. (eds) (1990) *Tourism Management* 11(4).

Goss R.M. (1990) *The UK Travel and Tourism Report.* Euromonitor, London.

Government of the Republic of Trinidad and Tobago (1963) *Hotel Development Act No. 3 of 1963,* Government Printery, Trinidad.

Government of the Republic of Trinidad and Tobago (1968) *Third Five-Year Development Plan 1969–73.* Trinidad and Tobago Government Printery, Port-of-Spain, Trinidad.

Government of the Republic of Trinidad and Tobago (1988) *Tourism Policy.* Trinidad and Tobago Government Printery, Port-of-Spain, Trinidad.

Government of Singapore (1991) *Singapore The Next Lap.* Times Editions Pte Ltd., Singapore.

Graburn, N.H.H. (1978) Tourism: the sacred journey. In: Smith, V.L. (ed.) *Hosts and Guests: The Anthropology of Tourism.* Basil Blackwell, Oxford, pp. 17–31.

Great Britain Advisory Council for applied R&D (1980) *Information Technology.* HMSO, London.

Green R.H. (1979) towards planning Tourism in African countries. In: Emmanuel de Kadt (ed.) *Tourism: Passport to Development?* Oxford University Press, Oxford.

Greenwood, D.J. (1978) Culture by the pound: an anthropolgical prespective on tourism as cultural commoditization. In: Smith, V.L. (ed.) *Hosts and Guests: The Anthropology of Tourism.* Basil Blackwell, Oxford. pp. 129–138.

Grover, R. (1991) *The Disney Touch — How a Daring Management Team Revived an Entertainment Empire.* Business One Irwin, Homewood, Illinois. USA.

Guardian (1986) UK, 15 September, p. 7.

Guerin-Calvert, M.E. and Noll, R.G. (1991) *Computer Reservations Systems and their Network Linkages to the Airline Industry.* Center for Economic Policy Research Publication, No. 252, June.

Hansen-Sturm, C. (1990) The electronic information revolution. *The Airline Quarterly,* Summer 1990.

Hansen-Sturm, C. (1991) Electronic travel markets. Paper delivered at an international forum on *Electronic Information, Marketing and Payments Systems for Tourism,* 22–25 May 1991, Perugia, Italy.

Harris, R. (1982) Foreign exchange flows and the Jamaican tourist sector. *Social and Economic Studies* 31(4), 219–238.

Hart, C., Heskett, J. and Sasser, W.E. Jr. (1990) The profitable art of service recovery. *Harvard Business Review* July–August, 148–156.

Harvey, D. (1986) The battle for the beaches. *Business Computing and Communications* 30–33.

Hawkins, D.E. and Frechtling, J.D. (eds) (1991) *World Travel and Tourism Review* Indicators, Trends and Forecasts Vol. 1. CAB, Wallingford, UK.

Hayes, R.H. and Abernathy, W.J. (1980) Managing our way to economic decline. *Harvard Business Review* 67–77.

Heskett, J.L., Sasser, W.E. (Jr.), Hart, C.W.L. (1990a) *Service Breakthroughs Changing The Rules Of The Game.* Free Press, New York.

Heskett, J.L., Sasser W.E. (Jr.), Hart, C.W.L. (1990b) The profitable art of service recovery, *Harvard Business Review* 148–156.

Hiller, H.L. (1978) Sunlust tourism in the Caribbean. *Caribbean Review* 8(4), 12–15.

Hiller, H.I. (1979) Tourism development or dependence. In: Millet, R. and Mills, W.R. (eds) *The Restless Caribbean: Changing Patterns of International Relations.* Praeger Special Studies, New York, pp. 51–61.

Hindley, B. and Smith A. (1984) Comparative advantage and trade in services. *The World Economy* 7(4), 369–391.

Hirschman, A.O. (1968) The political economy of import substitution in Latin America. *Quarterly Journal of Economics* 83(1), 1–32.

Hitchins, F. (1991) The Influence of Technology on UK Travel Agents. *Travel and Tourism Analyst,* No. 3, Economist Intelligence Unit, London, pp. 88–105.

Hoffman, K. and Rush, H. (1980) Microelectronics, industry and the Third World. *Futures* 12(4), 289–302.

Holder, J.S. (1990) Far greater dependence on tourism likely. *ACP-EEC Courier Special Issue on Tourism.* No. 122, July–August, 74–79.

Holder, J.S. (1991) Tourism, the world and the Caribbean. *Tourism Management* 12(4), 291–300.

Holder, J.S. (1992a) *Island Tourism and Price and Value Relationship: A Global Perspective.* Paper presented at Island Tourism International Forum, 18 May.

Holder, J.S. (1992b) The need for public-private sector co-operation in tourism. *Tourism Management* 13(2), 157–162.

Holder, J.S. and Poon, A. (1989) *Tourism Linkages — Traditional and Non-Traditional.* Presented at Business Links to Tourism Workshop, US Business and Commercial Center, Antigua and Barbuda, 14–15 November, p. 17.

Hong, E. (1985) *See the Third World While it Lasts: The Social and Environmental Impact of Tourism with Special Reference to Malaysia.* The Consumer Association of Penang, Phoenix Press, Penang.

Hudson, B.J. (1979) The end of Paradise — what kind of development for Negril (Jamaica). *Caribbean Review* 8(3), 32–33.

Hughes, H.L. (1983) The service economy, de-industrialization and the hospitality industry. *International Journal of Hospitality Management* 1(3), 145–150.

Hyatt (1991) *Time off the Psychology of Vacations.* A Hyatt Travel Futures Project prepared by Research and Forecasts Inc., New York.

Imai, M. (1986) *Kaisen: The Key to Japan's Competitive Success.* McGraw-Hill, New York.

Institute of Development Studies (1982) Comparative advantage in an automating world. *IDS Bulletin,* 13(2).

Institute of Development Studies (1991) *A Strategy for Industrial Restructuring in the Dominican Republic.* University of Sussex, Brighton.

Interdisciplinary Science Review (1983) Special issue on information technology, 1(1).

Jacobson, S. and Sigurdson, J. (eds) (1983) *Technological Trends and Changes in Microelectronics.* Research Policy Institute, University of Lund, Sweden.

Jamaica Ministry of Tourism (1990) *Annual Travel Statistics 1990.* JMT, Kingston, Jamaica.

Japan Travel Bureau Inc. (1990) *JTB Report '90 All About Japanese Overseas Travellers.* Japan Travel Bureau.

Jenkins, C.L. (1982a) Tourism policies in developing countries — a critique. *Tourism Management* 1(1), 22–29.

Jenkins, C.L. (1982b) The effects of scale in tourism projects in developing countries. *Annals of Tourism Research* 9(3), 229–249.

Johnson, S.C. (1984) Dining by computers: choosing a restaurant with the aid of a computer terminal. *Restaurant Hospitality* 68(11), 150–154.

Jurgan, R.K. (1983) Data Driven Automation, *IEEE Spectrum,* 34–96.

Jussawala, M and Chee, C.-W. (1983) Towards an information economy — the case of Singapore. *Information Economics and Policy* 1, 161–176.

Kanter, R. (1991) Even closer to the consumer. *Havard Business Review,* January–February, 9–10.

Kaplinsky, R. (1982) *Computer Aided Design: Electronics, Comparative Advantage and Development.* Frances Pinter, London.

Kaplinsky, R. (1984) *Automation: The Technology and Society.* Longman, London.

Kasper, D.M. (1987) *The US Regional Airline Industry to 1996.* EIU The Economist Intelligence Unit Travel and Tourism Report No. 4, pp. 1–50.

Khan, H. (1979) Optimistic holiday sets worldwide expansion goal, *Service World International* 13(5).

Khan, A.E. (1982) Is it time to re-regulate the airline industry? *The World Economy* 5(4), 341–360.

Khan, R.E. (1983) The quest — a new generation in computing: microelectronics and artificial intelligence may produce a new generation of computers that are both fast and smart. *IEEE Spectrum,* 36–119.

King, A. and Schneider, B. (1991) *The First Global Revolution.* A Report to the

Council of The Club of Rome. Simson and Schuster, London.

Kleiner, A. (1991) What does it mean to be green? *Harvard Business Review*, 38–47.

Kobayashi, K. (1986) *Computers and Communications — A vision of C+C.* MIT Press, Cambridge, Massachusetts.

Konsynski, B.R. and McFarlan E.W. (1990) Information partnerships — shared data, shared scale, *Harvard Business Review*, 114–120.

Kotler, P. (1984) Dream vacations: The booming market for designed experiences. *Futurist* 18(5), 7–13.

Kotler, P. (1986) Megamarketing. *Harvard Business Review* 117–124.

Krippendorf, J. (1986) Tourism in the System of Industrial Society. *Annals of Tourism Research* 13(4), 393–414.

Krippendorf, J. (1987a) *The Holidaymakers: Understanding the Impact of Leisure and Travel.* Heinemann, London. 160 pp.

Krippendorf, J. (1987b) Ecological approach to tourism marketing. *Tourism Management* 8(2), 174–176.

Lanvin, B. (ed.) (1989) *Global Trade — The Revolution Beyond the Communication Revolution.* IDATE, Montpelier, France.

Levitt, K. and Gulati, I. (1970) Income effects of tourist spending: mystification multiplied — a critical comment on the Zinder Report. *Social and Economic Studies* 19(3).

Lewis, A. (1950) The industrialisation of the British west indies. *Caribbean Economic Review* 2.

Lewis, A. (1954) Economic development with unlimited supplies of labour. In: Agarawala, J. and Singh, S. (eds) *The Economics of Underdevelopment.* (4th edition) Oxford University Press, Oxford.

Lewis, A. (1977) *The Evolution of the International Economic Order, Princeton.* The Elliot Janeway Lecture on Historical Economics in Honour of Joseph Schumpeter, Princeton University Press, New Jersey.

Lewis, A. (1980) The slowing down of the engine of economic growth. Nobel Prize Lecture. *American Economic Review* 70(4).

Luxenberg, S. (1985) *Roadside Empires: How the Chains Franchised America.* Viking, New York.

MacCannell, D. (1973) Staged authenticity: Arrangements of social space in tourist settings. *American Journal of Sociology* 79, 589–603.

Macdonald, S., Lamberton, D. and Mandeville, T. (1983) *The Trouble with Technology — Explorations in the Process of Technical Change.* Frances Pinter, London.

McFarlan, W.F. (1984) Information technology changes the way you compete. *Harvard Business Review* 98–103.

McKean, P.F. (1978) Towards a theoretical analysis of tourism: economic dualism and cultural involution in Bali. In: Smith, V.L. (ed.) *Hosts and Guests: The Anthropology of Tourism.* Basil Blackwell, London, pp. 93–107.

McQueen, M. (1983) Appropriate policies towards multinational hotel corporations in developing countries. *World Development* 7, 141–152.

Mansfield, E. (1961) Technical change and the rate of imitation. *Econometrica*, 29(4), 741–766.

Marriott, J.W. (Jr.) (1989) Managing change in the travel industry. In: Vladimir, A.

(ed.) *The Complete Travel Marketing Handbook.* NTC Business Books, Illinois, USA, pp. 288–291.

Masuda, Y. (1980) *The Information Society as Post-Industrial Society.* Japan Institute for the Information Society, Tokyo.

Masuda, Y. (1982) The conceptual framework of information economics. In: Kogane, Y. (ed.) *Changing Value Patterns and Their Impact on Economic Structure,* A Report to the OECD. University of Tokyo Press, Tokyo, pp. 151–171.

Matthews, H.G. (1977) Radicals in Third World tourism — a Caribbean focus, *Annals of Tourism Research* 5 (Special Issue), 20–29.

Maynard, C.A. (1991) A perspective on Caribbean Ecotourism. Paper presented at the *Caribbean's First Conference on Ecotourism,* 9–12 July, Belize City, Belize, Central America.

Medlik, S. (1985) *Paying Guests: A Report on the Challenge and Opportunity of Travel and Tourism.* Confederation of British Industry, London.

Metcalfe, J.S. (1984) Impulse and diffusion in the study of technical change. In: Freeman, C. (ed.) *Long Waves in the World Economy,* pp. 102–114.

Middleton, V.T.C. (1988) *Marketing in Travel and Tourism.* Heinemann Professional Publishing, Oxford.

Middleton, V.T.C. (1991) Whither the package tour? *Tourism Management* 12(3), 185–192.

Miles, I. (1987) *Information Technology and the Service Economy.* SPRU January, Brighton.

Miller, L.G. (1984) *An Alternative to the Mass Market Philosophy for Micro Caribbean States.* CTRC, Barbados.

Mitchell, J.F. (1972) To Hell With Paradise: A New Concept in Caribbean Tourism. Statement by the Honourable Premier of St Vincent and the Grenadines, delivered at the *21st Meeting of the Caribbean Travel Association.*

Monk, J. and Alexander, C.S. (1986) Free Port fallout: gender, employment and migration on Margarita Island. *Annals of Tourism Research* 13(3), 393–414.

Naibaru, T. and Schutz, B. (1974) Prostitution: problem or profitable industry, *Pacific Perspectives* 3(1), 201–210.

Naisbitt, J. (1984) *Megatrends: Ten New Directions Transforming Our lives.* Macdonald, London.

Naisbitt, J. (1985) Megatrends in the Travel Industry. A brief summary of his talk in the *Proceedings of the 1985 Travel Outlook Forum.* Travel Data Center, USA.

Nash, D. (1977) Tourism as a form of imperialism. In: Smith, V.L. (ed.) *Hosts and Guests: The Anthropology of Tourism,* Basil Blackwell, London, pp. 33–47.

National Audubon Society (1989) *Travel Ethic for Environmentally Sound Travel.* National Audubon Society, New York.

National Audubon Society (1991) *Are You A Little On The Wild Side?* National Audubon Society, New York.

National Geographic (1988) Special Issue: Can we save this fragile earth? 174(6).

National Geographic (1989) La Rutta Maya. Special Issue, October.

Nelson, R.R. and Winter, S.G. (1977) In search of a useful theory of innovation, *Research Policy* 36–76.

New Scientist (1987) Reach for the Skies 114 (1559), 17.

Noronha, R. (1977) *Social and Cultural Dimensions of Tourism: A Review of the Literature in English,* IBRD Draft Working Papers, 18 May. International

Bank for Reconstruction and Development, Washington.

Noronha, R. (1979) Paradise reviewed: tourism in Bali. In: de Kadt, E. (ed.) *Tourism: Passport to Development.* Oxford University Press, London, pp. 177–204.

Noyce, R.N. (1977) Microelectronics. *Scientific American* 237(3), 63–69.

O'Grady, R. (ed.) (1980) *Third World Tourism.* Christian Conference of Asia, Manila.

O'Grady, R. (1981) *Third World Stopover — The Tourism Debate.* The Risk Book Series. World Council of Churches, Geneva.

O'Loughlin, C. (1970) Tourism in the Tropics: Lessons from the West Indies. *Insight and Opinion* 5(2), 105–110.

Olsen, M.D. (1991) *Strategic Management in the Hospitality Industry: A Literature Review.* Belhaven Press, London.

Opaschowski, H.W. (1991) *Mythos Urlaub — Die unerfullbare Sehnsucht nach dem Paradies?* BAT Freizeit-Forschungsinstitut, Hamburg, Germany.

Organization for Economic Corporation and Development, OECD(1966) *Tourism Development and Economic Growth.* OECD, Paris.

Palmer, C. (1982) Booking package holidays. *Data Processing* 24(10), 24–26.

Palmer, R.W. (1982) Absorbing the Caribbean labour surplus — the need for an indigenous engine of growth. *Caribbean Review* 11(3), 22–25.

Pannel Kerr Forster Associates (1984) *Caribbean Comparative Tourism Pricing Study.* Prepared for the CTRC and the OAS, November. Pannel Kerr Forster, Bridgetown, Barbados.

Papson, S. (1979) Tourism: world's biggest industry in the 21st century. *Futurist* 13(4), 249–257.

Parsons, G. (1983) Information technology — a new competitive weapon. *Sloan Management Review.*

Pavitt, K. (1990) What we know about strategic management. *California Management Review* 32(3), 17–26.

Peisley, A. (1989a) UK tour operators and the European Market in the 1990s. *Travel and Tourism Analyst,* No. 5. Economist Intelligence Unit, London, pp. 56–67.

Peisley, A. (1989b) The world cruising industry in the 1990s. *Travel and Tourism Analyst,* No. 6. Economist Intelligence Unit, London, pp. 5–18.

Perez, C. (1983a) Towards a Comprehensive Theory of Long Waves. Paper presented at the IIASA meeting on *Long Waves, Depression and Innovation.* Florence, 26–29 October 1983, Brighton.

Perez, C. (1983b) Structural change and the new technologies, *Futures* 15(5), 357–375.

Perez, C. (1985) Microelectronics, long waves and world structural change: new perspectives of developing countries. *World Development* 13(3), 441–463.

Perez, C. (1986) The new technologies: an integrated view. English version of the original Spanish, Las nuevas technologies: una vision de cobjunto. In: Ominami, C. (ed.) *La Tercera Revolucion Industrial: Impactos Internacionales del Actual Viraje Technologico.* Grupo Editor Latinamerican, Buenos Aires, pp. 44–89.

Perez, L.A. (Jr.) (1974) Aspects of underdevelopment: tourism in the West Indies. *Science and Society* 37, 473–480.

Peters, M. (1969) *International Tourism: The Economics and Development of the International Tourist Trade.* Hutchinson, London.

Peters, M. (1980) The potential for less-developed Caribbean countries. *International Journal of Tourism Management* 1(1), 13–21.

Phongpaichit, P. (1982) *From Peasant Girls to Bangkok Masseuses.* International Labour Organization, Geneva.

Pi-Sunyer, O. (1974) Tourist images: a separate reality. Paper read at the *Annual Meeting of the American Anthropological Association*, 24 November. Article reviewed in Noronha (1977).

Pollard, H.J. (1985) The erosion of agriculture in an oil economy. *World Development* 13(7), 818–835.

Poon, A. (1984) *The Microelectronics Revolution — Its Nature and Consequences for Developing Countries.* Work in progress paper, Science Policy Research Unit, Sussex University.

Poon, A. (1985) *Services and the Development Process — A Review of the Literature and Issues for Developing Countries.* Work in progress paper, Science Policy Research Unit, Sussex University.

Poon, A. (1987a) *Information Technology and International Tourism — Implications for the Caribbean Tourism Industry.* PhD Thesis, Science Policy Research Unit, Sussex University, UK.

Poon, A. (1987b) *Long-term Prospects and Policies for Caribbean Tourism.* Consultancy Report Prepared for the Commonwealth Secretariat, June.

Poon, A. (1988a) The future of Caribbean tourism — a matter of inovation. *Tourism Management* 9(3), 213–220.

Poon, A. (1988b) Diagonal integration — a new common-sense for tourism and services. Paper presented to the *Fourth Annual Seminar on the Service Economy* hosted by PROGRES (Research Program on the Service Economy), Geneva, 30–31 May and 1 June, 1988.

Poon, A. (1988c) Information technology and tourism, *Annals of Tourism Research* 15(4), 531–549.

Poon, A. (1989a) Competitive strategies for a new tourism. In: Cooper, C. (ed.), *Progress in Tourism, Recreation and Hospitality Management*, Belhaven Press, London, pp. 91–102.

Poon, A. (1989b) Blueprint for tourism in Trinidad and Tobago. Presented at the *1989 Hospitality Festival* hosted by the Hotel and Tourism Association of Trinidad and Tobago, 2–3 November, 1989.

Poon, A. (1989c) *Global Developments in All-inclusive Hotels — With Special Reference to the Caribbean and St Lucia.* Doc No: CTO/12/(ii)/D/9/89. Caribbean Tourism Organization, Barbados.

Poon, A. (1990) Flexible specialization and small size — the case of Caribbean tourism. *World Development* 18(1), 109–123.

Poon, A. (1991a) *A New Tourism for the Toledo District, Belize.* Paper prepared for USAID and the Belize Tourism Industry Association, BTIA, Belize City, Belize, Central America.

Poon, A. (1991b) *International Tourism — A New Global Best Practice.* Intelligent Island Lecture, National Computer Board, Singapore, 3 July.

Poling, B. (1989) New entrants since airline deregulation. *Travel Weekly* (USA), 30 November, pp. 10–12.

Porter, M. (1980) *Competitive Strategy — Techniques for Analysing Industries and Competitors*. The Free Press, New York, 387 pp.

Porter, M. (1985a) Technology and Competitive Advantage. *Journal of Business Strategy*, 60–78.

Porter, M. (1985b) *Competitive Advantage: Creating and Sustaining Superior Performance*. The Free Press, New York. 540 pp.

Porter, M. (1986) Changing patterns of international competition. *California Management Review* 28(2), 9–40.

Porter, M. (1987) From competitive advantage to corporate strategy, *Harvard Business Review*, 43–59.

Pyke, F. and Sengenberger, W. (1992) *Industrial Districts And Local Economic Regeneration*. ILO Publications, Geneva.

Qualtiere, M. (1984) Computer case study: Marriott hotels. *Resort Hospitality* 68(11), 150–154.

Quelch, J.A. and Hoff, E.J. (1986) Customizing global markets. *Harvard Business Review* 59–68.

Quinn, J.B. (1986) Technology adoption: the service industries. In: Landau, R. and Rosenberg, N. (eds) *The Positive Sum Strategy — Harnessing Technology for Economic Growth*. National Academy Press, Washington, pp. 357–371.

Rada, J.F. (1980) *The Impact of Microelectronics — A Tentative Appraisal of Information Technology*. International Labour Organization, Geneva.

Rada, J.F. (1984a) Advanced technologies and development: are conventional ideas about comparative advantage obsolete? *Trade and Development — An UNCTAD Review*, No. 5.

Rada, J.F. (1984b) *Development, Telecommunications and the Emerging Service Economy*. Mimeo, International Management Institute (IMI), Geneva, Switzerland.

Ragatz, R.L. (1981) The socioeconomic impact of timesharing. Remarks appearing in the *Travel and Tourism Association Twelfth Annual Conference Proceedings*, 7–10 June 1981, p. 183.

Reed Travel Group (1990) *The European Travel Market in the 1990s*. An independent report prepared by Cleverdon Steer.

Reichheld, F.F. and Sasser, W.E. (Jr.) (1990) Zero defections: quality comes to services. *Harvard Business Review*, 148–156.

Renard, Y. (1991) Strategies for Increasing Community Involvement in Ecotourism, paper delivered at the First Caribbean Conference on Ecotourism, 9–12 July 1991, Belize City, Belize.

Riddle, D.I. (1986) *Service-led Growth: The Role of the Service sector in World Development*. Praeger, New York.

Rispoli, M. and Volpato, G. (1986) Innovation acquisition: an unavoidable challenge to small firms. Paper presented at the *Conference on Innovation Diffusion*, Venice, March 17–22.

Robinson, I. (1983) An era recalled — from 1958 to 1983. *Travel Weekly* 25th Anniversary Issue: Twenty-five years of the jet age.

Rogers, E.M. (1962) *The Diffusion of Innovations*. The Free Press, New York.

Rogers, E.M. (1986) Three decades of research on the diffusion of innovations: progress, problems and prospects. Paper presented at the *Conference on Innovation Diffusion*, 18–22 March, Venice.

Rosenburg, N. (1982) *Inside the Black Box: Technology and Economics.* Cambridge University Press, Cambridge.

Rosenberg, N. and Steinmuler, W.E. (1980) The economic implications of the VSLI revolution. *Futures* 12(5), 358–369.

Rothwell, R. (1983) *The Role of Small Firms in the Emergence of New Technologies.* Mimeo, International Management Institute. SPRU, Brighton.

Roy, R. and Wield, D. (eds) (1986) *Product Design and Technological Innovation — A Reader.* Open University Press, Milton Keynes, England.

Royal College of Physicians Report (1987) *The Links Between Sun and Skin Cancer.* A Report of the Royal College of Physicians, London, April.

Sabolo, Y. (assisted by Gaude, J. and Wery, R.) (1975) *The Service Industries.* International Labour Office, Geneva.

Saglio, C. (1979) Tourism for discovery: a project in lower Casamance Senegal. In: De Kadt (ed.) *Tourism: Passport to Development? Perspectives on the Social and Cultural Effects of Tourism in Developing Countries.* Published for the World Bank and UNESCO, Oxford University Press, London.

Saltmarsh (1986) Travel Retailing in the UK Economist Intelligence Unit, *Travel and Tourism Analyst,* September, pp. 49–62.

Sapir, A. and Lutz, E. (1980) *Trade in Non-Factor Services: Past Trends and Current Issues.* World Bank Staff Working Papers, No. 410, August.

Sapir, A. and Lutz, E. (1981) *Trade in Services: Economic Determinants and Development-Related Issues.* World Bank Staff Working Papers, No. 480, August.

Sauvant, K. (1983) *Transborder Data Flows: The Basis of the Emerging International Information Economy.* Mimeo, United Nations Center for Trans-National Corporations, February.

Schiller, H.I. (1981) *Who Knows? Information in the Age of the Fortune 500.* Ablex, New Jersey.

Schlesinger, L.A. and Haskett, J.L. (1991) The service-driven service company, *Harvard Business Review* 71–79.

Schonberger, R. (1982) *Japanese Manufacturing Techniques: Hidden Lessons of Simplicity.* Free Press, London.

Schumpeter, J.A. (1928) The instability of capitalism. *Economic Journal,* 361–386.

Schumpeter, J.A. (1939) *Business Cycles: A Theoretical, Historical and Statistical Analysis of the Capitalist Process.* (2 Vols.) Porcupine Press, Philaedelphia.

Schumpeter, J.A. (1965) *The Theory of Economic Development: An Enquiry Into Profits, Credit, Interest and the Business Cycle.* Oxford University Press, Oxford.

Schumpeter, J.A. (1976) *Capitalism, Socialism and Democracy,* 5th edn. George, Allen and Unwin London.

Seers, D. (1964) Open Petroleum Economy Model, *Social and Economic Studies.*

Seow, G. (1981) *The Service Sector in Singapore's Economy: Performance and Structure.* ERC Occasional Paper Series, No. 2. Chopmen Publishers, Singapore.

Seward, S.B. and Spinrad, B.K. (eds) (1982) *Tourism in the Caribbean: The Economic Impact.* International Development Research Center, Canada.

Shakelford, P. (1979) Planning for Tourism. *Futures* 11(1), 32–43.

Shapiro, B.P. (1988) What the hell is market-oriented? *Harvard Business Review* 119–125.

Sheldon, P.J. (1984) Impact of Technology on the Hotel Industry, *Tourism Management* 4(4), 269–278.

Sheldon, P.J. (1986) The tour operator industry: an analysis. *Annals of Tourism Research* 13(3), 344–366.

Shelp, R.K. *et al.* (1984) *Service Industries and Economic Development: Case Studies in Technology Transfer.* Praeger Special Studies, New York.

Singh, K. (1984) Successful strategies — the story of Singapore Airlines. *Journal of Long-Range Planning* 17(5), 17–22.

Smith, C. and Jenner, P. (1989) Tourism and the Environment. *Travel and Tourism Analyst,* No. 5. Economist Intelligence Unit, London, pp. 68–86.

Smith, P.D. (1989) Airline Diversification and Investment Strategies, *Travel and Tourism Analyst.* No. 4. Economist Intelligence Unit, London, pp. 5–15.

Smith, V.L. (1978) *Hosts and Guests: The Anthropology of Tourism.* Basil Blackwell, London.

Soete, L. (1981) Technological dependence: a critical view. In: Seers, D. (ed.) *Dependency Theory.* Frances Pinter, London, pp. 181–206.

Sommerville, I. (1983) *Information Unlimited: The Applications and Implications of Information Technology.* Addison-Wesley, Wokingham, UK.

St Cyr, E. (1982) *Towards a Long-Term Economic Strategy for Trinidad and Tobago: Some Alternative Perspectives.* University of the West Indies, St Augustine, Trinidad.

Steinberg, B. (1983) The mass market is splitting apart. *Fortune Magazine* 76–82.

Streeten, P. (1982) A cool look at outward-looking strategies of development. *The World Economy* 5(2), 159–169.

StFT (Studienkreis für Tourismus E.V.) (1991a) *Reiseanalyse 1990 — Erste Ergbnisse der Reiseanalyse 1990 des Studienkreis für Tourismus.* Presentation at ITB, Berlin 5 March, 1991.

Studienkreis für Tourismus (1991b) *Reiseanalyse,* (Travel Analysis) Summary Report Issues at ITB, Berlin, StfT, Starnberg, Munich.

Studienkreis für Tourismus (1989) *Tourism in Europe,* StfT, Starnberg, Munich, Germany.

Sunday Times (1986) 20 July, p. 6.

Teece, D.J. (1986) *Capturing Value from Technological Innovation: Integration, Strategic Partnering and Licensing Decisions.* Paper presented at the Conference on Innovation Diffusion, 17–22 March, Venice.

Teicher, James S. (1982) The Telecommunications Revolution, Parts 1 and 2, *The Cornell Hotel and Restaurants Administrative Quarterly,* Feb. and May, 13–16 and 53–56 respectively.

Times International (1991a) Hitting the Credit Limit. 138, 54–55.

Times International (1991b) Major Overhaul. 56–58.

Times International (1991c) Orlando, The Fantasy Land that Grew out of Disney World. 21, 48–54.

Thomas, C.Y. (1974) *Dependence and Transformation.* Monthly Review Press, New York.

Thomas-Frances, A. (1988) *St Lucia Visitor Expenditure and Motivation Survey 1988.* St Lucia Tourist Board, St Lucia.

Tobago House of Assembly (1982) Tourism Policy in Tobago: A Unique Brand of Tourism. *Proceedings of the Tobago House of Assembly Conference on*

Tourism held at Mount Irvin Bay Hotel, Tobago, 10–11 December, Tobago.

Towner, J. (1985) The history of the grand tour. *Annals of Tourism Research* 12(3), 301–316.

Trade Policy Research Center (1987) *Trade in Services, Open Markets and the Uruguay Round of Negotiations.* Collection of papers presented at the above-named conference sponsored by the American Enterprise Institute for Public Policy Research, Washington; The Trade Policy Research Center, London; The Coalition of Service Industries, New York; and the Liberalization of Trade in Services Committee, London, 8 July.

Travel Agent (1992) *Caribbean and Bahamas Stepping Out: Sandals Antigua Marks Chain's Debut Outside Jamaica,* New York, USA, 13 January, p. 1.

Travel and Tourism Research Association (1980) Research and the changing world of travel in the 1980s. *Proceedings of the Eleventh Annual Conference.*

Travel and Tourism Research Association (1981) Innovation and creativity in travel research and marketing — keys to survival and opportunity. *Proceedings of the Twelfth Annual Conference,* 7–10 June, UTAH: Bureau of Economics and Business Research, Graduate Business School University of Utah.

Travel and Tourism Research Association (1985) The battle for market share: strategies in research and marketing. *Proceedings of the Sixteenth Annual Conference,* 9–12 June, 1985.

Travel News (1987a) 27 February, p. 80.

Travel News (1987b) 5 September, pp. 6, 43.

Travel Industry World Yearbook (1991) Child and Waters Inc., New York.

Travel Trade Gazette (1986a) Caribbean Report. K. Magnay and J. Stern, TTG UK and Ireland, 29 May, pp. 41–44.

Travel Trade Gazette (1986b) LinkLine. Feature Article. TTG UK and Ireland, 12 June, pp. 49–56.

Travel Trade Gazette (1986c) Travicom fights US competition. TTG UK and Ireland, 3 July, p. 20.

Travel Trade Gazette (1986d) Grasp the technology nettle. TTG UK and Ireland, 3 July, p. 21.

Travel Trade Gazette (1986e) Winter sun: Long haul. Feature Article. TTG UK and Ireland, 10 July, pp. 19–22.

Travel Trade Gazette (1987) Agents must diversify to survive. TTG UK and Ireland, article by Peter Ellegard, 29 January, p. 1.

Travel Trade Gazette (1991a) Euroscope and Europa. 5 September, p. 4.

Travel Trade Gazette (1991b) Report on Mintel Survey. TTG UK and Ireland, 31 October, p. 25.

Travel Trade Gazette (1991c) TTG UK and Ireland, 21 November, p. 96.

Travel Trade Gazette (1991d) TTG UK and Ireland, 19 December, p. 6.

Travel Trade Gazette (1992a) Innovations have kept Virgin Atlantic Flying High on the North Atlantic Stage, TTG UK and Ireland, 19 March, p. 44.

Travel Trade Gazette (1992b) LTU swoops on UK giant. TTG Europa and Ireland, 11 June, p. 1.

Travel Trade Gazette (1992c) Thompson unveils technological breakthrough. TTG UK and Ireland, 25 June, p. 1.

Travel Trade Gazette (1993) Independents fear too much power in the hands of too few. Special Report, Airtours, TTG UK and Ireland, 14 January, p. 4.

Travel Weekly (1983) 25th Anniversary Issue: Twenty-five years of the jet age.

Travel Weekly (1984) Louis Harris Study Issue. 43(57), 28 June, Section 2.

Travel Weekly (1985a) Racing to automate the retailers. Focus on Deregulation, article by N. Godwin, 31 May, 52.

Travel Weekly (1985b) Deregulation — the new era, special issue, 44(48), 31 May, Section 2.

Travel Weekly (1986) Current Round of Trade Talks Could Prove Significant for Travel — Issues of Services to be Considered by GATT for the First Time. 11 December, pp. 12–20.

Travel Weekly (1987a) 26 March, p. 1.

Travel Weekly (1987b) Economic survey of the travel industry — ten key trends in the coming years. 46(12), 31 January, Section 2.

Travel Weekly (1988a) Ten Years of Deregulation. (Supplement) 47(87), 30 September, Section 2.

Travel Weekly (1988b) Making it all possible. Article by N. Godwin. 30 September, p. 30–31.

Travel Weekly (1988c) The CRS drama unfolds overseas, article by N. Godwin, 31 October.

Travel Weekly (1989) And there were four? Vendors continue their efforts to consolidate, article by N. Godwin, 26 October, 32–41.

Travel Weekly (1990a) A summary of the tenth comprehensive study of the travel agency business.

Travel Weekly (1990b) Growing pains: built-in limitations are limiting the development of better back office systems. Article by N. Godwin. 49(2).

Travel Weekly (1990c) Managing travel. (Supplement), 49(10), February, Section 2.

Travel Weekly (1990d) US travel agency survey. (Supplement) 49(52), 28 June, Section 2.

Travel Weekly (1990e) US Travel Agency Survey. (Supplement) Article by L. Harris, August 1990.

Travel Weekly (1990f) TW poll shows little change in vendor's market share, article by N. Godwin, 28 August.

Travel Weekly (1991a) Disney update. (Supplement) 50(24), 25 March, Section 2.

Travel Weekly (1991b) The 1991 Economic Survey of the Travel Industry. (Supplement) 50(1), 3 January, Section 2.

Travel Weekly (1991c) DOT's pending rules could open doors for multi-CRS access. Article by N. Godwin. 27 May, p. 54.

Travel Weekly (1991d) Focus on the frequent traveller. (Supplement) 50(43), 30 May, Section 2.

Travel Weekly (1991e) 2 September, 50(70).

Travel Weekly (1991f) 5 September, 50(71).

Travel Weekly (1992a) Top 50 travel agencies. 51(35), 30 April, Section 2.

Travel Weekly (1992b) Editorial. June 18, p. 10.

Truitt, L., Teye, V.B. and Farris, M.T. (1991) The role of computer reservations systems — international implications for the travel industry. *Tourism Management*, 12(1), 21–36.

Tse, E.C.-Y. and Olsen, M.D. (1991) *Relating Porter's Business Strategy to Organizational Structure: A Case of US Restaurant Firms.* Mineo, Department of Hotel, Restaurant and Institutional Management, College of Human Resources, Virginia Polytechnic Institute and State University, Blacksburg Virginia, USA, 18 pp.

Tucker, A. (1982) International regulation of air transport *Tourism Management* 3(4), 294–297.

Turner, L. (1975) The international division of leisure: tourism and the Third World. *World Development*, 3(3), 253–260.

Turner, L. and Ash J. (1975) *The Golden Hordes: International Tourism and the Pleasure Periphery.* Constable and Co., London.

United Nations Center on Transnational Corporations, UNCTC (1981) *Transnational Banks: Strategies and their Effects in Developing Countries.* United Nations Publications, New York.

United Nations Center on Transnational Corporations, UNCTC (1982) *Transnational Corporations in International Tourism.* United Nations Publications, New York.

United Nations Center on Transnational Corporations, UNCTC (1983) *Transborder Data Flows: Access to the International On-line Database Market.* UNCTC, New York.

UNCTAD (1983) *Protectionism and Structural Adjustment: Production and Trade in Services, Policy and their Underlying Factors Bearing upon International Service Transactions.* UNCTAD Trade and Development Board, 26th Session, 18 April, Geneva. Report by the UNCTAD Secretariat, TD/B/94.

UNCTAD (1984a) *Services and the Development Process.* UNCTAD, Trade and Development Board, 29th Session, 10 September, Geneva. Study by the UNCTAD Secretariat. TD/B 1008, 2 August. United Nations Conference on Trade and Development, Geneva.

UNCTAD (1984b) *Technology in the Context of Services and the Development Process.* UNCTAD, Trade and Development Board, Report by the UNCTAD Secretariat, TD/B/1012.

UNCTAD (1984c) *Insurance in the Context of Services and the Development Process.* UNCTAD, Trade and Development Board, Report by the UNCTAD Secretariat, TD/B/1014.

UNCTAD (1984d) *International Trade and Foreign Direct Investment in Services: Transborder Data Flows in the Context of Services and the Development Process.* Report by the UNCTC for UNCTAD Trade and Development Board, TD/B/1016, 27 August.

United Nations Educational, Scientific and Cultural Organization (1985) *Tourism: Transnational Corporations and Cultural Identities.* Article by Francois Archer. UNESCO, Paris.

United States Congressional Hearings (1983) First Session.

United States Government (1980) United States National Study on Trade in Services, No. 455-773-201145. US Government, Washington DC.

United States Government Printing Office (1983) *Impact of De-regulation on the Air Transportation Marketing System.* Hearings before the Subcommittee on Antitrust and Restraint of Trade Activities Affecting Small Business of the Committee on Small Business House of Representatives, 98th Congress, First Session, Washington DC, 24 May.

United States Government Printing Office (1983) *Review of Airline De-regulation and Sunset of the Civil Aeronautics Board (The State of the Airline Industry Under De-Regulation).* Hearings before the Subcommittee on Aviation, 98th Congress, First Session, 24 May, 9 and 15 June.

United States Government Printing Office (1983) *Review of Airline De-regulation and Sunset of the Civil Aronautics Board (Airline Computer Reservation Systems).* Hearings before the Subcommittee on Aviation, 98th Congress, First Session, 21–23 July.

United States Government Printing Office (1983) *Review of Airline De-regulation and Sunset of the Civil Aeronautics Board (Government Regulation of the Relationship Between Airlines and travel agents).* Hearing before the Subcommittee on Aviation, 98th congress, First Session, 26 and 28 July, 20 October.

United States Tour Operators Association (1975) *Tour Wholesaler Industry Study,* Prepared by Touche Ross and Co.

United States Travel Data Center (1985) Outlook for Travel and Tourism. *Proceedings of the 1985 Travel Outlook Forum,* 13 September 1984.

United States Travel Data Center (1986) *1985–1986 Outlook for Travel and Tourism.* Proceedings of the US Travel Data Center's 11th Annual Travel Outlook Forum, 20 September, 1985.

United States Travel Data Center (1989) *Discover America 2000 — The Implications of America's Changing Demographics and Attitudes on the US Travel Industry,* US Travel Data Center, Washington, 80 pp.

US Department of Transportation (1988) *Study of Airline Computer Reservation Systems.* May.

US Department of Transportation (1990) *Airline Marketing Practices: Travel Agencies, Frequent Flyer Programmes and Computer Reservations Systems.* Secretary's Task Force on Competition in the United States domestic Airline Industry, February.

US Department of Transportation (1991) *Computer Reservation System Regulation,* Docket No. 46494, Notice No. 91–6.

Vernon, R. (1966) International investment and international trade in the product cycle. *Quarterly Journal of Economics,* 80(2).

Vukonic, B. and Pirjevec, B. (1980) The tourist product as a limiting factor in tourism growth. *The Tourist Review,* 35(14), 14–16.

Walker, B.J. and Etzel, M.J. (1973) The Internationalization of the US Franchise System: Progress and procedures. *Journal of Marketing* 37, 38–46.

Wanhill, S.R.C. (1983) Measuring the Economic Impact of Tourism. *The Service Industries Journal* 3(1), 9–12.

WEFA Group (1987) *The Contribution of the World Travel and Tourism Industry to the Global Economy: Executive Summary.* Prepared for American Express Travel Related Services Company, Inc. New York.

Wheatcroft, S. (1990) Towards Transnational Airlines. *Tourism Management,* 11(4), 353–358.

Whitaker, M. (1984) *The Impact of Information Technology on the Hotel and Catering Industry.* Pilot Project Report, Innovation Research Group, Department of Business Management, Brighton Polytechnic.

Wigand, R.T., Shipley, C. and Shipley, D. (1984) Transborder data flows, informatics and national policies. *Journal of Communication,* 153–175.

Willig, R.D. (1979) Multiproduct Technology and Market Structure. *American Economic Review* Papers and Proceedings 346–351.

Wilson, D. (1979) The early effects of tourism in the Syechelles. In: de Kadt E. (ed.) *Tourism: Passport to Development.* Oxford University Press, Oxford, pp. 205–236.

Womack, James P. *et al.* (1990) *The Machine that Changed the World.* Rawson Associates, USA.

Wood, D.B. (1985) The rise of franchises: the homogenizing of America. *Christian Science Monitor,* 2 April, pp. 37–44.

World Tourism Organization (1966–1986) Economic Review of World Tourism: Study of the Economic Impact of Tourism on National Economies and International Trade. *Travel Research Journal,* all volumes.

World Tourism Organization (1971) An introduction to tourism theory. *Travel Research Journal* 1, 17–30.

World Tourism Organization (1973) The Meridian Hotel chain: an airline's stake in the hotel industry. *Travel Research Journal,* 3–11.

World Tourism Organization (1978) What would tourism be without paid holidays? *World Travel* 145, 30–32.

World Tourism Organization (1979) Adapting tourism facilities to changing demand. *Travel Research Journal* 2, 31.

World Tourism Organization (1981) Telecommunications and Tourism – a SITA case study. *Travel Research Journal* 2, 3–32.

World Tourism Organization (1990) *Tourism Trends World-wide and in the Americas, 1950–1989 – Outlook of Trends up to the Year 2000.* Paper presented at the WTO Commission for the Americas, 21st meeting, Santo Domingo, Dominican Republic, 21–23 June 1990, 22 pp.

World Travel Overview (1988/89) The Annual Review of the Travel Industry Worldwide. Cosmos Communications, 105 pp.

World Wildlife Foundation (1990) *Ecotourism – the potentials and pitfalls,* 2 Volumes. World Wildlife Foundation, Washington DC.

Young, G. (1973) *Tourism: Blessing or Blight?* Penguin, Harmondsworth, UK.

INDEX

Note: Page references in *italics* indicate tables and figures.

Abacos, the (Family Islands) 143
acid rain, effects 6, 64, 65
activities, vacation 121–2
adventure, quest for 90, 121–2, 146,
    332
agents, incoming 207, 230
air access 326–7
aircraft, jet 4, 33, 41, 42–3, 53, 59, 60
Airline Deregulation Act
    (1978) 100–1, 106
Airline Farebank 168, 230
airlines
    code-sharing 102, 104, 278
    concentration 51, 104, 105–6,
        183–6, 219–20
    credit cards 227, 228
    deregulation 11, 16, 41, 47, 60,
        89, 100–7, 154–6, 178, 180,
        292
    diversification 222
    frequent-flyer programmes 102,
        103–4, 188, 227, 232, 269,
        278
    horizontal integration 219–20
    hotel ownership 217, 275
    influence 206, 235–6
    and information
        technology 11–13, 21, 43,
        46–7, 52, 158, 171, 175, 215
    and mass tourism 51–2

mergers 51, 104–5, 106, 220
new affiliations 104
promotional fares 52–3, 102,
    103–4
safety 118
service delivery 177–8
vertical integration 217, *219*
see also charter flights; CRSs
    (computerized reservations
    systems)
Airlines Reporting Corporation 165,
    191
Alan, Peter 156
Allegis Corporation 280
Amadeus system 161, 182, 183, 186,
    189
American Airlines 44, 51, 104, 188,
    267, 280
American Express
    charge card 43–4, 243
    diagonal integration 96, 208, 216,
        224, 279
    information flows 156
Andros (Family Islands) 143
APEX fares 52–3
Apollo system 182, 183, 186, 189
Armstrong, and Symonds, 264
Artus, 52
Asia, growth in tourism 8
attention, personal 119–20, 249–50

authenticity, quest for 120, 122–3, 288
automation
back-office 191–2, 198
front-office 191
middle-office 191, 192
ticket machines 165–6, 177, 192–3

Bahamas
air access 326
and environment 301
mass tourism 141–2, 290, 307
new tourism 23, 114, 142, 143–4, 147–51
Bartels, Jurgen 114
beaches
blue flag scheme 107
degradation 64
Belize, and ecotourism 6, 17, 63, 303–5
Bell, John 306
Bermuda
capacity control 296
and ecotourism 6, 17, 63
Bessant, 254
Biminis, the (Family Islands) 143
boundaries, redefining 19, 205, 208, 215, 228, 235, 278–9
brands
splintering 89, 94, 96, 146–7
and standardization 48–50, 55–6, 60
Branson, Richard 222
Britain
paid holidays 132
quality strategies 256
tour operators 194, 217, 220–1
travel agents 190, 191
British Airways
and British Caledonian 106, 217, 220
vertical integration 217
British West Indian Airways (BWIA) 67, 327
buildings, 'smart' 201
Burkart, and Medlik, 58

Canadian Pacific Hotels and Resorts 6, 273
capacity, control 296
CardLink service 166–7, 170
Caribbean
air access 326–7
all-inclusive resorts 8, 233, 248, 270–1
boutique hotels 250
developing new institutions 334–5
economic potential of tourism 306–23
environmental awareness 66–7, 68–70, 296, 305
foreign investment 329–31
and information technology 319–23
multinational hotels 37, 196, 230
and new tourism 332–3
services sector 314–23
see also Bahamas; Jamaica
Caribbean Development Bank (CDB) 68, 69–70, 306
Caribbean Tourism Organization 68–9, 336
CHARMS (Caribbean hotel reservations and management system) 230
charter flights, and growth of mass tourism 5, 48, 52–3, 57, 58–9, 61
choice, demand for 120–1
Civil Aeronautics Board (CAB) 100, 103, 189
Clairmonte, and Cavannah, 222
Club Med 15, 16, 50, 86, 267, 270–1, 272–3
Coates, 119, 140–1
Cohen, 289
communications
in hotels 197–8
and new technologies 11, 72, 156–8, 167, 171, 176, 178
company
assessment 238
environment 237–8
structure 275

comparative advantage, as no longer natural 291–2, 305
competition
    competitive strategies 236–83
    fair 189–90
    influencing environment 281–2
    and information technology 12–13, 17, 23, 24, 103, 188–9
    learning from 273
    price 103, 106
    and response 228–34
computer technology 44–8, 60, 72, 73–9, 156–8
concentration 218–22, 224, 229
    of airline industry 51, 104–6, 183–6, 219–20
    of cruise lines 222
    of tour operators 221
    of travel agents 221–2
Conservation Foundation Holiday Club 68
conservation measures 297, 298–301
consolidation 168
consumers
    ageing 10, 113, 134–8
    and airline deregulation 106
    awareness 67
    experienced 3, 116–22, 123–4, 138, 150, 272, 332
    flexible 139–40
    hybrid 10, 135, 138, 139–40, 144
    independence 140–1
    as individuals 10, 85–6, 90, 96
    inexperienced 4, 5, 33, 40–1, 124
    learning from 272–3, 283
    in mass tourism 38–41, 47, 60, 144–6
    new 9–11, 16–18, 23, 76, 90–2, 96, 113–52
    in new tourism 85, 88–9, 114–16, 144–51
    protection 16, 89, 107–8, 207, 218, 230
    putting first 232, 240–53, 276, 282
    role in tourism system 208
    understanding 243
    see also lifestyle
control, individual 140–1, 144
Cook, Thomas 30–1
cost-leadership 24, 238, 239
costs, reduction 163–4
Covia system 186
Crandall, Bob 180, 186, 253
credit cards 4, 41, 43–4, 60, 96, 165–7, 227, 228, 310
crime, as result of mass tourism 5, 6, 287
crisis in tourism 3, 33, 61, 62, 84
CRSs (computerized reservations systems) 12, 13, 17, 18, 19, 46–7, 89, 92
    and airlines 11–12, 21, 52, 102–3, 161, 163, 176–7, 178–90
    architectural bias 188, 189
    as competitive weapon 188–9, 228
    concentration 183–6
    and cost reduction 163–4, 167–8, 169
    development costs 182–3, 186, 189
    diffusion 158–61, 171
    entry barriers 182–3, 281
    hotels 12, 196–7
    ownership *184–5*, 188, 190
    as profit centres 12, 186–8, 189
    regulation 190
    and tour operators 168, 229–30, 235
    and travel agents 156–64, 176, 180, 182–3, 187, 188, 190–3, 231–3, 276
    and vertical integration 225–6
CRTs (computerized reservations terminals) 92, 190, 191, 231, 233
cruises
    and airlines 104, 270
    effects on destination 296, 298, 300
    employees 260
    growth in 8, 15, 16
    and horizontal integration 222
    and hotels 269–70
    and market segmentation 86, 248

cruises (*contd*)
    rubbish disposal 16, 67
    and value-chain 215
Cullen, 43
culture, indigenous
    and mass tourism 4–5, 6, 18, 32,
       60, 69, 144, 288–90
    and new tourism 90, 126, 297–8

database, interactive 193
DATAS II system 103, 182
decision-making, and information
    technology 175
defection, zero 9, 82–3, 244, 276
demography, changes 10–11, 88, 113,
    116–17, *133*, 134–9, 152, 170
destination
    economy 98, 290, 291–4, 300,
      302, 305–6
    effects of mass tourism 5, 6–7, 9,
      16, 23, 32, 64–6, 94, 144,
      287–91
    image 251–2
    and new tourism 288, 291–4
    preserving assets 296–8
    strategies for 287–336
developing countries, role of
    tourism 36–7, 291–4, 306–23
differentiation 24, 238–9
DINKS (double income, no
    kids) 10–11, 17, 88, 113, 152,
    247
Disney Company 260–1, 267
distribution 24, 202, 326–9
diversification 51, 222, 224, 333
dubois, 63

East Europe, and new tourism 23, 124
economy
    and effects of ecotourism 300,
      302, 305–6
    and effects of tourism 98, 290,
      291–4, 306–7
    tourism as lead sector 306–23
ecotourism 6–7, 9, 17–18, 62, 301

effects on environment 67
    niche exploitation 302–5
Ecumenical Coalition of Third World
    Tourism 66
education, increased levels 118, 144,
    147, *149*
electronics, impact 71–2
Eleuthera (Family Islands) 143
Elrod, Thomas R. 260–1
employees 250, 258–63
    and demand for quality 14,
      119–20, 164, 276, 281–2
    education and training 261–2
    learning from 273
    loyalty 282
    motivation and reward 263, 274
    responsibility and authority 9, 234,
      264–5
enrichment, holiday as 127–8, 129–30,
    138–9
entry barriers 182–3, 281
environment
    competitive 281–2
    conservation agencies 68–70
    consumer awareness 67, 88–9, 96,
      114, 170
    destination awareness 296–301
    of firm 237–8
    as focus 301–6
    impact assessments 297, 298, 305
    and limits on growth 3, 62, 63–70,
      89, 94, 96
    and mass tourism 5, 6–7, 9, 16,
      23, 32, 64–6, 94, 144
    and new tourism 288
    pressure groups 66–7
    producer awareness 67–8, 252–3
    putting first 24, 294–306
escape, holidays as 126–7, 144
Europe
    airlines 106–7
    mass tourism 48–50, 56–9, 61
    new technology 159
    paid holidays 132
    tour operators 193
    travel agents 191–2
European Community
    conservation funding 68–9

European Community (*contd*)
  consumer protection 107–8
  coordination of vacation days 107
exchange dining 245
experience, growth in *see* consumers,
    experienced

Family Islands (Bahamas)
  length of stay 147, *148*
  new tourism 23, 142, 143–52
Farrell, 253
Feldman, 42
financial services, suppliers 208
Firnstahl, Timothy 264–5
flexibility
  demand for 132, 138, 229–30,
    245, 247, 282
  increase in 12–13, 85–8, 108, 113,
    152, 171, 207
  and new technology 153, 163,
    164–5, 167–8
  and travel agents 232, 235
  see also consumers, flexible;
    production, flexible
focus as competitive strategy 24, 239
Forbes, 55, 272
forests, destruction 65
franchising of hotels 33, 50, 55–6
Fredericks, 266
Freeman, and Perez, 73–5
Freitag, Rolf 119–20
Frigenbaum, 256
funds, electronic transfer 177

Galileo system 159, 161, 182, 183–6,
    189
garbage dumping 16, 65
Gemini system 186
Germans, and new tourism 126, *127*
Germany
  paid holidays 132
  quality strategies 256
  tour operators 194, 218, 221
  travel agents 191–2
Godfrey, Glen 303
Godsman, James 260
Godwin, Nadine 102, 192

Grand Tour 30–1
Grenada, national parks 69
Grosvenor, Gilbert M. 64

Harbour Island (Family Islands) 143
Harris, Jim 164–5
Hart, *et al.* 262
health, concern for 113, 130–1
Heskett, 258
Hi-Net communications network 196
Holder, Jean 334
holiday brands 50, 61, 94
Holiday Corporation 196
Holiday Inn chain 53–4
holiday-makers
  and flexible production 15, 206–7,
    251
  and quality 256–7
holidays, paid 5, 35–6, 50, 60, 132
holistic approach 250–3
Horizon Holidays 31, 50, 163, 193,
    220, 249
hotels
  all-inclusive 270–1
  boutique 120, 249–50
  branding 48, 50, 60–1
  communications 197–8
  and demand for quality 117
  energy management 199
  food-and-beverage systems 199
  franchising 55–6, 60
  and growth of mass tourism 5,
    36–7, *38*, 48–50, 53–6
  guest-accounting systems 198
  incentives to 37
  and information technology 12,
    20–1, 47, 194–201, 229
  infrastructure 201
  marketing 196–7, 228, 229, 235,
    246–7, 278
  ownership by airlines 217
  representatives 208
  room-management systems 198
  safety and security systems 199
  strategic response 233–4, 276
  and value-chain 215, 234
  vertical integration 217

human resource management 296, 213
  see also employees
Hyatt Travel Futures Project 121, 140

image communication 167, 171, 177,
  197
Imai, 274
import substitution 36, 312–13, 323
improvement, continuous 15, 82, 254,
  263–5, 274–5, 282–3
income levels, increase 10, 132–3,
  135–8, *149*, 150
independence of new tourists 146,
  170
individual, needs of 9, 18, 85–6, 90,
  96, 141, 144, 146, 152
Indonesia, role of tourism 36
information
  manipulation 214–15
  proliferation 99–100, 153–6
  provision 9, 232
information technology
  and airline deregulation 102–3
  in Caribbean 319–23
  development 180–2
  and diagonal integration 19, 216,
    224, 228
  diffusion 11–12, 92–4, 158–61,
    169–71, 178, 202, 240
  effect on work 131–2
  and flexibility 153, 171
  and hotels 12, 20–1, 47, 194–201
  and increased efficiency 11, 41,
    163–4, 169, 171, 193, 194, 201
  and management 173, 175–6
  and new 'best practice' 13–16, 17,
    23, 41, 73–9, 169–71
  and new tourism 19–21, 23, 44–8,
    62, 71, 85, 88, 92–6, 161
  and productivity 9, 11–13, 16, 19,
    193–4
  and service provision 173, 175
  stages of adoption 199–200
  system 156–8, 169
  and systems development 214
  and tour operators 168, 193–4,
    229–30

tourism production system
  (TPS) 172–8, *179*
  and travel agents 190–3
infrastructure, firm 213
innovation
  as competitive strategy 238, 239,
    266–75
  continuous 272, 273–5, 283, 314
  incremental 266
  and new ideas 267–71
  in new tourism 88–9, 213
  radical 24, 266–7, 283
Intasun 220–1
integration
  diagonal 9, 18, 19, 88–9, 205,
    208, 215–28, 234–5, 276
  as competitive strategy 96,
    278–81, 283
  distinctness 223–6
  and economies of scope 216,
    224, 226–7, 279
  implications 228
  and information technology 19,
    216, 224
  and logically combined
    services 279–80
  synergies 224, 227, 230, 279–80
  and systems gains 19, 224, 227
  horizontal 33, 51, 94–6, 218–22,
    224
  mechanism 224
  vertical 33, 51, 94–6, 216–18, 224
InterAmerican Development Bank 69,
  298
International Air Transportation
  Association (IATA) 53
investment, attracting 329–31
Issa, John 270–1, 332
ITX fares 52–3, 57

Jamaica
  all-inclusive hotels 270–1
  ecotourism 303
  employee motivation 263
  local entrepreneurship 331, 332–3
  market segmentation 247–8
  Tourism Action Plan 70, 334–5

Japan
and flexible production 14–15, 61, 79, 82
and innovation 274–5
and mass tourism 5, 41
and new technologies 201
and new tourism 23, 116, 118–19, *121*, 122, 124, 129–30, 133
paid holidays 132
and quality 254–6
Jefferis, John 298
Journeys International 68

Kahn, Alfred 100–1
Kanter, 263–4
Kasper, Daniel 105
Kleiner, 68
Konsynski, and McFarlan, 227
Krippendorf, 122, 126–8

leakage 307–10
learning, continuous 271–3, 283
Lee, 69
leisure, increased importance 128–30, 152
Levine, Michael 106
lifestyle
and market segmentation 10–11, 17, 88, 114, 247–8
and new consumers 113–14, 128–33, 138, 152
Lipman, Geoffrey 252
LOME Convention 68–9
loyalty, consumer 150–1, 188, 232, 244, 249
LTU group 208, 221
Luxenberg, 56

management
and new technology 173, 175–6
in new tourism 89, 96–8, 234
manufacturing sector
competitive strategies 236–9
lessons from 13–16, 79–83

vertical integration 216–17, *218*
market segmentation
by cluster 247
as competitive strategy 9, 245–9
demographic 10–11, 113–14, 152, 246–7
and information technology 85, 170
and new consumers 16, 17–18, 84, 86, 113–14, 152
psychographic 11, 144, 139–40, 152, 246–7
marketing
airlines 101–2
clarity in 243–4
hotels 196–7, 228, 229, 235, 278
and information technology 176–7, 196–7
mass 32, 33, 50, 55, 56, 60
decline 18, 85
and product development 96, 240–4, 327–9
in value chain 208, 210–12, 323–9
Marriot, J.W. Jr 101, 273
Marshall, Sir Colin 88, 105
mass consumption 39–40
mass customization 16, 86, 88–9, 96, 152
mass tourism
changes in 3, 9, 16–17, 89, 109
compared with new 21–3, 141–6, 151
definition 32–3
effects 5–7, 287–91
in Europe 48–50, 56–9, 61
frame conditions 4–5, 16–17, 35–7, 61, 62, 84, 96
future prospects 21–3, 62
growth of 4–5, 33, *34*
history 30–2
and technology 44–6
in USA 48–50, 51–6, 60–1
Matthews, 290
Maya Peace Park 304–5
McCarthy, Fenella 117
McEleny, James A. 264
McMullen, Bob 251

microelectronics *see* computer
     technology; information
     technology; technology
MILKIES (modern introverted luxury
     keepers) 10–11, 17, 88,
     113–14, 134, 152
Mount Pleasant Credit Union,
     Tobago 333

Naisbitt, 119–21
Nassau (Bahamas), mass tourism 23,
     142, 144–6, *147–9*, 150
national parks 65, 69, 301, 303–4, *304*
nature, experience of 63, 122–3, 124,
     152
nesting, virtual 188
New Providence *see* Nassau (Bahamas)
new tourism 17–21
     compared with mass tourism 21–3,
          141–6, 151
     and competitive strategies 236–40,
          332–3
     definition 85–6
     and destination 288, 291–4,
          299–300
     emergence 86–9
     frame conditions 62, 84, 86–9,
          100–8, 170–1
     and technology 44–6, 92–6
     and value creation 205–6, 214–15
     see also consumers, new
niche exploitation 302–5, 319, *320,
     321*
Nicholls, Neville 70, 306
Noyce, 72

O'Grady, 5
Organization of American states
     (OAS) 69
ozone layer, destruction 6, 63, 125

package tours
     EC Directive 107–8
     and growth of mass tourism 5, 32,
          48, 57–8

history 31
Japan 124
and new technology 161
and new tourism 17–18, 230, 232
Pan Am 51, 161, 326
paradigm, new 23, 73–9, 109
PARS system 180, 182, 189
payment systems, electronic 11, 44, 60,
     154, 177
Peisley, 108
People's Express airline 101, 104, 105,
     237
personalization 119–20, 124, 131–2
personnel, creative practices 260–1
Pi-Sunyer, 288
planning, strategic 237
platform products 192
pollution 64–6, 107
Porter, 239
private sector
     development 24, 329–31, 332–3,
          334–6
     'greening' 67–8
processes, continuous
     improvement 263–5
product development
     and marketing 96, 240–4, 327–9
     and value-chain 213, 329
production
     flexible 17–19, 23, 92, 94–6, 170,
          314
     as new best practice 13–16, 61,
          63, 76–9, *81*, 82–3, 202
     integrated 89
     mass 77–83, 96, 163, 170, 255–6
     as best practice 13–15, 60–1,
          73–6, 77–9, 85–8
     in mass tourism 4–5, 16, 29,
          38–40, 46–7, 50, 55–6
productivity, and new technology 9,
     11–13, 16, 19, 193–4, 202, 216
promotion by government 36–7
prosperity, post-war 4, 5, 31–2, 35,
     59–60, 96
prostitution, and tourism 5, 6, 287, 289
public sector, collaboration with 252–3,
     334–6
Purdom, Keith 163

quality 334
   and computer technology 47, 164, 171
   consumer demand 117-19, 120, 134, 144, 152, 239, 282
   in hotel services 194
   leadership 234, 254-66
   in manufacturing sector 82-3, 254
quality control 20, 191, 192, 207, 230

Raitz, Vladimir 31
reefs, destruction 65, 67
regions, cooperation 336
Renanado, Oscar 303
reservations *see* CRSs (computerized reservations systems)
resort offices 130, 201
resorts, all-inclusive 8, 15, 233, 248, 270
   and value-chain 215
   see also Sandals; SuperClub
risk-raking 140-1, 229-30
Robinson, 42
Robinson, James 243
Ruta-Maya project 304

Sabre system 167, 182, 183, 186, *187*, 188, 189, 267
SabreVision 12, 167, 177
Saga Holidays 230, 248-9
St Lucia, service sector 314-16
sales, in value-chain 210-12
San Salvador (Family Islands) 143-4
Sandals 15, 21, 33, 233, 245, 248, 261, 263, 267, 270-1, 332
satellite
   entertainment 72, 197, 198
   ticket printers 11, 165, 171, 177, 193
satisfaction, consumer 150, *151*, 152, 212, 232, 244-50
Satisfaction Guaranteed Eateries 264-5
scale economies
   and diagonal integration 224, 226

   in mass tourism 4-5, 32, 38, 46-7, 50, 58, 60
   and new tourism 16, 18, 85, 86, 94, 182
Schumpeter, 266
scope economies
   and diagonal integration 216, 224, 226-7, 279
   in new tourism 86, 94, 182
seasonality 89, 107, 290
service provision
   control of 253
   financial 208
   'high touch' 12, 119-20, 164, 190, 245, 249-50, 265
   and new technology 173, 175, 177-8
   potential of tourism 310-11, 314-23
   and value chain 210, 212, 213
   and vertical integration 225
sewage disposal 64
sex tourism 5
Shapiro, 243
Singapore Airlines 201, 249
ski resorts, environmental effects 65
Skytours 194
smart cards 11, 165, 193
Smith, and Jenner, 65
Spain, as mass tourism destination 59, 61
spear fishing, illegal 65
specialization, flexible 313-14
Speth, James Gustave 66
sport, and new tourism 90, 139, 146
Start reservation system 159, 183, 194
Stempel, Robert 255
Stewart, Butch 261, 331, 332
strategies, competitive 236-83
   alliances 9, 21, 271, 278, 280, 283
   for destinations 287-336
   explicit/implicit 237
   generic 238-9
   and hotels 233-4, 276
   need for 3, 23, 24, 188-9, 228-35, 291-4
   networks 280-1

strategies, competitive (*contd*)
  niche exploitation 302–5, 319, *320, 321*
  putting consumers first 240–53, 276, 283
  strengthening position 275–82, 283
  and tour operators 21, 228, 229–31, 276
  and travel agents 231–3, 276
  and wealth-creation 276–8
sun
  effects of 90, 125
  quest for 4, 33, 38–9, 60, 123, 124–5, 146
SuperClub 15, 21, 233, 248, 263, 270–1, 331, 332
suppliers, and information technology 176–7
Switzerland, quality strategies 256
Sympathy Magazines 66
synergies, and diagonal integration 224, 227, 230, 279–80
System One 103, 182, 183, 186
systems development 214
systems gains, and diagonal integration 19, 224, 227

technology
  creative use 265–6
  diffusion 92–4, 158–61
  effects on tourism 3, 4, 5, 11–13, 16, 70–2, 153–71
  effects on work 131–2
  and flexibility 153
  and hotel infrastructures 201
  and mass tourism 41–8, 60
  and new 'best practice' 13–16, 73–9, 88, 92–4, 169–71
  and payment systems 44, 60, 154, 177
  and systems development 214
  see also computer technology; information technology
teleconferencing 72, 167, 178, 197
telephone
  digital networks 11, 177, 197

freephones 177
hotel systems 197
Thai Airways International 262
Thomas Cook tour operator 94, 208, 221
Thomson Holidays 50, 163, 177, 193, 217–18, 220–1, 249
Thomson Open-line Programme (TOP) 193–4
tickets
  automated machines 164–6, 177, 192–3
  satellite printers 11, 165, 171, 177, 193
time share holidays 166
tour operators
  and airlines 57, 218
  concentration 221
  and consumer protection 107–8
  and flexibility 229
  horizontal integration 220–1
  and hotel ownership 218
  influence 206, 235
  market segmentation 248
  and mass tourism 5, 40, 48–50, 56–8, 61
  and new technology 168, 193–4, 229–30, 235
  and new tourism 18, 19–20, 21
  strategic response 21, 228, 229–31, 276
  vertical integration 217–18, *220*
  wholesaling and packaging 210
tourism
  changes 9, 16–17, 24, 236–7, 291–2
  future prospects 3, 7–9, 24–5
  life cycle *22*
  limits to growth 5–7
  system 206–8
  see also mass tourism; new tourism
Tourism with Insight group 66
tourist boards 208
Touristic Union International; (TUI) 94, 194, 218
Towner, 30
Toyota, Eiji 274

transportation
    and growth of mass tourism 30-2,
        41, 42-3
    as primary activity 210
    see also airlines
travel, as way of life 130, 144
travel agents
    and airlines 104, 221-2, 232
    business/leisure 161
    and CRSs 11, 156-8, 176, 180,
        182-3, 187, 188, 190-3, 231-2,
        276
    horizontal integration 221-2
    and hotels 21, 233, 271, 276
    influence 206
    and information
        technology 12-13, 20, 46-7,
        92, 154-64, 168, 215
    strategic response 228, 231-3,
        235, 275, 276
    and tour operators 19, 168,
        217-18, 229-30
Travicom system 159, 183, 186, 189
Trinidad and Tobago, responsible
        tourism 6, 297-8, 305
Tse, and Olsen, 24, 237, 239
Turner, and Ash, 30-1, 32, 38-9

Udall, Stuart L. 63
UNCTC 58
United Nations Development
        Programme (UNDP) 70
United States Agency for International
        Development (USAID) 70, 334
USA
    airlines 98-106, 161, 178, 183-6,
        189, 219-20
    Demographic groups *133, 136-7*
    Hotels 246-7
    mass tourism 48-50, 51-6, 60-1
    new technology 159-61, 176-7

and new tourism 126
paid holidays 132
quality strategies 256
tour operators 193-4, 221
travel agents 190, 192, 221-2

vacation days, coordination 89, 107
value chain 205-6, 208-14, *211*
    changes 24, 275-6, 282-3
    and diagonal integration 215-28,
        278-9
    and new tourism 92, 214-15
    position in 276-8
    primary activities 209-12
    support activities 212-14
values, changes in 122-8, 134, 138,
        152
video brochures 177, 196
videotext 72, 168, 193, 197, 198
viewdata systems 193, 194
Virgin Atlantic 222, 269

Womack, *et al.* 15
Woolridge, C.V. 296
work, changing nature of 131-2
workstations systems 192
World Tourism Organization 8, 52, 59,
        70
World Travel Overview 116
World Travel and Tourism
        Council 252-3
World Travel and Tourism
        Environment Research
        Centre 252
Worldspan system 183

Young, 30, 36
YUPPIES (Young urban upwardly
        mobile professionals) 10-11,
        17, 88, 113-14, 134, 138, 152